CW00418587

THE SILENT CITIES

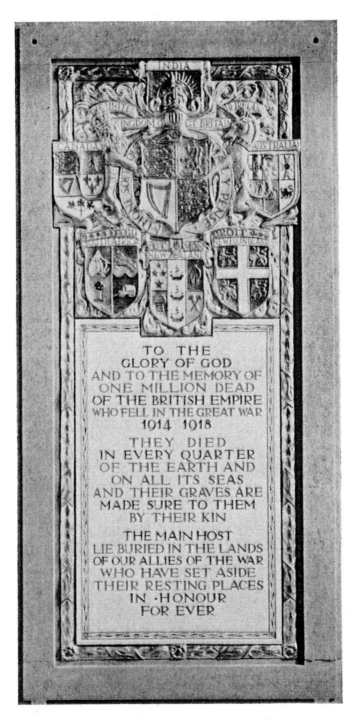

THE MEMORIAL TABLET IN
WESTMINSTER ABBEY

THE SILENT CITIES

AN ILLUSTRATED GUIDE TO THE WAR CEMETERIES
AND MEMORIALS TO THE 'MISSING' IN
FRANCE AND FLANDERS : 1914-1918
CONTAINING 959 ILLUSTRATIONS
AND 31 MAPS

Compiled with the kind permission of
THE IMPERIAL WAR GRAVES COMMISSION

BY

SIDNEY C. HURST, P.A.S.I.

With a Preface by
MAJOR-GENERAL SIR FABIAN WARE
K.C.V.O., K.B.E., C.B., C.M.G.
VICE-CHAIRMAN OF THE IMPERIAL WAR GRAVES COMMISSION

METHUEN & CO. LTD.
36 ESSEX STREET W.C.
LONDON

First Published in 1929

THE KING'S PILGRIMAGE

BY

RUDYARD KIPLING

OUR King went forth on pilgrimage
    His prayer and vows to pay
To them that saved our Heritage
    And cast their own away.
And there was little show of pride,
    Or prows of belted steel,
For the clean-swept oceans every side
    Lay free to every keel.

And the first land he found, it was shoal and banky ground
    Where the broader seas begin,
And a pale tide grieving at the broken harbour mouth
    Where they worked the Death Ships in :
And there was neither gull on the wing,
    Nor wave that could not tell
Of the bodies that were buckled in the lifebuoy's ring
    That slid from swell to swell.

(All that they had they gave—they gave ; and they shall not return,
For these are those that have no grave where any heart may mourn.)

And the next land he found, it was low and hollow ground
    Where once the cities stood,
But the man-high thistle had been master of it all,
    Or the bulrush by the flood ;
And there was neither blade of grass
    Nor lone star in the sky,
But shook to see some spirit pass
    And took its agony.

And the next land he found, it was bare and hilly ground
  Where once the bread-corn grew,
But the fields were cankered and the water was defiled,
  And the trees were riven through ;
And there was neither paved highway,
  Nor secret path in the wood,
But had borne its weight of the broken clay,
  And darkened 'neath the blood.

(Father and Mother they put aside, and the nearer love also—
An hundred thousand men who died, whose grave shall no man know.)

And the last land he found, it was fair and level ground
  Above a carven Stone,
And a stark Sword brooding on the bosom of the Cross
  Where high and low are one ;
And there was grass and the living trees,
  And the flowers of the Spring,
And there lay gentlemen from out of all the seas
  That ever called him King.

('Twixt Nieuport sands and the eastward lands where the Four Red
   Rivers spring
Five hundred thousand gentlemen of those that served the King.)

All that they had they gave—they gave—
  In sure and single faith.
There can no knowledge reach the grave
  To make them grudge their death
Save only if they understood
  That, after all was done,
We they redeemed denied their blood,
  And mocked the gains it won.

' The King's Pilgrimage ' from *Inclusive Verse* is reprinted by kind permission of Mr. Kipling and Messrs. Hodder & Stoughton, Ltd.

PREFACE

BY

MAJOR-GENERAL SIR FABIAN WARE

K.C.V.O., K.B.E., C.B., C.M.G.

I HAVE been asked by the Author and Publishers to write an introduction to their Guide to the British War Cemeteries in France and Belgium. In doing so I feel that it will be of interest to the reader if I explain the extent to which the Imperial War Graves Commission has been associated with its production and say something of the special circumstances in which it has been compiled.

During the War, as Director-General of Graves Registration and Enquiries, I was able, with the help of funds generously and sympathetically provided by the Joint War Committee of the British Red Cross Society and Order of St. John, to furnish the next-of-kin of a soldier who had fallen, with a photograph of his grave. On the card in which this photograph was placed were given certain particulars, including the best available indication as to the situation of the grave and, when it was in a cemetery, directions as to the nearest railway station, which might be useful for those wishing to visit the country after the War. This branch of our work had, however, to be abandoned as an official undertaking soon after the conclusion of hostilities and when the military organization was finally merged into the Imperial War Graves Commission.

To relatives of the dead who, as we have every reason to know, have watched the Commission's work closely and anxiously and have shown a wonderfully patient appreciation of the many complexities and difficulties which it involved, no excuse need, I believe, be offered for having concentrated our energies and our resources on the main objects of our task. We did, nevertheless, at the same time, do everything in our power to encourage and assist private enterprise to fill the gap thus created, and, thanks mainly to the warmhearted and devoted efforts of one or two well-known voluntary organizations, it has to some extent done so.

But in spite of this, and of the regular publication by the Commission of Cemetery Registers giving particulars of each individual grave and of the names inscribed on the 'Missing Memorials', evidence has been constantly before us that two widespread demands were not satisfied. The first was for a photograph showing the general appearance of each cemetery when its construction was finished : the headstones erected, the Cross of Sacrifice (together with the Stone of Remembrance in the larger of the cemeteries) set up and the buildings and flower-beds completed. The second was for such clear indications of the situation of each cemetery as would enable its geographical surroundings to be to some extent visualized and a visit to it easily planned or undertaken.

It was therefore with very great interest that I learnt some months ago that Mr. S. C. Hurst, who was working for us in France, had been giving up such leisure as he had in order to photograph the cemeteries, memorials, and to make specially designed maps to indicate their situation. He showed me specimens of both, and they appeared to me to be so admirable and to show such sympathetic understanding of what was so persistently required, that I encouraged him to proceed with the venture on which he had spontaneously embarked. Very shortly afterwards he informed me that Messrs. Methuen & Co. Ltd. had agreed to publish his guide-book ; but my friend, Mr. E. V. Lucas, chairman of that firm, who is able to speak with unequalled authority on such a matter, told me that, while he thought highly of the quality of Mr. Hurst's work, if it was to be completed satisfactorily it would require his individual attention for several months. Mr. Hurst was therefore allowed to sever his connexion temporarily with the Commission and to devote himself exclusively to the production of this book. That is the only help, such as it is, which the Commission has given him, unless one takes into account the supplying of information to which any member of the public has the right of access, the checking of his figures and statements and the making of a few suggestions.

    While this book cannot therefore be said to be authoritative, it is right to add that it has the sympathetic approval of the Commission, and that, personally, I do not think that the two demands to which I referred above could have been more adequately met within such convenient limits. There is only one addition I should like to make to the information which Mr. Hurst has supplied.

    The British War Cemeteries in France and Belgium are so important a feature of the towns, villages and country-side, and are regarded as so important by the peoples of those countries themselves, that permission was willingly accorded by the proper authorities for road-signs to be erected where desirable indicating the direction to be followed by those in search of them. These signposts conform to the general pattern adopted in those countries, but were specially designed by Sir Charles Holmes, the late Director of the National Gallery. This is one more instance of the ready response which the Commission has never failed to receive to its appeal for help and guidance from those who are the leading authorities in their own special spheres throughout the Empire. Not only did Sir Charles design them, but he came to France with me when the first were erected and made, on the spot, such modifications as seemed to him needful to adapt them to their surroundings. They are effective and dignified, and besides fulfilling their purpose will in future remind all travellers on the French and Belgium roads of the sacrifice which the British Empire made in the Great War. The accompanying illustration shows one of these signposts ; they are all of the same colours, white lettering and crown on an apple-green background, the support being painted in the same two colours.

As I have said, I believe that this book meets a real demand. If I am right, there will be some—in these present times there may be many—whose husband, son or father lies in one of those silent cities oversea and who would wish to have a copy but cannot afford to buy it. I am often asked how the richer, in this fellowship of sacrifice, can help the poorer. Might I suggest that this is one way ? But I hope that it will also get into the hands of many who have no association of kinship with these cemeteries and memorials, but for whom the claims of national brotherhood fall on ears not deaf to the sounds of a past fading into the distance or on hearts not yet unmoved by gratitude for a sacrifice on which their present rests secure. Then perhaps some of them, touring in these foreign lands, may be reminded by this book that a short way to the left or the right off the main road, but far enough off to be rarely visited, lies one of those cemeteries tended reverently and lovingly by a British gardener, a man who himself fought in the War, but who rarely sees one of his own countrymen and to whom a word of encouragement, thanks and wonder at the beauty of his work may give new strength and be long remembered.

FABIAN WARE

82 BAKER STREET, W.1
March 26th 1929

INTRODUCTORY NOTE

THIS book, by the aid of maps, illustrations, and descriptive notes, endeavours to be a complete guide to all Cemeteries containing war graves and all Memorials recording 'Missing' of the Forces of the British Empire who fell in France and Flanders during the Great War 1914–1918.

The Cemeteries (so aptly termed 'The Silent Cities' by Mr. Rudyard Kipling) and Memorials in France and Belgium north of a line drawn east and west through Paris are, with few exceptions, shown on the enclosed maps. The maps divide the book into geographical sections, and each section contains illustrations and descriptions of those Cemeteries and Memorials, within the limits of the map, that record over forty British Dead. The Cemeteries and Memorials not within the area mapped and generally outside the Battle Zone of the British Armies are described in relation to a large town by brief notes.

The descriptions of Cemeteries, Memorials, and Towns are mostly compiled from the Introductions to the Cemetery and Memorial Registers published by order of the Imperial War Graves Commission, 82 Baker Street, London, W.1. 'Special Memorials' in these abbreviated descriptions indicate memorials to officers and men whose graves have been destroyed by shell-fire and to those known or believed to be buried in the Cemetery.

I acknowledge my gratitude to Major-General Sir Fabian Ware, Vice-Chairman of the Imperial War Graves Commission, for his Preface, and for the facilities granted to me in compiling this book. By his advice and support the whole was made possible.

I am indebted for valuable help to Major H. F. Chettle, Director of Records, London, and to Lieutenant-Colonel F. Higginson, Chief Administrative Officer, France and Belgium.

S. C. HURST

May 1929

CONTENTS

NOTE

THE following explanation of a typical entry will assist the reader to use this book to the best advantage :

705 . . . The Cemeteries and Memorials are numbered consecutively in alphabetical order, and the numbers are repeated on the Maps. The relevant map will be found stated in the Index after the name of the Cemetery or Memorial. The mark ■ indicates a Cemetery and ✚ a Memorial.

DUNKERQUE TOWN CEMETERY. . . . This is the official British name.

(Nord). . . . This is the name of the Department, corresponding roughly to a County.

1¼ miles. . . . Furnes. This is a brief statement of the position of the cemetery, supplementing the information given by the Map.

The town . . . war. A summary of the War history of the neighbourhood.

Three plots . . . cem. This detail is necessary where a Cemetery is not a purely British War Cemetery.

Records . . . burials. A statement of the War graves by nationalities.

The names of all places where British War Graves exist are *underlined* in the Maps.

The following abbreviations are used in the descriptions of cemeteries and memorials :

Aust. . . . . Australian.	Newfld. . . . . Newfoundland.
Belg. . . . . Belgian.	N.Z. . . . . New Zealand.
B.W.I. . . . . British West Indies.	Port. . . . . Portuguese.
Can. . . . . Canadian.	Roum. . . . . Roumanian.
Chin. . . . . Chinese.	Russ. . . . . Russian.
Guernsey . . . . Royal Guernsey Light Infantry.	S.A. . . . . South African.
	S.A.N.L.C. . . . . South African Native Labour Corps.
Ind. . . . . Indian.	
Nat. Sea. . . . . Native Seamen.	U.K. . . . . United Kingdom.

THE SILENT CITIES

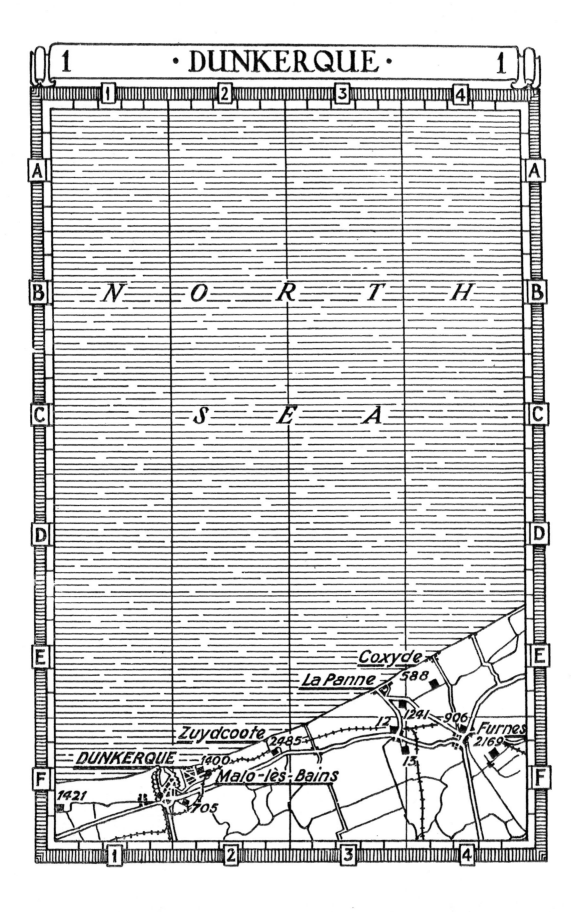

NORTH

SEA

Coxyde
La Panne
588
1241
906
Furnes
2169
Zuydcoote
12
2485
DUNKERQUE
1400
13
Malo-lès-Bains
1421
705

DUNKERQUE

MAP SHEET No. 1

DUNKERQUE is a large fortified town of 39,000 inhabitants, an important and progressive seaport on the north coast, at the confluence of five canals, in the Department of the Pas-de-Calais. The town is of great historic interest and was frequently attacked and besieged from the 8th to the 18th centuries. Ceded to Cromwell by Louis XIV, fortified by the English and returned to France (1662) by Charles II. During the War 1914–1918 Dunkerque was severely bombarded by the Germans from land, sea, and air, notably by a long-range gun 22 miles away on the Belgian coast.

705 DUNKERQUE TOWN CEMETERY (Nord). 1¼ miles SE. of sta., S. of Dunkerque Canal and road to Furnes. The town remained in Allied hands throughout the war. Three plots of British graves are near the entrance and 2 are in the NE. corner of the Cem. Records 423 U.K., 7 Aust., 4 Can., 4 N.Z., 2 S.A., 2 Ind., 1 B.W.I., and 5 Egypt burials.

2485 ZUYDCOOTE MILITARY CEMETERY (Nord). 6 miles NE. of Dunkerque, 600 yards E. of Zuydcoote Sta., 400 yards W. of village on farm track. Majority of British burials date from Aug. to Nov. 1917. Records 313 U.K., 6 Can., 3 N.Z., 2 S.A., 1 Aust., 1 Egypt., and 1 Belg. burials.

588 COXYDE MILI-
TARY CEMETERY (W.
FLANDERS). 1½ miles
from coast, 1 mile W. of
Coxyde village and sta.,
on road to La Panne.
Used by 4th Army from
June to end of 1917.
Records 1,452 U.K., 19
N.Z., 18 Aust., 14 Can.,
2 S.A., and 1 B.W.I., also
10 German burials.

13 ADINKERKE
MILITARY CEME-
TERY (W. FLAN-
DERS). 2¾ miles W. of
Furnes, S. of village and
Adinkerke-Panne Sta. on
road to Bulscamp. The
village was 8 miles behind
the 4th Army front from
June to Nov. 1917. Re-
cords 158 U.K., 5 Aust.,
2 Can., 2 B.W.I., 1
Egypt., 4 Russ., and 98
German burials.

12 ADINKERKE
CHURCHYARD EX-
TENSION (W. FLAN-
DERS). 2¾ miles W. of
Furnes, 200 yards from
Adinkerke - Panne Sta.,
near church and road to
La Panne. In June 1917
the 4th Army took over
the sector before Adin-
kerke from St. Georges
to the sea, and held it
until Nov. 1917. British
plot in Belgian Mil. Cem.
and records 69 U.K. and
8 B.W.I. burials.

NIEUPORT—OSTENDE

MAP SHEET No. 2

NIEUPORT MEMOR-
IAL (W. FLANDERS).
½ mile NE. of Nieuport
Station, where the Os-
tende road crosses the R.
Yser, within the British
lines held by 32nd Di-
vision after July 10th
1917. Records 566 U.K.
'Missing' who fell in
the operations of 1914
and 1917.

NIEUPORT is a small town in the Province of West Flanders, on the south-west side of the River Yser, two miles from the sea.

To relieve Antwerp the 87th French Territorial Division, the Brigade of Fusiliers Marins, and the British Royal Naval, 7th, and 3rd Cavalry Divisions arrived on the coast at different dates early in October. The Royal Naval Division alone reached Antwerp, where they made a short but gallant stand. The French Marines and the two British Divisions covered the retreat of Belgian forces from Ghent, and the British Divisions were placed under Sir John French's command on the 9th October. The whole British Army was drawn south to Ypres and La Bassée.

In June 1917 the British Fourth Army (now reduced to the XV Corps) took over the sector from St. Georges to the sea from the XXXVI French Corps. The town of Nieuport, almost destroyed above ground, had been equipped by the French troops with a considerable system of tunnels.

The 1st and 32nd Divisions came to Nieuport in the middle of June, and the 66th (East Lancashire) Division at the end of June.

On the 10th July the enemy began an intense bombardment, which was followed in the evening by what is known as the 'German Attack on Nieuport'. The blow fell, in particular, on the 1st Division. Parties from two battalions of this Division (the 1st Northamptons and the 2nd King's Royal Rifles) were holding the left of the line from the sea for a mile south-eastwards; they were cut off by the demolition of the bridges, and annihilated, except for 76 officers and men who swam the river. The 32nd Division, immediately north of Nieuport, lost its advanced trenches, but retained the bridgehead. Fighting continued until the 17th, but the new line was held. In that month of July the 1st Division sustained over 2,000 casualties, and the 32nd Division nearly 1,000.

In the middle of July the 49th (West Riding) Division joined the XV Corps, and the 33rd Division came at the end of July. No further offensive move was made on either side, though the monthly casualties of the Divisions were heavier than in other quiet sectors. The advance made from Ypres was too slow and too costly to justify a diversion from Nieuport. The Divisions continued to change. The 33rd Division left at the end of August, the 49th Division in the middle of September, and the 66th Division at the end of September. The 42nd (East Lancashire) Division came early in September and the 41st Division at the end of the month. The 1st and 32nd Divisions left in October, and the 9th (Scottish) Division came. In the middle of November the 41st Division left for Italy, and the 9th and 42nd, relieved by two French Divisions, returned to the original British Front. The occupation of Nieuport by the British forces was ended.

5

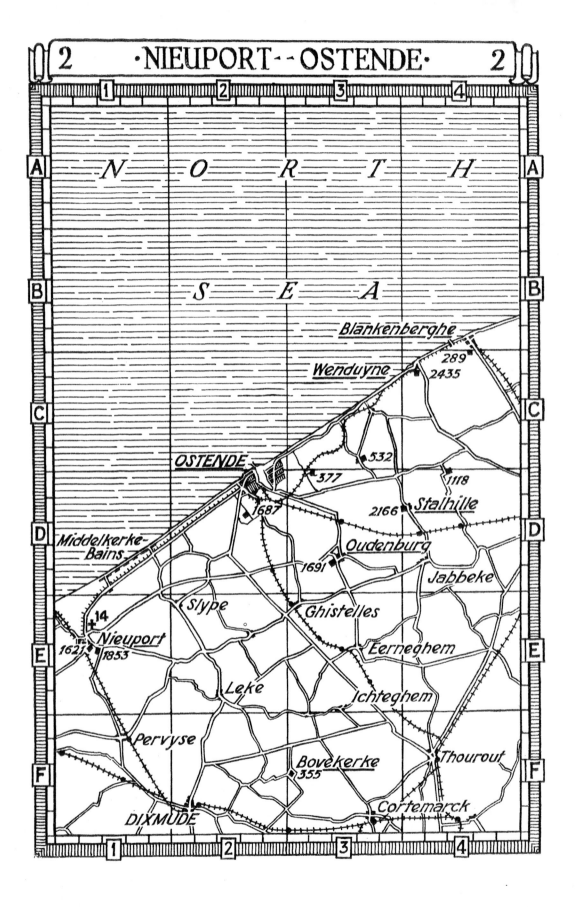

A   N   O   R   T   H   A

B   S   E   A   B

Blankenberghe

Wenduyne — 289
2435

C   C

532

OSTENDE   *377*

1118

2166   *Stalhille*
1687

D   D
Middelkerke-   *Oudenburg*
Bains
1691   *Jabbeke*

Slype   *Ghistelles*

14
E   *Nieuport*   *Eerneghem*   E
1621   1853

Leke   *Ichteghem*

Pervyse

Bovekerke   *Thourout*
F   *355*   F

Cortemarck
DIXMUDE

1621 NIEUPORT COMMUNAL CEMETERY (W. FLANDERS). 10 miles SW. of Ostende, E. of Nieuport town and sta., S. of road to St. Pierre-Capelle. The 4th Army took over this sector June 1917 and held it through the German attack on Nieuport July 10–17th until Nov. 1917. Records 70 U.K. and 3 Belg. burials.

1853 RAMSCAPPELLE ROAD MILITARY CEMETERY, ST. GEORGES (W. FLANDERS). 1 mile E. of Nieuport, at junction of Ramscappelle and St. Georges roads. Created after the Armistice from isolated graves and small cems. from the battlefields in the vicinity. Records 804 U.K., 7 Aust., 2 Can., 1 S.A., and 2 German burials.

1687 OSTENDE NEW COMMUNAL CEMETERY (W. FLANDERS). 1 mile S. of town with entrance in Rue des Deniers. Used by Germans from Oct. 1914 to Oct. 1918. Contains burials from H.M.S. *Vindictive*, which was sunk inside Ostende Harbour May 10th 1918. Records 52 U.K. burials.

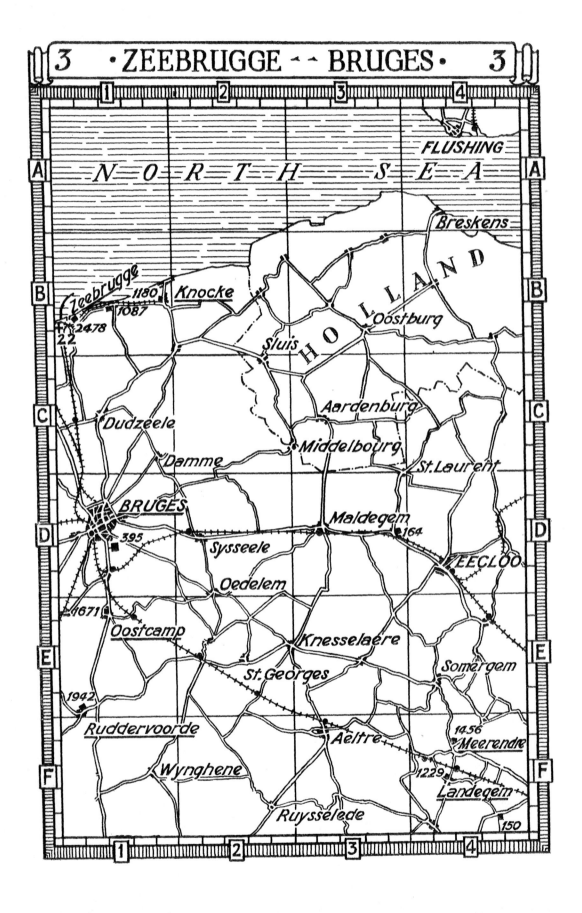

FLUSHING

NORTH SEA

Breskens

Zeebrugge
1180
Knocke
1087
2478
22

HOLLAND

Sluis

Oostburg

Aardenburg

Dudzeele

Middelbourg

Damme

St. Laurent

BRUGES

Maldegem

164

395

Sysseele

ZEECLOO

Oedelem

1671

Oostcamp

Knesselaere

St. Georges

Somergem

1942

Ruddervoorde

1456
Aeltre
Meerendre

Wynghene

1229

Landegem

Ruysselede

150

ZEEBRUGGE—BRUGES

MAP SHEET No. 3

ZEEBRUGGE MEMORIAL

ZEEBRUGGE. The Bruges Canal at Zeebrugge was an important German Submarine Base until the night before St. Georges Day, April 23rd, 1918, when the enemy submarine menace was seriously checked by the blocking of that canal at Zeebrugge. This audacious affair was carried out to a successful conclusion at night through new and uncharted enemy mine-fields, and under the severe fire from the then heavily fortified Belgian coast. Sir Roger Keyes commanded a flotilla, comprising the block-ships *Intrepid,* *Iphigenia*, and *Thetis*, also the *Brilliant* and *Sirius* for Ostende Harbour, the cruiser *Vindictive* to attack the Mole, two ferry-boats, the *Daffodil* and *Iris*, the submarine ' C.3 ', supported by monitors and destroyers, with a flotilla of fast launches and motor-boats.

The *Vindictive*, assisted by the *Daffodil* and *Iris*, attacked and landed boarding-parties on the extremity of the Mole, and the submarine ' C.3 ' was blown up as arranged, destroying the viaduct and preventing reinforcements from reaching the Mole. Meanwhile the block-ships, under the glare of searchlights and point-blank range of enemy guns, entered the channel of the canal and there blew up, to remain until the end of the War, an insurmountable barrier to enemy submarines and destroyers.

9

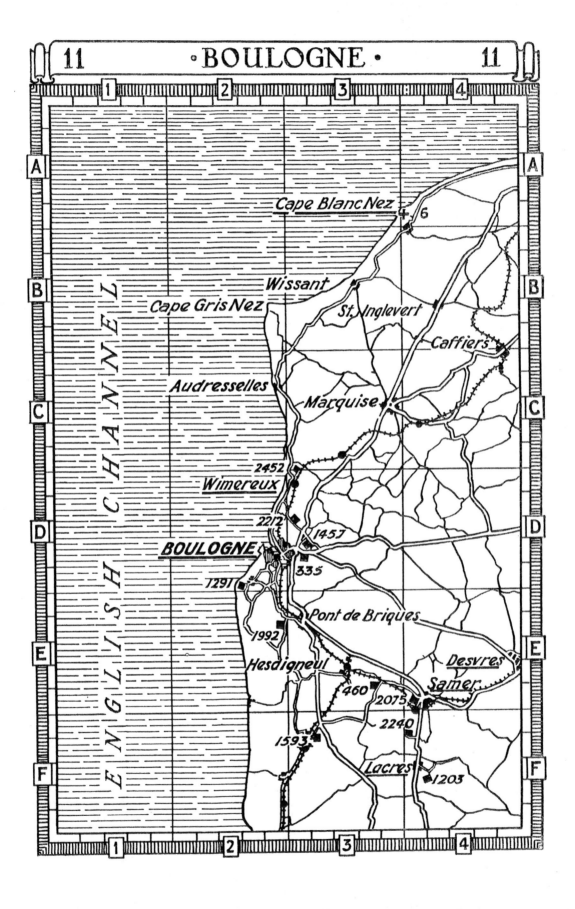

Cape Blanc Nez + 6

Wissant

Cape Gris Nez

St. Inglevert

Caffiers

Audresselles

Marquise

ENGLISH CHANNEL

2452

Wimereux

2212

1457

BOULOGNE

335

1291

Pont de Briques

1992

Desvres

Hesdigneul

Samer

460

2075

2240

1593

Lacres

1203

BOULOGNE
MAP SHEET No. 11

BOULOGNE-SUR-MER, a large town and seaport in the Department of the Pas-de-Calais, was one of the three Base ports most extensively used by the British Armies on the Western Front. It was closed and cleared on August 27th, 1914, in consequence of the retreat of the Allies; but it was opened again in October, and from that month to the end of the War Boulogne and Wimereux formed one of the chief hospital areas.

DOVER PATROL MEMORIAL, CAP BLANC-NEZ, ESCALLES (P. de C.). 9 miles W. of Calais Station on Coast road to Boulogne. Erected in Memory of the glorious co-operation of the French Navy in the Dover Patrol 1914–1919 (there is a similar Memorial at Dover).

335 BOULOGNE EASTERN CEMETERY (P. de C.). On high ground overlooking V., in which town is situated. Boulogne was one of three Base ports most extensively used by British Armies on the Western Front. Records 4,696 U.K., 438 Can., 307 Aust., 74 N.Z., 38 B.W.I., 15 S.A., 4 Newfld., 2 Bermuda and 4 Egypt. burials.

1457 MEERUT MILITARY CEMETERY, ST. MARTIN - LES - BOULOGNE (P. de C.). 2 miles NE. of Boulogne Ville Sta., ¾ mile N. of St. Martin-les-Boulogne Sta., near road to Terlincthun. Contains Casualties from Indian Army 1914–1915, Egypt. Lab. Corps of Aug.- Sept. 1917, and Indian Drivers who died 1919. Records 281 Ind., 26 Egypt. burials and 32 special memorials.

1992 ST. ETIENNE-AU-MONT COMMUNAL CEMETERY (P. de C.). 3 miles S. of Boulogne above R. Liane. No. 2 Native Lab. Gen. Hosp. was posted here from 1917 to 1919. Records 163 Chin. and 5 S.A.N. L.C. burials (contains Chinese memorial).

2212 TERLINCTHUN BRITISH CEMETERY, WIMILLE (P. de C.). 1¾ miles from Boulogne Town Sta., E. of main Boulogne - Calais road. Burials mostly those who died at the Base hospitals at Boulogne and Wimereux. Records 2,551 U.K., 277 Can., 88 Aust., 29 N.Z., 10 Newfld., 1 S.A., 1 Guernsey, 33 S.A., 5 B.W.I., 16 Unknown, 1 American, 27 Italian, 4 Russian, 3 Poles, 2 Serbs, and 188 German burials.

2452 WIMEREUX COMMUNAL CEME-TERY (P. de C.). Near coast, 3 miles N. of Boulogne, ¾ mile from Wimille-Wimereux Sta., and 50 yards from E. of Ambleteuse road. Was important hospital centre. Records 2,310 U.K., 216 Can., 208 Aust., 79 N.Z., 21 B.W.I., 10 S.A., and 3 Newfld. Contains memorial seat to Lt.-Col. John McCrae inscribed with verse of his poem 'In Flanders Fields'.

McCrae Memorial Seat, Wimereux Communal Cemetery

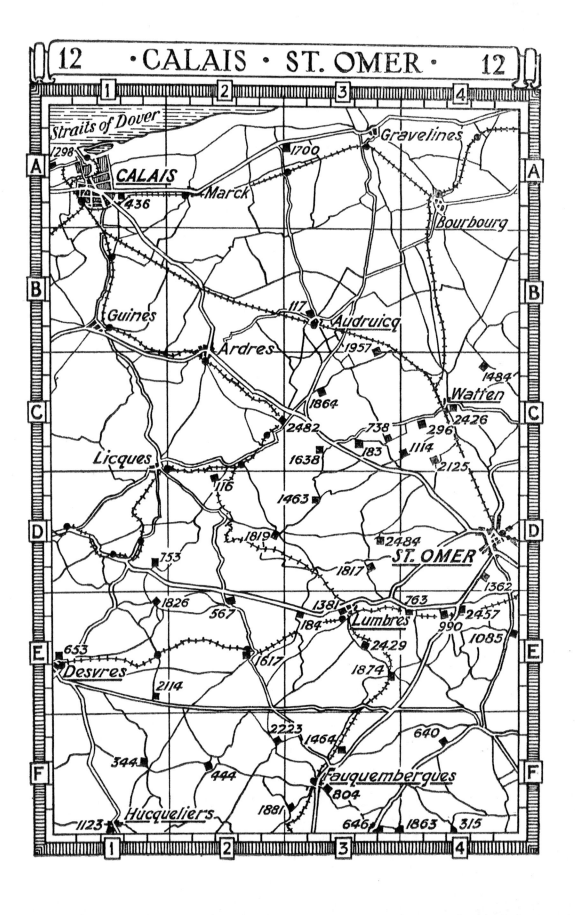

CALAIS—ST. OMER

MAP SHEET No. 12

CALAIS is a considerable town and seaport of 72,000 inhabitants in the Department of the Pas-de-Calais.

In April 1915 it was found necessary to open a new Base which would be nearer to the British Front than Havre or Rouen and would relieve those Bases and Boulogne, and No. 6 Base Supply Depot was started at Calais. The 30th, 35th, and 38th General Hospitals, No. 9 British Red Cross Hospital, and No. 10 Canadian Stationary Hospital were the Medical Units stationed in the town; the hospital accommodation at its greatest strength was about 2,500 beds. The Base remained open until the last formations of the Army left France in March 1921.

436 CALAIS SOUTHERN CEMETERY (P. de C.). 1½ miles from Calais-Ville Sta., at tram terminus on road to Gravelines. No. 6 Base Supply Depot was opened at Calais April 1915, and the 30th, 35th, and 38th Gen. Hosps., No. 9 B.R. C.S. and No. 10 Can. Sta. Hosp. were stationed in the town. Records 640 U.K., 35 Aust., 27 Can., 12 N.Z., 1 S.A., 1 Newfld, 1 B.W.I., and 1 Nat. Sea. burials.

ST. OMER is a small town of great antiquity in the Department of the Pas-de-Calais, on the main road and railway between Calais and Lille.

St. Omer became on October 13th, 1914, and remained until the end of March 1916, the General Headquarters of the British Expeditionary Force. Lord Roberts died there in November 1914. It was a considerable hospital centre, more especially in 1918: the 4th, 10th, 7th Canadian, 9th Canadian and New Zealand Stationary Hospitals, the 7th, 58th (Scottish) and 59th (Northern) General Hospitals, and the 17th, 18th and 1st and 2nd Australian Casualty Clearing Stations were all, at some time during the War, quartered in St. Omer. It was raided by aeroplanes in November 1917 and May 1918, with serious loss of life.

1362 LONGUENESSE (ST. OMER) SOUVENIR CEMETERY (P. de C.). 2 miles S. of St. Omer Sta., E. of Wizernes road. Town was Gen. Hdqtrs. of Brit. Exp. Force Oct. 1914 to March 1916. (Lord Roberts died here Nov. 1914.) Considerable hospital centre. Records 2,364 U.K., 156 Aust., 148 Can., 52 N.Z., 24 S.A., 12 B.W.I., 5 Ind., 2 Guernsey, 1 Newfld., 5 Unknown, 64 Chin., and 180 German burials.

1298 LES BARAQUES MILITARY CEMETERY, SANGATTE (P. de C.). 3 miles W. of Calais-Ville Sta. near coast road to Sangatte and N. of Les Baraques. Burials from Base Hospitals at Calais and used from Sept. 1917. Records 1,002 U.K., 27 Aust., 25 Can., 16 S.A., 6 Ind., 4 N.Z., 1 Newfld., 1 Guernsey, 1 B.W.I., 1 Ind., 1 Fijian, 17 Egypt., 203 Chin., 28 American, 26 Portuguese, 1 Belg., 1 Jap., 236 German, and 15 Unknown burials.

296 BLEUE MAISON MILITARY CEMETERY, EPERLECQUES (P. de C.). 6½ miles NW. of St. Omer, 2,000 yards W. of Watten Sta., NE. of Eperlecques, near road to Watten. Used from May to Oct. 1918 during period of German advance and retreat in Flanders. Few burials after Armistice. Records 52 U.K., and 1 Can. burials.

HAZEBROUCK

MAP SHEET No. 13

HAZEBROUCK is a town and commune in the Department of the Nord, about 35 miles south-east of Calais. It is an important railway junction on the lines from Calais to Lille and from Dunkerque to Paris.

From October 1914 to September 1917 Casualty Clearing Stations were posted at Hazebrouck. From September 1917 to September 1918 enemy shelling and bombing rendered the town unsafe for hospitals; but in September and October 1918 No. 9 British Red Cross Hospital was in the town.

1040 HAZEBROUCK COMMUNAL CEME-TERY (Nord). 1 mile from sta. on S.W. out-skirts of town. In Sept. and Oct. 1918, No. 9 British Red Cross Hosp. here, but before was un-safe for hospitals. Re-cords 719 U.K., 59 Can., 50 Aust., 30 N.Z., 7 Ind., 1 B.W.I., 11 Unknown, and 2 Chin. burials.

760 ESQUELBECQ MILITARY CEME-TERY (Nord). 1¼ miles from Esquelbecq Halte on S. side of road be-tween sta. and village. Opened in April 1918 when the German offen-sive in Flanders had be-gun. Records 569 U.K., 4 N.Z., 2 Aust., 1 Can., 1 S.A., 1 Ind., 3 French, and 7 German burials.

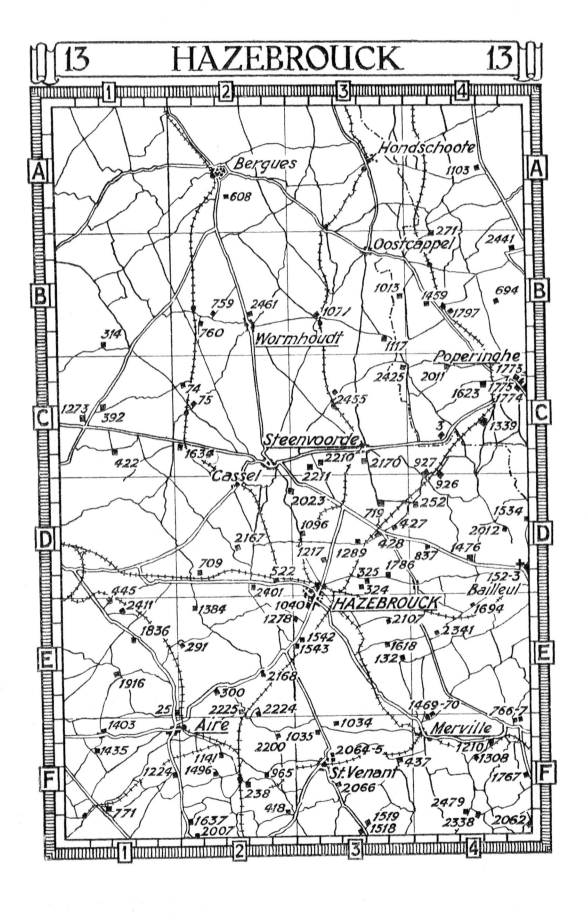

A

A
1217 LA KREULE MILITARY CEMETERY, HAZEBROUCK (Nord). 1½ miles N. of Hazebrouck Sta., W. of road to St. Sylvestre-Cappel. Begun in April 1918 by 1st and 2nd Aust. Casualty Clearing Stations and used by Heavy Artillery and fighting units. Records 456 U.K., 78 Aust., 41 S.A., 1 Newfld., and 12 German burials.

B
522 CINQ RUES BRITISH CEMETERY, HAZEBROUCK (Nord). 2 miles W. of Hazebrouck Sta. N. of road to St. Omer. Begun in April 1918, closed Aug. 1918. Chiefly used by Field Ambulances and fighting units of 29th Div. Records 226 U.K. burials.

C
709 EBBLINGHEM MILITARY CEMETERY (Nord). ¾ mile N. of Ebblinghem Sta., ½ mile E. of village. Begun by 2nd and 15th Casualty Clearing Stations in April 1918 during Battles of the Lys. Records 266 U.K., 158 Aust., 3 Channel Isls., 2 Can., 2 S.A., 1 Chin., 1 French and 11 German burials.

D
324 BORRE BRITISH CEMETERY (Nord). 2 miles E. of Hazebrouck Sta. W. of road from Borre to Sec Bois. Begun May 1918 and used by Field Ambulances and fighting units (1st Aust. Div.). Records 234 Aust., 130 U.K., and 3 German burials.

B

C

D

25 AIRE COMMUNAL CEMETERY (P. de C.). ½ mile N. of town and 1 mile from sta. on road to St. Omer. The 4 British plots are on E. side. From March 1915 to Feb. 1918 Aire was Corps Hdqtrs. In 1918 town was within eight miles of German lines. Records 865 U.K., 15 Can., 6 Aust., 3 Ind., 3 B.W.I., 1 N.Z., 1 Guernsey, 4 French, and 26 German burials.

2200 TANNAY BRITISH CEMETERY, THIENNES (Nord). Tannay is hamlet of Thiennes. Cemetery is E. of hamlet on S. side of Haverskerque road, 2¼ miles from Thiennes Sta. Made by units of 5th Div., during German offensive April 1918. Records 362 U.K. and 1 Can. burials.

2224 THIENNES BRITISH CEMETERY (Nord). 5½ miles SW. of Hazebrouck and ½ mile E. of station in angle formed by Nieppe Canal and the Forest of Nieppe. Opened in May 1918 during German offensive and used by the 5th, 59th and 61st Divs. Records 114 U.K. burials.

694 DOZINGHEM MILITARY CEMETERY, WESTVLETEREN (W. FLANDERS). Near French frontier, S. of village and 5 miles from Poperinghe, light railway within 500 yards of cem. Records 3,021 U.K., 61 Can., 34 B.W.I., 19 Newfld., 15 S.A., 14 N.Z., 6 Aust., 1 Unknown, 3 Chinese, and 65 German burials.

1013 HARINGHE (BANDAGHEM) MILITARY CEMETERY, ROUSBRUGGE - HARINGHE (W. FLANDERS). 6 miles NW. of Poperinghe, near road to Bergues, 500 yards S. of Haringhe. Used by Casualty Clearing Stations from July 1917 to Oct. 1918. Records 732 U.K., 11 N.Z., 7 S.A., 5 Newfld., 4 B.W.I., 2 Aust., 1 Can., 1 Bermuda, 5 Unknown, 4 Chin. and 38 German burials.

1459 MENDINGHEM BRITISH CEMETERY, PROVEN (W. FLANDERS). 5½ miles NW. of Poperinghe Sta. on road to Bergues, ½ mile. NW. of village and sta. Name of Mendinghem, like those of Dozinghem and Bandaghem, was coined by the troops. Records 2,267 U.K., 33 S.A., 27 Can., 26 B.W.I., 14 Aust., 12 N.Z., 3 Newfld., 8 Chin., and 51 German burials.

74 ARNEKE BRITISH CEMETERY (Nord). 1 mile from Arneke Sta. and 1 mile NW. of Church, on S. side of farm road which turns E. from Gravelines road. Used by Clearing Sta. and Stationary Hospitals from Oct. 1917. Records 418 U.K., 9 Aust., 3 Can., 2 N.Z., 2 S.A., 1 Unknown, some French, and 2 German burials.

608 CROIX-ROUGE MILITARY CEMETERY, QUAEDYPRE (Nord). 6½ miles S. of Dunkerque, 2 miles SE. of Bergues Sta., on byroad E. of Cassel road. Named after Red Cross Hospital which existed in vicinity. Records 81 U.K. burials.

1534 MONT-NOIR MILITARY CEMETERY, ST. JANSCAPPEL (Nord). 3 miles N. of Bailleul, on S. slope of hill near road to Westoutre. Nearly all casualties fell between April–Sept. 1918, the period of German advance and retirement in this sector. (Mem. to 34th Div. on top of Mont). Records 146 U.K., 2 Newfld., 1 Aust., and 58 French burials.

1623 NINE ELMS BRITISH CEMETERY, POPERINGHE (W. FLANDERS). 2 miles from Poperinghe Sta. on S. of road leading W. from town. Due partly to Battles of Ypres 1917. Records 955 U.K., 289 Can., 149 Aust., 118 N.Z., 26 S.A., 8 Guernsey, 7 Newfld., 2 B.W.I., 1 Bermuda, 6 French, and 37 German burials.

1774 POPERINGHE NEW MILITARY CEMETERY (W. FLANDERS). 7 miles due W. of Ypres and 12 miles NE. of Hazebrouck. Cem. on Reninghelst road just outside the town. First a Casualty Clearing Station centre, but Field Ambs. took their place in 1916. Records 596 U.K., 55 Can., 20 Aust., 3 N.Z., 2 B.W.I., and 1 Chinese burials.

1775 POPERINGHE OLD MILITARY CEMETERY (W. FLANDERS). Just outside town SW. of Reninghelst road. Town was Casualty Clearing Station centre until 1916 when Field Ambs. took their place. Records 397 U.K., 46 Can., 1 Chin., 2 German burials and 7 special memorials.

1339 LIJSSENTHŒK MILITARY CEMETERY, POPERINGHE (W. FLANDERS). 2¾ miles SW. of Poperinghe Sta. Poperinghe-Ypres road was the main communication with Flanders battle-fields. Between June 1915 and the Armistice it was the second greatest Brit. War Cem. Records 7,305 U.K., 1,128 Aust., 1,051 Can., 291 N.Z., 28 S.A., 22 B.W.I., 5 Newfld., 2 Ind., 32 Chin., and 3 Unknown burials.

3 ABEELE AERODROME MILITARY CEMETERY, WATOU (W. FLANDERS). On Franco-Belgian frontier, SW. of Abeele and sta., on N. side of road to Steenvoorde. Records 104 British burials.

926 GODEWAERSVELDE BRITISH CEMETERY (Nord). Close to Belgian frontier, ⅝ mile E. of Godewaersvelde sta., a little E. of village, beyond railway. Begun in July 1917 between Battle of Messines and the Battle of Ypres. Records 894 U.K., 65 Aust., 4 Can., 2 N.Z., 2 S.A., 1 Ind., and 19 German burials.

152 BAILLEUL COM-
MUNAL CEMETERY
(Nord). 1 mile N. of
sta. on E. outskirts of
town. An important rail-
head, air depot and hosp.
centre; after Battle of
Bailleul (13–15th April
1918) it fell into German
hands for over four
months. Records 586
U.K., 21 Can., 4 Ind.,
1 French, 2 Belg., 8 Ger-
man burials and 13 special
memorials.

153 BAILLEUL COM-
MUNAL CEMETERY
EXTENSION (Nord).
1 mile N. of sta. on E.
outskirts of town, E. of
Com. Cem. Was a Corps
Hdqtrs. until July 1917
when it was severely
bombed and shelled. Re-
cords 3,411 U.K., 396
Aust., 290 Can., 252
N.Z., 4 Ind., 3 B.W.I.,
1 S.A., 1 Newfld., 1
Guernsey, 31 Chin., 1
Russ., 3 French, 111 Ger-
man burials and 11 special
memorials.

1694 OUTTERSTEENE
COMMUNAL CEME-
TERY EXTENSION,
BAILLEUL (Nord). 3½
miles SW. of Bailleul Sta.
N.E. of village, on NW. of
road to Bailleul. Taken
by 3rd Corps Oct. 13th
1914, retaken by Ger-
mans April 12th 1918,
finally captured by 9th,
29th, and 31st Divs.
Aug. 18–19th. Records
854 U.K., 230 Aust., 19
Channel Isls., 4 Can., 2
N.Z., 2 B.W.I., 1 S.A.,
262 Unknown, 1 Chin.
burials and 14 special
memorials.

132 AVAL WOOD MILITARY CEMETERY, VIEUX - BER - QUIN (Nord). 1½ miles S. of Strazeele Sta. at SE. corner of Bois d'Aval. Made largely by 11th Batts. of E. Yorks and E. Lancs. June and Aug. 1918 after the Battles of the Lys. Records 406 U.K., 3 Aust., 1 German burials and 2 special memorials.

1618 NIEPPE - BOIS (RUE-DU-BOIS) MILI-TARY CEMETERY, VIEUX - BERQUIN (Nord). 1½ miles SW. of Strazeele Sta. on N. edge of Aval Wood on S. side of Rue-du-bois. Records 55 U.K., and 15 Aust. burials, all but one fell in April–Sept. 1918.

1476 METEREN MILI-TARY CEMETERY (Nord). 2¾ miles W. of Bailleul Sta. on road to Berthen. First taken by 10th Bgde. of 4th Div. Oct. 13th 1914, finally retaken by 9th (Scot) Div. July 19th 1918 after a fortnight's bombard-ment. Records 583 U.K., 104 Aust., 31 S.A., 22 N.Z., 15 Ind., 5 Can., 1 Newfld., 65 French, and 7 special memorials.

1210 LA GORGUE COMMUNAL CEME-TERY (Nord). ¾ mile SW. of station, S. of town. British railhead and a Field Amb. station. From April 10th to Sept. 1918 was in enemy hands. Records 144 U.K., and 1 German burials.

1289 LE PEUPLIER MILITARY CEMETERY, CAESTRE (Nord). 30 yards off the Caestre-Staple road, and about 1¾ miles from Caestre Sta. Begun in May 1918 and used by fighting units during the period between German and British offensives of that year. Records 60 U.K. and 45 Aust. burials.

1469 MERVILLE COMMUNAL CEMETERY (Nord). 1 mile NE. of sta. on NE. of town. Railhead until May 1915, billeting and Hosp. centre from 1915 to 1918. Hdqtrs. of Indian Corps Oct. 1914 and autumn 1915. Records 1,143 U.K., 93 Ind., 21 Aust., and 11 Can. burials.

1470 MERVILLE COMMUNAL CEMETERY EXTENSION (Nord). E. of Com. Cem. opened Aug. 1916 and enlarged after Armistice. Records 896 U.K., 3 Can., 2 S.A., 1 Aust., 9 German burials and 18 special memorials.

252 BERTENACRE MILITARY CEMETERY, FLETRE (Nord). 6 miles NE. of Hazebrouck, 1½ miles S. of Godewaersvelde Sta., near road to Eecke. Earliest burials were 38 men of 10th R.W. Surrey Regt. Aug. 18th 1917, and last burial made Sept. 1918. Records 108 U.K. and 2 Can. burials.

766–7 ESTAIRES COMMUNAL CEMETERY AND EXTENSION (Nord). 7½ miles SW. of Armentières, 1 mile NE. of La Gorgue-Estaires Sta., E. of village near road to Armentières. Cem. was used from Nov. 1914 to June 1917. Ext. from June 1917 to Oct. 1918. Records 232 U.K., 5 Can., 3 Aust., 1 N.Z., 1 Ind., 2 French and 3 German burials.

1278 LE GRAND HASARD MILITARY CEMETERY, MOR-BECQUE (Nord). Le Grand Hasard is a hamlet on Hazebrouck side of Morbecque, and Cem. is 500 yards along road which runs W. from the hamlet. Begun by 31st Div. and also used by the 40th. Records 264 U.K. and 36 Aust. burials.

1542 MORBECQUE BRITISH CEMETERY (Nord). Morbecque is 2 miles from Hazebrouck on road to Aire, and Cem. lies 200 yards from that road on a side road lead-ing SE. from village. Begun by the 5th Div. in April 1918 during the German advance in Flan-ders. Records 104 U.K. burials.

2062 ST. VAAST POST MILITARY CEME-TERY, RICHEBOURG L'AVOUE (P. de C.). 6 miles NE. of Béthune, 4 miles S. of Laventie Sta., 1 mile N. of village, E. of 'Edward Road'. Begun May 9th 1915 from Battles of Aubers Ridge and Festubert and used until July 1917. Re-opened Sept. 1918. Records 752 U.K., 47 Ind., and 91 German burials.

2064 ST. VENANT COMMUNAL CEMETERY (P. de C.). $\frac{7}{8}$ mile NE. of station, E. of town, along canal bank. From January 1915 to Oct. 1917 used as Brit. and Ind. Casualty Clearing Stations. Records 85 Ind. and 71 U.K. burials.

2065 ST. VENANT COMMUNAL CEMETERY EXTENSION. S. end of Com. Cem. Used from Dec. 1916 to Dec. 1918. Records 91 U.K., 2 S.A., 8 Unknown and 1 French burials.

2066 ST. VENANT-ROBECQ ROAD BRITISH CEMETERY, ROBECQ (P. de C.). $1\frac{1}{4}$ miles S. of St. Venant Sta. on road between St. Venant and Robecq. Begun about April 12th 1918 and used as a front-line Cem. until end of July. Records 475 U.K. and 1 Aust. burials.

1034 HAVERSKERQUE BRITISH CEMETERY (Nord). 2 miles N. of St. Venant town and Sta., ¾ mile from village, 500 yards N. of road running E. of Merville. Casualties from German advance in this sector April 1918. Records 89 U.K., and 1 German burials.

1518 MONT BERNENCHON BRITISH CEMETERY, GONNEHEM (P. de C.). 5 miles NW. of Béthune, SW. of village. Begun by 2nd Lancs. Fus. April 1918, used by fighting units and 13th Corps. Records 166 U.K. (mostly 4th Div.), and 2 French burials.

2338 VIEILLE-CHAPELLE NEW MILITARY CEMETERY (P. de C.). 6¼ miles N. of Béthune, 3 miles S. of Lestrem Sta., 300 yards N. of village on road to Lestrem. Begun by Middlesex Regt. and Gordon Highlanders end of 1914. Enlarged after Armistice by concentration of smaller Cems. Records 909 U.K., 1 Can., 71 Ind., and 9 special memorials.

1767 PONT-DU-HEM MILITARY CEME-TERY, LA GORGUE (P. de C.). 2 miles SW. of Laventie Sta., 2½ miles S. of La Gorgue-Estaires Sta., on road to La Bassée. Begun summer 1915, used during German advance April 1918, enlarged after Armistice from battle-fields of Neuve-Chapelle and Richebourg-l'Avoué. Records 1,549 U.K., 40 N.Z., 38 Aust., 22 Can., 11 Ind., 1 U.S.A., and 112 German burials.

2479 ZELOBES IN-DIAN CEMETERY, LACOUTURE (P. de C.). Between Béthune and Estaires, on Béthune-Estaires road, sta. at Lacouture. Hamlet was in Brit. hands from early days of War until April 11th 1918. Records 105 Indian burials.

THE LAND IN FRANCE OCCUPIED BY BRITISH WAR CEMETERIES IS, BY A LAW OF 29TH DECEMBER 1915, THE FREE GIFT OF THE FRENCH PEOPLE FOR THE PERPETUAL RESTING-PLACE OF THOSE WHO ARE LAID THERE.

YPRES—ARMENTIERES

MAP SHEET Nos. 14 AND 14A
YPRES

YPRES is an old town and a commune in the Province of West Flanders. It was, from October 1914 to the Autumn of 1918, the centre of a Salient held by the British (and for some months by the French) forces in Belgium. From April 1915 it was bombarded and destroyed more completely than any other town of its size on the Western Front ; but even to the end certain buildings remained distinguishable. The ruins of the Cathedral and the Cloth Hall stood together in the middle of the city. The Infantry Barracks stood, in part, at the re-entrant angle of the south walls. The Prison, the Reservoir, and the Water Tower were together at the Western Gate ; and the prison was ' a fine example of the resistance to shell-fire of thick walls if they are thick enough ' (*War Diary of the 1st Irish Guards*, quoted by Mr. Rudyard Kipling).

It was surrounded by ramparts and a moat ; and from these, on its eastern side, issued the road to Menin. The Menin Gate is rebuilt as a memorial to some of those who fell in the salient and have no known graves.

MENIN GATE MEMORIAL, YPRES (W. FLANDERS). A ' Hall of Memory ' ⅝ mile NE. of sta. on ·Menin road where hundreds of thousands passed through to the Ypres Salient. Records 56,000 Missing ·of the Brit. Emp. who fell in the Salient from Oct. 1914 to the night of Aug. 15 – 16th 1917, when Battle of Langemarck began.

The remaining ' Missing ' who fell in the Salient after the Battle of Langemarck are recorded on the Memorial in Tyne Cot Cem., Passchendaele, which is the largest British War Cem. in the world.

THE SALIENT. Between the 19th September and the 18th October 1914 the original Ypres Salient was formed. The British 7th Division and 3rd Cavalry Division, which had landed at Zeebrugge and Ostende on the 6th, 7th, and 8th October, helped to cover the Belgian retreat through West Flanders and arrived at Ypres on the 14th. The British II and III Corps from the Aisne reached on the 10th–11th October a line behind Hazebrouck and La Bassée. The German IV Cavalry Corps, which had entered Ypres, Bailleul, and Hazebrouck early in October, was forced back by our Cavalry Corps to the Ypres–Comines Canal, and the III Corps moved up behind them. The British I Corps entered Ypres on the 20th.

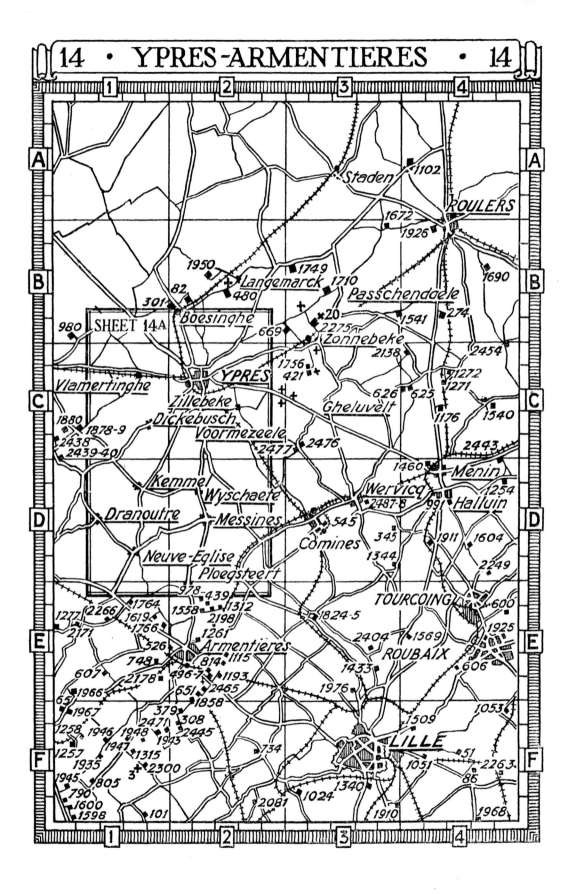

The Armies were now in position 'from the sea to Switzerland'. The Battle of Messines (1914), at the opposite end of the line in Belgium, had begun on the 12th October. There followed the Battle of Langemarck (21st–24th October); the Battle of Gheluvelt, astride the Menin Road (29th–31st October); and the Battle of Nonne-Boschen (11th November), in which the British Artillery and what was left of the British Infantry broke the culminating attack of the best German troops.

The closing month of 1914 witnessed the unsuccessful Anglo-French attack on Wytschaete, followed by Artillery fighting.

The Battles of Ypres, 1915, lasted from the 22nd April to the 25th May. They included the Battle of Gravenstafel Ridge (22nd–23rd April), in which gas was employed for the first time; the Battle of St. Julien (24th April–4th May); the Actions of Steenstraat (23rd April–5th May) in which the Belgians held their ground; the German Gas Attacks on Hill 60 (1st and 5th May); the Battle of Frezenberg Ridge (8th–13th May); and the Battle of Bellewaarde Ridge (24th–25th May). The Empire lost in this fighting 60,260 soldiers killed, wounded, and missing; and in the course of it we withdrew our line to north of Wieltje-Frezenberg to south and west of Hooge. The northern side of the Salient was re-drawn. Four actions were fought at Hooge (2nd June–9th August). The British attacks on Bellewaarde (16th June and 25th–26th September) and the German local attacks in July and August were not successful.

The year 1917 began with five months of trench warfare in the Salient, and these were followed by six months of successful but costly attack by the Allied forces. In the British official history this offensive is known as the Battle of Messines, 1917, and the Battles of Ypres, 1917; the Germans call the period from the 27th May to the 3rd December that of the Battle of Flanders, 1917. Its immediate object was 'the capture of the Messines-Wytschaete Ridge, and of the high ground which extends thence north-eastwards for some seven miles and then trends north through Broodseinde and Passchendaele'.

The first step was taken at the beginning of June, when a Corps was sent to take over from French troops a line, about four miles long, from St. Georges to the sea about Nieuport.

The next step was the Battle of Messines (7th–14th June), in which for the first time Australian and New Zealand troops took part in the fighting north of Ploegsteert Wood. It began with the explosion of nineteen mines, long prepared.

On the 31st July the Battles of Ypres, 1917, began, and on the 10th November, they ended in the capture of Passchendaele. They included the Battles of Pilckem Ridge, Langemarck, the Menin Road Ridge, Polygon Wood, Broodseinde, Poelcapelle, and Passchendaele.

The year 1918, however, the last of the War, witnessed the three great efforts of the German Army to snatch the final victory. In March they attacked the right and centre of the British line and drove back the Fifth Army, and part of the Third, nearly to Amiens. Their second attempt to break through was on the British left wing; the Battle of the Lys (known to the French as the Third Battle of Flanders and to the Germans as the Battle of Kemmel) began on the 9th April and lasted until the 30th.

The German effort, repeated in June far to the south, failed; and five months later their gains were lost for ever. In Flanders, after a few successful local advances, the British, French, and Belgian forces, under the King of the Belgians, attacked on the 28th September. 'By the end of the day the British divisions had passed far beyond the farthest limits of the 1917 battles.'

By the 6th October the British left had reached Ledeghem (due east of Ypres), and the right was on the Lys at Comines and Warneton. The Belgians and French were on the line from Ledeghem to Roulers. Eleven days later the Belgians were in Ostende, and the British warships in the harbour. The Ypres Salient existed only as a battle-field and a memory.

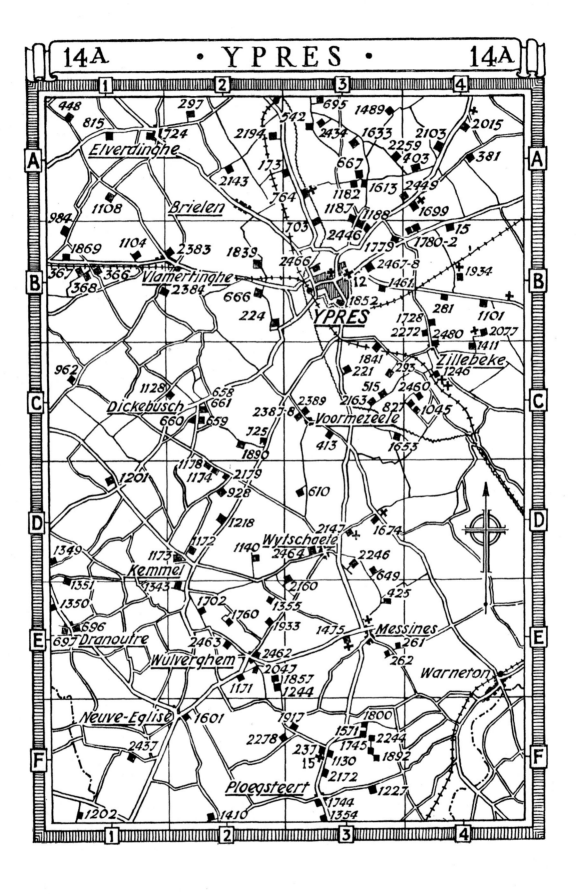

980 GWALIA CEME-
TERY, POPERINGHE
(W. FLANDERS). 2
miles NE. of Poperinghe
Sta. on road to Elver-
dinghe, behind farm
known to Army as Gwalia
Farm. Begun in July
1917 between the Battle
of Messines and the
Battles of Ypres. Re-
cords 436 U.K., 14
B.W.I., 5 Can., 5 N.Z.,
2 Aust., 1 S.A., 2 Belg.,
4 Chin., and 3 German
burials.

448 CANADA FARM
CEMETERY, ELVER-
DINGHE (W. FLAN-
DERS). 5 miles NW. of
Ypres and $3\frac{3}{4}$ miles from
Poperinghe station, $\frac{1}{2}$
mile SW. of Poperinghe-
Woesten road. Used as
dressing station during
Flanders offensive June
to Oct. 1917. Records
879 U.K., 5 Can., 4
Newfld., and 19 B.W.I.
burials.

815 FERME-OLIVIER
CEMETERY, ELVER-
DINGHE (W. FLAN-
DERS). On road to
Poperinghe, 1 mile W. of
Elverdinghe, $3\frac{1}{2}$ miles
from Poperinghe Sta., 3
from Vlamertinghe Sta.
and $4\frac{1}{2}$ from Ypres. Used
continuously between
June 9th 1915 and Aug.
5th 1917 by Field Ambs.
Records 405 U.K. and 3
German burials.

1108 HOSPITAL FARM CEMETERY, ELVERDINGHE (W. FLANDERS). 4 miles NW. of Ypres, 1½ miles from Vlamertinghe Sta., near road to Elverdinghe. Hospital Farm was used as dressing station and Cem. is behind farm. Records 115 U.K. and 1 French civilian burials.

1104 HOP STORE CEMETERY, VLA-MERTINGHE (W. FLANDERS). 3¼ miles from Ypres Sta., W. of village and ⅝ mile from Vlamertinghe Sta. Was for a time used as Hdqtrs. both by our Heavy Artillery and Field Ambs. Records 247 U.K., 1 Can., and 1 French burials.

297 BLEUET FARM CEMETERY, ELVER-DINGHE (W. FLAN-DERS). 1 mile E. of village, 150 yards from road to Boesinghe. Was a dressing station during Flanders offensive 1917. Records 437 U.K., 3 S.A., 1 Can., 1 Newfld., 1 French, and 1 German burials.

366 BRANDHŒK MILITARY CEME-TERY, VLAMER-TINGHE (W. FLAN-DERS). On road and railway between Pope-ringhe and Ypres. Brand-hœk is a hamlet about 1½ miles from Vlamertinghe Sta. and 2½ from Pope-ringhe Sta. Its three Cems. are on S. side of village. Was a centre for Field Ambs. during the War. Records 601 U.K., 62 Can., 4 Aust., 2 Bermuda and 1 German burials.

367 BRANDHŒK NEW MILITARY CEMETERY (W. FLANDERS). 300 yards W. of, and opened subsequent to, Brand-hœk Mil. Cem. (which see). Was used in July-Aug. 1917. Records 514 U.K., 11 Aust., 6 Can., and 28 German burials.

368 BRANDHŒK NEW MILITARY CEMETERY, No. 3, VLAMERTINGHE (W. FLANDERS). (See Brandhœk Mil. and New Mil. Cems.). This cem. was begun in Aug. 1917, when other cems. were filled, and closed in May 1918. Records 849 U.K., 54 Can., 46 Aust., 18 N.Z., 5 S.A., 1 B.W.I., 4 French, and 1 Chinese burials.

2384 VLAMER-TINGHE NEW MILITARY CEMETERY (W. FLANDERS). 1½ miles SW. of sta. on Ouderdom road. During greater part of war was just outside range of shell fire. Used both by Artillery units and Field Ambs. Records 1,609 U.K., 155 Can., 44 Aust., 3 S.A., 1 N.Z., 1 Guernsey, and 7 German burials.

2194 TALANA FARM CEMETERY, BŒSINGHE (W. FLANDERS). N. of Ypres. Talana Farm on E. of Ypres-Bœsinghe road, 1 mile from Bœsinghe and 3 miles from Ypres Sta. Was about 1 mile from edge of Salient during the war. Records 529 U.K. burials.

2143 SOLFERINO FARM CEMETERY, BRIELEN (W. FLANDERS). 3¼ miles NW. of Ypres Sta., 2 miles SW. of old German front line of June 1917, ½ mile N. of village on road running from 'Dawson's Corner' to Bœsinghe. Records 293 U.K., 1 Newfld., and 1 B.W.I. burials.

A

A

2383 VLAMER-TINGHE MILITARY CEMETERY (W. FLANDERS). On main road between Poperinghe and Ypres, with sta. on railway between those towns. Cem. on side road running NW. from church. Begun by French in 1914. Records 1,114 U.K., 52 Can., 4 Aust., 2 S.A., 2 Newfld., 1 Ind., 1 Unknown, and 3 German burials.

B

1869 RED FARM MILITARY CEMETERY, VLAMERTINGHE (W. FLANDERS). 2 miles W. of Vlamertinghe Sta., N. of Poperinghe-Ypres road. Centre for Medical Posts and Cems. Used April–May 1918 during battles of the Lys. Records 46 U.K. and 3 Civ. burials.

B

C

C

1182 LA BELLE ALLIANCE CEMETERY, BŒSINGHE (W. FLANDERS). 2½ miles N. of Ypres Sta. La Belle Alliance Farm is E. and S. of Bœsinghe, near the W. end of Buffs Road. Cem. is near SW. corner of farm and was made in Feb. and March 1916 by the 10th and 11th K.R.R.C. Records 60 U.K. burials.

D

984 HAGLE DUMP CEMETERY, ELVERDINGHE (W. FLANDERS). 2¼ miles W. of Vlamertinghe Sta., N. of Poperinghe-Ypres road. Behind Brit. front line throughout war. Begun April 1918 during battles of the Lys. Records 397 U.K., 26 Aust., 14 Can., and 2 German burials.

D

703 DUHALLOW A.D.S. CEMETERY, YPRES (W. FLANDERS). On Bœsinghe road, 1½ miles from Ypres Sta. Begun during Battle of Pilckem Ridge, July 1917. Records 1,442 U.K., 26 Can., 13 Aust., 12 Newfld., 6 N.Z., 3 S.A., 2 B.W.I., 2 French, 2 Belg., 52 German burials, and 41 special memorials.

695 DRAGOON CAMP CEMETERY, BŒSINGHE (W. FLANDERS). E. of Yser Canal, within German lines until July 1917. S. of Bœsinghe-Pilckem road, and approached by track leading from point near Dragoon House past Villa Gretchen. Records 66 U.K. burials.

2434 WELSH CEMETERY (CÆSAR'S NOSE), BŒSINGHE (W. FLANDERS). 4 miles N. of Ypres Sta., near crossing of Ypres-Pilckem and Bœsinghe-Wieltje roads. Begun July 1917 by 38th (Welsh) Div. at a spot then known as Cæsar's Nose. Records 62 U.K. and 6 Unknown burials.

1633 NO MAN'S COT CEMETERY, BŒSINGHE (W. FLANDERS). N. of Ypres and is on E. side of canal. Station on Ypres-Thourout railway, on S. side of village. Cem. was named from building on S. side of Admiral's Road. Records 79 British burials, mostly of 51st (Highland) Div.

2259 TRACK 'X' CEMETERY, ST. JEAN - LES - YPRES (W. FLANDERS). 3 miles N. of Ypres Sta. Cem. is 1 mile NW. of village on NE. side of Wieltje-Bœsinghe road. Site of Cem. was between British and German front lines in June 1917. Records 126 U.K., 5 Can., and 12 Unknown burials.

667 DIVISIONAL COLLECTING POST CEMETERY AND EXTENSION, BŒSINGHE (W. FLANDERS). 1½ miles N. of Ypres, E. of Yser Canal. Begun Aug. 1917 by 48th (S. Midland) and 58th (London) Divs. Cem. records 86 U.K. and 1 German burial. The Ext. made after Armistice from battle-fields of Salient records 493 U.K., 102 Aust., 73 Can., 5 N.Z., 2 Newfld., 1 S.A. burials and 2 special memorials.

1613 NEW IRISH FARM CEMETERY, ST. JEAN-LES-YPRES (W. FLANDERS). 2¼ miles NE. of Ypres Sta. on SW. corner of junction of roads to St. Julien and Langemarck, once known as Hammond's Corner, and 300 yards N. of Irish Farm. Begun in Aug. 1917, and records 4,272 U.K., 254 Can., 65 Aust., 23 N.Z., 6 S.A., 5 Ind., 3 Newfld., 1 W.Ind., 12 Unknown, 6 Chin., 1 German burial, and 69 special memorials.

173 BARD COTTAGE CEMETERY, BŒSINGHE (W. FLANDERS). On Bœsinghe road 2½ miles from Ypres Sta. and 1¾ miles from Bœsinghe Sta. It reflects the holding of N. sectors of the Salient by successive Divs. Records 1,616 U.K., 9 Can., 6 Newfld., 3 B.W.I., 2 S.A., 3 German burials, and 3 special memorials.

1187–1188 LA BRIQUE MILITARY CEMETERIES Nos. 1 AND 2 (W. FLANDERS). 1¾ miles NE. of Ypres Sta. on road leading to Langemarck. No. 1 Cem. records 90 U.K. burials, No. 2 Cem. records 777 U.K., 23 Can., 18 Aust., 9 N.Z., 7 S.A., 2 Unknown burials and 4 special memorials.

2446 WHITE HOUSE CEMETERY, ST. JEAN-LES-YPRES (W. FLANDERS). 1⅝ miles NE. of Ypres on road to St. Jean. Was begun in March 1915 and used until April 1918 by units holding this part of line. Records 973 U.K., 73 Can., 40 Aust., 24 N.Z., 5 S.A., 1 Bermuda, 1 B.W.I. burials and 44 special memorials.

2449 WIELTJE FARM CEMETERY, ST. JEAN - LES - YPRES (W. FLANDERS). 2¼ miles from Ypres N. of road from St. Jean to Wieltje. Cem. is between farm buildings and road. Made and used by fighting units in July–Oct. 1917. Records 113 U.K., 1 Can., 1 N.Z., 1 German burials and 20 special memorials.

1699 OXFORD ROAD CEMETERY, YPRES (W. FLANDERS). 2½ miles from Ypres, in angle of 'Oxford' and Potijze-Wieltje roads. Used by units fighting on this front from Aug. 1917 to April 1918. Records 404 U.K., 74 Can., 74 Aust., 37 N.Z., 9 Newfld., 2 Guernsey, 248 Unknown, 2 German burials, and 3 special memorials.

A

A

764 ESSEX FARM CEMETERY, BŒSINGHE (W. FLANDERS). 1½ miles N. of Ypres and a little less than midway from Ypres to Bœsinghe, between road and the Yser Canal bank, was Essex Farm. Used as a dressing sta. The 49th Div. Memorial is behind Cem. on canal bank. Records 1,088 U.K., 9 Can., 83 Unknown, 1 German burials, and 19 special memorials.

B

542 COLNE VALLEY CEMETERY, BŒSINGHE (W. FLANDERS). 4 miles N. of Ypres Sta., SW. of Cæsar's Nose, near Bœsinghe-La Brique road. Begun by Territorials of W. Riding Regt. (49th Div.). Records 47 U.K. burials.

B

C

C

1489 MINTY FARM CEMETERY, ST. JEAN - LES - YPRES (W. FLANDERS). 3¾ miles NE. of Ypres Sta. on road to St. Julien, 1½ miles N. of St. Jean village. Farm was used as a German blockhouse, and in 1917 as a British Co. Hdqtrs. Records 188 U.K., 4 Unknown and 1 German burials.

D

2015 ST. JULIEN DRESSING STATION CEMETERY, LANGEMARCK (W. FLANDERS). S. of village and sta., on road to Wieltje. Can. Mem. at Vancouver Cross Roads is ¾ mile N. of village. Records 290 U.K., 14 Can., 10 Aust., 3 N.Z., 3 S.A., 1 Newfld., 96 Unknown burials, and 11 special memorials.

D

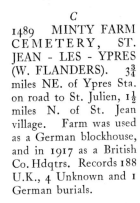

1839 RAILWAY CHA-
TEAU CEMETERY,
VLAMERTINGHE (W.
FLANDERS). 1¼ miles
W. of Ypres, 1¾ miles E.
of Vlamertinghe, near
road between Voorme-
zeele and Brielen, E. of
the moated 'Railway
Chateau'. Used from
Nov. 1914 to Oct. 1918.
Records 105 U.K.
burials.

666 DIVISIONAL
CEMETERY, DICKE-
BUSCH ROAD, VLA-
MERTINGHE (W.
FLANDERS). 1 mile
W. of Ypres Sta., a little
S. of Ypres-Vlamertinghe
road, and on W. side of
by-road (rue Brielen),
leading S. to Dickebusch.
Records 188 U.K., 65
N.Z., 26 Can., 1 Ber-
muda, and 3 Unknown
burials.

224 BELGIAN BAT-
TERY CORNER
CEMETERY, YPRES
(W. FLANDERS). Was
name given to point
where rue Brielen joins a
spur of Ypres-Dickebusch
road, 1 mile from ram-
parts of Ypres. Cem. is
in NE. corner of road
angle. Begun by the 8th
Div. in June 1917. Re-
cords 430 U.K., 122
Aust., 8 N.Z., 7 Can., 2
Ind., 1 Unknown burials,
and 2 special memorials.

2466 YPRES RESERVOIR CEMETERY (W. FLANDERS). At Western Gate and stretches N. to new boulevard which cuts across to ' Plaine d'Amour '. Begun in Oct. 1915 and used until Armistice. Records 2,248 U.K., 151 Can., 142 Aust., 28 N.Z., 12 S.A., 6 B.W.I., 4 Newfld., 2 Guernsey, 1 Ind., 7 Unknown, 1 German burials, and 12 special memorials.

2467 YPRES TOWN CEMETERY (MENIN GATE) (W. FLANDERS). Town Cem. is close to Menin Gate, in which British forces began to bury their dead in Oct. 1914 to Feb. 1915 and again in 1918. Records 142 U.K. burials.

2468 YPRES TOWN CEMETERY EXTENSION (MENIN GATE) (W. FLANDERS). On E. side of Town Cem. Used from Oct. 1914 to April 1915, again in 1918 and enlarged after Armistice. Records 462 U.K., 15 Can., 13 Aust., 1 S.A., 91 Unknown burials, and 16 special memorials.

1852 RAMPARTS CEMETERY (LILLE GATE) YPRES (W. FLANDERS). On W. side of Lille Gate, at top of old rampart. Begun by French in Nov. 1914 and used by British from Feb. 1915 to April 1918. Records 154 U.K., 14 N.Z., 11 Aust., 10 Can., and 3 Unknown burials.

15 AEROPLANE CEMETERY, YPRES (W. FLANDERS). From Menin Gate, two roads led to the front, to Zonnebeke and Menin respectively. Cem. is on S. side of former road, W. of Verlorenhœk. Was in No Man's Land until July 31st 1917. Records 825 U.K., 204 Aust., 47 Can., 17 N.Z., 1 S.A., 1 Newfld., 2 Unknown burials, and 8 special memorials.

1461 MENIN ROAD SOUTH MILITARY CEMETERY, YPRES (W. FLANDERS). 1½ miles from Ypres Sta., or ½ mile from Menin Gate. The Menin road which ran E. and a little S. from Ypres to a front line which varied but a few miles during greater part of war. Records 1,051 U.K., 263 Aust., 145 Can., 52 N.Z., 3 B.W.I., 65 Unknown, 1 German burials, and 79 special memorials.

1779 P O T I J Z E BURIAL GROUND, YPRES (W. FLANDERS). 2 miles from Ypres Sta. and 1 mile from Menin Gate near road to Zonnebeke. Burial ground on N. side of village on road to St. Jean. Potijze was within British lines during practically the whole of the War. Records 580 U.K., 3 Aust., 1 Can., and 2 German burials.

1780–1781 POTIJZE CHATEAU GROUNDS AND LAWN CEME-TERIES, YPRES (W. FLANDERS). E. of village on N. of Zonnebeke road. Chateau Grounds records 301 U.K., 49 Can., 23 Aust., 2 N.Z., 2 Guernsey, 1 S.A., 86 Unknown, 1 French, 1 German burials, and 12 special memorials. Chateau Lawn records 173 U.K., 22 Can., 9 S.A., 4 Aust., 17 Unknown, 3 German burials, and 1 special memorial.

281 BIRR CROSS ROADS CEMETERY, Z I L L E B E K E (W. FLANDERS). On Menin Road, at its crossing with the Wieltje-Zillebeke road (Cambridge road). Cem. is near SW. angle of Cross Roads. R e c o r d s 625 U.K., 140 Aust., 15 Can., 12 N.Z., 1 S.A., 1 New-fld., 1 W.Ind., 11 Unknown burials, and 27 special memorials.

A

B

A

381 BRIDGE HOUSE CEMETERY, LANGE-MARCK (W. FLANDERS). 3¾ miles from Ypres Sta. and 1 mile S. of St. Julien, close to bridge over the Steenbeck, 50 feet from Ypres-Passchendaele road. Was made by 59th (N. Mid.) Div. Sept. 1917. Records 45 U.K. burials.

B

2103 SEAFORTH CEMETERY, CHEDDAR VILLA, LANGE-MARCK (W. FLANDERS). Name given by Army to farm on W. side of road from Wieltje to St. Julien. On April 25th and 26th, 1915, during Battle of St. Julien, Brit. dead were buried on spot. Records 147 U.K. (101 of 2nd Seaforths), 1 Can. burials, and 42 special memorials.

C

D

C

403 BUFFS ROAD CEMETERY, ST. JEAN - LES - YPRES (W. FLANDERS). 2 miles NE. of Ypres Sta. on Buffs Road E. of the crossing of Boundary and Admiral's Roads. Made and used by fighting units July 1917 to March 1918. Records 265 U.K., 13 Aust., 10 Can., 1 S.A., burials, and 10 special memorials.

D

1782 POTIJZE CHATEAU WOOD CEMETERY, YPRES (W. FLANDERS). Little way W. of Grounds and Lawn Cems. Used from April 1915 to June 1917 and in 1918. Records 145 U.K., 6 Can., and 5 Unknown burials.

1101 HOOGE CRATER CEMETERY, ZILLEBEKE (W. FLANDERS). $2\frac{1}{2}$ miles from Ypres on Menin road. July 1915 the crater on N. side of road was made by a mine sprung by 3rd Div. On Aug. 9th Hooge Château and Crater were taken by 6th Div. Records 5,153 U.K., 509 Aust., 119 N.Z., 95 Can., 2 B.W.I. burials, and 45 special memorials.

2077 SANCTUARY WOOD CEMETERY, ZILLEBEKE (W. FLANDERS). 4 miles from Ypres, $\frac{3}{4}$ mile from Menin road and Hooge Halte, on road leading to Can. Mem. on Hill 62. Some of the heaviest fighting of the Great War 1915–1916 took place around the Cem., and it was heavily shelled. Records 102 U.K., 41 Can., and 1 German burials. (Now being enlarged.)

1411 MAPLE COPSE CEMETERY, ZILLE-BEKE (W. FLAN-DERS). $2\frac{1}{2}$ miles SE. of Ypres, $1\frac{1}{2}$ miles E. of Zillebeke Halte, on track to Observatory Ridge. Scene of incessant fighting from 1915 to 1918, finally captured Sept. 1918. Records 168 U.K., and 151 Can. burials.

1841 RAILWAY DUG-OUTS BURIAL GROUND (TRANSPORT FARM), ZILLEBEKE (W. FLANDERS). 2¼ miles SE. of Ypres Sta. and 1 mile W. of village, between SW. corner of Zillebeke Lake and Ypres-Comines railway. Begun in April 1915. Records 1,629 U.K., 694 Can., 154 Aust., 3 N.Z., 3 Ind., 1 B.W.I., 2 Unknown, 4 German burials, and 332 special memorials.

1728 PERTH CEMETERY (CHINA WALL) ZILLEBEKE (W. FLANDERS). 2½ miles from Ypres Sta., on E. of road from Zillebeke to Hell-fire Corner. Begun by French in Nov. 1914 and used as front-line Cem. until Oct. 1917. Records 2,360 U.K., 134 Aust., 129 Can., 22 N.Z., 7 S.A., and 3 Unknown burials, also 135 special memorials.

1246 LARCH WOOD (RAILWAY CUT-TING) CEMETERY, ZILLEBEKE (W. FLANDERS). 2½ miles S. of Ypres, alongside the Ypres-Comines railway. Hill 60, 600 yards SE., was scene of desperate fighting April 17th to May 5th, 1915. Records 728 U.K., 86 Can., 36 Aust., 1 B.W.I., 2 German burials, and 5 special memorials.

221 BEDFORD HOUSE CEMETERY, ZILLE-BEKE (W. FLAN-DERS). 2,000 yards S. of Ypres, E. of Lille road. Used practically through-out the war and enlarged after Armistice. Bedford House was scarcely touched by gun-fire until Jan. 1917 when it was severely shelled. Records 3,980 U.K., 328 Can., 194 Aust., 29 N.Z., 18 S.A., 19 Ind., 6 B.W.I., 2 German burials, and 27 special memorials.

2460 WOODS CEME-TERY, ZILLEBEKE (W. FLANDERS). $3\frac{1}{2}$ miles SE. of Ypres Sta. on W. edge of wood, 1 mile S. of village. Begun by 1st Dorsets and 1st E. Surreys in April 1915. Records 212 U.K., 111 Can., and 3 Aust. burials.

1045 HEDGE ROW TRENCH CEMETERY, ZILLEBEKE (W. FLANDERS). SW. of Woods Cem. on W. edge of wood, 2 miles from Zillebeke. Begun March 1915, used until Aug. 1917. Suffered severely from shell-fire. Records 94 U.K., 2 Can., and 2 Unknown burials.

2163 SPOILBANK CEMETERY, ZILLE-BEKE (W. FLAN-DERS). 3½ miles SE. of Ypres Sta., 1½ miles SW. of Zillebeke village on N. bank of Ypres-Comines Canal on by-road to Verbrandenmolen. Burials were made practically continuously from Feb. 1915 to May 1918. Records 436 U.K. and 68 Aust., also 16 Can. burials.

515 CHESTER FARM CEMETERY, ZILLE-BEKE (W. FLAN-DERS). Name given to farm ½ mile S. of Blauwe-poort Farm, on road from Zillebeke to Voorme-zeele. Cem. is opposite farm on NW. side of road. Records 306 U.K., 87 Can., 21 Aust., 4 German burials, and 6 special memorials.

1653 OAK DUMP CEMETERY, VOOR-MEZEELE (W. FLAN-DERS). 3½ miles S. of Ypres Sta. between roads to Messines and Kemmel, E. of village, and S. of Ypres - Comines Canal. Made by fighting units in July to Sept. 1917. Records 109 U.K., 2 Aust. burials and 2 special memorials.

A

A

2272 TUILERIES BRITISH CEMETERY, ZILLEBEKE (W. FLANDERS). 2½ miles SE. of Ypres, ¾ mile N. of Zillebeke Halte, W. of road leading from 'Hellfire Corner' to Zillebeke. Used from Feb. to May 1915, but utterly destroyed by shell-fire and reconstructed after Armistice. Records 106 U.K., and 3 French burials.

B

293 BLAUWEPOORT FARM CEMETERY, ZILLEBEKE (W. FLANDERS). 2½ miles SE. of Ypres Sta. and 1 mile SW. of village, adjoining N. side of farm. Begun by Chasseurs Alpins in Nov. 1914 and used by British from Feb. 1915 to Feb. 1916. Records 83 U.K. and 7 Unknown burials.

B

C

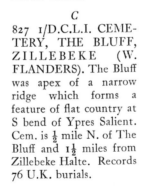

827 1/D.C.L.I. CEMETERY, THE BLUFF, ZILLEBEKE (W. FLANDERS). The Bluff was apex of a narrow ridge which forms a feature of flat country at S bend of Ypres Salient. Cem. is ½ mile N. of The Bluff and 1½ miles from Zillebeke Halte. Records 76 U.K. burials.

D

413 BUS HOUSE CEMETERY, VOORMEZEELE (W. FLANDERS). 2½ miles S. of Ypres and 1,000 yards SE. of village behind 'Bus House' farm. Made June–Nov. 1917. Records 190 U.K., 2 Aust., 2 Can., 1 N.Z., 1 B.W.I. burials, and 2 special memorials.

C

D

2387 VOORMEZEELE ENCLOSURES, Nos. 1 AND 2 (W. FLANDERS). 3¼ miles S. of Ypres Sta., NW. of village, near roads to Ypres and Kruisstraathœk. Were, originally, r e g i m e n t a l groups of graves. Re-cords 511 U.K., 54 Can., 17 Aust., 2 N.Z., 6 Ger-man burials, and 21 special memorials.

2389 VOORMEZEELE ENCLOSURE No. 3 (W. FLANDERS). 3⅛ miles S. of Ypres Sta. The 'Enclosures' are immediately NW. of village, at junction of roads to Ypres and Kruisstraathœk. Begun by Princess Patricia's Can. L. Inf. in Feb. 1915. Records 1,480 U.K., 100 Can., 8 Aust., 2 N.Z., 1 S.A., 1 Unknown burials, and 19 special memorials.

725 ELZENWALLE BRASSERIE CEME-TERY, V O O R M E-ZEELE (W. FLAN-DERS). The hamlet of Elzenwalle is almost half-way from Ypres to Kem-mel on main road, and little farther S. is 'Kem-mel-Brouwerij' halte on light railway. Opposite Brasserie is Cem. Re-cords 106 U.K., 41 Can., and 2 B.W.I. burials.

659 DICKEBUSCH NEW MILITARY CEMETERY (W. FLANDERS). 3 miles SW. of Ypres. New Mil. Cem. is on S. side of village, on E. side of road to Vierstraat, and Extension faces on W. side of road. A light railway runs from Ypres to Dickebusch. Records 528 U.K., 84 Can., and 11 Aust. burials.

660 DICKEBUSCH NEW MILITARY CEMETERY EXTENSION (see Dickebusch New Mil. Cem.). Begun in May 1917 (in succession to other Dickebusch cems.) and used until Jan. 1918. Records 520 U.K., 24 Aust., 2 Can., 1 S.A., and 1 German burials.

1128 HUTS CEMETERY, DICKEBUSCH (W. FLANDERS). 3¾ miles SW. of Ypres, ½ mile NW. of Dickebusch, on road to Brandhœk. Near gun positions, and 687 (nearly two-thirds) of soldiers buried in it were gunners. Records 816 U.K., 242 Aust., 19 N.Z., 5 Can., 4 S.A., 1 Ind., 1 B.W.I., 6 Unknown, and 6 German burials.

1201 LA CLYTTE MILITARY CEMETERY, RENING-HELST (W. FLANDERS). 5 miles from Ypres and Poperinghe Stats., N.W. of La Clytte on Reninghelst road. La Clytte was used as Bgde. Hdqtrs. Records 819 U.K., 51 Can., 12 Aust., 7 B.W.I., 6 S.A., 3 N.Z., and 159 Unknown burials.

962 GROOTEBEEK BRITISH CEMETERY, RENINGHELST (W. FLANDERS). 3¾ miles SE. of Poperinghe Sta., in hamlet of Ouderdom. In Brit. occupation from Autumn 1914 to end of war. Made after Battles of Lys April 1918. Records 97 U.K., 7 Ind., 1 N.Z., 1 S.A., 1 Bermuda burials, and 2 special memorials.

1880 RENINGHELST NEW MILITARY CEMETERY (W. FLANDERS). 3 miles SE. of Poperinghe Sta. Was in Brit. occupation from late autumn of 1914 to end of war. Records 453 U.K., 230 Can., 104 Aust., 2 N.Z., 1 S.A., 1 Unknown, 51 French, 7 Chin., and 2 German burials.

2438 WESTOUTRE BRITISH CEMETERY (W. FLANDERS). 4¾ miles S. of Poperinghe, on outskirts of village, E. of Westoutre-Poperinghe road, W. of Mont Kemmel, N. of Mont Noir. Begun Oct. 1917 towards the end of the 3rd Battle of Ypres. Records 166 U.K., 4 Can., 3 N.Z., and 3 Chinese burials.

2440 WESTOUTRE CHURCHYARD EXTENSION (W. FLANDERS). 8 miles SW. of Ypres, 4¾ miles S. of Poperinghe Sta., on road to Locre. Used intermittently for British burials from Nov. 1914 to April 1918. Records 64 U.K., 15 Can., 1 Aust., 1 N.Z., and 3 German burials.

1890 RIDGE WOOD MILITARY CEMETERY, VOORMEZEELE (W. FLANDERS). 4¼ miles S. of Ypres Sta., S. of Ridge Wood, on high ground between Kemmel road and Dickebusch Lake, ½ mile from Kemmel-Brouwerij Halte. Records 292 Can., 259 U.K., 44 Aust., 3 N.Z., 20 Unknown, and 2 German burials.

1351 LOCRE HOS-
PICE CEMETERY (W.
FLANDERS). ½ mile
SE. of village and 200
yards SE. of Hospice.
Scene of severe fighting
May 20th 1918. Begun
June 1917 by Field Ambs.
and used until April 1918.
Records 238 U.K., 2
Aust., 1 Can., 1 N.Z., 1
B.W.I., 2 German burials
and 10 special memorials.

1349 LOCRE CHURCH
YARD (W. FLAN-
DERS). 7 miles SW. of
Ypres. In Brit. hands
during greater part of
war and Field Ambs. were
stationed at Convent of
St. Antoine. In 2 Plots
N. and S. of church.
Records 184 U.K. and 31
Can. burials.

1350 LOCRE No. 10
CEMETERY (W.
FLANDERS). ¾ mile
S. of village on W. of
road to Dranoutre. Be-
gun by French in Spring
1918. Brit. and German
graves added after Armis-
tice from battle-fields.
Records 55 U.K., 150
German burials, and 3
special memorials.

A

B

A

661 DICKEBUSCH OLD MILITARY CEMETERY (W. FLANDERS). 3½ miles SW. of Ypres, on S. side of lane opposite the church. Was a front-line Cem. from Jan. to March 1915. Dickebusch is connected by a light railway with Ypres. Records 41 U.K., 2 Can., and 1 German burials.

B

1879 RENINGHELST CHURCHYARD EXTENSION (W. FLANDERS). Lying in V. of small stream, 4 miles SE. of Poperinghe. Nearest railway sta. is at Poperinghe, on Hazebrouck-Ypres line. Was in Brit. occupation from Autumn of 1914 to end of War. Records 55 U.K. and 1 Aust. burials.

C

D

C

2179 SUFFOLK CEMETERY, VIERSTRAAT, KEMMEL (W. FLANDERS). 5 miles SW. of Ypres Sta. and 700 yards from Vierstraat (light rly. to Ypres). This Cem. lies between Vierstraat and Klein-Vierstraat Cabaret, begun by 3rd Suffolks in March 1917. Records 47 U.K. burials.

D

696 DRANOUTRE CHURCHYARD (W. FLANDERS). 3 miles NE. of Bailleul Sta., nearest convenient sta. on main line from Calais to Lille. Churchyard is in village. Records 79 U.K. burials.

697 DRANOUTRE MILITARY CEME-TERY (W. FLAN-DERS). 3 miles NE. of Bailleul. Nearest convenient sta. at Bailleul, on main line from Calais to Lille. Cem. is on NW. outskirts of village. Was captured by 1st Cav. Div. on Oct. 14th 1914. Records 421 U.K., 19 Can., 17 Aust., 1 N.Z., and 1 German burials.

1218 LA LAITERIE MILITARY CEME-TERY, KEMMEL (W. FLANDERS). 6 miles SW. of Ypres, near a dairy farm on Kemmel-Ypres road, by a railway halte. Begun Nov. 1914 and used until Oct. 1918 by units holding this sector of front. Records 468 U.K., 197 Can., 7 Aust., 1 Newfld., 78 Unknown burials and 2 special memorials.

928 GODEZONNE FARM CEMETERY, KEMMEL (W. FLAN-DERS). 4½ miles SW. of Ypres and 1,000 yards due W. of Vierstraat on E. of secondary road ('Cheapside') running from Kemmel to Ypres. Begun in Feb. 1915 by 2nd R. Scots and 4th Middlx. Records 74 U.K., 3 S.A., 1 Can., and 1 Aust. burials.

1178 KLEIN - VIER-STRAAT BRITISH CEMETERY, KEM-MEL (W. FLANDERS). 6 miles SW. of Ypres and $\frac{1}{2}$ mile from Vierstraat (light rly. to Ypres) S. of Vierstraat-Hallebast road. Village and adjoining hill, Mont-Kemmel, were the scene of fierce fighting in latter half of April 1918. Records 777 U.K., 8 Can., 8 Aust., 7 N.Z., 1 S.A., 1 Ind., 1 Chin. burials and 2 special memorials.

1172 KEMMEL CHA-TEAU MILITARY CEMETERY (W. FLANDERS). 6 miles SW. of Ypres. The Cha-teau is on NE. side of village and sta., on E. side of main road to Ypres. Begun in Dec. 1914 and used until March 1918. Records 1,030 U.K., 80 Can., 24 Aust., and 1 N.Z. burials.

1174 KEMMEL No. 1 FRENCH CEMETERY (W. FLANDERS). 4 miles SW. of Ypres, 1,000 yards NW. of Vierstraat, S. of road to Ouderdom. Created after Armistice by concentration of iso-lated graves from sur-rounding battle-fields. All French graves have been removed. Records 134 U.K. and 47 German burials.

1674 OOST'TAVERNE WOOD CEMETERY, WYTSCHÆTE (W. FLANDERS). 1 mile NE. of Wytschæte on W. of Voormezeele-Warneton road. Captured June 7th 1917 by 19th Western and 11th Divs. Records 923 U.K., 133 Can., 43 Aust., 19 N.Z., and Unknown number of German burials, also 1 special memorial.

2147 SOMER FARM CEMETERY, WYTSCHÆTE (W. FLANDERS). In an orchard on S. side of road to Hollebeke, ½ mile NW. of Wytschæte. Begun in June 1917 and used until March 1918. Records 65 U.K. and 19 Aust. burials also 5 special memorials.

2464 WYTSCHÆTE MILITARY CEMETERY (W. FLANDERS). 4 miles S. of Ypres, W. of village and sta., on road to Kemmel. Village was captured by Germans Nov. 1914, recaptured 1917, lost again April 1918 and retaken Sept. 1918. Records 486 U.K., 31 Aust., 19 Can., 11 S.A., 7 N.Z., 423 Unknown burials and 25 special memorials.

A

A

610 CROONÆRT CHAPEL CEMETERY, WYTSCHÆTE (W. FLANDERS). 1 mile N. of Wytschæte, W. of Voormezeele road. In No Man's Land before Battle of Messines 1917. Begun by 19th Div. June 1917. Records 74 U.K., and 1 Chin. burials.

B

2160 SPANBRŒK-MOLEN BRITISH CEMETERY, WYTS-CHÆTE (W. FLAN-DERS). 4 miles S. of Ypres. Spanbrœkmolen was name of windmill 1 mile SW. of Wytschæte on Messines Ridge. Bur-ials are those of 1st and 2nd days of the Battle of Messines. Records 58 U.K. burials, all but one of the 36th (Ulster) Div.

B

C

C

1140 IRISH HOUSE CEMETERY, KEM-MEL (W. FLANDERS). 1 mile E. of village and sta. In Row 'A' are 33 1st Gordons, killed Dec. 1914, in 3rd Div.'s attack on Wytschæte, reburied by 16th (Irish) Div. when Cem. was begun in June 1917. Records 102 U.K., 14 Aust., 4 German bur-ials and 1 special memor-ial.

D

2246 TORREKEN FARM CEMETERY No. 1 WYTSCHÆTE (W. FLANDERS). 4 miles S. of Ypres, 570 yards E. of village and sta. Was begun by 5th Dorset Rgt. in June 1917 and used as a front-line Cem. until April 1918. Records 70 U.K. and 20 Aust., and a few German burials.

D

649 DERRY HOUSE CEMETERY No. 2, WYTSCHÆTE (W. FLANDERS). 4 miles S. of Ypres, 1 mile SE. of village and sta., beyond Torreken Farm Cem., and was begun in June 1917 by 11th Div. (32nd Bgde.) and used as a front line Cem. until Dec. Records 126 U.K. and 37 Aust. burials.

1343 LINDENHŒK CHALET MILITARY CEMETERY, KEMMEL (W. FLANDERS). 6¾ miles SW. of Ypres Sta. on road to Kemmel Hill. Kemmel was the scene of fierce fighting in latter half of April 1918. Records 278 U.K., 15 Can., 9 Aust., 7 N.Z., 2 German burials, and 6 special memorials.

1760 POND FARM CEMETERY, WUL-VERGHEM (W. FLAN-DERS). 7½ miles from Ypres, the Cem. is NW. of Pond Farm, which in turn is in the fields about ½ mile E. of Packhorse Farm. Begun by 3rd Rifle Bgde. and 8th Buffs, in July 1916. Records 293 U.K., 5 German burials, and 3 special memorials.

1355 LONE TREE CEMETERY, WYTS-CHÆTE (W. FLAN-DERS). Near site of Spanbrœkmolen wind-mill, S. of Kemmel road, on Messines Ridge. Re-cords 88 U.K. burials, many of them being from the R.I. Rifles (36th) Div.

1933 R.E. FARM CEMETERY, WYTS-CHÆTE (W. FLAN-DERS). 4 miles S. of Ypres and 1½ miles from Wytschæte (light rly. to Ypres). 'R.E. Farm' was name given to Ferme des douze Bonniers, on W. side of road between Wulverghem and Wyts-chæte. Saw exception-ally fierce fighting in Nov. 1914 and April 1918. Records 132 U.K., and 47 Can. burials.

2463 WULVERGHEM-LINDENHŒK ROAD MILITARY CEME-TERY, WULVER-GHEM (W. FLAN-DERS). 1½ miles from Kemmel Sta., 2 miles NW. of Wulverghem, on Lindenhœk road. Re-cords 835 U.K., 69 N.Z., 54 Can., 35 Aust., 9 S.A., burials, and 9 special memorials.

1475 MESSINES RIDGE BRITISH CEMETERY, MESSINES (W. FLANDERS). 6 miles S. of Ypres, on W. outskirts of village, on road to Neuve-Eglise. Created after Armistice from isolated graves and small cems. in battle-fields of the Salient. Contains Mem. to N.Z. 'Missing'. Records 990 U.K., 338 Aust., 125 N.Z., 60 S.A. burials, and 13 special memorials.

2047 ST. QUENTIN CABARET MILITARY CEMETERY, PLŒGSTEERT (W. FLANDERS). St. Quentin Cabaret was an inn 500 yards E. of Kandahar Farm, on S. side of road from Neuve-Eglise to Messines. Cem. is E. of inn and close to Wulverghem. Records 316 U.K., 68 Can., 64 N.Z., 7 Aust., 5 Unknown, and 2 German burials.

1171 KANDAHAR FARM CEMETERY, NEUVE-EGLISE (W. FLANDERS). 'Kandahar Farm' is on road to Wulverghem, 1½ miles from Neuve-Eglise. Brit. front line ran little E. of Wulverghem from the Autumn of 1914 to Summer of 1917, when Messines was captured. Records 211 U.K., 186 Aust., 33 N.Z., 6 Can., 7 Unknown, and 3 German burials.

A

B

A

425 CABIN HILL CEMETERY, WYTS- CHÆTE (W. FLAN- DERS). 1 mile from Messines Halte, near road to Gapaard, beyond Derry House Cem. Be- gun by 11th Div. June 1917 and used as a front- line Cem. until March 1918. Records 42 U.K., and 25 Aust. burials.

B

1702 PACKHORSE FARM SHRINE CEMETERY, WUL- VERGHEM (W. FLAN- DERS). 1¼ miles from Wulverghem, E. of Lin- denhœk road. Was scene of German gas attack on night of April 29–30th, 1916, which was repulsed by 3rd and 24th Divs. Records 59 U.K. burials.

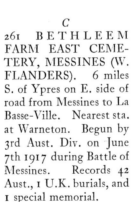

C

261 BETHLEEM FARM EAST CEME- TERY, MESSINES (W. FLANDERS). 6 miles S. of Ypres on E. side of road from Messines to La Basse-Ville. Nearest sta. at Warneton. Begun by 3rd Aust. Div. on June 7th 1917 during Battle of Messines. Records 42 Aust., 1 U.K. burials, and 1 special memorial.

D

262 BETHLEEM FARM WEST CEME- TERY, MESSINES (W. FLANDERS). (See Bethleem Farm East Cem.), but on W. of Messines La-Basse-Ville road. Was begun by the 3rd Aust. Div. on June 7th 1917, in Battle of Messines. Records 114 Aust., 27 N.Z., 24 U.K. burials, and 1 special memorial.

C

D

1244 LA PLUS DOUVE FARM CEMETERY, PLŒGSTEERT (W. FLANDERS). Little S. of village of Wulverghem, 8 miles from Ypres and 6 from Armentières, and 2 miles from Messines Sta. on narrow-gauge railway from Ypres. La Plus Douve Farm was generally within British lines and was used as Batt. Hdqtrs. for a time. Records 101 U.K., 88 Can., 86 Aust., 61 N.Z., and 9 German burials.

1857 RATION FARM (LA PLUS DOUVE) ANNEXE, PLŒGSTEERT (W. FLANDERS). N. of La Plus Douve Farm Cem. and 150 yards from road. Used from Jan. 1915 to Jan. 1918. Records 185 U.K., 12 Aust., 4 N.Z., 1 Unknown, and 1 German burials.

2437 WESTHOF FARM CEMETERY, NEUVE-EGLISE (W. FLANDERS). Sta. at Neuve-Eglise on light rly. from Ypres and 1½ miles SW. of village. Westhof Farm was used as Hdqtrs, N.Z. Div., in May and June, 1917. Records 69 U.K., 43 Aust., 14 N.Z., 1 Can., 5 German burials, and 6 special memorials.

237 BERKS CEMETERY EXTENSION, AND PLŒGSTEERT MEMORIAL TO 'MISSING' (W. FLANDERS). 9 miles S. of Ypres, 4½ miles N. of Armentières, on road between these towns. Cem. records 295 U.K., 51 Aust., 45 N.Z., and 3 Can. burials. Memorial records 11,447 'Missing' who fell in Battles of Armentières, Aubers Ridge 1914, Loos 1915, Fromelles 1916, Estaires, Hazebrouck, Scherpenberg and Outtersteene Ridge 1918.

1130 HYDE PARK CORNER (ROYAL BERKS) CEMETERY, PLŒGSTEERT (W. FLANDERS). On road from Messines to Armentières. 'Hyde Park Corner' was 1 mile N. of village. Cem. was begun April 1915 by 1/4th R. Berks Rgt. It is opposite Berks Cem. Ext. and the Plœgsteert Memorial to 'Missing'. Stas. are Messines and Pont-Rouge Records 81 U.K., 1 Can., 1 Aust., and 4 German burials.

2278 UNDERHILL FARM CEMETERY, PLŒGSTEERT (W. FLANDERS). 8 miles from Bailleul Sta. and 3¼ miles from Neuve-Eglise Sta. Underhill Farm and Red Lodge were names given to dressing stations on NW. edge of Plœgsteert Wood. Records 102 U.K., 47 Aust., 39 N.Z., 1 Can., 1 Unknown burials, and 5 special memorials.

1800 PROWSE POINT MILITARY CEMETERY, WARNETON (W. FLANDERS). 300 yards N. of Mud Corner, 1¾ miles from La Basse-Ville Halte, and 9½ miles to Ypres Sta. Was named after the late Brig.-Gen. C. B. Prowse, D.S.O. Records 159 U.K., 42 N.Z., 13 Aust., 1 Can., and 12 German burials.

2244 TORONTO AVENUE CEMETERY, WARNETON (W. FLANDERS). 10½ miles from Ypres, 2 miles from Plœgsteert, near NE. edge of Plœgsteert Wood. Begun by 3rd Aust. Div. during Battle of Messines, June 7th–10th 1917. Records 78 Aust. burials.

1745 PLŒGSTEERT WOOD MILITARY CEMETERY, WARNETON (W. FLANDERS). (See Lancashire Cottage Cem.). This Cem. about centre of wood. Was made by the enclosing of a number of small regimental Cems. Records 117 U.K., 28 Can., 18 N.Z., 1 Aust., and 1 Unknown burials.

2172 STRAND MILITARY CEMETERY, PLŒGSTEERT WOOD (W. FLANDERS). Close to French border, 4 miles N. of Armentières Sta., on Ypres road, S. of Plœgsteert Wood. The Cem. was established near Strand Trench in October 1914. Records 659 U.K., 284 Aust., 77 N.Z., 15 Can., 1 S.A., 4 unknown, 4 German burials, and 19 special memorials.

1892 RIFLE HOUSE CEMETERY, WARNETON. (See Lancashire Cottage Cem.). This Cem. is in wood, a little SW. of Plœgsteert Wood Mil. Cem. Records 229 U.K. and 1 Can. burials.

1227 LANCASHIRE COTTAGE CEMETERY, PLŒGSTEERT (W. FLANDERS). In Plœgsteert Wood, on S. side of Plœgsteert-Warneton road, just W. of cottage. Nearest stas. are Armentières and Warneton. This Cem. was in German hands from April 10th to Sept. 29th 1918. Records 229 U.K., 23 Aust., and 2 Can. burials.

1354 LONDON RIFLE BRIGADE CEMETERY, PLŒGSTEERT (W. FLANDERS). 3 miles N. of Armentières Sta., 600 yards S. of Plœgsteert on road to Messines. Begun by London Rifle Bgde., Dec. 20th, 1914, and used until March 1918. Cem. was dedicated by Bishop of London, Easter Day 1915. Records 263 U.K., 38 Aust., 34 N.Z., and 18 German burials.

82 ARTILLERY WOOD CEMETERY, BŒSINGHE (W. FLANDERS). $7\frac{1}{4}$ miles from Ypres. Cemetery is little N. of wood, $\frac{1}{2}$ mile E. of Yser Canal, 1 mile from Bœsinghe Sta. The Guards Div. captured Artillery Wood during Battle of Pilckem Ridge, July 31st, 1917. Records 1,243 U.K., 30 Can., 10 Newfld., 5 Aust., 2 N.Z., 1 S.A., 4 Unknown burials, and 12 special memorials.

480 CEMENT HOUSE CEMETERY, LANGEMARCK (W. FLANDERS). Sta. on line from Ostende (or Bruges) to Ypres. Was on N. side of the Ypres Salient. Cemetery on Langemarck-Bœsinghe road, little way beyond stream called Hannebeek. Records 2,910 U.K., 14 Newfld., 5 Guernsey, 4 Can., 1 S.A., 1 Unknown, 1 German burials, and 11 special memorials.

2275 TYNE COT CEMETERY, AND MEMORIAL, PASSCHENDAELE (W. FLANDERS). 5½ miles NE. of Ypres Sta., ¾ mile NE. of Zonnebeke Sta. Cem. records 8,901 U.K., 1,353 Aust., 966 Can., 519 N.Z., 90 S.A., 14 Newfld., 6 R. Guernsey L.I., 2 B.W.I., 1 French, 4 German burials, and 101 special memorials. Mem. Records 34,888 'Missing' of the Brit. Emp. who fell in the Ypres Salient from Aug. 16th 1917 to end of War.

1710 PASSCHENDAELE NEW BRITISH CEMETERY (W. FLANDERS). 7½ miles from Ypres Sta., ½ mile NW. of village. Passchendaele and its neighbourhood are associated with every phase of the War in Flanders. Records 1,018 U.K., 647 Can., 292 Aust., 126 N.Z. 6 Guernsey, 3 S.A., 1 Newfld. burials, and 7 special memorials.

1749 POELCAPELLE BRITISH CEMETERY (W. FLANDERS). 7 miles NW. of Ypres, E. of village and sta., on road to Westroosebeke. Made after the Armistice by graves from battle-fields. Records 6,541 U.K., 525 Can., 237 N.Z., 117 Aust., 10 S.A., 8 Newfld., 4 Channel Isl. burials, and 36 special memorials.

A

B

A

1571 MUD CORNER CEMETERY, WARNETON (W. FLANDERS). Near R. Lys. On N. edge of Plœgsteert Wood, 2 miles from La Basse-Ville Halte. Used from June 7th (when N.Z. Div. captured Messines) to Dec. 1917. Records 53 N.Z., 31 Aust., and 1 U.K. burials.

B

1410 MAPLE LEAF CEMETERY, ROMARIN (W. FLANDERS). 4 miles NW. of Armentières Sta., 2 miles S. of Neuve-Eglise, near road to Pont d'Achelles. Used from Dec. 1914 to Dec. 1917. Records 80 U.K. 43 N.Z., 39 Can., 4 Aust., 1 S.A., and 9 German burials.

C

D

C

1950 RUISSEAU FARM CEMETERY, LANGEMARCK (W. FLANDERS). 1 mile W. of Langemarck Sta., and $3\frac{1}{4}$ miles from Bœsinghe Sta. Ruisseau Farm was taken by the Guards Div. on Oct. 8th 1917. Records 82 U.K. burials.

D

1756 POLYGON WOOD CEMETERY, ZONNEBEKE (W. FLANDERS). 5 miles NE. of Ypres, 1 mile S. of Zonnebeke, at NE. end of wood. Used from Nov. 1917 to Sept. 1918. Records 44 U.K., 59 N.Z., and 1 German burials. (150 yards N. of Buttes New Brit. Cem. and Mem. to 5th Aust. Div.)

421 BUTTES NEW BRITISH CEMETERY, POLYGON WOOD (W. FLANDERS). 150 yds. S. of Polygon Wood Cem. Created after Armistice. Mem. to 5th Aust. Div. on Butte, and Mem. to N.Z. 'Missing' in Record Building. Records 1,317 U.K., 561 Aust., 167 N.Z., and 48 Can. burials.

659 DOCHY FARM NEW BRITISH CEMETERY, LANGEMARCK (W. FLANDERS). 5 miles from Ypres on Zonnebeke road, ¾ mile from Zonnebeke Sta. Begun after Armistice from battlefields of Bœsinghe, St. Julien, Frezenberg and Passchendaele. Records 523 U.K., 305 Aust., 98 N.Z., 81 Can., 17 S.A., 1 Newfld., 412 Unknown burials, and 2 special memorials.

626 DADIZEELE NEW BRITISH CEMETERY (W. FLANDERS). 4 miles N. of Menin, 1½ miles W. of Ledeghem Sta., W. of village. Dadizeele was 7 miles behind German line during greater part of war. Hill 41, S. of village, was captured by 36th Div. Oct. 1st 1918, after desperate fighting. Records 1,007 U.K., 19 Newfld., 1 Can. burials, and 4 special memorials.

A

A

1272 LEDEGHEM MILITARY CEME-TERY (W. FLAN-DERS). 4 miles N. of Menin, 500 yards E. of sta., N. of village, S. of Dadizeele road. Captured by 6th Cav. Bgde. Oct. 19th 1914, and again by 9th Div. Sept. 28th–29th 1918. Records 67 U.K. burials.

B

B

1176 KEZELBERG MILITARY CEME-TERY, MOORSEELE (W. FLANDERS). 3 miles N. of Menin Sta., 2 miles E. of Moorseele Halte near road to Roulers. Casualties from final advance to Victory, Oct. 26th 1918 to Armistice. Records 145 U.K., 1 Can., 1 Chin., and 14 German burials.

C

C

978 GUNNERS' FARM CEMETERY, PLŒG-STEERT (W. FLAN-DERS). Plœgsteert village is on the Armentières-Ypres road, 3 miles from Armentières Sta., on the Hazebrouck-Lille line. The Cem. lies SE. of village on N. side of Warneton road. Begun in July 1915 by 9th Essex and Suff. Rgts. Records 163 U.K., 9 S.A., 2 Aust., and 1 N.Z. burials.

D

D

439 CALVAIRE (ESSEX) MILITARY CEMETERY, PLŒG-STEERT (W. FLAN-DERS). This Cem. is a little E. of Gunners' Farm Cem. (which see) on S. side of road to Warneton, beside a building known as Essex House. Records 218 Brit. burials.

1540 MOORSEELE MILITARY CEMETERY (W. FLANDERS). 4 miles NE. of Menin, 2½ miles E. of Moorseele Sta., near Gulleghem road behind the Convent of the Holy Family. Convent was used as hosp. by British and Germans. Burials made from Oct. 18th to 30th 1918. Records 89 U.K., 8 Can., 1 French, and 1 German burials.

2476 ZANTVOORDE BRITISH CEMETERY (W. FLANDERS). 6 miles SE. of Ypres, 2¼ miles from Houthem Sta., NE. of village. Made after Armistice by concentration of graves from battle-fields. Records 1,525 U.K., 22 Can., 2 Aust., 1 Ind. burials and 33 special memorials.

2198 TANCREZ FARM CEMETERY, PLŒGSTEERT (W. FLANDERS). 3 miles N. of Armentières Sta., 2 miles SE. of village, N. of road from Le Bizet (frontier) to Le Touquet. In line with row of 'pill boxes' which formed part of German front line between Frelinghien and Plœgsteert June 1916. Records 307 U.K., 19 Aust., 4 S.A., 3 N.Z., and 2 German burials.

1764 PONT D'ACHELLES MILITARY CEMETERY, NIEPPE (Nord). 4 miles NW. of Armentières Sta., N. of Bailleul road. Pont de-Nieppe was seized by 1st Hants Regt. on Oct. 16th, 1914, finally recaptured Sept. 3rd, 1918, by 29th Div. Records 173 U.K., 72 Aust., 48 N.Z., and 27 German burials.

1766 PONT-DE-NIEPPE COMMUNAL CEMETERY (Nord). 2¼ miles NW. of Armentières Sta. on N. side of hamlet. Used by British from Oct. 1914 to March 1918, by Germans during Summer of 1918 and again by British in Sept.–Nov. 1918. Records 122 U.K., 12 Aust., and 1 Unknown burials.

1619 NIEPPE COMMUNAL CEMETERY (Nord). ¾ mile N. of Nieppe Halte on SE. side of cross-roads to Courte-Rue. Used by the British from Oct. 1914 to Nov. 1917, and again in Sept. and Nov. 1918. Records 43 U.K., 11 N.Z., 6 Aust., and 2 S.A. burials.

2266 TROIS-ARBRES CEMETERY, STEEN-WERCK (Nord). 1 mile SE. of sta., E. of village. Site chosen by 2nd Aust. Casualty Clearing Sta. in 1916. April 10th 1918 captured by enemy and held until Oct. Records 954 U.K., 470 Aust., 214 N.Z., 33 Guernsey, 20 Can., 1 S.A., 1 Newfld., 1 Ind. burials and 10 special memorials.

1277 LE GRAND BEAUMART BRITISH CEMETERY, STEEN-WERCK (Nord). 2¼ miles SW. of sta., W. of village. Made by fighting units and Field Ambs. in April and Oct. 1918. Records 528 U.K., 1 Can., 1 Guernsey burials, and 23 special memorials.

1115 HOUPLINES COMMUNAL CEME-TERY EXTENSION (Nord). 2 miles NE. of Armentières Sta., ¾ mile E. of Houplines Sta., NE. of road to L'Epinette. In the race to the sea the Germans were held here by III Corps Oct. 1914. Records 506 U.K., 3 Can., 3 N.Z., 1 Aust. burials, and 1 special memorial.

526 CITE BONJEAN MILITARY CEMETERY, ARMENTIÈRES (Nord). ¾ mile from Armentières Sta. on W. outskirts of town, NE. side of Avenue Bayart. Used from Oct. 1914 to March 1918, when Germans retook town, but was recaptured Oct. 3rd 1918. Records 1,182 U.K., 475 Aust., 460 N.Z., 14 Can., 3 French, 2 Belg., and 507 German burials. (Mem. to N.Z. 'Missing' in Cem.)

607 CROIX-DU-BAC BRITISH CEMETERY, STEENWERCK (Nord). 4 miles SW. of Armentières, ½ mile N. of Bac-St. Maur Sta., on road to Steenwerck. Begun July 1916, used by Germans March 1918, and again after their retirement by British until Oct. 1918, and enlarged after Armistice. Records 540 U.K., 11 Aust., and 5 N.Z. burials.

1935 ROYAL IRISH RIFLES GRAVEYARD, LAVENTIE (P. de C.). 7 miles SW. of Armentières, 1¾ miles SE. of Laventie Sta. on La Couture-Fleurbaix road. Begun Nov. 1914, used by 10th Service Batt. R.I. Rifles 1915, enlarged after Armistice from battle-fields of Neuve Chapelle, Laventie, and Richebourg-l'Avoué. Records 800 U.K., 2 Can., 2 German burials and 2 special memorials.

497 CHAPELLE-D'ARMENTIÈRES OLD MILITARY CEMETERY (Nord). 1 mile SE. of Armentières Sta., 150 yards W. of Chapelle d'Armentières Church, on Lille road. Begun Oct. 1914 and used until Oct. 1915 when it was subject to shell-fire and ceased to be used for sanitary reasons. Records 103 U.K. burials.

496 CHAPELLE-D'ARMENTIÈRES NEW MILITARY CEMETERY (Nord). 200 yards N. of Old Cem., opened subsequent to that Cem. and used until Jan. 1916. Lost April 10th 1918 in Battles of the Lys, retaken in final advance Oct. 3rd 1918. Records 73 U.K. burials.

1858 RATION FARM MILITARY CEMETERY, LA CHAPELLE-D'ARMENTIÈRES (Nord). On NW. side of Bois Grenier road, 1 mile from La Chapelle d'Armentières Sta. Was about 1,200 yards from British front line. Records 575 U.K., 260 Aust., 32 N.Z., 441 Unknown, 4 German burials, and 8 special memorials.

1601 NEUVE-EGLISE CHURCH-YARD (W. FLANDERS). 8 miles S. of Ypres, in centre of village on road to Messines. Neuve-Eglise was occupied by Germans early in 1914 but retaken by Allies same year, and held until April 1918. Finally retaken Sept. 1st 1918. Records 76 U.K., 9 Aust., 6 N.Z., and 1 Can. burials.

1193 LA CHAPELLE D'ARMEN-TIÈRES COMMUNAL CEMETERY (Nord). 8 miles NW. of Lille, 1½ miles SE. of Armentières Sta., 300 yards from Chapelle d'Armentières Halte, E. of village. Used for British burials from Oct. 1914 to Sept. 1915, mostly by 1st Roy. Fus. Records 60 U.K. and 1 Can. burials.

1976 ST. ANDRE COMMUNAL CEME-TERY (Nord). 2 miles from Lille, N. of village and sta. on road to Ypres. Used by Germans as Prisoners of War Cem., enlarged during Advance to Victory and after Armistice. Records 155 U.K., 1 Can., 1 S.A., and 3 Chin. burials.

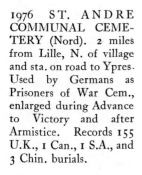

748 ERQUINGHEM-LYS CHURCHYARD EXTENSION (Nord). 1¾ miles W. of Armentières Sta., N. of road to Aire. Taken by 1st Somerset L.I. Oct. 1914, evacuated after stubborn defence by 101st Inf. Bgde. and 1/4th Duke of Wellington's April 10th 1918, retaken Sept. 1918. Records 521 U.K., 32 Aust., 3 N.Z., 2 Can., 1 Fiji., 1 Russ., and 131 German burials.

2178 SUFFOLK CEMETERY, LA ROLANDERIE FARM, ERQUINGHEM - LYS (Nord). 2 miles W. of Armentières, 1 mile S. of village, W. of Rue du Biez, S. of Rolanderie Farm. Casualties chiefly of Suffolk Regt. killed by bombs and machine-gun fire from German aeroplanes during advance April 10th 1918. Records 43 U.K. burials.

1258 LAVENTIE MILITARY CEMETERY (P. de C.). 6 miles SW. of Armentières, E. of village, near Laventie Sta. Used from June 1916 to Oct. 1918. Laventie was 2 miles behind British front from 1914 to 1918 until the Battle of the Lys. Records 413 U.K., 4 Aust., and 3 German burials.

65 ANZAC CEMETERY, SAILLY-SUR-LA-LYS (P. de C.). On road to Estaires, opposite Can. Cem. Begun by Aust. units in July 1916, before attack at Fromelles. Records 111 Aust., 167 U.K., 8 N.Z., 24 Unknown, 1 German burials, and 10 special memorials.

1967 SAILLY-SUR-LA-LYS CANADIAN CEMETERY (P. de C.). On SE. side of road to Estaires, ½ mile SW. of village. Begun by Can. units in March 1915 and used as a front-line Cem. until July 1916. Records 285 U.K., 19 Aust., 9 Can., and 1 German burials.

2465 'X' FARM CEMETERY, LA CHAPELLE D'ARMENTIÈRES (Nord). 1½ miles SE. of Armentières Sta., ½ mile S. of village on road to Bois-Grenier. Was for greater part of the War close to British front line. Used from April 1915 to June 1916. Records 105 U.K. and 8 Aust. burials.

A

A

1966 SAILLY-SUR-LA-LYS CHURCH-YARD (P. de C.). 1 mile N. of Sailly Sta.

Captured by Germans April 9th 1918 and remained in enemy hands until Sept. Records 46 U.K. and 2 Can. burials.

B

B

1312 LE TOUQUET RAILWAY CROSSING CEMETERY, WARNETON (W. FLANDERS). (See Gunners' Farm Cem.). This Cem. is in NW. angle of railway line from Armentières to Warneton, and the road from Le Bizet to Fréling-hien, close to Le Touquet Rly. Sta. Records 71 U.K. burials, and 3 special memorials.

C

1558 MOTOR CAR CORNER CEME-TERY, PLŒG-STEERT (W. FLAN-DERS). (See Gunners' Farm Cem.). This Cem. is 500 yards E. of village of Le Bizet, on N. side of road to Frélinghien. Be-gun in June 1917 at out-break of the Battle of Messines. Records 84 N.Z., 36 U.K., 9 Aust., and 2 Unknown burials.

C

308 BOIS-GRENIER COMMUNAL CEME-TERY (Nord). 2 miles S. of Armentières Sta., S. of village near Church, on right of entrance to Com. Cem. Used from Oct. 1914 to Dec. 1915. Brit. Plot Records 119 U.K. and 2 Can. burials.

379 BREWERY ORCHARD CEME-TERY, BOIS-GRENIER (Nord). 2½ miles from Armentières Sta., E. end of village, N. of road to La Chapelle d'Armentières. The cellar of brewery was used as dressing station. Records 201 U.K., 125 Aust., 13 N.Z., and 5 German burials.

2445 WHITE CITY CEMETERY, BOIS-GRENIER (Nord). 3 miles S. of Armentières Sta., ½ mile SE. of village on road to Fromelles. Used by fighting units from Oct. 1914 to Dec. 1915. Records 92 U.K., and 3 German burials.

2300   V.C. CORNER
AUSTRALIAN
CEMETERY, FRO-
MELLES (Nord).   2½
miles N. of Aubers Sta.,
1 mile N. of Fromelles, N.
of Rue Delvas.   Made
after Armistice from
battle-fields of the attack
of Fromelles (5th Aust.)
and 61st (S. Mid.) Divs.,
July 19th 1916.   Con-
tains 410 graves and re-
cords 1,298 Australian
' Missing '.

1943 RUE-DAVID
MILITARY CEME-
TERY, FLEURBAIX
(P. de C.).   5 miles SW.
of Armentières Sta., 1
mile SE. of village on
road between La Croix
Maréchal and La Boutil-
lerie.   Begun by 2nd R.
Scots Fus. in Dec. 1914.
Records 456 U.K., 353
Aust., 38 Ind., 18 N.Z.,
10 Can., 1 Unknown, 10
German burials, and 21
special memorials.

1947   RUE DU BOIS
MILITARY CEME-
TERY, FLEURBAIX
(P. de C.).   5¼ miles SW.
of Armentières Sta., 3½
miles E. of Laventie Sta.
Reflects attack at Fromel-
les (July 19th–20th 1916),
5th Aust.Div., and gallant
defence of village by 12th
Suffolks, April 9th, 1918.
Records 585 U.K., 242
Aust., 5 N.Z. burials, and
13 special memorials.

1948 RUE-PETILLON MILITARY CEMETERY, FLEURBAIX (P. de C.). 3 miles SW. of Armentières, 1½ miles S. of Fleurbaix. Begun in Dec. 1914, and used by fighting units until Mar. 1918, adjoined 'Eaton Hall' Hdqtrs. and dressing station. Records 1,129 U.K., 291 Aust., 40 Can., 24 N.Z., 2 Guernsey, 12 German burials, and 23 special memorials.

1946 RUE-DU-BAC-QUEROT (13TH LONDON) GRAVEYARD, LAVENTIE (P. de C.). 7 miles SW. of Armentières, 1½ miles E. of Laventie Sta., on La Couture-Fleurbaix road. Begun by R.I. Rifles Nov. 15th, 1914, used by 13th London Regt. Dec. 1914, and subsequently by other units until July 1916. Records 168 U.K. and 28 Aust. burials.

1945 RUE-DU-BAC-QUEROT No 1. MILITARY CEMETERY, LAVENTIE (P. de C.). 7 miles SW. of Armentières, 2 miles S. of Laventie village and sta., through farmyard on N. of Rue du Bacquerot. Used continuously from Oct. 1914 to Oct. 1918. Records 488 U.K., 129 Ind., 7 German burials, and 12 special memorials.

2471 'Y' FARM MILITARY CEME-TERY, BOIS-GRENIER (Nord). 4¼ miles S. of Armentières Sta., 1 mile S. of village. Begun in March 1915 and was used by units holding this sector until Feb. 1918. Records 529 U.K., 163 Aust., 58 Ind., 42 N.Z., 24 Can., 3 S.A., 2 German burials, and 1 special memorial.

814 FERME BUTERNE MILITARY CEME-TERY, HOUPLINES (Nord). 2 miles NE. of Armentières Sta., ¾ mile S. of village, 400 yards from road to l'Epinette. Houplines was taken by III Corps, Oct. 17th, 1914. Records 128 U.K., and 1 Can. burials.

651 DESPLANQUE FARM CEMETERY, LA CHAPELLE D' ARMENTIÈRES (Nord). 1½ miles SE. of Armentières Sta., 1,100 yards S. of village church near road to Bois-Grenier. Begun Oct. 1914 on front of the III Corps of the original B.E.F. and used until June 1916. Records 47 U.K. and 8 Aust. burials.

1315 LE TROU AID POST CEMETERY, FLEURBAIX (P. de C.). 3 miles SW. of Armentières, S. of village. Le Trou Aid Post was established very early in the War, and Cem. was begun in Oct. 1914. Records 288 U.K., 56 Aust., 7 Can., 2 French burials, and 5 special memorials.

101 AUBERS RIDGE BRITISH CEMETERY, AUBERS (Nord). ½ mile SE. of Aubers Sta., on road to Herlies. Taken by 9th Bgde., Oct. 17th, 1914, on 19th the 2nd R. Irish took Le Pilly. Retaken Oct. 1918 by 47th (London) Div. Records 593 U.K., 124 Aust., 1 Ind. burials, and 1 special memorial.

790. EUSTON POST CEMETERY, LAVENTIE (P. de C.). 9½ miles SW. of Armentières, 2½ miles S. of Laventie Sta. on La Bassée road. Begun Oct. 1914 on front of the III Corps of the original B.E.F. and used until Oct. 1915. Records 41 U.K. and 1 German burials.

1598 NEUVE - CHA-PELLE BRITISH CEMETERY (P. de C.). 8 miles NE. of Béthune, 3½ miles S. of Laventie Sta., 400 yards NW. of Neuve-Chapelle Church. Used from Oct. 1914 through Battle of Neuve-Chapelle March 10th–14th to Oct. 1915. Records 50 U.K. burials, and 5 special memorials.

1600 NEUVE - CHA-PELLE FARM CEME-TERY (P. de C.). 8 miles NE. of Béthune, 3½ miles S. of Laventie Sta., ½ mile NW. of Neuve-Chapelle Church. Created by 13th London Regt. and used only during Battle of Neuve-Chapelle March 10th–14th 1915. Records 66 U.K. burials.

805 FAUQUISSART MILITARY CEME-TERY, LAVENTIE (P. de C.). 7 miles SW. of Armentières, 2¾ miles SE. of Laventie Sta., W. of main road to Béthune. Used from Nov. 1914 until 1915, mostly by 2nd R. Berks Rgt. and 2nd Rifle Bgde. Records 105 U.K. burials.

1926 ROULERS COMMUNAL CEMETERY (W. FLANDERS). 1 mile W. of Sta., close to a church near road to Dixmude. Used by Germans as Prisoners of War Cem. Roulers was occupied by Germans Oct. 1914, and finally retaken by French Oct. 14th 1918. Records 58 U.K., 28 Can., 2 French burials, and 4 special memorials.

2249 TOURCOING (PONT-NEU-VILLE) COMMUNAL CEMETERY (Nord). 10 miles NE. of Lille, 2 miles N. of Tourcoing Sta., near road to Courtrai. Used by Germans as Prisoners of War Cem. from Nov. 1914 to Aug. 1918. British plot has prominent position in centre of Com. Cem., and records 176 U.K., 1 N.Z., 1 S.A., 3 Chin., 18 French, and 1 German burials.

1340 LILLE SOUTH-ERN CEMETERY (Nord). S. of town in ' Rue du Faubourg des Postes ', near Lille (Porte des Postes) Sta. Town was occupied by Germans Aug. 1914 and was finally captured by British Oct. 17th 1918. Cem. was used for British burials from Aug. 1914 to April 1919, and records 314 U.K., 10 N.Z., 7 Aust., 2 Chin., and 9 German burials.

86　ASCQ COMMUNAL CEMETERY (Nord). 4 miles E. of Lille, on road
and rly. to Brussels.　Cem. is close to Ascq Sta.　Used from Oct. 22nd, 1918, to
Aug. 7th, 1919, during the Advance to Victory and after the Armistice.
Records 45 U.K., 1 Aust., 1 Can., 2 Ind., and 4 Chinese burials.

THE LAND IN BELGIUM OCCUPIED BY BRITISH WAR CEMETERIES
OR GRAVES HAS BEEN GENEROUSLY CONCEDED IN PERPETUITY BY
THE BELGIAN PEOPLE UNDER AN AGREEMENT MADE AT LE HAVRE ON
9TH AUGUST, 1917

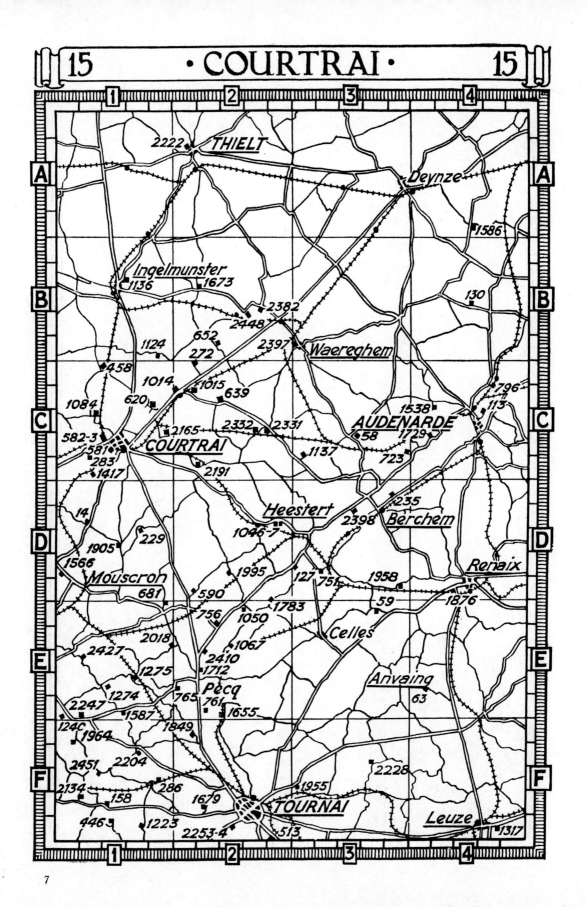

A

A

582 COURTRAI COMMUNAL CEMETERY (St. Jean) (W. FLANDERS). 1¼ miles NW. of Courtrai Sta., E. of town on road to Menin. Used throughout the War by Germans as Prisoners of War Cem. and by British from Nov. 1918 to April 1919. The Cem. is still open for concentration of burials.

B

1047 HEESTERT MILITARY CEMETERY (W. FLANDERS). Near main road between Courtrai and Audenarde, behind ch. and 1 mile from Moen-Heestert Sta. All casualties fell in Advance to Victory, Oct. and Nov. 1918. Records 127 U.K., and 57 German burials.

B

C

1317 LEUZE COMMUNAL CEMETERY (HAINAUT). 6¾ miles E. of Tournai, 1 mile E. of Leuze Sta., S. of road to Ath. Used by Germans for burial of British Prisoners of War April to Nov. 1918. Records 63 U.K., 1 N.Z., and 1 Russ. burials.

D

2253 TOURNAI COMMUNAL CEMETERY, ALLIED EXTENSION (HAINAUT). 2¾ miles SW. of Tournai Sta., SW. of town and S. of road to Orchies. British burials date from Jan. 1916 to March 1919. Records 446 U.K., 21 Can., 4 Aust., 4 Newfld., 1 N.Z., 2 Belg., 1 French, 6 Russ., 64 Port., and 3 special memorials.

C

D

1015 HARLEBEKE NEW BRITISH CEMETERY (W. FLANDERS). 3 miles NE. of Courtrai, 500 yards NE. of Harlebeke Sta., N. of road to Deerlyck. Created after Armistice for isolated graves from battlefields and German cemeteries. Records 1,024 U.K., 23 Can., 7 Aust., 4 S.A., 3 Newfld. burials, and 21 special memorials.

1137 INGOYHEM MILITARY CEMETERY (W. FLANDERS). 7 miles E. of Courtrai, NE. of village and sta., on track which leaves the Renaix road near church. All casualties fell Oct. 1918 in Advance to Victory. Records 81 U.K., 3 Newfld., and 54 German burials.

2332 VICHTE MILITARY CEMETERY (W. FLANDERS). 7 miles E. of Courtrai, 1,000 yards SW. of village near farm track and close to Vichte Sta. Begun Oct. 1918, during final Advance to Victory and enlarged after Armistice. Records 191 U.K., 11 Newfld., and 1 Can. burials.

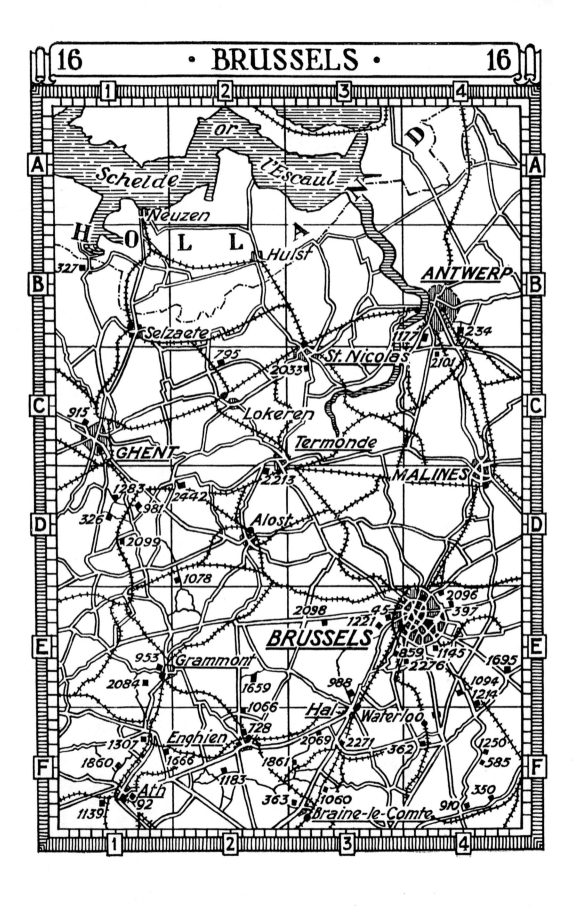

BRUSSELS

MAP SHEET No. 16

397 BRUSSELS COMMUNAL CEMETERY, EVÉRE (BRABANT).   3¼
miles E. of Nord Sta., N. of road to Louvain.   British Plot is on E. side of
Cem.   Majority of burials were Can. who died at end of war.   Few
Prisoner of War burials.   Records 48 Can., 5 U.K., 1 Newfld., and 1 Port.
burials.

BRUSSELS, Capital of Belgium, County Town of the Province of Brabant, and is of great historica
and architectural interest.
    Occupied by the Germans throughout the War, from 20th August, 1914, to the Armistice, and was
subject to a rigorous military government under von der Goltz and von Bissing.   Miss Edith Cavell was
shot here by the Germans 12th October, 1915.
    The King of the Belgians, after four years of war, made a solemn but triumphal return to Brussels
25th November, 1918.

988 HAL COM-MUNAL CEMETERY (BRABANT). 10 miles SW. of Brussels, 1¼ miles N. of Hal Sta., on road to Mekingen. Cem. used by Germans for burial of Prisoners of War April to Nov. 1918, and by British from Nov. 1918 to March 1919. Records 102 U.K., 2 Aust., and 1 Can. burials.

915 GHENT CITY CEMETERY (BRUGES GATE), (E. FLANDERS). NW. of town and sta., on road to Bruges.   In Allied plot near War Mem.   Ghent was occupied by Germans from Oct. 1914 to Nov. 1918, and Cem. was used for Prisoners of War.   Records 78 U.K., 8 Can., 1 Belg., 25 Italian, 13 Russ., and 1 Port. burials.

2101 SCHOONSELHOF CEMETERY, ANT-WERP (ANVERS).   3 miles S. of Antwerp (tram service) on Chaus-sée St. Bernard. British plot at S. end of cem. Contains casualties of R. Nav. Div. and R. Marines who fell Oct. 1914, and Prisoners of War who died March to Oct. 1918. Records 97 U.K., 1 Can., and 7 Port. burials.

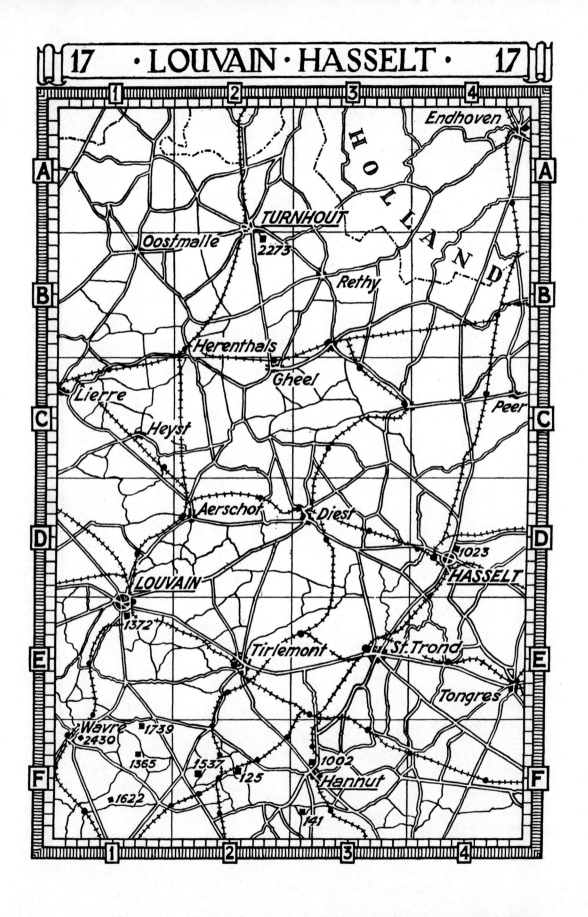

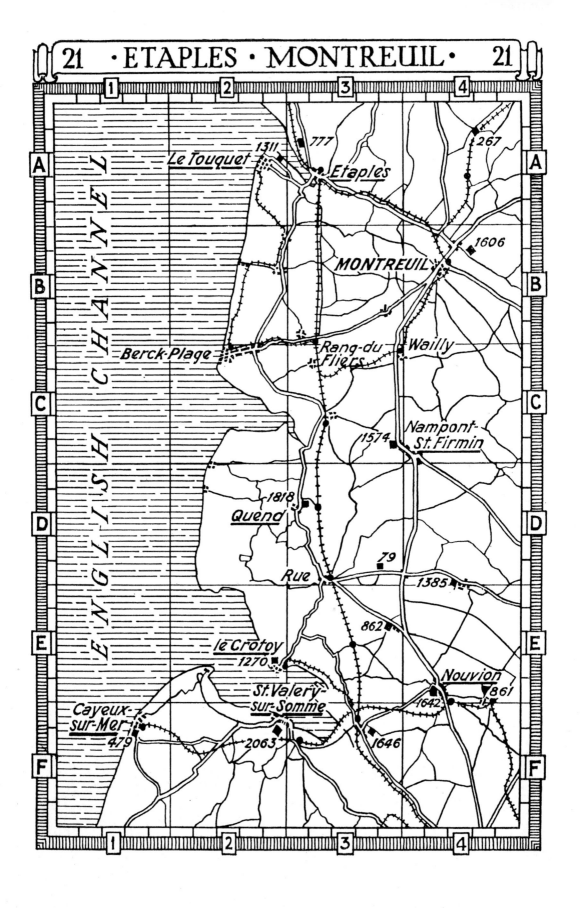

777 ETAPLES MILITARY CEMETERY (P. de C.). On main road and rly. from Boulogne to Paris, 2 miles from Etaples Sta. Was the site of immense British reinforcement camps and hospitals, being remote from attack except by aircraft. Records 8,767 U.K., 1,122 Can., 461 Aust., 261 N.Z., 67 S.A., 28 B.W.I., 18 Newfld., 5 Ind., 1 U.S.A., 2 Belg., 47 Port., 1 Chin., 655 German burials, and 11 special memorials.

1311 LE TOUQUET-PARIS PLAGE COMMUNAL CEMETERY (P. de C). On S. bank of R. Canche, 200 yards from ' Château ' Halte on tramway from Etaples. Burials made from the Duchess of Westminster's Hosp. (No. 1, B.R.C.S.) Oct. 1914–July 1918. Records 139 U.K., and 3 Can. burials.

1646 NOYELLES-SUR-MER CHINESE CEMETERY (SOMME) 9 miles W. of Abbeville, NE. of village and sta., N. of by-road running E. from Noyelles. Cem. created and headstones executed by Chinese. Hdqtrs. of Chinese Labour Corps was in fields S. of Cem. during War. Records 838 Chinese burials.

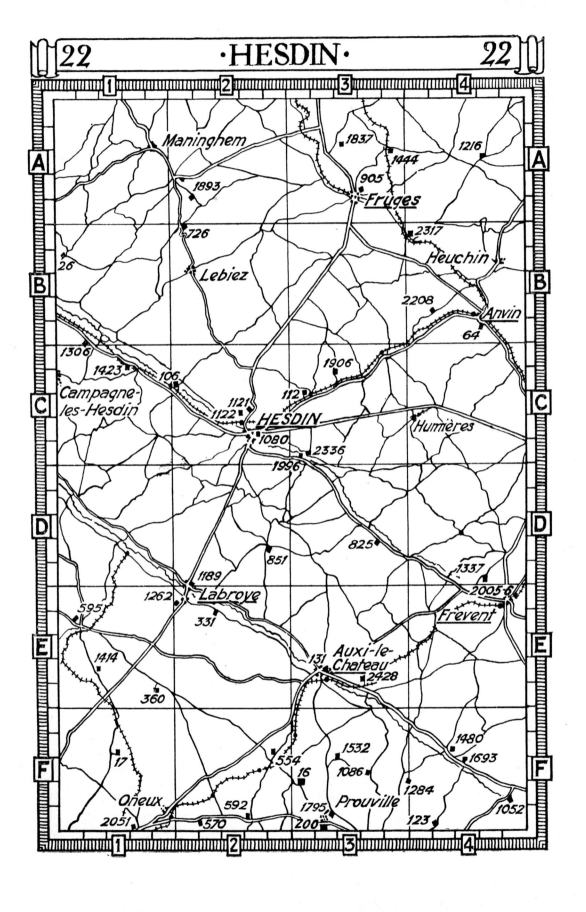

1121 HUBY-ST. LEU BRITISH CEMETERY (P. de C.). 1½ miles N. of Hesdin town and sta., E. of road to St. Omer overlooking V. of R. Canche. Majority of burials from Air Force (Hdqtrs. in neighbourhood), but some from Can. Base at Aubin-St. Vaast. Records 39 U.K., 10 Can., and 1 Chin. burials.

825 FILLIEVRES BRITISH CEMETERY (P. de C.). 8 miles SW. of Hesdin Sta., 6¼ miles NE. of Frévent Sta., S. of village on road to Aubrometz. Original burials of June 1918 to Feb. 1919. Enlarged after Armistice by concentration of isolated graves. Records 75 U.K., and 1 N.Z. burials.

1337 LIGNY - SUR - CANCHE BRITISH CEMETERY (P. de C.). 3 miles NW. of Frévent Sta. N. of village on road to Haute-Côte. Begun Aug. 1918 by 3rd Can., 19th and 43rd Casualty Clearing Stations. Records 77 U.K. and 3 Can. burials.

2005   ST. HILAIRE
CEMETERY, FRÉ-
VENT (P. de C.). 1 mile
NE. of Frévent Sta. on
E. side of town. Frévent
was a place of importance
on Line of Com. Records
195 U.K., 4 N.Z., 4
Ind., 4 S.A., 2 Can., and
1 Aust. burials.

2006   ST. HILAIRE
CEMETERY EXTEN-
SION, FRÉVENT (P.
de C.). E. of Com. Cem.
Used from March to
Aug. 1918. Records 266
U.K., 24 Can., 9 Aust.,
3 N.Z., and 2 B.W.I.
burials.

A

2051   ST. RIQUIER
BRITISH CEMETERY
(SOMME). 6 miles NE.
of Abbeville, ¾ mile N. of
St. Riquier Sta., E. of
by-road to Millencourt.
Original burials made
April to July 1918. En-
larged after Armistice.
Records 30 U.K., 11
Aust., 4 Can., 3 S.A., and
35 Ind. burials.

B

2428   WAVANS BRIT-
ISH CEMETERY (P. de
C.). 2 m. E. of Auxile-
Château, ¾ m.NW. of Wa-
vans Halte, on road to Bois
d'Auxi. Used from May
to Sept. 1918. Records 39
U.K., 2 N.Z., 1 B.W.I.,
and 1 German burials.

A

B

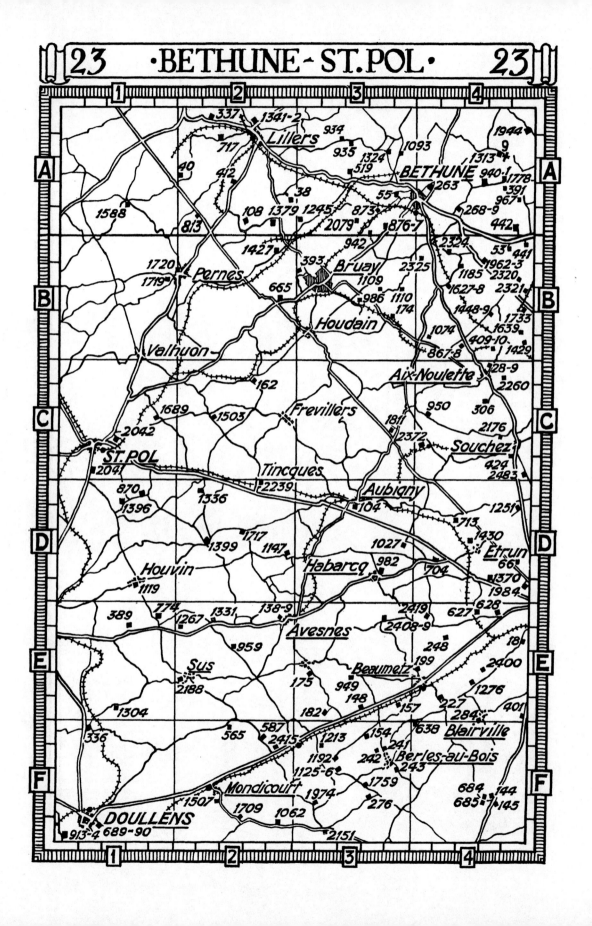

BETHUNE—ST. POL

MAP SHEET No. 23

BETHUNE is an ancient town in the Department of the Pas-de-Calais, on the railway line from Dunkerque to Paris.

During the greater part of the War Béthune was comparatively free from bombardment, and remained an important railway and hospital centre as well as Corps or Divisional Headquarters. The 33rd Casualty Clearing Station was in the town until December 1917. Early in 1918 Béthune began to suffer from constant shell-fire and in April 1918 (in the Battle of Béthune, one of the Battles of the Lys) German forces reached Locon, three miles to the north. The bombardment of the 21st May did great damage to the town, and it was not till October that the enemy pressure was relaxed.

1313 LE TOURET MILITARY CEMETERY, RICHEBOURG-L'AVOUE AND MEMORIAL TO THE 'MISSING' (P. de C.). 4½ miles NE. of Béthune Sta., E. of Le Touret, on Rue du Bois. Begun Nov. 1914. Used by Guards Division Indian Corps (2nd Leicesters) and during Battle of Festubert. Cem. records 899 U.K., 11 Can., 1 B.W.I., and 4 German burials. Mem. records 13,479 'Missing' who fell in the Battles of La Bassée, Neuve-Chapelle, Aubers Ridge, and Festubert 1914–1915.

263 BÉTHUNE TOWN CEMETERY (P. de C.). On N. outskirts, near junction of R. Lawe and Aire-La Bassée Canal. Rly. and hosp. centre, Corps and Div. Hdqtrs. Battle of Béthune was fought in April 1918. Records 2,941 U.K., 55 Can., 7 Ind., 1 S.A., and 6 French burials.

268   BEUVRY COM-
MUNAL CEMETERY
(P. de C.). 2 miles SE. of
Béthune Sta., W. end of
village.   Largely occu-
pied by R.E.'s Supply
Units and Artillery Horse
Lines during War. Bur-
ials from Field Ambs. and
Units Nov. 1914 to Aug.
1916. Records 61 U.K.,
and 7 Can. burials.

269   BEUVRY COM-
MUNAL CEMETERY
EXTENSION (P. de C.).
On W. side of Com. Cem.
Remained in Brit. posses-
sion during the German
offensive of April 1918.
Used March 1916 to Oct.
1918. Records 204 U.K.,
2 S.A., and 1 French
burials.

1944   RUE-DES-
BERCEAUX MILI-
TARY CEMETERY,
RICHEBOURG L'
AVOUE (P. de C.).   6
miles NE. of Béthune, 5
miles S. of Laventie Sta.,
¾ mile W. of village, 700
yards S. of Richebourg.
St. Vaast. Begun by Irish
and Grenadier Guards
Jan. 1915, used by units
fighting on Neuve-Cha-
pelle front and enlarged
after Armistice. Records
464 U.K., 3 German
burials, and 3 special
memorials.

940-941 GORRE BRIT-ISH AND INDIAN CEMETERIES, BEUVRY (P. de C.). 3¾ miles NE. of Béthune, 1 mile N. of Beuvry. Gorre Château was occupied early in war by Brit. and Ind. troops, and Cems. were begun in Autumn of 1914. Brit. Cem. records 830 U.K., 2 S.A., 1 Aust., 1 French, and 8 German burials, also 4 special memorials. Ind. Cem. records 93 Indian burials.

519 CHOCQUES MILITARY CEME-TERY (P. de C.). ½ mile from Chocques Sta. on N. outskirts of village. Was in British occupa-tion from late Autumn of 1914 to end of War. Records 1,681 U.K., 51 Can., 4 S.A., 1 Madras, 36 Ind., 16 Chin., and 82 German burials.

877 FOUQUIERES CHURCHYARD EX-TENSION (P. de C.). 2 miles SW. of Béthune and 1½ miles S. of Fou-quereuil Sta. on N. of road to Bruay. Majority of graves belong to 46th (N. Mid.) Div., which spent three years in neigh-bourhood. Records 387 U.K. burials.

1341 LILLERS COM-MUNAL CEMETERY (P. de C.). ½ mile N. of station on road to St. Venant. Used as Billet and Hdqtrs. offices from Autumn of 1914 to April 1918, also a hosp. centre. Records 699 U.K., 151 Ind., 42 Can., 1 Aust., 1 S.A., and 15 German burials.

1342 LILLERS COM-MUNAL CEMETERY EXTENSION (P. de C.). N. of Com. Cem. and bounded on further side by small stream. Used when Germans advanced to Robecq and Lillers, was under shell-fire April 1918. Records 63 U.K., 3 Aust., 2 Can., and 3 Unknown burials.

1245 LAPUGNOY MILITARY CEME-TERY (P. de C.). 1 mile NW. from Lapugnoy Sta. on side road to Allouagne. Many burials from the Battles of Arras. Records 961 U.K., 349 Can., 7 Aust., 2 S.A., 2 Port., 1 Chin., and 2 German burials.

1778   POST OFFICE RIFLES CEMETERY, FESTUBERT (P. de C.). 5 miles E. of Béthune, 2¼ miles N. of Cuinchy Sta. Used in April–June 1915, before and during Battles of Aubers Ridge and Festubert. Records 399 U.K., and 1 Can. burials.

391   BROWN'S ROAD MILITARY CEMETERY, FESTUBERT (P. de C.). 5 miles E. of Béthune, 2 miles N. of Cuinchy Sta. Festubert was held by 55th (West Lancs.), 1st and other Divs. against German assaults during Battles of Lys April 1918. Records 1,041 U.K., 21 Can., 6 S.A. burials, and 3 special memorials.

967   GUARDS CEMETERY, WINDY CORNER, CUINCHY (P. de C.). ¾ mile N. of Cuinchy Sta. at cross-roads, known to the Army as 'Windy Corner', which was a usual target for German mach.-gunners. Records 3,364 U.K., 32 Can. burials, and 47 special memorials.

441 CAMBRIN CHURCHYARD EXTENSION (P. de C.). 2 miles W. of Cuinchy Sta. and 5 miles E. of Béthune on road to La Bassée. Less than ½ mile from front-line trenches; is remarkable for a very large number of grouped graves of battalions from Battle of Loos. Records 1,206 U.K., about 150 French and 3 German burials.

442 CAMBRIN MILITARY CEMETERY (P. de C.). 5 miles from Béthune, N. of road to La Bassée, 2 miles SW. of Cuinchy Sta. Used as Bgde. Hdqtrs.; was not until end of war more than a mile from German front-line trenches. Records 819 U.K., and 1 S.A. burials.

2079 SANDPITS BRITISH CEMETERY, LABEUVRIERE (P. de C). S. of road to Fouquereuil Sta. (1½ miles) on steep bank. Made and used by the XIII Corps during German advance by which Béthune was threatened. Records 393 U.K., and 1 Ind. burials.

1719 PERNES BRITISH CEMETERY (P. de C.). ½ mile W. of Pernes on road to Sains-les-Pernes and 1¾ miles from Pernes-Camblain Sta. Begun by 1st and 4th Can. Casualty Clearing Stations in April 1918 during German advance. Records 1,028 U.K., 27 Can., 11 Ind., 5 S.A., 3 Aust., 1 B.W.I., 5 Port., 4 French, 2 Chin., and 21 German burials.

393 BRUAY COMMUNAL CEMETERY EXTENSION (P. de C.). Sta. SE. corner of village, and Cem. NW. corner on road to Marles-les-Mines. Extension lies E. of the Com. Cem. The Can. Corps occupied this sector in early 1917. Records 276 Can., 126 U.K., 9 Ind., 1 S.A., and 26 German burials.

1109 HOUCHIN BRITISH CEMETERY (P. de C.). 3½ miles S. of Béthune and ½ mile SW. of village, on road to Hallicourt. Chiefly burials from 55th (W. Lancs.) Div. during Battles of the Lys. Records 659 U.K., 39 Can., 1 Port., 1 Belg., and 39 German burials.

A

A

934 GONNEHEM BRITISH CEMETERY (P. de C.). 2 miles N. of Chocques Sta., on road to Busnes. Begun in April 1918 when Germans came within 2 miles of village during Battles of the Lys. Records 200 U.K. burials.

B

1324 LE VERTANNOY BRITISH CEMETERY, HINGES (P. de C.). 3½ miles NW. of Béthune Sta., S.W. of hamlet near road to Chocques. Begun April 1918 during Battles of the Lys and used by Field Ambs. and fighting units until Sept. Records 141 U.K. (mostly from 4th Div.).

B

C

C

1093 HINGES MILITARY CEMETERY (P. de C.). 3 miles NW. of Béthune Sta. S. of village. The Château nearby was Hdqtrs. of Ind. I, XI, and other Corps, and village was used for rest billets until April 1918. Records 75 U.K., 26 Can. burials and 4 special memorials.

D

1628 NŒUX - LES - MINES COMMUNAL CEMETERY EXTENSION (P. de C.). W. of Com. Cem. Begun in Aug. 1917 and used until Dec. 1918, chiefly by 6th and 7th Casualty Clearing Stations. Records 232 U.K., 71 Can., and 1 S.A. burials.

D

1627   NŒUX - LES - MINES COMMUNAL CEMETERY (P. de C.). ½ mile W. of station on NE. outskirts of town Used by British (in succession to the French) from June 1915 to Aug. 1917. Records 754 U.K., 226 Can., and 1 B.W.I. burials.

1962–1963 SAILLY-LABOURSE COMMUNAL CEMETERY AND EXTENSION (P. de C.). 4 miles SE. of Béthune. Close to battle-field of Loos. Records 126 U.K. in Com. Cem., and 210 U.K., 3 Aust., 2 S.A., and 2 German burials in Extension.

2320 VERMELLES BRITISH CEMETERY (P. de C.). 1 mile N. of sta. SW. of village, on road to Mazingarbe. Begun Aug. 1915, used through Battle of Loos and until April 1917. Records 2,114 U.K., 7 Can., 3 Bermuda, 7 French, 4 German burials, and 6 special memorials.

A

A

1811 QUATRE VENTS MILITARY CEME-TERY, ESTREE-CAUCHY (P. de C.). $3\frac{1}{4}$ miles from Aubigny-en-Artois Sta., SW. of village, near old Roman road to Thérouanne. Begun by French troops in June 1915, carried on by Field Ambs. to April 1918. Records 77 Can., 49 U.K., 4 S.A., 1 Ind., and 1 Unknown burials.

B

306 BOIS-DE-NOU-LETTE BRITISH CEMETERY, AIX-NOULETTE (P. de C.). $3\frac{7}{8}$ miles from Bully-Grenay Sta., on S. side of village under Lorette Ridge. Made by Field Ambs. between April 1916 and May 1917. Records 112 U.K., 19 Can., and 1 Unknown burials.

B

C

C

1430 MAROEUIL BRITISH CEMETERY (P. de C.). Is between the village and the Bois de Maroeuil, 800 yards from Maroeuil Sta. Begun by the 51st (High.) Div., when the British Army took over the Arras front in March 1916. Records 531 U.K., 30 Can., 1 Ind., 1 Chin., and 11 German burials.

D

1448 MAZINGARBE COMMUNAL CEME-TERY (P. de C.). $\frac{7}{8}$ mile NE. of Mazingarbe Halte, SW. of village, adjoining road to Sains-en-Gohelle. Used by British units and Field Ambs. from June 1915 to Feb. 1916. Records 108 U.K. burials.

D

1449   MAZINGARBE COMMUNAL CEMETERY EXTENSION. SW. of Com. Cem. Begun by 16th (Irish) Div., April 1916, used until Oct. 1918. Records 182 U.K., 66 Can., and 2 German burials.

1733 PHILOSOPHE BRITISH CEMETERY, MAZINGARBE (P. de C.). ½ mile S. of Vermelles Sta. on R. of Bully-Grenay road between village and rly. In 1916 was taken over by 16th (Irish) Div., who held Loos salient at the time. Records 1,988 U.K., 6 Can., 2 Aust., 1 B.W.I., and 2 German burials.

174   BARLIN COMMUNAL CEMETERY EXTENSION (P. de C.). The Com. Cem. and Ext. are about 600 yards from rly. sta. on the road to Houchin. The Ext. was begun by French troops in Oct. 1914 and continued by the 6th Casualty Clearing Station in March and April 1918, during the German attack on this front. Records 677 Can., 410 U.K., 5 S.A., 1 Bermuda, 2 Unknown, 58 French, and 13 German burials.

409–410 BULLY-GRE-NAY COMMUNAL CEMETERY, BRITISH AND FRENCH EXTENSIONS (P. de C.). 1¼ miles from sta. on NW. side of village. Begun by French troops and taken over by British in 1915. Records 91 U.K., in French Ext., and 495 U.K., 171 Can., 2 B.W.I., 95 Unknown burials, and 2 special memorials in British Ext.

1429 MAROC BRITISH CEMETERY, GRENAY (P. de C.). N. side of road between Maroc and Grenay, 1 mile E. of Bully-Grenay sta. Was during greater part of war a front-line Cem. Records 1,014 U.K., 178 Can., 98 Unknown, and 23 German burials.

1074 HERSIN COMMUNAL CEMETERY EXTENSION (P. de C.). ¾ mile N. of Hersin-Coupigny Sta., 100 yards E. of church. Begun by French, taken over by British Field Ambs. in March 1916. Records 130 U.K., 55 Aust. (54 of 3rd Aust. Tunnelling Cy.), and 39 Can. burials.

868   FOSSE No. 10 COMMUNAL CEME-TERY EXTENSION, SAINS-EN-GOHELLE (P. de C.). ¾ mile NE. of Sains-Bouvigny Sta., on by-road between the village and Fosse. Used by French until March 1916, then taken over by Brit. Records 214 Can., 203 U.K., 1 Aust., and 49 Chin. burials.

29 AIX NOULETTE COMMUNAL CEME-TERY   EXTENSION (P. de C.). 1⅞ miles from Bully-Grenay Sta., N. of village.   Taken over by 1st and 2nd Divs. in Feb. 1916, used by fighting units and Field Ambs. until Oct. 1918. Records 492 Can., 257 U.K., and 503 French burials.

2260 TRANCHEE DE MECKNES CEME-TERY, AIX-NOU-LETTE (P. de C.). 2 miles from Bully-Grenay Sta., 1 mile E. of village. Named by French troops after Méquinez (Morocco), used by British from Feb. 1916. Records 153 U.K., 45 Can., 2 German burials, and 1 special memorial.

424 CABARET-ROUGE BRITISH CEMETERY, SOUCHEZ (P. de C.). 7 miles N. of Arras, 1 mile S. of Souchez Sta., on Arras-Béthune road. Begun by 47th Div. March 1916, used by fighting units until Sept. 1918 (from Dec. 1916 onwards by Can. Corps), and enlarged after Armistice. Records 6,705 U.K., 721 Can., 115 Aust., 42 S.A., 8 N.Z., 2 Newfld., 4 German burials, and 60 special memorials.

2372 VILLERS STATION CEMETERY, VILLERS-AUBOIS (P. de C.). On N. side of rly., 250 yards W. of sta. and 1 mile NW. of village. Used by British after taking over line from French in March 1916. Records 1,009 Can., 168 U.K., 20 S.A., 9 Unknown, and 32 German burials.

2176 SUCRERIE CEMETERY, ABLAIN-ST. NAZAIRE (P. de C.). 900 yards W. of Ablain-Souchez Sta., 8 miles N. of Arras under Lorette Ridge. Begun in April 1917 and one time known as Saskatchewan Cem. Records 220 U.K., 163 Can., and 1 Unknown burials.

2041 ST. POL BRITISH CEMETERY, ST. POL-SUR-TERNOISE (P. de C.). 1 mile S. of St. Pol Sta., E. of Doullens road. Town was Hdqtrs. of Gen. Byng (Third Army) at commencement of final advance to Victory Aug. 1918. Burials from No. 12 Gen. Hosp. March 1918 to April 1919. Once contained Mem. to 58th Batt. A.I.F. Records 217 U.K., 20 Aust., 14 Can., 5 N.Z., 1 S.A., 1 B.W.I., and 20 German burials.

2042 ST. POL COMMUNAL CEMETERY EXTENSION (P. de C.). Important rly. junction 45 miles SE. of Boulogne, 20 miles W. of Arras. Was a busy hospital and billeting centre during War. Cem. on E. of town near Arras road. Used from March 1916 to April 1918. Records 201 U.K., 7 Can., 4 N.Z., 3 Aust., 1 S.A., and 10 B.W.I. burials.

1336 LIGNY-ST. FLOCHEL BRITISH CEMETERY, AVERDOINGT (P. de C.). Sta. is N. of road to Arras, and Cem. is S. of that road and village. Begun in April 1918 when the 7th Casualty Clearing Station arrived before the German advance. Records 347 Can., 283 U.K., 1 S.A., and 1 Unknown burials.

104 AUBIGNY COM-
MUNAL CEMETERY
EXTENSION (P. de C.).
½ mile from Aubigny Sta.
S. of village, behind Com.
Cem.   From March 1916
to Armistice was held by
British.   Burials were
made from the following
Casualty Clearing Stas. :
42nd, 30th, 24th and 1st
Can.   Records 2,048
U.K., 666 Can., 50 S.A.,
4 Aust., 2 N.Z., 1 B.W.I.,
and 63 German burials.

1027   HAUTE-AVES-
NES BRITISH CEME-
TERY (P. de C.).   S. of
village on road to Ha-
barcq, 2 miles S. of
Frevin-Capelle Sta. and 6
miles W. of Arras. Begun
by 51st (High.) Div., and
used by Field Ambs.
Records 119 U.K., 7
S.A., 3 Can., 1 Ind., 13
Chin., and 8 German
burials.

713   ECOIVRES
MILITARY CEME-
TERY, MONT - ST.
ELOI (P. de C.).   1 mile
from Mont St. Eloi Sta.,
on the edge of the hamlet
of Ecoivres. Brit. troops
took over this front in
March 1916.   Records
891 U.K., 828 Can., 4
S.A., 2 Aust., and 10
German burials.

704 DUISANS BRIT-
ISH CEMETERY,
ETRUN (P. de C.). 1½
miles W. of Marœuil Sta.
and ½ mile N. of Duisans,
in angle of Arras-Ha-
barcq road and a track
leading to Haute-Avesnes.
Under Brit. occupation
from March 1916.   Re-
cords 2,872 U.K., 306
Can., 12 Newfld., 7 Aust.,
7 N.Z., 5 S.A., 2 Ind., 1
Chin., 81 German bur-
ials, and 2 special memorials.

1370   LOUEZ MILI-
TARY   CEMETERY,
DUISANS (P. de C.).
3 miles NW. of Arras, 1½
miles E. of Duisans Halte,
½ mile S. of Louez.   Be-
gun by French troops,
taken over by 51st (High.)
Div. as a 'front-line
cemetery'   in   March
1916. Records 155 U.K.,
and 49 Can. burials.

139   AVESNES - LE -
COMTE COMMUNAL
CEMETERY EXTEN-
SION (P. de C.).   Be-
tween road to Givenchy-
le-Noble and a side road
to sta. (300 yards) about
½ mile NW. of village, on
W. side of Com. Cem.
A large centre of Casualty
Clearing Stations from
June 1916 to July 1917.
Records 326 U.K., 3
Can., 3 S.A., and 1 B.W.I.
burials.

949   GOUY-EN-AR-TOIS COMMUNAL CEMETERY EXTEN-SION (P. de C.). 2 miles N. of Gouy-Bailleulval Halte on S. outskirts of village, S. of Com. Cem. Begun in April 1917 at time of British advance from Arras.   Records 44 U.K., and 4 German burials.

A

A

2409   WANQUETIN COMMUNAL CEME-TERY   EXTENSION (P. de C.). 7 miles W. of Arras and 3½ miles from Beaumetz - Rivière Sta. Begun Nov. 1916. The last graves are those of 23 men of the 3rd Can. Machine - Gun Battn., killed on Sept. 24th, 1918, in a German daylight air raid. Records 145 U.K., 76 Can., and 1 S.A. burials.

B

B

627 DAINVILLE BRITISH CEMETERY (P. de C.). On W. out-skirts of Arras. Cem. is at the end of a track run-ning N. from road to Warlus, ¼ mile W. of vil-lage. Begun by 56th (London) Div. in April 1918, and used by that Div. until Can. took over in July 1918.   Records 116 U.K., 15 Can., and 4 German burials.

148 BAC - DU - SUI BRITISH CEMETERY BAILLEULVAL (P. de C.). ½ mile W. of Gouy Bailleulval Halte on N side of Doullens-Arra road. Begun by 7th 20th, and 43rd Casualty Clearing Stations in Mar 1918. Records 640 U.K. 48 Can., and 55 German burials.

1276 LE FERMONT MILITARY CEME-TERY, RIVIÈRE (P. de C.). 2 miles S. of Wailly Halte, E. of Le Fermont. Begun by the 55th (W. Lancs.) Div. as front-line Cem. Records 78 U.K. and 2 Chin. burials.

227 BELLACOUR'I MILITARY CEME-TERY, RIVIÈRE (P. de C.). ¾ mile SE. of Beau-metz-Rivière Sta., N. of Bellacourt. Used by 46th (N. Mid.), 55th (W Lancs.), 58th (London) 49th (W. Riding), and other Divs. and Can Corps. Records 25 c U.K., 173 Can., 117 French, and 1 German burials.

2400 WAILLY OR-
CHARD CEMETERY
(P. de C.). 4¼ miles SW.
of Arras Sta., 1¼ miles
SE. of Wailly Halte.
Begun May 1916 by 55th
(W. Lancs.) Div. as front-
line Cem., enlarged by
Can. and other units in
1918. Records 189 Can.,
162 U.K., and 15 Un-
known burials.

2415 WARLINCOURT
HALTE BRITISH
CEMETERY, SAULTY
(P. de C.). 500 yards
from Warlincourt Halte
on N. side of Arras-
Doullens road. Used by
various Casualty Clearing
Stations, noticeably dur-
ing Battles of Arras April-
May 1917. Records
1,262 U.K., 4 Can., and
29 German burials.

1974 ST. AMAND
BRITISH CEMETERY
(P. de C.). 9 miles E. of
Doullens, 3 miles S. of
Saulty-l'Arbret Halte, at
cross-roads N. of village.
Burials were made from
Hosps. at St. Amand from
April 29th 1916 to Aug.
24th 1918. Records 221
U.K., 1 Can., 1 N.Z., and
1 Ind. burials.

689 DOULLENS COMMUNAL CEMETERY EXTENSION, No. 1 (SOMME). NE. of town and 1 mile from sta. Was Marshal Foch's Hdqtrs. early in the War, and the scene of the Conference of Unified Command in March 1918. Records 1,143 U.K., 77 N.Z., 69 Aust., 36 Can., 4 Newfld., 3 S.A., 1 Guernsey, 2 Ind., 2 B.W.I., and 13 German burials.

690 DOULLENS COMMUNAL CEMETERY EXTENSION, No. 2 (SOMME). Opp. side of Com. Cem. Begun in March 1918 during German advance, when Ext. No. 1 was filled. Records 320 U.K., 27 N.Z., 23 Can., 2 S.A., 1 Aust., 1 Chin., and 86 German burials.

914 GÉZAINCOURT COMMUNAL CEMETERY EXTENSION (SOMME). 2 miles S. of Doullens Sta. and 1 mile N. of Gézaincourt Halte. Burials due in most cases from Casualty Clearing Stations. Records 501 U.K., 40 N.Z., 23 Aust., 18 Can., 6 Newfld., 2 Ind., 4 Chin., and 76 German burials.

241 BERLES-AU-BOIS CHURCHYARD EXTENSION (P. de C.). 2 miles S. of Gouy-Bailleulval Halte, in old orchard at back of chyd. Remained in British hands from summer of 1915, when taken over from French troops until end of war. Records 144 U.K., 44 French, 1 German burials, and 1 special memorial.

242 BERLES NEW MILITARY CEMETERY, BERLES-AU-BOIS (P. de C.). 1¾ miles S. of Gouy-Bailleulval Halte, NW. of village where roads to Bailleulval and La Cauchie join. Begun by fighting units Jan. 1917. Records 167 U.K. and 11 French burials.

243 BERLES POSITION MILITARY CEMETERY, BERLES-AU-BOIS (P. de C.). 3¼ miles S. of Gouy-Bailleulval Halte, S. of village near road to Monchy-au-Bois. Begun by 46th (N. Mid.) Div. July 1916 and used until Feb. 1917. Records 52 U.K. burials.

638 DE CUSINE RAVINE BRITISH CEMETERY, BASSEUX (P. de C.). 2⅛ miles S. of Beaumetz-Rivière Sta., ½ mile SE. of Basseux. Was begun by 13th K.R.R.C. in Feb. 1916 and used by units holding this front until March 1917. Records 65 U.K. and 3 German burials.

1126 HUMBERCAMPS COMMUNAL CEMETERY EXTENSION (P. de C.). 2 miles from Saulty-l'Arbret Sta. on N. edge of village. Used mainly by Field Ambs. from Sept. 1915 to Feb. 1917 and in March 1918. Records 79 U.K. burials.

276 BIENVILLERS MILITARY CEMETERY (P. de C.). 4½ miles from Gouy-Bailleulval Halte, SW. of village on road to Souastre. Begun by 37th Div. Sept. 1915, afterwards used by other Divs. in line. Records 1,567 U.K., 25 Aust., 9 N.Z., 3 Can., 1 S.A., 1 German burials, and 2 special memorials.

684 DOUCHY-LES-AYETTE BRITISH CEMETERY (P. de C.). 3½ miles SW. of Boisleux Sta., E. of village. Occupied by Germans Oct. 1914 to March 1917, never completely evacuated by inhabitants. Begun Aug. 1918 by 3rd Div. Records 726 U.K., 5 Aust., 2 S.A., 1 Can., and 1 German burials.

144 AYETTE BRITISH CEMETERY (P. de C.). 8½ miles S. of Arras, 3 miles SW. of Boisleux-au-Mont Sta., N. of village near road to Arras. The Lancs. Fus., 1/8th Manchesters, 11th E. Yorks., and 1/1st E. Lancs. buried here March 1918, and the Irish, Grenadier, and Coldstream Guards during following months. Records 53 U.K., and 1 Chin. burials.

145 AYETTE INDIAN AND CHINESE CEMETERY (P. de C.). 8½ miles S. of Arras, 3 miles SW. of Boisleux-au-Mont Sta., S. of village near track to Ablainzevelle. Ayette was brought into front line by German advance of March 1918. Records 52 Ind., 33 Chin. and 1 German burials.

66 ANZIN ST. AUBIN BRITISH CEMETERY (P. de C.). 3 miles NW. of Arras Sta., N. of village in field behind farm-house. Begun in April 1917 by 51st (Highland) Div. Records 291 U.K., 63 Can., and 4 Ind. burials.

1251 LA TARGETTE BRITISH CEMETERY (AUX-RIETZ) NEU-VILLE-ST. VAAST (P. de C.). 5 miles N. of Arras Sta., W. of road to Béthune, adjoining Fr. National Cem. Begun April 1917 and used by Field Ambs. and fighting units until Sept. 1918, nearly one-third of graves are burials from Artillery units. Records 310 U.K., 296 Can., 3 S.A., and 3 Ind. burials.

18 AGNY MILITARY CEMETERY (P. de C.). 3 miles SW. of Arras Sta., NW. of village. Begun by French, used by British units and Field Ambs. from March 1916 to June 1917. Contains 407 U.K., 1 Aust., and 5 German burials.

401 BUCQUOY ROAD CEMETERY, FICHEUX (P. de C.). 1⅛ miles N. of Boisleux Sta., E. of village on W. side of Bucquoy road. In April and May 1917 the VII Corps Main Dressing Sta. was posted near for Battles of Arras. Records 1,318 U.K., 446 Can., 1 Ind., 91 Unknown burials, and 44 special memorials.

2483 ZOUAVE VALLEY CEMETERY, SOUCHEZ (P. de C.). 7 miles SE. of Arras, 1½ miles SE. of Souchez Sta. Named after French Rgts. which fought here 1914–1915. Begun May 1916. Records 128 U.K., 93 Can., 8 S.A., 4 Unknown, 1 German burials, and 11 special memorials.

1984 STE. CATHERINE BRITISH CEMETERY (P. de C.). 1¼ miles from Arras on L. of Roman road to Thérouanne, just beyond church. Was from March 1916 to Armistice in British occupation. Records 312 U.K., 32 Can., 2 S.A., 1 Aust., 1 Unknown, and 1 German burials.

982 HABARCQ COM-
MUNAL CEMETERY
EXTENSION (P. de C.).
4½ miles S. of Aubigny
Sta., NE. of village. Be-
gun by French 1914,
taken over by the British
XVII Corps March 1916.
Records 171 U.K., 6
S.A., and 2 N.Z. burials.

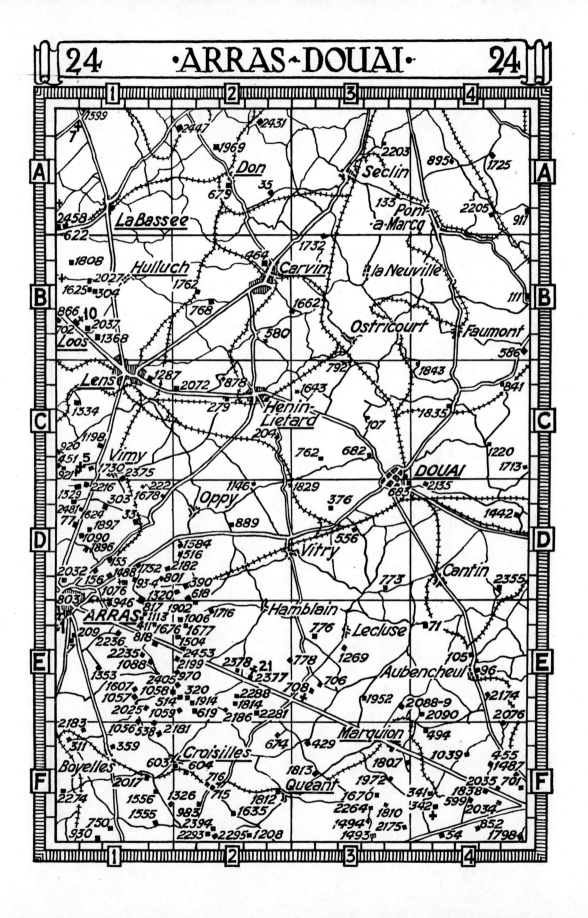

ARRAS—DOUAI

MAP SHEET No. 24

ARRAS, the capital of the Pas-de-Calais Department, is a city and commune of 26,000 inhabitants, the seat of a bishopric, an important manufacturing and commercial town and a road and railway junction. It was a centre of population and government before Caesar invaded Gaul. It has played a considerable part in Burgundian and French history. It was fortified by Vauban, and the Citadel is part of his work.

The city was raided by German forces at the end of August 1914, and occupied by the Germans during the last fortnight in September. It was fiercely and unsuccessfully attacked in October, and it remained in Allied hands until the end of the War. It passed from French to British occupation in the Spring of 1916. It has given its name to the Battles of April and May 1917, in which the German front at Vimy and on the Scarpe was broken; to the Battle of the 28th March, 1918, in which the German attack on the Third Army was defeated; and to the Battles of August and September 1918, in which the Third Army helped to break the Hindenburg Line.

The city is built, to some extent, on its own underground quarries, and it covers a very large system of tunnels, which was used and developed by the British Army; their use, in the preparation for the Battle of April 1917, is mentioned in the official despatches.

The city has been 'adopted' by the City of Newcastle-upon-Tyne; and a memorial tablet to the 56th (London) Division was placed on the wall of the Convent of St. Augustine, in the Rue du Saumon near the railway station, in 1923.

803 FAUBOURG D'AMIENS CEMETERY AND MEMORIAL TO 'MISSING', ARRAS (P. de C.). 1¼ miles NW. of Arras Sta. S. of road to Doullens. Records 2,395 U.K., 152 Can., 60 S.A., 23 N.Z., 9 Ind., 6 B.W.I., 1 Newfld., 1 Unknown, 1 French, 1 Russ., 28 German burials, and 2 special memorials. The Memorial records 35,928 'Missing' who fell in the Battles of Arras, Vimy Ridge, 1st, 2nd, and 3rd Battles of the Scarpe, Battles of Arleux, Bullecourt, and Hill 70, 1917, and all 'Missing' of the R.F.C. and R.A.F., who fell on the Western Front.

CANADIAN NATIONAL MEMORIAL, VIMY RIDGE (P. de C.). 8½ miles N. of Arras Sta., 3¼ miles W. of Vimy Sta., on Vimy Ridge, in NE. corner of the Canadian Memorial Park. Ridge was captured by the Canadians, April 1917.

The Memorial, erected by the Can. Battle-fields Memorials Comm., will record 11,500 Can. 'Missing'. The dug-outs within the Park form a remarkable relic of the War.

NEUVE - CHAPELLE INDIAN MEMORIAL (P. de C.). 8 miles NW. of Béthune Sta. on La Bassée-Estaires road. Records 4,843 Brit. and Ind. 'Missing' of Ind. units. Mainly from Battles of La Bassée, Messines, Armentières, Festubert, and Givenchy (1914), Neuve-Chapelle, Ypres, Aubers Ridge, Festubert, and Loos (1915) and Cambrai (1917).

702 DUD CORNER CEMETERY AND LOOS MEMORIAL TO THE 'MISSING' (P. de C.). 3¾ miles NW. of Lens Sta. on Béthune-Lens road. Large concentration Cem. Name due to dud shells fired on spot during Battle of Loos. Records 1,772 U.K. and 28 Can. burials. The Loos Memorial records 20,693 'Missing' who fell in the Battle of Loos Sept.–Oct. 1915, Lys, Estaires, and Béthune April 1918.

2377 VIS-EN-ARTOIS BRITISH CEMETERY AND MEMORIAL TO 'MISSING', HAU-COURT (P. de C.). 7½ miles SE. of Arras Sta., N. of Cambrai road. Begun by Can. Corps who took Vis-en-Artois Aug. 1918. Cem. records 1,749 U.K., 573 Can., 9 Newfld., 6 Aust., 2 S.A. burials, and 4 special memorials. Mem. records 9,903 'Missing' who fell 1918 in the advance in Picardy, Hindenburg Line, Selle, and the final advance in Artois.

1368 LOOS BRITISH CEMETERY (P. de C.). 2½ miles NW. of Lens Sta., ½ mile S. of Loos Church. Village gave its name to Battle of Sept. 25th to Oct. 8th 1915, when captured by 15th (Scot.) and 47th (Lond.) Divs.   Records 2,387 U.K., 398 Can., 1 Unknown, 1 French burials, and 62 special memorials.

622 CUINCHY COMMUNAL CEMETERY (P. de C.). 1 mile SE. of sta., N. of Béthune-La Bassée road. Remained within range of enemy guns during almost the whole of the war. Brit. burials from Field Ambs. and fighting units. Records 104 U.K. burials.

2027 ST. MARY'S A.D.S. CEMETERY, HAISNES (P. de C.). 4 miles S. of La Bassée Sta., 5 miles N. of Lens sta. on Vermelles-Hulluch road, S. of Hohenzollern Redoubt. Made after Armistice from battle-field of Loos. Records 1,761 U.K., 19 Can. burials, and 30 special memorials.

304 BOIS - CARRÉ MILITARY CEMETERY, HAISNES (P. de C.). 2¼ miles S. of Haisnes Halte, 200 yards S. of road from Vermelles to Hulluch. Begun Sept. 1915 and used largely by 16th (Irish) Div. until Aug. 1916. Records 227 U.K. burials, and 47 special memorials.

1625 NINTH AVENUE CEMETERY, HAISNES (P. de C.). NW. of Bois - Carré Mil. Cem. Named after a trench NW. of Cem. Records 1 officer and 41 men of 1st Cameron Highlanders in one large grave.

1808 QUARRY CEME-
TERY, VERMELLES
(P. de C.). 2¼ miles NE.
of Vermelles Sta., E. of
road to Haisnes. Due
chiefly to fighting at
Fosse 8 and Hohenzollern
Redoubt. Records many
graves of dismounted
cavalry 1915-16. Re-
cords 139 U.K. and 1
German burials.

2037 ST. PATRICK'S
CEMETERY, LOOS
(P. de C.). 3½ miles NW.
of Lens Sta., W. of Loos.
Begun during Battle of
Loos by Brit. and French
and used largely by 16th
(Irish) Div. in 1916. Re-
cords 571 U.K., 13 Can.,
53 French, 1 German
burials, and 24 special
memorials.

866   FOSSE 7 MILI-
TARY CEMETERY
(QUALITY STREET)
MAZINGARBE (P. de
C.). 1 mile SE. of Ver-
melles Sta., 2 miles E. of
village, near road from
Lens to Béthune. Begun
by French troops in May
1915 and carried on by
Brit. from June 1915 to
April 1917. Records 128
U.K., 12 French burials,
and 17 special memorials.

A

A

2458 WOBURN ABBEY CEMETERY, CUINCHY (P. de C.). ¾ mile SE. of sta., N. of Béthune-La Bassée road. 'Woburn Abbey' was house E. of cem. used as Batt. Hdqtrs. and dressing sta. Begun by R. Berks Rgt. June 1915. Records 544 U.K., 12 Can. burials, and 3 special memorials.

B

679 DON COM-MUNAL CEMETERY, ANNOEULLIN (Nord). 8 miles SW. of Lille, 1 mile S. of Don-Sainghin Sta., on road to Annoeullin. British plot commenced during advance on Lille Oct. 1918. Records 121 U.K., 3 Aust., 1 Can., and 2 Chin. burials.

B

C

683 DOUAI COM-MUNAL CEMETERY (Nord). E. of town, 1 mile from sta., near road to Valenciennes. Cem. used by enemy for Prisoner of War burials. Records 198 U.K., 8 Can., 7 Aust., 5 Newfld., 3 N.Z., and 1 S.A. burials.

D

1334 LIEVIN COM-MUNAL CEMETERY EXTENSION (P. de C.). 3 miles SW. of Lens Sta., SW. of town on road to Givenchy-en-Gohelle. Captured by Can. Corps on April 14th 1917. Records 521 U.K., 155 Can., and 1 French burials, and 14 special memorials.

C

D

682 DOUAI BRITISH CEMETERY, CUINCY (Nord). 2 miles SW. of Douai Sta., W. of road to Lens on road to Cuincy. Begun during British advance on Douai Oct. 1918 and used by Brit. Hosp. in vicinity until July 1919 and enlarged by concentrations. Records 196 U.K., 17 Can., 2 S.A., 3 Chin., 6 German burials, and 1 special memorial.

920 GIVENCHY-EN-GOHELLE CANADIAN CEMETERY, SOUCHEZ (P. de C.). 3¼ miles W. of Vimy Sta., ½ mile SW. of village on W. slopes of Vimy Ridge. Taken by 2nd Can. Div. April 13th 1917. Records 129 Can., 8 U.K., 2 Unknown burials, and 15 special memorials.

921 GIVENCHY ROAD CANADIAN CEMETERY, NEUVILLE-ST. VAAST (P. de C.). 5 miles N. of Arras, 3 miles W. of Vimy Sta., W. of road from village to Givenchy-en-Gohelle, in NW. corner of Can. Mem. Park. Records 111 Can. burials.

451 CANADIAN CEMETERY No. 2, NEUVILLE-ST.VAAST (P. de C.). 3 miles W. of Vimy Sta., 1 mile N. of Neuville-St. Vaast on northern slopes of Vimy Ridge on N. edge of Can. Mem. Park. Begun by Can. Corps after successful storming of Vimy Ridge April 9th 1917. Records 531 Can., 215 U.K. burials, and 29 special memorials.

1198 LA CHAUDIERE MILITARY CEMETERY, VIMY (P. de C.). On W. side of Arras road, N. of village and 2 miles from Vimy Sta. at foot of Vimy Ridge. The Ridge was attacked by the 25th and 47th (London) Divs. May 1916, and taken by the 4th Can. Div. on April 9th–10th 1917. Records 590 Can., 90 U.K., 184 Unknown burials, and 12 special memorials.

1730 PETIT-VIMY BRITISH CEMETERY, VIMY (P. de C.). 1¾ miles W. of Vimy Sta., W. of main road from Lens to Arras, near Vimy Ridge. Made and used by units in front line from May to Oct. 1917. Records 90 Can. and 4 U.K. burials.

2216 THELUS MILI-TARY CEMETERY (P. de C.). 2⅝ miles E. of Farbus Sta., W. of Arras-Lens road near Vimy Ridge. Captured by Can. Corps on April 9th 1917. See 1st Can. Div. and Can. Artillery Mems. nearby. Records 245 Can., 50 U.K., and 1 German burials.

1329 LICHFIELD CRATER, THELUS (P. de C.). ½ mile E. of Neuville-St. Vaast. Mine crater used by Can. Corps in 1917 as one large grave. Records 52 Can., 1 U.K., 4 Unknown, and 1 Russ. burials. (All but one fell 9th or 10th April 1917.)

1624 NINE ELMS MILITARY CEME-TERY, THELUS (P. de C.). 2 miles E. of Farbus Sta., on Arras road, 1 mile SW. of village. Begun after capture of Vimy Ridge by 14th Can. Inf. Batt. Records 484 Can., 145 U.K., 54 Fr. burials, and 55 special memorials.

A

A

2481 ZIVY CRATER, THELUS (P. de C.). S. of Lichfield Crater and S. of road from Thélus to Neuville-St. Vaast. Mine crater used by Can. Corps in 1917 as one large grave. Records 50 Can. and 3 Unknown burials.

B

77 ARRAS ROAD BRITISH CEMETERY, ROCLINCOURT (P. de C.). 4½ miles N. of Arras Sta., 1¼ miles NW. of Roclincourt, W. of Arras-Lens road. Begun by 7th Can. Inf. Batt. (1st Brit. Columbia), who fell in action during capture of Vimy Ridge April 1917. Enlarged after Armistice from isolated graves. Records 504 U.K., 92 Can., 15 Aust., and 1 N.Z. burials.

B

C

C

2032 ST. NICOLAS BRITISH CEMETERY (P. de C.). 1¼ miles from Arras, on rue d'Enfer, which joins road to Roclincourt. Was from Mar. 1916 to Armistice in Brit. occupation. Records 350 U.K., 9 S.A., 3 Can., and 2 Aust. burials.

D

156 BAILLEUL ROAD WEST CEMETERY, ST. LAURENT-BLANGY (P. de C.). 2 miles NE. of Arras Sta., ¾ mile N. of village, S. of Hénin-Liétard road. Casualties mostly from 9th (Scot.) Div., who fell on April 9th 1917 during Battle of Arras. Records 97 U.K. and 1 S.A. burials.

D

303 BOIS CARRE BRITISH CEMETERY, THÉLUS (P. de C.). 2 miles W. of Farbus Sta. Thélus (on Vimy Ridge) was captured by Can. Corps April 9th 1917 and Cem. was begun by units of 1st Can. Div. same month. Records 372 Can., 115 U.K., and 15 special memorials.

222 BEEHIVE CEMETERY, WILLERVAL (P. de C.). 6 miles NE. of Arras, 1½ miles NE. of Farbus Sta., ¾ mile N. of village. Named after German pill-box 25 yards N. of Cem. Used from May to Dec. 1917. Records 42 Can. and 7 U.K. burials.

1678 ORCHARD DUMP CEMETERY, ARLEUX - EN - GO - HELLE (P. de C.). 7 miles NE. of Arras, 2 miles NE. of Bailleul-sire - Berthoult Sta., |¾ mile SW. of village on road to Hénin-Liétard. Begun April 1917, used until Nov. 1917, considerably enlarged after Armistice from battlefields around Arras. Records 2,693 U.K., 282 Can., 1 S.A. burials, and 44 special memorials.

1896 ROCLINCOURT MILITARY CEMETERY (P. de C.). 3 miles N. of Arras Sta. on W. side of village. Begun by 51st (Highland) and 34th Divs. in April 1917 and contains many graves of April 9th (first day of the Battles of Arras). Records 776 U.K., 134 Can., 6 Unknown, and 4 German burials.

1897 ROCLINCOURT VALLEY CEMETERY (P. de C.). 3¾ miles N. of Arras Sta., E. of road from Arras to Lens. The 51st (Highland) and 34th Divs. advanced on April 9th 1917 from village during Battles of Arras. Records 509 U.K., 22 S.A., 2 Can., 2 N.Z., 9 Unknown burials, and 4 special memorials.

33 ALBUERA CEMETERY, BAILLEUL-SIRE - BERTHOULT (P. de C.). 5 miles NE. of Arras, W. of village. Captured by 2nd Div. April 13th 1917. Cem. made by fighting units April–Nov. 1917. Records 237 U.K., 1 German burials, and 15 special memorials.

A

A

1090 HIGHLAND CEMETERY, ROCLINCOURT (P. de C.). 4 miles N. of Arras Sta., ½ mile NE. of village. Within Brit. lines before Battles of Arras 1917. 51st (Highland) and 34th Divs. advanced from here. Records 271 U.K., 33 Can., 16 S.A., 1 B.W.I. burials, and 1 special memorial.

B

1076 HERVIN FARM BRITISH CEMETERY, ST. LAURENT-BLANGY (P. de C.). 3 miles NE. of Arras Sta., S. of road to Fampoux. Front line ran through village until April 9th 1917, and Hervin farm was taken by 9th (Scot.) Div. that day. Records 51 U.K. burials.

B

C

C

801 FAMPOUX BRITISH CEMETERY (P. de C.). 2 miles W. of Rœux Sta. on road ('York Lane') to Point-du-Jour. Made by 4th and 34th Divs., April–June 1917, and used by Guards Div. 1918. Records 99 U.K. and 19 S.A. burials.

D

516 CHILI TRENCH CEMETERY, GAVRELLE (P. de C.). 5 miles NE. of Arras, W. of road to Fampoux, made by 37th Div., April–May 1917. Gavrelle was captured by R.N. Div. April 23rd 1917, recaptured by 51st (Highland) Div. Aug. 27th 1918. Records 192 U.K. burials and 86 special memorials.

D

155 BAILLEUL ROAD EAST CEMETERY, ST. LAURENT-BLANGY (P. de C.). 3 miles NE. of Arras, 1½ miles SW. of Bailleul-sire-Berthoult Sta., 1½ miles NE. of village on road to Hénin - Liétard. Used from Jan. to Nov. 1917, and enlarged after Armistice. Records 1,225 U.K. 43 Aust., 12 Can., 6 S.A., 1 Newfld. burials, and 7 special memorials.

1488 MINDEL TRENCH BRITISH CEMETERY, ST. LAURENT - BLANGY (P. de C.). 2½ miles NE. of Arras Sta., N. of road to Gavrelle. Mindel Trench was taken by 9th (Scot.) Div. April 9th 1917, and Cem. was made alongside after battle. Records 190 U.K. and 2 S.A. burials.

946 GOUROCK TRENCH CEMETERY, TILLOY - LES - MOFFLAINES (P. de C.). 3 miles E. of Arras Sta., 1¼ miles N. of village, 140 yards from by-road. Made by units of 15th (Scot.) and 37th Divs. April 1917. Records 40 U.K. and 4 Can. burials.

2182 SUNKEN ROAD CEMETERY, FAMPOUX (P. de C.). 4½ miles E. of Arras, at summit of sunken road to Bailleul. Captured by 4th Div. April 9th 1917. Cem. made by fighting units April 1917–Jan. 1918. Records 196 U.K. burials and 16 special memorials.

1584 NAVAL TRENCH CEMETERY, GAVRELLE (P. de C.). 5 miles NE. of Arras, ½ mile SW. of village. Named from 2nd line trench made by 63rd Div. summer 1917, Hdqtrs. of Queen's Wests., March 1918, and retaken by 6th Black Watch Aug. 26th 1918. Records 59 U.K. burials.

817 FEUCHY BRITISH CEMETERY (P. de C.). 3 miles E. of Arras, SW. of village. Captured by 15th (Scot.) Div. April 9th 1917. Cem. made by 12th Div. same month. Records 213 U.K., 1 Can. burials, and 2 special memorials.

818 FEUCHY CHAPEL BRITISH CEMETERY, WANCOURT (P. de C.). 3½ miles SE. of Arras Sta. on Cambrai road. German Redoubt near Chapel taken by 12th (Eastern) Div. April 9th 1917 (Mem. near Cem.). Records 1,056 U.K., 26 Can., 1 S.A. burials, and 20 special memorials.

390 BROWN'S COPSE CEMETERY, RŒUX (P. de C.). ⅝ mile W. of sta., ½ mile W. of village. Village built over caves and difficult to capture. Attacked by 9th (Scot.) Div. April 12th, cleared by 51st (Highland) Div. May 14th 1917, and re-taken by same Div. Aug. 26th 1918. Records 1,923 U.K., 129 S.A., 2 Can., 1 Unknown burials, and 9 special memorials.

1902 RŒUX BRITISH CEMETERY (P. de C.). 6 miles E. of Arras, W. of village and sta. Village attacked by 9th (Scot.) Div. April 12th. Chemical Works by rly. taken by 51st (Highland) Div. April 22nd. Records 349 U.K. burials and 82 special memorials.

A

A

1320 LEVEL CROSS-ING CEMETERY, FAMPOUX (P. de C.). 1 mile SW. of Rœux Sta., SE. of village. The 9th, 15th and 51st (all Scots.) Divs. fought in this area. Records 400 U.K., 4 S.A. burials, and 1 special memorial.

B

B

618 CRUMP TRENCH BRITISH CEMETERY (P. de C.). $1\frac{1}{8}$ miles S. of Rœux Sta. between Fampoux and Rœux. Fampoux was taken by 4th Div. April 9th 1917, finally cleared by 51st (Highland) Div. Aug. 26th 1918. Records 182 U.K. burials.

C

C

7 ACHICOURT ROAD CEMETERY, ACHI-COURT (P. de C.). $1\frac{1}{2}$ miles S. of Arras Sta., E. of road to Amiens. Be-gun March 1917 when German retreat began, and used until June. Re-used Aug. and Sept. 1918. Records 78 U.K., 52 Can., and 1 Unknown burials.

D

D

1006 HAPPY VALLEY BRITISH CEMETERY, FAMPOUX (P. de C.). $3\frac{1}{2}$ miles S. of Rœux Sta. and 1 mile NW of Monchy - le - Preux. 'Happy Valley' runs E. from Orange Hill along which British troops fought their way on April 10th–11th 1917. Records 75 U.K. burials, and 1 special memorial.

1752 POINT-DU-JOUR MILITARY CEME-TERY, ATHIES (P. de C.). 3¼ miles NE. of Arras Sta. on road to Douai. German redoubt captured by 34th Div. April 9th 1917. Mems. to 9th Div. and Seaforth Highs. nearby. Records 627 U.K., 68 S.A., 24 Guernsey, 14 Can., 2 N.Z., 3 French burials, and 28 special memorials.

2236 TILLOY BRIT-ISH CEMETERY, TILLOY - LES - MOF-FLAINES (P. de C.). 2¼ miles SE. of Arras Sta., 300 yards SE. of village. Taken by Brit. April 9th 1917, was partly in German hands again from March to Aug. 1918. Records 1,446 U.K., 91 Aust., 57 Can., 15 S.A., 4 Newfld., 3 N.Z., 2 German burials, and 25 special memorials.

209 BEAURAINS ROAD CEMETERY, BEAURAINS (P. de C.). 1¼ miles S. of Arras Sta. on road to Bapaume. Captured after slight re-sistance on March 18th 1917. Burials carried out by fighting units, especi-ally 14th (Light) Div. Records 303 U.K., 14 Can., 4 German burials, and 14 special memorials.

A

A

1113 HOUDAIN LANE CEMETERY, TILLOY-LES-MOFFLAINES (P. de C.). 2 miles SE. of Arras between Tilloy and Feuchy. Made in April 1917 by units of the 12th (Eastern), 15th (Scot.) and 37th Divs. Records 74 U.K. and 2 Can. burials.

B

B

1732 PHALEMPIN COMMUNAL CEMETERY (Nord). 8 miles S. of Lille, ¾ mile from Phalempin Sta. on N. outskirts of village. Used from May 1915 to June 1918 by Germans as Prisoners of War Cem. Records 41 U.K. and 2 Can. burials.

C

C

411 BUNYANS CEMETERY, TILLOY-LES-MOFFLAINES (P. de C.). 2¾ miles E. of Arras Sta., ¾ mile NE. of village. Captured April 9th 1917 by 3rd Div. followed by 37th. Begun after battle by Inf. units, used by 62nd and 63rd Bgds., R.F.A. Records 54 U.K. burials.

D

D

1676 ORANGE HILL CEMETERY, FEUCHY (P. de C.). 3 miles E. of Arras, 1 mile SE. of village. Reached by 12th Div. April 10th 1917. Cem. made by Can. Corps after recapture of hill Aug. 1918. Records 42 Can. and 1 U.K. burials.

970 GUEMAPPE BRIT-ISH CEMETERY, WANCOURT (P. de C.). 6 miles SE. of Arras, 5 miles N. of Croisilles Sta., W. of village, S. of road to Wancourt. Wancourt lay in the Hindenburg Line and was taken by assault April 12th 1917. Records 170 U.K. burials.

1677 ORANGE TRENCH CEMETERY, MONCHY-LE-PREUX (P. de C.). 3¼ miles S. of Rœux Sta., N. of village. Made after April 9th–11th 1917, when the 12th, 15th and 37th Divs. carried Monchy-le-Preux and the Scarpe. Records 112 U.K. burials and 6 special memorials.

1088 HIBERS TRENCH CEMETERY, WAN-COURT (P. de C.). 4½ miles SE. of Arras Sta., ½ mile NW. of village. Captured by Brit. April 12th 1917, Wancourt Tower taken by 50th (Northumbrian) Div. on 13th. Finally secured by Can. Corps Aug. 26th 1918. Records 133 U.K., 3 Can. burials, and 2 special memorials.

A

A

2199 TANK CEME-
TERY, GUEMAPPE (P.
de C.). 6 miles SE. of
Arras, 5 miles N. of
Croisilles Sta., NW. of
village and W. of road to
Monchy - le - Preux.
Majority of casualties fell
in heavy fighting for
Hindenburg Line April
23rd–28th 1917 during
Battle of Arras. Records
218 U.K. and 1 Newfld.
burials.

B

2235 TIGRIS LANE
CEMETERY, WAN-
COURT (P. de C.). 4
miles SE. of Arras Sta.,
NE. of village, on road to
Tilloy. Named from a
trench and made by 14th
(Light) Div. May 1917.
Records 86 U.K. and 33
Can. burials.

B

C

C

1058 HENINEL COM-
MUNAL CEMETERY
EXTENSION (P. de C.).
6 miles SE. of Arras, 3
miles N. of Croisilles
Sta., 500 yards E. of
village on ' Chemin de
Douay '. Village was
taken with 1,000 yards of
Siegfried Line by aid of
tanks April 12th 1917 in
Battle of Arras. Records
140 U.K. burials.

D

1059 HENINEL-
CROISILLES ROAD
CEMETERY, HENI-
NEL (P. de C.). 2½ miles
on road due N. of Croi-
silles Sta. 21st Div. captured Heninel April 12th
1917, 33rd Div. took over
the attack eastwards.
Both Divs. represented in
cem. Records 297 U.K.,
10 Aust., and 11 German
burials.

D

2405 WANCOURT BRITISH CEMETERY (P. de C.). 5¾ miles SE. of Arras Sta. S. of main road from Arras to Cambrai. Captured on April 12th 1917, after very heavy fighting. Records 1,026 U.K., 246 Can., 1 Bermuda, 566 Unknown burials, and 96 special memorials.

1353 LONDON CEMETERY, NEUVILLE-VITASSE (P. de C.). 3½ miles from Arras, 1,000 yards NW. of village on road to Croisilles. Majority of casualties from London Rgts., who fell in Battle of Arras 1917 when village was taken, others from German offensive of March 1918. Records 575 U.K., 19 Can., 12 Aust., 3 Newfld. burials, and 138 special memorials.

1056 HÉNIN COMMUNAL CEMETERY EXTENSION, HÉNIN-SUR-COJEUL (P. de C.). 5 miles S. of Arras, 2½ miles NE. of Boyelles Sta., 750 yards S. of village, near St. Léger road. Hénin was ½ mile behind front line at beginning of Battle of Arras April 1917, and was used from April to Nov. 1917. Records 191 U.K. burials and 2 special memorials.

A

B

A

1057 HÉNIN CRUCI-FIX CEMETERY (P. de C.). 5 miles SE. of Arras Sta. and 1 mile E. of main road to Bapaume. Captured on April 2nd 1917, lost March 1918, and retaken following Aug. Made by units of 30th Div. after capture of village in 1917. Records 61 U.K. burials and 8 special memorials.

B

514 CHERISY ROAD EAST CEMETERY, HÉNINEL (P. de C.). 6 miles SE. of Arras, 3 miles N. of Croisilles Sta., S. of road to Cherisy. All casualties from Arras offensive April 14th to 28th 1917. Records 85 U.K. burials.

C

320 B O O T H A M CEMETERY, HÉNI-NEL (P. de C.). 6 miles SE. of Arras, 3 miles N. of Croisilles Sta., on by-road to Cherisy. Created during first battle of Arras April 1917. Casualties from 2nd R. Scots Fus. and 1st Queen's West. Rifles April 14th–23rd. Records 186 U.K. bur-ials.

D

2183 SUNKEN ROAD CEMETERY, BOIS-LEUX-ST. MARC (P. de C.). 5 miles S. of Arras, 1 mile E. of Boisleux-au-Mont Sta., NW. of vil-lage, W. of road to Mer-catel. Begun during Battle of Arras May and June 1917. Re-used Sept. and Oct. 1918 during final advance to Victory. Records 398 U.K., 14 Can., 2 N.Z., 1 Ind., and 4 German burials.

C

D

94 ATHIES COMMUNAL CEMETERY EXTENSION (P. de C.). 3¼ miles E. of Arras Sta., N. of village. Captured by 9th (Scot.) Div. which included S.A. Bgde. on April 9th 1917. Records 287 U.K., 21 S.A., 1 Aust., 1 German burials, and 3 special memorials.

1914 ROOKERY BRITISH CEMETERY, HÉNINEL (P. de C.). 6 miles SE. of Arras, 3 miles N. of Croisilles Sta., E. of Héninel and E. of by-road to Fontaine-lès-Croisilles. The Rookery was a network of trenches and strong point in Hindenburg Line 200 yards NW. of Cem. Records 55 U.K. burials.

619 CUCKOO PASSAGE CEMETERY, HÉNINEL (P. de C.). 6 miles SE. of Arras, 3 miles N. of Croisilles Sta., 1¼ miles E. of village, SW. of Fontaine-lès-Croisilles road. Cuckoo Passage, a trench in the Hindenburg Line, ran NE. to SW. by cem. Casualties from April 14th to May 3rd 1917. Records 54 U.K. burials.

11

1607 NEUVILLE-VITASSE ROAD CEMETERY, NEU-VILLE-VITASSE (P. de C.). 5 miles SE. of Arras Sta., 1 mile SE. of village. Captured by 56th (Lond.) Div. on April 9th 1917. Made by units of 33rd Div. after first capture of village. Records 86 U.K. burials.

2025 ST. MARTIN CALVAIRE BRITISH CEMETERY, ST. MARTIN - SUR - CO-JEUL (P. de C.). 3 miles NE. of Boyelles Sta., SE. of village, on road from Hénin to Héninel. Begun by units of 30th Div. April 1917 and used until March 1918. Records 228 U.K. and 3 German burials.

2181 SUMMIT TRENCH CEMETERY, CROISILLES (P. de C.). 8 miles SE. of Arras, NW. of village and sta., W. of track to St. Martin-sur-Cojeul. Begun by 56th (London) Div. during attack on Hindenburg Line, Aug. 1918. Casualties chiefly of 1/1st and 1/2nd London Rgt. Records 74 U.K. burials.

A

A

2288 VALLEY CEME-
TERY, VIS-EN-AR-
TOIS (P. de C.). 1 mile
S. of sta. between Vis-en-
Artois and Cherisy. Be-
gun on Aug. 31st 1918
when 3rd Can. Inf. Batt.
buried 31 who fell pre-
vious day in capture of
Orix Trench. Records
37 Can., 24 U.K., 7
Aust. burials, and 1
special memorial.

B

2089 S A U C H Y -
C A U C H Y C O M-
MUNAL CEMETERY
EXTENSION (P. de C.).
2 miles N. of Marquion
Sta., S. of village, E. side
of Com. Cem. Village
was captured by 56th
(Lond.) Div. on Sept.
27th 1918. Records 51
U.K. and 3 Can. burials.

C

2274 T W O T R E E
CEMETERY, MOYEN-
NEVILLE (P. de C.). 8
miles S. of Arras, 1 mile
N. of Courcelles-le-
Comte Sta., ¾ mile SW.
of village on ' Chemin des
Bois '. The 15th W.
Yorks held the front of
the 31st Div. at Moyen-
neville on March 26th–
27th 1918 for 36 hours
averting disaster at the
cost of 700 casualties
Records 49 U.K. burials.

D

2453 W I N D M I L L
BRITISH CEMETERY,
MONCHY-LE-PREUX
(P. de C.). 5¼ miles E.
of Arras Sta., N. side of
Arras-Cambrai road.
Infantry Hill captured
April 23rd 1917. Records
320 U.K., 61 Can., 4 New-
fld., 1 S.A., 15 Unknown
burials, and 1 special
memorial.

B

C

D

1504 MONCHY BRIT-
ISH CEMETERY,
MONCHY - LE-PREUX
(P. de C.). 4¾ miles E. of
Arras Sta., N. side of
main road from Arras to
Cambrai. Was captured
on April 11th 1917 in
first Battle of Scarpe.
Memorial to 37th Div. in
village. Records 529
U.K., 23 Can. burials,
and 2 special memorials.

359 BOYELLES
COMMUNAL CEME-
TERY EXTENSION (P.
de C.). ½ mile N. of sta.,
E. of main road from
Arras to Bapaume. Taken
by 7th Div. March 19th
1917. Cem. largely used
by 21st, 33rd and 56th
(London) Divs. Records
142 U.K. and 4 German
burials.

2017 ST. LEGER
BRITISH CEMETERY
(P. de C.). 8 miles S. of
Arras, ½ mile W. of St.
Léger Sta., 300 yards W.
of main village street.
Enemy positions on this
front were carried by 4th
Aust. and 7th Divs. April
2nd 1917. Records 183
U.K., 1 Ind., and 20
German burials.

1556 MORY STREET MILITARY CEME-TERY, ST. LÉGER (P. de C.). 8 miles S. of Arras, S. of St. Léger village and sta. on road to Mory. Majority of identified casualties are from Guards Div. who fell Aug. and Sept. 1918. Records 66 U.K. burials.

1555 MORY ABBEY MILITARY CEME-TERY, MORY (P. de C.). 4 miles N. of Bapaume, 2½ miles S. of St. Léger Sta., 500 yards NW. of village on road to Ecoust-St. Mein. Mory was taken by 62nd Div. after hard and deter-mined fighting Aug. 25th 1918. Records 617 U.K., 1 Aust., 1 N.Z., and 15 German burials.

983 H.A.C. CEME-TERY, ECOUST-ST. MEIN (P. de C.). 1¼ miles S. of sta., on road to Beugnâtre. Enemy positions from Doignies to Hénin-sur-Cojeul were captured on April 2nd 1917 by 4th Aust. and 7th Divs. Records 1,508 U.K., 162 Aust., 26 Can., 4 N.Z., 145 Unknown burials, and 65 special memorials.

716 ECOUST - ST. MEIN BRITISH CEMETERY (P. de C.). 1,000 yards SW. of sta., R. of Croisilles road. On April 2nd 1917 Croisilles and Ecoust were captured in a blizzard by 7th Div. Regained Aug. 1918 by 3rd Div. Records 145 U.K. and 6 Can. burials.

715 ECOUST MILITARY CEMETERY, ECOUST-ST. MEIN (P. de C.). 6 miles NE. of Bapaume, 800 yards SW. of sta., near road to Bullecourt. The 2/6th N. Staffs. Rgt. held embankment by Cem. on March 21st 1918 in effort to stem German advance. Many lie in the Cem. including their C.O. Records 141 U.K., 9 Aust., and 71 German burials.

1326 L'HOMME MORT BRITISH CEMETERY, ECOUST ST. MEIN (P. de C.). 6 miles NE. of Bapaume, 2½ miles S. of St. Léger Sta., SW. of village, N. of Mory road. Croisilles and Ecoust were first captured by 7th Div. 2nd April 1917, finally captured by 3rd Div. Aug. 1918. Records 126 U.K., 37 N.Z., and 3 Can. burials.

603 CROISILLES BRITISH CEMETERY (P. de C.). 8 miles SE. of Arras, 700 yards W. of Croisilles Sta. on track from road to St. Léger. Begun by 2nd Queen's Rgt. April 2nd 1917, used until March 1918 and enlarged after Armistice. Records 1,156 U.K. 3 Can., 2 S.A., 1 Aust., 2 Chin., 16 German burials, and 6 special memorials.

604 CROISILLES RAILWAY CEMETERY (P. de C.). 8 miles SE. of Arras, 500 yards SE. of Croisilles Sta. on W. of rly. Begun by 21st Manchester Rgt. April 2nd 1917, and used by other units until Jan. 1918, then taken by Germans who buried Prisoners of War there. Records 182 U.K., and 26 German burials.

1635 NOREUIL AUSTRALIAN CEMETERY (P. de C.). 6 miles NE. of Bapaume, 1½ miles SE. of Ecoust-St. Mein Sta., S. of Noreuil on road to Morchies. Begun by Aust. units April 2nd 1917, used until Dec. 1917 and again in Sept. 1918. Records 182 Aust. and 64 U.K. burials.

2295 VAULX HILL CEMETERY, VAULX-VRAUCOURT (P. de C.). 4 miles NE. of Bapaume, 3¼ miles N. of Beugny Sta., 700 yards E. of village on road to Lagnicourt. Germans evacuated village Sept. 2nd–3rd 1918, consequent to attack by Third Army in final advance to Victory. Records 686 U.K., 106 Aust., 58 N.Z., 1 Can. burials, and 4 special memorials.

1208 LAGNICOURT HEDGE CEMETERY (P. de C.). 6¼ miles NE. of Bapaume, on SW. outskirts of village, near road to Beugny. Finally taken by 2nd Guards Bgde. Sept. 3rd 1918. Begun by 7th Somerset L.I. June 1917. Records 61 U.K., 1 Aust., and 15 German burials.

1813 QUÉANT ROAD CEMETERY, BUISSY (P. de C.). 1¼ miles from Quéant Sta., near Buissy Sta., on road from Buissy to Quéant. Quéant was strongly fortified by Germans and was taken by 52nd, 57th and 63rd Divs. Sept. 2nd 1918. Records 1,266 U.K., 997 Aust., 87 Can., 1 N.Z., 2 B.W.I., 3 German burials and 26 special memorials.

1812 QUÉANT COM-
MUNAL CEMETERY,
BRITISH EXTEN-
SION (P. de C.). 12
miles SE. of Arras, NW.
of town and sta., W. of
Riéncourt road. Begun
during advance to Vic-
tory Sept. 1918. Maj.-
Gen. Lipsett, C.B.,
C.M.G., R. Irish Rgt.,
G.O.C., 4th Div., is
buried here. Records 160
U.K., 112 Can., 3 N.Z.,
and 1 Chin. burials.

376 BRÉBIÈRES
BRITISH CEMETERY
(P. de C.). 4 miles SW.
of Douai Sta., ¾ mile N.
of Brébières village on
by-road to l'Homme
Mort. Begun during
British advance on Douai
Oct. 1918. Nearly all
burials from Oct. 29th to
Nov. 25th 1918. Re-
cords 50 U.K., 13 Can.,
and 2 German burials.

1814 QUEBEC CEME-
TERY, CHERISY (P.
de C.). NW. from Sun
Quarry and 1¼ miles E.
of Cherisy. Mainly of
22nd and 24th (Quebec)
Can. Batts. who fell Aug.
27th to Sept. 11th 1918.
Records 189 Can. and 6
U.K. burials.

2186 SUN QUARRY CEMETERY, CHERISY (P. de C.). 3 miles N. of Croisilles Sta., SE. of Cherisy. Retaken by Can. Corps on Aug. 27th 1918. Records 160 Can. and 31 U.K. burials.

2281 UPTON WOOD CEMETERY, HENDE-COURT - LES - CAG-NICOURT (P. de C.). 10 miles SE. of Arras, 3 miles NE. of Ecoust-St. Mein Sta., 1 mile N. of village near rough road to Haucourt. Begun by Can. Corps Sept. 1918 after storming of Dro-court-Quéant Line. Records 217 Can. and 10 U.K. burials.

674 DOMINION CEMETERY, HENDE-COURT - LES-CAGNI-COURT (P. de C.). 10 miles SE. of Arras, 3 miles NW. of Inchy Sta., 1½ miles NE. of village, on road to Cagnicourt. Begun by Can. Corps after storming of the Dro-court-Quéant Line on Sept. 2nd 1918. Records 213 Can. and 18 U.K. burials.

429 CAGNICOURT BRITISH CEMETERY (P. de C.). 12 miles SE. of Arras, 2 miles NW. of Inchy Sta., E. of village on road to Buissy. 56th and 57th Divs. reached Riencourt-lès-Cagnicourt on night of Aug. 31st 1918 and Germans subsequently retired from Cagnicourt early in Sept. Records 248 U.K., 24 Can., 5 Aust., 4 Newfld., 1 N.Z., and 1 Port. burials.

778 ETERPIGNY BRITISH CEMETERY (P. de C.). 9½ miles E. of Arras station, E. of village, near crucifix. Begun by 4th and 1st Divs. and used from end of Aug. 1918 to middle of Oct. Records 53 U.K., 12 Can. burials, and 1 special memorial.

706 DURY CRUCIFIX CEMETERY (P. de C.). S. of village N. of Mill Cem. on Haucourt-Saudemont road. Begun by Can. units mainly 46th and 47th Batts. immediately after capture of village Sept. 2nd 1918. Records 1,885 U.K., 162 Can., and 11 Newfld. burials.

708   DURY MILL BRITISH CEMETERY (P. de C.). 4 miles from Inchy and Marquion stats., 1 mile N. of road to Cambrai, 600 yards W. of site of mill. Drocourt-Quéant Line broken by Can. and XVII Corps Sept. 2nd 1918. Records 324 Can. and 11 U.K. burials.

2076   SANCOURT BRITISH CEMETERY (P. de C.). 3 miles NW. of Cambrai, ¾ mile NW. of Sancourt Sta., 700 yards NW. of village. Captured by Can. Corps Sept. 29th 1918. Records 230 Can. and 6 U.K. burials.

1039   HAYNECOURT BRITISH CEMETERY (Nord). 5½ miles NW. of Cambrai Sta., SW. of village. On Sept. 27th 1918 the 1st Can. and 11th Divs. took Haynecourt. Records 265 Can., 22 U.K., and 2 Unknown burials.

1487 MILL SWITCH BRITISH CEMETERY, TILLOY - LES - CAMBRAI (Nord). 1½ miles N. of Cambrai, SW. of village. Captured by Can. Corps, Sept. 1918. Name due to switch line from large German Supply Camp ½ mile NW. Records 107 Can. burials.

494 CHAPEL CORNER CEMETERY, SAUCHY-LESTRÉE (P. de C.). 1 mile E. of Sauchy Lestrée Sta., ½ mile SE. of village by a shrine. Captured on Sept. 27th 1918 by 56th (London) Div. Records 116 U.K. and 62 Can. burials.

455 CANTIMPRE CANADIAN CEMETERY, SAILLY (Nord). 4 miles NW. of Cambrai Sta. N. of village near road to Sancourt. On Sept. 28th 1918 this village was taken by the 1st and 11th Can. Divs. Records 223 Can. and 1 U.K. burials.

A

A

2174 SUCRERIE CEMETERY, EPINOY (P. de C.). 1⅛ miles from Fressies Halte, ¾ mile NE. of village. Captured by 11th (North.) Div. Sept. 27th 1918, and made by fighting units after battle. Records 98 U.K., 1 Can. burials, and 1 special memorial.

B

1798 PROVILLE BRITISH CEMETERY (Nord). 2¼ miles SW. of Cambrai Sta., S. of village. Finally captured Oct. 8th–9th 1918. Cem. made by 61st Div. and 8th N. Staffs. Records 140 U.K. and 9 Unknown burials.

B

C

1670 ONTARIO CEMETERY, SAINS-LES - MARQUION (P. de C.). 2 miles from Buissy-Baralle Halte, S. of village. Begun Sept. 1918 by 1st Can. Div. (1st, 2nd, 3rd and 4th Ontario Batts.) after capture of village. Records 182 U.K., 144 Can., 9 Aust., 1 N.Z. burials, and 5 special memorials.

C

D

1972 SAINS-LES-MARQUION BRITISH CEMETERY (P. de C.). 2½ miles S. of Marquion Sta., on E. side of Canal du Nord, at cross-roads E. of village. Captured on Sept. 27th 1918 by 1st Can. Div. Records 185 Can., 69 U.K., and 1 Aust. burials.

D

701 DRUMMOND CEMETERY, RAILLENCOURT (Nord). 2 miles W. of Cambrai Sta., 1 mile E. of village. Made by Can. Corps in Oct. 1918, named after first burial (Lieut. R. J. Drummond, R.A.F.). Records 79 Can. (largely 2nd Can. Mounted Rif.), 6 U.K., 3 Unknown, and 3 German burials.

1838 RAILLENCOURT COMMUNAL CEMETERY EXTENSION (Nord). $3\frac{1}{2}$ miles W. of Cambrai Sta. on main road to Arras. Captured by Can. Corps on Sept. 28th in Battle of Canal du Nord. Records 188 Can. and 11 U.K. burials.

54 ANNEUX BRITISH CEMETERY (Nord). 2 miles W. of Fontaine N.D. Sta. on Cambrai-Bapaume road. Captured by 62nd (W. Rid.) Div. on Nov. 20th and 21st 1917. Recaptured on Sept. 27th 1918 by 57th (W. Lancs.) and 63rd (R.N.) Divs. acting with 52nd (Lowland) and 1st and 4th Can. Divs. Records 830 U.K., 89 N.Z., 86 Can., 1 Aust. burials, and 7 special memorials.

599 CREST CEME-TERY, FONTAINE-NOTRE - DAME (Nord). 1½ miles N. of Fontaine-N.D. Sta., and 3 miles W. of Cambrai. Captured for a short time on Nov. 21st 1917 by 51st (Highland) Div., again by Guards Div. on Nov. 27th, finally by 3rd and 4th Can. and 57th Divs. on Sept. 27th 1918. Records 87 Can. and 1 U.K. burials.

2034 ST. OLLE BRITISH CEMETERY, RAILLENCOURT (Nord). 3 miles W. of Cambrai Sta., 500 yards S. of village. Carried by Can. Corps on Sept. 28th and 29th in Battle of Canal du Nord, 1918. Records 97 Can. burials (73 of 116th Batt.).

342 BOURLON WOOD CEMETERY, BOUR-LON (P. de C.). 6 miles W. of Cambrai, S. of village and sta., NW. of Bourlon Wood. On Sept. 27th 1918 the Can. Corps forced the Canal du Nord and captured Bourlon Hill (see Can. Mem.). Records 226 Can., 16 U.K., and 3 Chin. burials.

2175 SUCRERIE BRIT-ISH CEMETERY, GRAINCOURT - LES - HAVRINCOURT (P. de C.). 3½ miles from Fontaine N.D. Sta., N. of village, and ½ mile N. of ruined Sucrerie. Captured by 62nd (W. Rid.) Div. Nov. 20th 1917, and again by 63rd (R.N.) Div. Sept. 27th, 1918. Records 57 U.K. burials.

1810 QUARRY WOOD CEMETERY, SAINS-LES-MARQUION (P. de C.). 8 miles W. of Cambrai, 2½ miles W. of Bourlon Sta., 1¼ miles S. of village, E. of Havrincourt road. Created by Can. Corps Sept. 27th to Oct. 2nd 1918, during second Battle of Cambrai. Records 263 Can. and 15 U.K. burials.

1494 MŒUVRES COMMUNAL CEME-TERY EXTENSION (Nord). 8 miles W. of Cambrai, 2½ miles SE. of Inchy-en-Artois Sta., N. of village on road to Inchy. Mœuvres resisted all attacks in Battle of Cambrai, Nov. 1917, but was taken by 52nd Div. Sept. 19th 1918. Records 529 U.K., 22 Can., 8 Aust., 94 German burials, and 3 special memorials.

1493   MŒUVRES BRITISH CEMETERY (Nord). 3½ miles S. of Inchy Sta., S. of village. Attacked by 36th (Ulster) Div., Battle of Cambrai 1917, partly taken by 57th (W. Lancs.) Div., Sept. 11th 1918. Cleared by 63rd (R.N.) Div., Sept. 12th. Records 102 U.K., 1 Can., and 4 German burials.

2264   TRIANGLE CEMETERY, INCHY-EN-ARTOIS (P. de C.). 2½ miles from Inchy Sta., SE. of village. The line between Inchy and Mœuvres was broken by 4th Can. Div. on Sept. 27th 1918, and Cem. was made after battle. Records 69 Can., 19 U.K., and 2 Unknown burials.

1807   QUARRY CEMETERY, MARQUION (P. de C.). 1 mile E. of Marquion Sta., ½ mile SE. of village. Captured by 1st Can. and 11th Divs. on Sept. 27th 1918. Records 45 Can. and 23 U.K. burials.

538 COJEUL BRITISH CEMETERY, ST. MARTIN-SUR-COJEUL (P. de C.). 3 miles NE. of Boyelles Sta., SE. of village. Taken by 30th Div. on April 9th 1917, lost in March 1918 and retaken in Aug. Made by 21st Div. Records 318 U.K. burials and 31 special memorials.

464 CARVIN COMMUNAL CEMETERY (P. de C.). 12 miles SW. of Lille, 1 mile N. of Carvin Sta., E. of village on by-road to Provin. Used intermittently from Sept. 1915 to end of War. Burials from various units. Records 39 U.K., 4 Can., 1 S.A., and 1 Russ. burials.

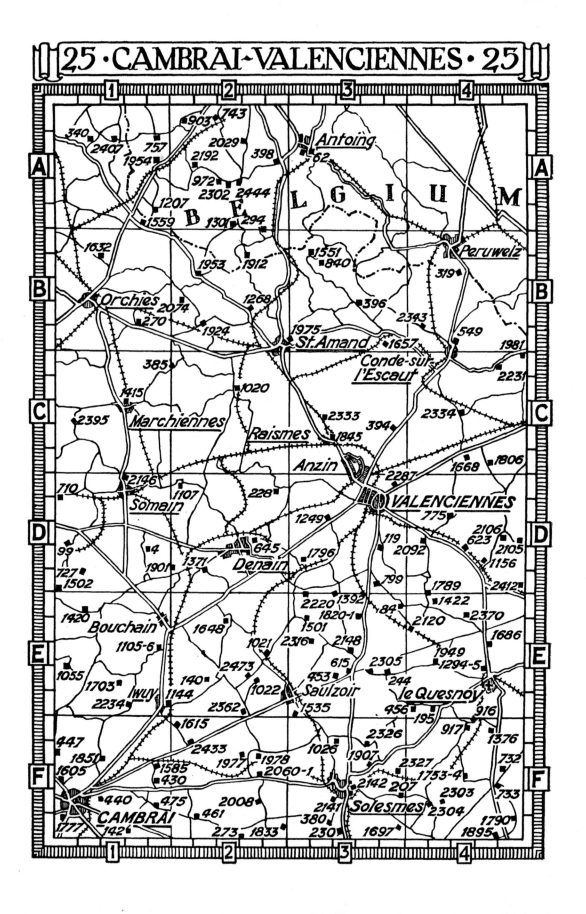

CAMBRAI—VALENCIENNES

MAP SHEET No. 25

CAMBRAI is a considerable industrial town in the Department of the Nord on the right bank of the canalized River Scheldt (or Escaut). It has a railway station on the main lines from Calais to Bâle and from Paris to Douai. It is the seat of an archbishopric, and a city of great importance in the history of France and the Low Countries.

The city was occupied by German forces on the 26th August 1914, and it remained in German hands until the 9th October 1918. The Battle of Cambrai, 1917 (20th November to 3rd December), left the British line still five miles from the city on the south-west side, and the German Offensive of March 1918 drove it far to the west; but the Battle of Cambrai, 1918, the last of the Battles of the Hindenburg Line, delivered the city into British hands. It was very severely damaged, and the main square was still burning two days after the fight. In October and November four Casualty Clearing Stations were posted at Cambrai.

The city has been 'adopted' by the County Borough of Birkenhead.

THE BATTLE OF CAMBRAI, 1917. The attack was opened at 6.20 a.m. on 20th November by the advance of 360 Tanks and six Infantry Divisions, and at the same moment the Artillery (1,009 guns) put down smoke barrages in front of the advance. Another Infantry Division followed almost at once. The German front trenches and dugouts were carried and cleared up and the portion of the Hindenburg Line attacked was completely captured. Before midday the villages of Havrincourt and Ribécourt were taken and Welch Ridge, on the right front of our line, was stormed; but at a single point, the village of Flesquières, the advance was checked.

On the 21st Flesquières was captured by 8 a.m., and the attack on the Beaurevoir-Masnières Line begun. By the evening, in spite of heavy German counter-attacks, Masnières had been cleared and Noyelles-sur-l'Escaut, Cantaing and Fontaine-Notre Dame had been taken, while on the extreme north British troops were near to Mœuvres.

The fighting from the 23rd to the 28th inclusive was concentrated almost entirely on Bourlon and Fontaine-Notre Dame. The latter village was gained and lost on the 23rd and 27th. A fresh Division was put in, and Bourlon village and the wood were the scene of desperate fighting during the whole of these days.

A German counter-attack began on the morning of the 30th November, and it was immediately successful on the southern half of the line, from the Canal de l'Escaut at Masnières to the neighbourhood of Vend'huile. It captured the Bonavis Ridge and the villages of Gonnelieu, Gouzeaucourt, and Villers-Guislain. It was checked in the afternoon, and Gouzeaucourt was recovered.

The fighting on the 1st December resulted in little gain or loss of ground. It was very severe, and villages were captured and recaptured. It was followed on the 2nd December by renewed and successful German attacks on Welch Ridge, and on the 3rd by further attacks and further slight withdrawal. Local fighting continued from the 4th to the 7th; during the same period, for tactical reasons, the positions north of the Flesquières Ridge (including the villages of Masnières, Marcoing, Noyelles Graincourt, Anneux, Cantaing, and Bourlon) were evacuated.

2287 VALENCIENNES COMMUNAL CEMETERY (Nord). NE. of town, 1 mile E. of sta. near road to Mons. Valenciennes was occupied by Germans from Aug. 1914 until just before Armistice. Cem. used by enemy for Prisoners of War burials. Records 668 U.K., 154 Can., 28 Aust., 3 S.A., 1 N.Z., 5 Ind., and 7 special memorials.

549 CONDE - SUR - L'ESCAUT COMMUNAL CEMETERY (Nord). 7½ miles NE. of Valenciennes, 2,000 yards N. of sta. on road to Bonsecours. Used by Germans as Prisoners of War Cem. and enlarged by British during advance to Victory Oct. – Nov. 1918. Records 96 U.K., 2 Can., 1 N.Z., and 1 Newfld. burials.

645 DENAIN COMMUNAL CEMETERY (Nord). 6 miles SW. of Valenciennes, NW. of town and 1 mile E. of Denain Sta. on road to Hénin. Germans occupied town from Aug. 1914. Cem. was used for burial of Prisoners of War and enlarged when British recaptured Denain Oct. 1918. Records 236 U.K., 65 Can., 1 Aust. burials, and 7 special memorials.

A

A

99 AUBERCHICOURT BRITISH CEMETERY (Nord). 7 miles E. of Douai, ½ mile W. of village. Village occupied by British Oct. 1918. Cem. was begun that month and used until Feb. 1919. Records 197 U.K., 87 Can., 2 Chin. burials, and 1 special memorial.

B

B

119 AULNOY COMMUNAL CEMETERY (Nord). 2 miles S. of Valenciennes, 1 mile E. of Le Poirier Sta. Cem. used by Can. and Imp. units in fighting around Valenciennes early Nov. 1918. Records 120 Can. and 40 U.K. burials.

C

C

799 FAMARS COMMUNAL CEMETERY EXTENSION (Nord). 3 miles S. of Valenciennes, S. of village and Halte, N. of Com. Cem. Famars is in the sector taken by the 4th, 49th and 61st Divs., Nov. 1st and 2nd 1918, in final advance to Victory. Records 38 U.K., 2 Can., and 1 French burials.

D

D

1789 PRESEAU COMMUNAL CEMETERY EXTENSION (Nord). 4 miles SE. of Valenciennes, 2 miles from Curgies Sta., S. of village near Church. Preseau was in the sector carried by the 4th, 49th and 61st Divs. after crossing R. Rhonelle Nov. 1st–2nd 1918. Records 115 U.K. burials who fell in the advance.

A

A
1144 IWUY COM-
MUNAL CEMETERY
(Nord).   5 miles NE.
of Cambrai, ¾ mile N. of
Iwuy Sta., near railway,
N. of road to Avesnes-le-
Sec.   Used from Oct.
10th–26th 1918 during
final advance to Victory.
Records 132 U.K., 6
Can., and 11 Russ. burials.

B
1022 HASPRES COP-
PICE CEMETERY,
HASPRES   (Nord).
2,000 yards S. of sta., S.
of village on road to
Villers - en - Cauchies.
Taken after severe fight-
ing with help of tanks on
Oct. 20th 1918.   Made
by 49th (W. Rid.) Div.
Records 64 U.K. burials.

B

C

C
140 AVESNES-LE-
SEC COMMUNAL
CEMETERY EXTEN-
SION (Nord). 1¼
miles W. of Avesnes Sta.
on W. edge of village.
Made by 51st (Highland)
Div. in Nov. 1918. Re-
cords 100 U.K. burials
(46 Seaforths and 41
Gordons).

D
2220 THIANT COM-
MUNAL CEMETERY
(Nord).   5 miles SW.
of Valenciennes, 2 miles
S. of Prouvy-Thiant Sta.,
½ mile E. of village on
road to Maing.   All
casualties from Oct. 24th
to Nov. 8th 1918 in final
advance to Victory. Re-
cords 69 U.K., 3 Can.,
and 6 German burials.

D

2105 SEBOURG BRIT-ISH CEMETERY (Nord). 6 miles E. of Valenciennes, 2 miles N. of Jenlain Sta., E. of village near road to Roisin. Many casualties of 9th Notts and Derby Rgt. Sebourg was captured by 11th and 56th Divs. Nov. 4th 1918 after a difficult crossing of R. Aunelle. Records 53 U.K. and 3 German burials.

2473 YORK CEME-TERY, HASPRES (Nord). W. of Coppice Cem., SW. of village on road to Naves. Made by 1/5th York and Lancs. Rgt. and other units of 49th (W. Riding) Div. Oct. 1918. Records 137 U.K. and 10 German burials.

1392 MAING COM-MUNAL CEMETERY EXTENSION (Nord). 4 miles SW. of Valenciennes, 2 miles E. of Famars, S. of village on road to Querenaing. Casualties mostly of Scottish Rgts. who fell during fighting around Valenciennes a few days before the Armistice. Records 84 U.K. burials.

2316 VERCHAIN BRITISH CEMETERY, VERCHAIN-MAUGRE (Nord). 7 miles S. of Valenciennes, 3 miles N. of Saulzoir Sta., ¾ mile NW. of Verchain on rough track to Pluvinage Farm. Casualties from final advance to Victory Oct. 24th to Nov. 2nd 1918. Records 109 U.K. and 1 Can. burials.

615 CRUCIFIX CEMETERY, VENDEGIES-SUR-ECAILLON (Nord). 5½ miles N. of Solesmes Sta., 7¼ miles S. of Valenciennes Sta. and ½ mile SW. of village. Captured by 19th (West.) and 61st (S. Mid.) Divs. on Oct. 24th 1918 after severe fighting. Records 50 U.K. and 31 French burials.

453 CANONNE FARM BRITISH CEMETERY, SOMMAING (Nord). 2 miles NW. of Saulzoir Sta., N. of Chaussée Brunehaut (Roman road) and ½ mile NE. of farm on Haussy-Sommaing rd. Records 64 U.K. burials (27 of 2/7th R. Warwicks Oct. 22nd to Nov. 7th 1918).

A

A

2305 VENDEGIES CROSS-ROAD BRITISH CEMETERY, BERMERAIN (Nord). 6½ miles S. of Valenciennes, 2¾ miles S. of Artres Sta., at cross-roads N. of Bermerain. Vendegies-sur-Ecaillon was taken by 19th and 61st Divs. in an enveloping attack, after strong resistance Oct. 24th 1918. Records 46 U.K. burials.

B

244 BERMERAIN COMMUNAL CEMETERY (Nord). 9 miles S. of Valenciennes, 4 miles from Artres Sta., NE. of village on road to Ruesnes. Used from Oct. 24th to Nov. 4th 1918. 21 burials from 9th Northumb. Fus., who fell in the open warfare in clearing of Bermerain. Records 41 U.K. burials.

C

C

1949 RUESNES COMMUNAL CEMETERY (Nord). 2 miles NW. of Le Quesnoy, NW. of village and sta., on road to Sepmeries. Used by British Oct. 1918 during advance to Victory. Records 75 U.K. and 11 N.Z. burials.

D

916 GHISSIGNIES BRITISH CEMETERY (Nord). 2 miles SW. of Le Quesnoy on NW. of Le Quesnoy road. Village taken by 37th Div. Oct. 24th 1918. Cem. commenced after capture of village by same Div. Records 117 U.K. burials and 1 special memorial.

2370 VILLERS - POL COMMUNAL CEME-TERY EXTENSION (Nord). 7 miles SE. of Valenciennes, 2 miles S. of Jenlain Sta., N. of village on road to Preseau. Majority of burials from Guards Div. who fell Nov. 1918 in advance to Victory. Records 96 U.K. and 74 German burials.

1294–5 LE QUESNOY COMMUNAL CEME-TERY AND EXTEN-SION (Nord). 9 miles SE. of Valenciennes, N. of town near road to Valenciennes. Town was surrounded by N.Z. Div. early morning Nov. 4th 1918 and gained that day by scaling ramparts. (Mem. to N.Z. Div). Records 61 U.K., 2 Aust. 1 Russ., and 2 German burials in Com. Cem., and 65 U.K., 50 N.Z., 2 Chin. burials and 1 special memorial in Ext.

456 CAPELLE-BEAU-DIGNIES ROAD CEMETERY, BEAU-DIGNIES (Nord). 18 miles E. of Cambrai, 3½ miles SW. of Le Quesnoy, 1 mile from Beaudignies on road to Capelle. In direct line of Retreat from Mons 1914. Le Quesnoy was taken by N.Z. Div. with 1,000 prisoners Nov. 5th, 1918. Records 55 U.K. burials.

447 CANADA CEMETERY, TILLOY-LES-CAMBRAI (Nord). 2½ miles N. of Cambrai Sta., N. of village on road to Blécourt. Captured by Can. Corps Oct. 1st 1918. Records 254 Can., 6 U.K., and 4 Unknown burials.

142 AWOINGT BRITISH CEMETERY (Nord). ½ mile S. of Halte, between Cambrai road and village. Begun in Oct. 1918 by 38th, 45th and 59th Casualty Clearing Stations. Records 636 U.K., 15 N.Z., 1 Ind. burials, and 1 special memorial.

1777 PORTE-DE-PARIS CEMETERY, CAMBRAI (Nord). On SW. outskirts of town, near old gate on road to Paris. A great part of Cem. was used by enemy in early years of War for burial of German and Allied dead. British graves on either side of Town War Mem. Records 94 U.K., 10 Can., 7 Aust., 1 S.A., 1 N.Z., and 6 Belgian burials.

A

A

440 CAMBRAI EAST MILITARY CEMETERY (Nord). $1\frac{1}{4}$ miles E. of sta. on road to Solesmes. Made by Germans during occupation. The Battle of Cambrai 1917 (Nov. 20th to Dec. 3rd) left Brit. line still 5 miles from city on SW. side. Records 475 U.K., 14 Can., 3 N.Z., 1 B.W.I. burials, and 8 special memorials.

B

1851 RAMILLIES BRITISH CEMETERY (Nord). 3 miles NE. of Cambrai, 200 yards E. of Ramillies Halte. Captured by Can. Corps on night of Oct. 8th–9th 1918. Records 104 U.K., 75 Can., and 1 Chin. burials.

B

C

1585 NAVEŚ COMMUNAL CEMETERY EXTENSION (Nord). 4 miles from Cambrai, $\frac{1}{2}$ mile SW. of Naves Halte, on Cambrai road behind Com. Cem. Used Oct. 1918 during second Battle of Cambrai. Records 318 U.K., 53 N.Z., 50 Can., 15 S.A., 4 Aust. burials, and 5 special memorials.

D

2433 WELLINGTON CEMETERY, RIEUX-EN-CAMBRESIS (Nord). $5\frac{1}{2}$ miles NE. of Cambrai, 2 miles SE. of Iwuy Sta., on road to Rieux. Begun by Duke of Wellington's (W. Riding) Rgt. Oct. 11th 1918, the 49th Div. being heavily engaged. Records 284 U.K., 20 Can. burials, and 1 special memorial.

C

D

1615 NIAGARA CEME-
TERY, IWUY (Nord).
5 miles NE. of Cambrai,
¾ mile N. of village and
sta. on road to Rieux.
Begun Oct. 1918 casual-
ties from 13th to 17th of
that month, the majority
being of the Can. Corps.
Records 174 Can. and 27
U.K. burials.

1977 ST. AUBERT
BRITISH CEMETERY
(Nord). 1⅛ miles N. of
St. Aubert Sta. on
Avesnes - lès - Aubert
road. Captured in pur-
suit to the Selle (Oct.
9th–12th 1918). Cem.
begun by 24th Div. on
Oct. 12th. Records 415
U.K., 8 Can., 8 N.Z.
burials, and 4 special
memorials.

1833 QUIEVY COM-
MUNAL CEMETERY
EXTENSION (Nord).
900 yards S. of sta., E. of
village on road to Viesly.
Made after capture of
village by 62nd (W. Rid.)
Div. in Oct. 1918. Re-
cords 89 U.K., 16 French,
and 99 German burials.

A

B

A

2061   ST. VAAST COMMUNAL CEMETERY EXTENSION (Nord). 2 miles S. of St. Aubert Sta., W. of village on road to Cambrai. Made by Guards Div. in Oct. 1918 after capture of village. Records 43 U.K. burials and 2 special memorials.

B

2326 VERTAIN COMMUNAL CEMETERY EXTENSION (Nord). 3 miles NE. of Solesmes, ¾ mile from Vertain Halte. Captured on Oct. 23rd 1918 by 24th R. Fus. (2nd Div.) who billeted there same night. Records 52 U.K. burials.

C

D

C

732 ENGLEFONTAINE BRITISH CEMETERY (Nord). 4 miles S. of Le Quesnoy on W. edge of Forest of Mormal, nearest sta. at Saleches. Captured by 18th and 33rd Divs. Oct. 26th 1918. Cem. begun by 38th (Welsh) Div. Nov. 1918. Records 179 U.K. burials.

D

2303 VENDEGIES-AU-BOIS BRITISH CEMETERY (Nord). 6 miles N. of Le Cateau Sta., on N. of village. Cem. on E., near road to Ghissignies. Village was taken by Third Army in final advance to Victory Oct. 24th 1918. Records 43 U.K. burials.

1907 R O M E R I E S COMMUNAL CEME-TERY EXTENSION (Nord). 2¼ miles N. of Solesmes Sta., ¾ mile W. of Romeries Halte on road to Solesmes. In Re-treat from Mons, part of II Corps retired through this area, and our Army retook it Oct. 1918. Records 656 U.K., 112 N.Z., 1 Can., 48 Unknown burials, and 15 special memorials.

2141 S O L E S M E S BRITISH CEMETERY (Nord). 300 yards W. of sta. on W. of town. On Oct. 19th–21st 1918 the 62nd (W. Rid.) Div. followed by 61st (S. Mid.) Div. captured and cleared the town after severe street fighting. Records 133 U.K., 3 Ind., 1 N.Z., 1 French, 1 Chin., and 1 German burials.

230 B E L L E V U E BRITISH CEMETERY, B R I A S T R E (Nord). 200 yards W. of Briastre Halte and 1 mile E. of Briastre Sta. Village was taken by the N.Z. and 37th Div. on night of Oct. 10th–11th 1918, and on 20th Belle Vue Farm was captured by 5th E. Lancs. Records 134 U.K. and 7 N.Z. burials.

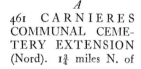

A

461 CARNIERES COMMUNAL CEME-TERY EXTENSION (Nord). 1¾ miles N. of sta. and N. of village. Captured on Oct. 10th 1918 and made by Guards Div. a week later. Records 54 U.K. burials.

B

B

207 BEAURAIN BRITISH CEMETERY (Nord). 12 miles S. of Valenciennes, 2½ miles E. of Solesmes Sta., 140 yards N. of Beaurain Church. Used from Oct. 23rd to Nov. 4th 1918 during victorious advance. Records 57 U.K. burials.

C

1790 PREUX-AU-BOIS COMMUNAL CEME-TERY (Nord). 4 miles N. of Landrecies Sta. on W. edge of Forest of Mormal. Village was captured after severe struggle by units of 18th Div. and Tanks Nov. 4th 1918. Records 65 U.K. burials.

C

1754 POIX-DU-NORD COMMUNAL CEME-TERY EXTENSION (Nord). 5 miles S. of Le Quesnoy, nearest sta. at Salesches. Begun after capture of village Oct. 1918 and enlarged after Armistice. Records 96 U.K. burials.

1697 OVILLERS NEW COMMUNAL CEME-TERY, SOLESMES (Nord). $4\frac{1}{2}$ miles N. of Le Câteau, 3 miles SE. of Solesmes Sta., NW. of village near road to Soles-mes. Casualties from ad-vance to Victory who were buried here between Oct. 21st and Nov. 8th 1918. Records 62 U.K., 7 Fr., and 11 German burials.

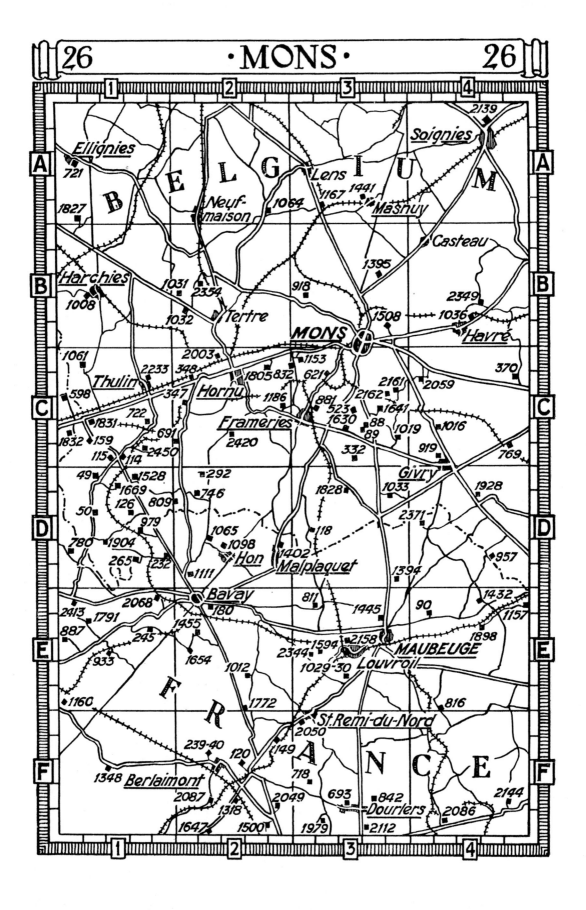

MONS

MAP SHEET No. 26

MONS, County Town of the Province of Hainaut, scene of severe fighting in the Retreat from Mons 1914 and the Return to Mons 1918.

The I and II Corps of the British Expeditionary Force under Sir John French were entrenched before Mons, Sunday 23rd August 1914. The German Army Corps of von Kluck and von Buelow massed to attack them about noon that day.

The attack, well supported by artillery fire, was hastily pressed, the enemy infantry advancing in dense masses from the shelter of the woods. Line after line were decimated, but reserves quickly replaced the fallen and continued the advance. They would have reached the British trenches, but our troops rose as a man and dispersed the remainder of the attacking force at the point of the bayonet. The Attacks were repeated throughout the day but met with no success.

The retirement of our Allies on the right, and knowledge of the immense German forces opposed to him, caused Sir John French to order a general retirement.

The Retreat commenced at dawn on Monday and continued through the Affair of Landrecies and Battle of Le Câteau, the Actions in the Forests of Compiègne and Villers Cotterêts until Thursday 3rd September 1914, when the British forces crossed the River Marne between Lagny and Meaux. There, after ten days of fighting and retreat, thirty miles a day, practically without food or sleep, haggard, begrimed, bearded, and footsore, the British forces, undefeated and undaunted, stayed to rest and reorganize prior to the Battle of the Marne.

The Canadians of General Horne's First Army returned to Mons. Advancing from south and west they had enveloped the town by Sunday night 10th November 1918 against a determined and tenacious machine-gun defence. Fighting continued throughout the night, and at dawn of Armistice morning the 3rd Canadian Division entered Mons.

1508 MONS COM-MUNAL CEMETERY (HAINAUT). 2 miles E. of sta. on by-road to Nimy, N. of road to Havré. Burials from Battle of Mons 1914, and used by Germans as Prisoners of War Cem. The town was recaptured by the Can. Corps on Armistice Day. Records 330 U.K., 57 Can., 4 Aust., 2 N.Z., 1 S.A., 25 French, 1 Belg., 2 Italian, 71 Russ., 9 Roum., and 3 German burials.

621 CUESMES COM-MUNAL CEMETERY (HAINAUT). 1¾ miles SW. of Mons Sta., 300 yards S. of village on road to Frameries. British burials made Aug. 1914 (1st S. Lancs.) and Nov. 1918 (Canadians). Brit. plot records 44 U.K. and 3 Can. burials.

881 FRAMERIES COMMUNAL CEME-TERY (HAINAUT). 3½ miles SW. of Mons Sta., ½ mile N. of Frameries Sta., E. of village on by-road to Mons. Majority of burials from Battle of Mons 1914 (mostly 1st Lincolns), but some Nov. 1918 casualties buried by 6th Bgde. Can. Field Art. Records 87 U.K. and 8 Can. burials.

A

A

2059 ST. SYMPHO-RIEN MILITARY CEMETERY (HAIN-AUT). 3 miles SE. of Mons, ½ mile S. of village and sta., at junction of roads to Malplaquet and Spiennes. Laid out as cem. by Germans after Battle of Mons 1914. Contains German monuments to R. Middlesex Rgt., Roy. Fus., and R. Irish Rgt. Records 220 U.K. burials, and 4 special memorials.

B

B

1831 QUIÉVRAIN COMMUNAL CEMETERY (HAINAUT). 9 miles NE. of Valenciennes 1 mile S. of Quiévrain Sta., SE. of village on road to Audregnies. Used for British burials Oct. 1918 (large number of 2nd Can. Mtd. Rifles). Records 35 Can. and 8 U.K. burials.

C

C

115 AUDREGNIES COMMUNAL CEMETERY (HAINAUT). 10 miles E. of Valenciennes, 13 miles SW. of Mons, E. of Audregnies village and sta. Casualties fell Aug. 28th 1914 and are of 1st Cheshire, 1st Norfolk Rgts., and one Lieut. of the 6ᵉ Chasseurs. Records 40 U.K. and 1 French burials.

D

D

722 ELOUGES COMMUNAL CEMETERY (HAINAUT). 10½ miles SW. of Mons, 12 miles NE. of Valenciennes, ½ mile N. of Elouges Sta., near road to Thulin. British burials made Aug. 24th 1914 (mainly 1st Norfolk) and Nov. 1918 (22nd and 25th Can. In. Batts.). Records 41 U.K., 14 Can., 1 French, and 3 German burials.

A

B

A

1445 MAUBEUGE-CENTRE CEMETERY (Nord). 1¼ miles N. of Maubeuge Sta., ½ mile N. of town, E. of road to Mons. British plot near entrance to Com. Cem. Used by Germans as Prisoners of War Cem. June 1917 to Nov. 1918 and enlarged after Armistice. Records 154 U.K., 18 Aust., 6 N.Z., 4 Can., and 1 Russ. burials.

B

2158 MAUBEUGE (SOUS-LE-BOIS) CEMETERY (Nord). 3¼ miles E. of Maubeuge Sta., ¾ mile N. of Sous-le-Bois Sta., on by-road to Douzies. British plot in centre of Allied Mil. Plot near War Mem. British burials made Dec. 1918 to March 1919. Records 63 U.K., 47 Aust., 3 N.Z., and 1 Can. burials.

C

1772 PONT-SUR-SAMBRE COMMUNAL CEMETERY (Nord). 9 miles NW. of Avesnes-sur-Helpe, ¾ mile N. of Pont-sur-Sambre Sta., E. of road to La Longueville. All casualties fell Nov. 1918 in the last days of the advance to Victory. Records 54 U.K. burials.

D

1029 HAUTMONT COMMUNAL CEMETERY (Nord). 3 miles SW. of Maubeuge, E. of town and sta., on 'Chemin Vert'. Used by Germans as Prisoners of War Cem. March to Nov. 1918. Town captured by 42nd Div. Nov. 1918. Records 244 U.K., 2 Can., 56 French, 1 Belg., and 100 Russ. burials.

C

D

1032 HAUTRAGE MILITARY CEME-TERY (HAINAUT). 9 miles W. of Mons, in wood, S. of main road to Tournai, between Haut-rage and Tertre. Made by Germans Aug.–Sept. 1914 and used by them as concentration ceme-tery for British who fell in action 1914 on the sur-rounding battle-fields. Records 224 U.K. and 85 German burials.

240 BERLAIMONT COMMUNAL CEMETERY EXTEN-SION (Nord). On E. edge of Mormal Forest, 1 mile from Berlaimont Sta., NE. of village on the Chemin de la Grande Carrière. Used by Germans as Prisoner of War Cem. July to Oct. 1918, then used by advancing British from Nov. 4th to 11th 1918. Records 50 U.K. burials.

693 DOURLERS COMMUNAL CEME-TERY EXTENSION (Nord). 4 miles N. of Avesnes-sur-Helpe Sta., 300 yards NE. of Dourlers Church. Dourlers fell subsequent to attacks of 5th, 21st and 33rd Divs., E. of Mormal Forest Nov. 1918. Records 161 U.K. and 108 German burials.

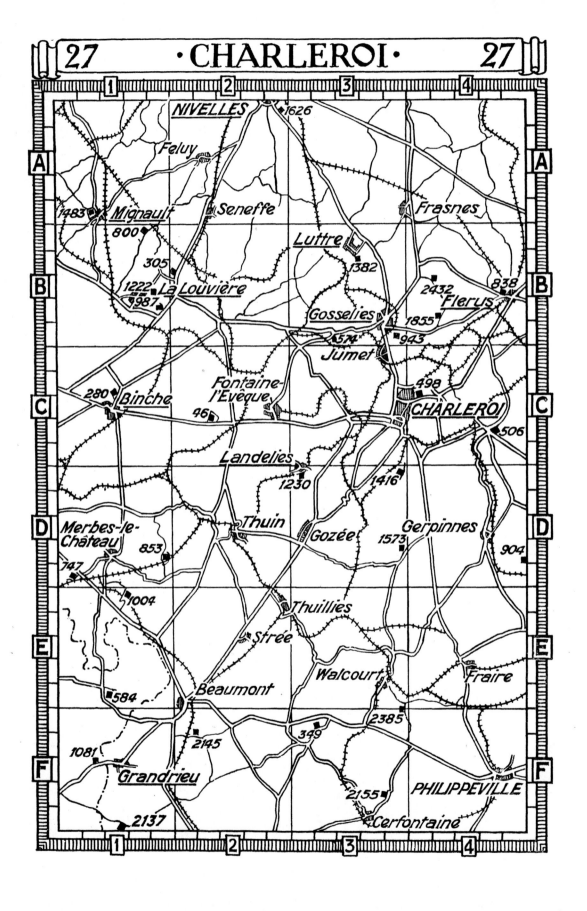

NIVELLES ◆1626

Feluy

A

1483 ◆ Mignault   ■ Seneffe   Frasnes
800 ■

305   Luttre
                                       1382
B 1222 ■ La Louvière   2432 ■   838
   ◆987   Flerus
                                   Gosselies 1855 ■
                              574   ■943
                              Jumet
                                          498
C 280 ◆ Binche   Fontaine-   CHARLEROI
        46 ■   l'Evêque   506

        Landelies
        1230   1416 ■

D Merbes-le-   Thuin   Gozée   Gerpinnes
   Château 853 ■   1573 ■
   747 ◆   904 ■

   1004 ■   Thuillies

E   Strée
                        Walcourt   Fraire
   584 ■   Beaumont

1081 ■   2385
F Grandrieu 2145 ■   349 ■
                                       PHILIPPEVILLE
   2137 ■   2155 ■
                        Cerfontaine

498 CHARLEROI COMMUNAL CEMETERY (HAINAUT). 1¾ miles NE. of Charleroi Sta., in N. suburbs of town, near road to Namur. Majority of burials are those who died from wounds received in advance to Victory. Records 169 U.K., 79 Aust., 18 Can., 2 N.Z., 1 S.A., 1 Ind., 3 Russ., 1 Roum., and 15 German burials.

1416 MARCINELLE NEW COMMUNAL CEMETERY (HAINAUT). 2¼ miles S. of Charleroi Sta., S. of Marcinelle in hamlet of Les Haies. British burials were made from March to Nov. 1919. Records 44 U.K., 13 Aust., 1 Can., 10 French, and 280 German burials.

1222 LA LOUVIÈRE COMMUNAL CEMETERY (HAINAUT). 13 miles NW. of Charleroi, 2 miles N. of La Louvière Sta., and ¾ mile S. of Bois d'Haine Sta. British burials were made from Jan. 14th 1919 to April 11th 1919. Records 43 U.K., 1 Aust., and 1 N.Z. burials.

747 ERQUELINNES COMMUNAL CEMETERY (HAINAUT). 14 miles SE. of Mons, $\frac{1}{4}$ mile N. of Erquelinnes Halte, E. of village, near road to Mons. British burials made Oct. 10th to Nov. 7th 1918 during advance to Victory. Records 66 U.K., 1 S.A., and 1 French burials.

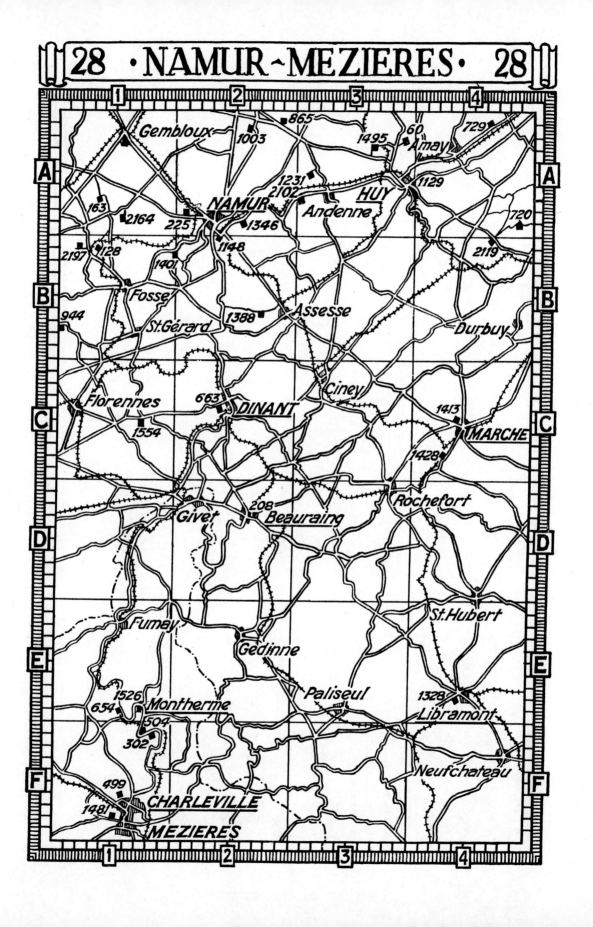

225 BELGRADE CEMETERY, NAMUR (NAMUR). 1½ miles W. of sta., tram service (Belgrade-Jambes) from sta., N. of road to Nivelles. Burials from Oct. and Nov. 1918 some who died as Prisoners of War, others who fell in advance to Victory. Records 194 U.K., 44 Can., 6 Aust., 2 S.A., 1 N.Z., and 2 Ind. burials.

499 CHARLEVILLE COMMUNAL CEMETERY (ARDENNES), 1½ miles from sta. on NW. outskirts of town, ¼ mile N. of Rocroi road. Charleville was occupied by Germans from Aug. 1914 to Nov. 1918 and Cem. was used by them for burial of Prisoners of War. Records 175 U.K., 2 S.A., 1 French, and 31 Russ. burials.

1129 HUY (LA SARTE) COMMUNAL CEMETERY (LIÈGE). 1¾ miles SE. of Huy (Nord) Sta., E. of road to Haute Sarte. British burials were made from Dec. 1918 to July 1919. Records 58 Can., 51 U.K., 8 French, 1 Russ., and 9 German burials.

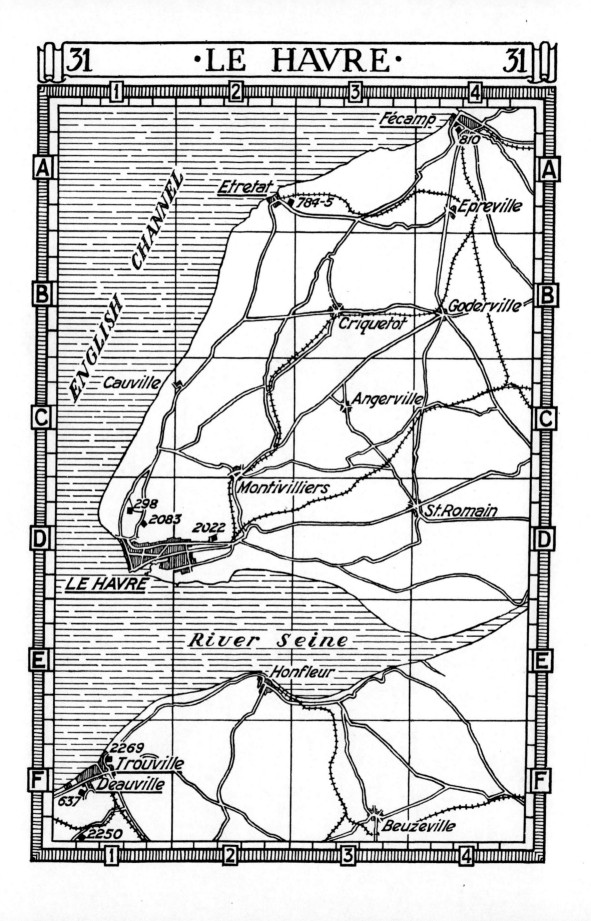

ENGLISH CHANNEL

Fécamp
810

Etretat
784·5
Epreville

Criquetot
Goderville

Cauville

Angerville

Montivilliers
298
2083
2022
St.Romain

LE HAVRE

River Seine

Honfleur

2269
Trouville
Deauville
637
2250

Beuzeville

LE HAVRE

MAP SHEET No. 31

LE HAVRE, in the Department of the Seine-Inférieure, was one of the ports at which the British Expeditionary Force disembarked in August 1914, and it remained throughout the War (except for a short interval during the German advance in 1914) No. 1 Base. Supplies and reinforcements passed through it to the railheads, and wounded men and prisoners came back to it. By the end of May 1917 it contained three General and two Stationary Hospitals, and four Convalescent Depots.

2022 STE. MARIE CEMETERY, LE HAVRE, GRAVILLE-STE. HONORINE (SEINE-INF.). Part of Brit. Exped. Force disembarked in Aug. 1914 at Le Havre which was known as No. 1 Base. Cem. on ridge overlooking town from N. Records 1,293 U.K., 131 Aust., 99 Can., 44 S.A., 7 N.Z., 2 Newfld., 28 B.W.I., 1 Egypt., 17 Ind., 65 Chin., 3 Allies, and 243 German and Austrian burials.

2250 TOURGEVILLE MILITARY CEMETERY (CALVADOS). Opposite Le Havre, 1½ miles from Trouville Sta. 14th Convalescent Depot was stationed at Trouville in Oct. 1917, and a fleet of drifters were at Deauville at the same time. Records 196 U.K. 8 Aust., 7 Can., 1 N.Z., 27 Americans, and 57 German burials.

784 ETRETAT CHURCHYARD (SEINE-INF.). 16 miles N. of Le Havre with sta. on branch line from Harfleur. No. 1 Gen. Hosp. here throughout War. No. 2 (Presbyterian U.S.A.) Base Hosp. from July 1917. Records 248 U.K., 14 Can., 4 Aust., 3 N.Z., 2 Newfld., and 1 German burials.

785 ETRETAT CHURCHYARD EXTENSION (SEINE-INF.). On SE. side of churchyard. Used from Dec. 1916 to Dec. 1918. Records 237 U.K., 37 Aust., 1 S.A., and 10 German burials.

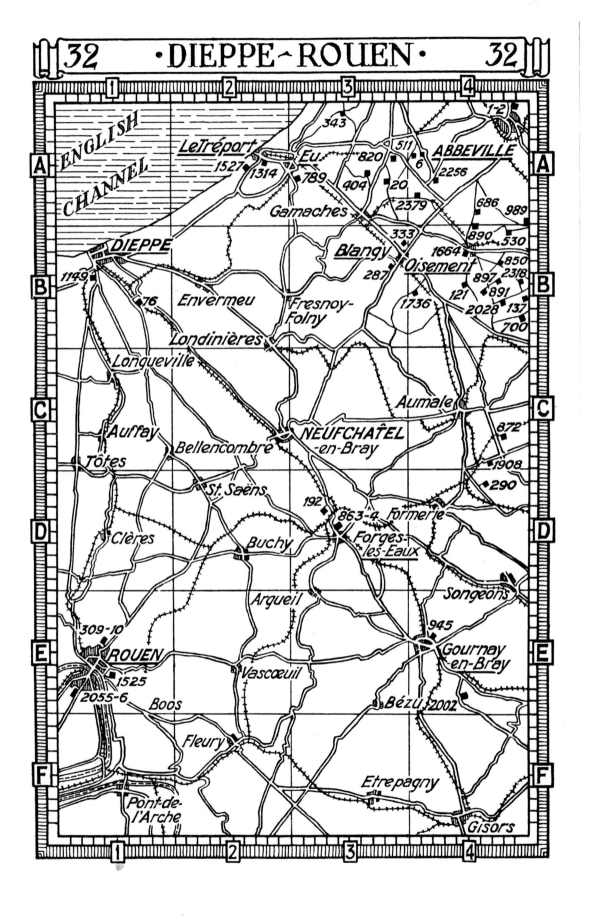

ENGLISH CHANNEL

1 2 3 4

343

Le Tréport
1527
1314
Eu.
789
820
511
6
ABBEVILLE
2256
404
20
2379
686 989
Gamaches
333
890 530
DIEPPE
Blangy
Oisement
1664
850
2318
1149
287
897 891
76
Envermeu
1736
121
2028 137
Fresnoy-Folny
700
Londinières
Longueville
Aumale
872
Auffay
NEUFCHÂTEL
-en-Bray
1908
Bellencombre
290
Tôtes
St. Saëns
192
863-4 Formerie
Clères
Buchy
Forges-les-Eaux
Songeons
Arqueil
945
309-10
Gournay
en-Bray
ROUEN
Vascœuil
1525
2055-6
Boos
Bézu 2002
Fleury
Etrepagny
Pont-de-l'Arche
Gisors

1 2 3 4

DIEPPE—ROUEN

MAP SHEET No. 32

DIEPPE is an important town and seaport in the Department of the Seine Inférieure, at the mouth of the River Arques.

Dieppe was used as a minor British Base (particularly for supplies of small arms ammunition, forage, and flour) from December 1914 onwards; and from January 1915 to May 1919 'A' Section of No. 5 Stationary Hospital was quartered in the town.

ROUEN is an old cathedral town on the River Seine, in the Department of the Seine-Inférieure. It is the chief town of the Department, and important both as an industrial centre and as a port. During the War, British camps and hospitals were placed on the southern outskirts of the city; a Base Supply Depot and the 3rd Echelon of General Headquarters were established at Rouen; and the railway sidings at Sotteville were largely increased to deal with the British supply and troop trains which passed through the Rouen stations or were dispatched from them.

The hospitals at Rouen remained there in almost all cases for practically the whole of the War. They included eight General, five Stationary, one British Red Cross and one Native Labour Hospitals, and No. 2 Convalescent Depot.

ABBEVILLE, an old and important town near the mouth of the Somme, lies on the main road and the main railway line between Boulogne and Paris. It was during the greater part of the War, under various titles, the Headquarters of the British Lines of Communication, and three Hospitals were stationed there from 1915 to 1919.

1149 JANVAL CEME-
TERY, DIEPPE
(SEINE-INF.). 1½ miles
SW. of Sta. in Rue-
Montigny-Prolongée, S.
of town. Used as minor
British Base from Dec.
1914. From Jan. 1915 to
May 1919 'A' Sect. of
No. 5 Stationary Hosp.
was in the town. Records
214 U.K., 2 S.A., 1 Can.,
and 1 Aust. burials.

1314 LE TREPORT
MILITARY CEME-
TERY (SEINE-INF.).
15½ miles NE. of Dieppe,
on high ground 1 mile S.
of sta., on road to Dieppe.
Was important hospital
centre (Nos. 3, 16 and
No. 2 Can. Gen. Hosps.,
No. 3 Convalescent De-
pot and Lady Murray's
B.R.C.S. Hosp.).   Re-
cords 429 U.K., 15 Can.,
1 Aust. burials, and 4
special memorials.

1527   MONT HUON
MILITARY CEME-
TERY, LE TREPORT
(SEINE-INF.). Le Tre-
port is 15½ miles NE. of
Dieppe, 1 mile S. of
town, and about ½ mile
from sta. This Ceme-
tery was used when
original Mil. Cem. was
nearly filled.   Records
1,842 U.K., 124 Aust.,
117 Can., 33 N.Z., 9 S.A.,
2 Newfld., 1 Ind., 1
B.W.I., 1 Italian, and 222
German burials.

309 BOISGUILLAUME COMMUNAL CEME-TERY, ROUEN (SEINE-INF.). Bois-guillaume adjoins the city of Rouen on the N., near the brow of the hill be-tween Rouen and Forêt-Verte. Burials for the most part from No. 8 Gen. Hosp. and are S. of the central French monu-ment. Records 302 U.K., 10 Aust., 6 Can., and 2 S.A. burials.

310 BOISGUILLAUME COMMUNAL CEME-TERY EXTENSION, ROUEN (SEINE-INF.) In March 1917 it was necessary to use this Ex-tension on NE. of Com. Cem. Burials are mostly from No. 8 General Hosp. Records 305 U.K., 28 Aust., 13 Can., 7 N.Z., 3 B.W.I., 2 Guernsey, 1 S.A., 1 Bermuda, 2 Ital., and 1 Port. burials.

76 ARQUES-LA-BA-TAILLE BRITISH CEMETERY (SEINE-INF.). 3 miles SE. of Dieppe on hill-side over-looking Rivers Béthune and Eaulne. No. 1 Gen. Native Lab. Hosp. was established here. Re-cords 235 S.A.N.L.C., 11 B.W.I., 7 Chin., 6 Cape A.H.T.C., 1 U.K., and 1 native seaman burials. Contains Memorial to S.A.N.L.C.

2055   ST. SEVER CEMETERY, ROUEN (SEINE-INF.). 2 miles S. of Cathedral, close to tram terminus in Rue d'Elbeuf. Hosp. Centre, Base Supply Depot, and Gen. Hdqtrs. of 3rd Echelon. Records 2,689 U.K., 132 Can., 112 Aust., 73 Ind., 51 N.Z., 19 S.A., 5 Newfld., 1 Bermuda and 1 Egypt. burials.

2056   ST. SEVER CEMETERY EXTEN-SION,   ROUEN (SEINE-INF.). S. of Com. Cem. and adjoin-ing. Begun Sept. 1916. Records 6,600 U.K., 783 Aust., 311 Can., 271 Ind., 134 N.Z., 88 B.W.I. 84 S.A., 11 Newfld., 3 Guernsey, 1 Bermuda, 6 Unknown, 1 Egypt, 44 Chin., 18 Italian, and 1 Port. burials.

290 BLARGIES COM-MUNAL CEMETERY EXTENSION (OISE). 32 miles SW. of Amiens, E. of sta. and N. of vil-lage. Used from March 1918 to Oct. 1918 for burial of dead from hosps. in the vicinity. Records 160 U.K., 7 S.A., 1 Aust., 1 N.Z., 44 Ind., 2 B.W.I., and 22 Chin. burials.

1 ABBEVILLE COMMUNAL CEME-TERY (SOMME). The Cem. is on high ground overlooking Abbeville from N. Was during the greater part of the war Hdqtrs. of the British lines of communication and three hosps. were stationed there from 1915 to 1919. Records 740 U.K., 13 Aust., 10 S.A., 8 Can., 1 N.Z., 1 Newfld., and 1 Ind. burials.

2 ABBEVILLE COMMUNAL CEME-TERY EXTENSION (SOMME). Used when Com. Cem. was filled in July 1916. Records 1,370 U.K., 227 Aust., 107 Can., 33 N.Z., 8 S.A., 3 B.W.I., 2 Newfld., 2 Guernsey, 1 Ind., 1 Unknown, and 1 Port. burials.

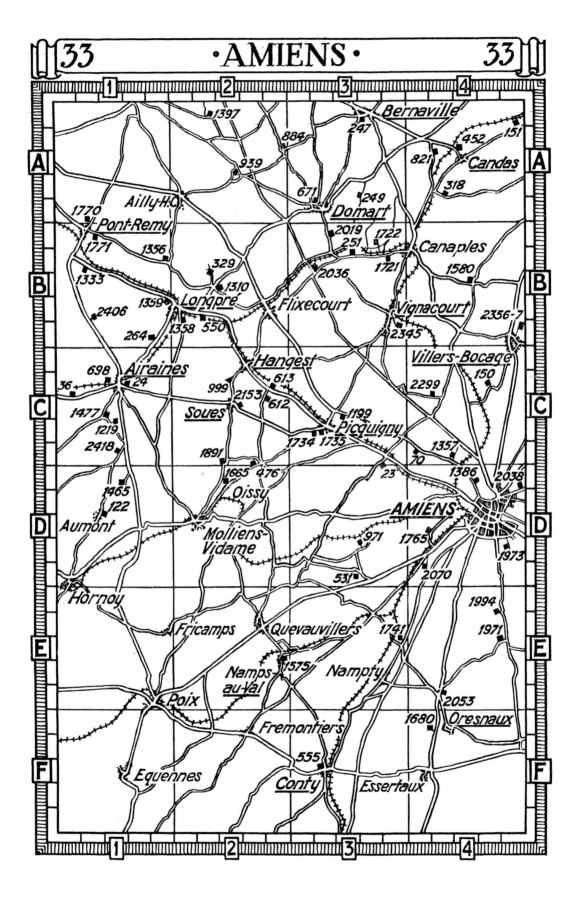

1397
884
247 Bernaville
939
452 151
821 Candas
671 318
Ailly-H.C. 249
1770 Domart
Pont-Remy 2019 1722
1771 1356 251 Canaples
329 1721
1333 2036 1580
1310
2406 1359 550 Longpré Flixecourt Vignacourt 2356-7
1358 2345
264
Hangest Villers-Bocage
698 Airaines 613 150
36 24 2299
999
1477 2153 612
1219 Soues 1199
2418 1891 Picquigny
1734 1735 1357
1665 476 70 1386 2038
23
1465 Oissy AMIENS
122
Aumont 971 1765
Molliens- 1973
Vidame
531 2070
Hornoy 1994
Fricamps Quevauvillers 1741 1971
1575
Namps- Nampty 2053
au-Val 1680 Oresnaux
Poix
Fremontiers
555
Equennes Conty Essertaux

AMIENS

MAP SHEET No. 33

AMIENS is an ancient cathedral town on the left bank of the Somme, containing nearly 100,000 inhabitants. It is the capital of the Department of the Somme, the Headquarters of the II French Army Corps, a railway junction and an important manufacturing town. During part of August 1914 it was the British Advanced Base. It was captured by the Germans on the 31st of that month, and retaken by the French on the following 13th September. The German offensive, which began in March 1918, had Amiens for at least one of its objectives; but the 'Battle of Amiens' (8th to 11th August 1918) is the British name for the action by which the counter-offensive, the Advance to Victory, was begun.

The 7th General Hospital was at Amiens in August 1914; the 56th (South Midland) Casualty Clearing Station from April to July 1916; the New Zealand Stationary Hospital from July 1916 to May 1917; the 42nd Stationary Hospital from October 1917 to March 1919; and the 41st Stationary Hospital in March 1918, and again in December 1918 and January 1919.

2038 ST. PIERRE CEMETERY, AMIENS (SOMME). 1¾ miles from sta. on N. side of main road to Albert in NW. (or St. Pierre) district of the City. First used Sept. 1915, closed Oct. 1919. Records 562 U.K., 95 Aust., 11 Can., 3 N.Z., 2 Ind., 1 S.A., 1 Unknown, 1 Chin., and 1 special memorial.

1575 NAMPS-AU-VAL BRITISH CEMETERY (SOMME). 11 miles SW. of Amiens, 500 yards S. of Namps-Quevauvillers Sta. Burials by 41st, 50th and 55th Casualty Stations during German offensive in Picardy. Records 315 U.K., 57 Aust., 24 Can., 1 S.A., 6 Unknown burials.

1734 PICQUIGNY BRITISH CEMETERY (SOMME). ½ mile from Picquigny Sta. on S. of road to Airaines. From 1914–March 1918 on lines of communication. March 1918, 5th and 46th Casualty Clearing Stats. were stationed here during German advance on Amiens. Records 94 U.K., 29 Aust., 1 Can., 1 Unknown, and 1 French burials.

612 CROUY BRITISH CEMETERY (SOMME) 2 miles SE. of Hangest Sta., ½ mile S. of village on road to Cavillon. Begun in April 1918, mostly from 5th and 47th Casualty Clearing Stations during German advance. Records 280 U.K., 275 Aust., 180 Can., 1 B.W.I., 2 Ind., 6 French, and 44 German burials.

1770 PONT - REMY BRITISH CEMETERY (S O M M E). 1¼ miles from village and sta., on road to St. Ricquier, overlooking V. of R. Somme. Burials from 41st Stationary Hosp., which was stationed in village from April to Nov. 1918 ; Nos. 4, 38 and 46 C.C.Ss. were there also in 1918. Records 45 U.K. and 5 Aust. burials.

1358 LONGPRE-LES-CORPS SAINTS BRITISH CEMETERY (SOMME). ½ mile S. of village and sta. at top of a steep rise. In April 1918 at turning point of the German offensive towards Amiens, the 12th and 55th Casualty Clearing Stats. came to Longpré. Records 56 U.K., 20 Aust., and 1 French burials.

2345 VIGNACOURT BRITISH CEMETERY (SOMME). Sta. E. side of village and cem. 500 yards S. of sta., close to rly. and road to Flesselles. Burials reflect desperate fighting of Aust. forces on Amiens front. Records 423 Aust., 146 U.K. 11 Can., 2 B.W.I., 1 Ind., 1 Unknown, and 44 German burials.

1721 PERNOIS BRIT-ISH CEMETERY, HALLOY - LES - PER-NOIS (SOMME). 600 yards S. of Pernois Halte on road to Vignacourt. Begun during the German advance in April 1918 by No. 4 Casualty Clearing Sta. Records 331 U.K., 63 Aust., 5 B.W.I., 4 Ind., and 18 German burials.

821 FIENVILLERS BRITISH CEMETERY (SOMME). 7 miles SW. of Doullens, 1 mile W. of Fienvillers Sta., E. of road to Pernois. The 34th and 38th Casualty Clearing Stas. were posted here April to Sept. 1918, during German advance on Amiens. Records 122 U.K., 1 Can., and 1 N.Z. burials.

151 BAGNEUX BRIT-ISH CEMETERY, GÉZAINCOURT (SOMME). 60 yards from Gézaincourt Halte, S. of Bagneux village and 2 miles SW. of Doullens. Begun in April 1918 after close of German offensive in Picardy. Records 1,141 U.K., 181 N.Z., 46 Can., 2 B.W.I., 1 Aust., 1 Ind., 1 American, and 2 Chin. burials.

2357 VILLERS - BO-CAGE COMMUNAL CEMETERY EXTENSION (SOMME). 8 miles from Amiens, $3\frac{1}{2}$ miles from Flesselles Sta., $\frac{1}{2}$ mile from village on by-road to Talmas. The 51st (Highland) Casualty Clearing Sta. was posted at Villers-Bocage April–May 1916. Cem. used from Oct. 1915 to Feb. 1917. Records 58 U.K. and 1 Aust. burials.

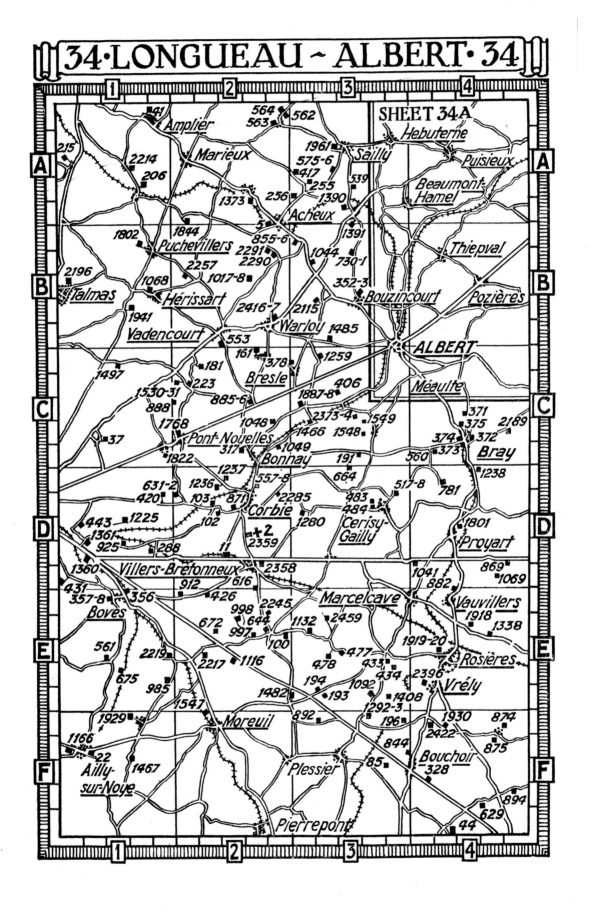

34·LONGUEAU ~ ALBERT · 34

SHEET 34A

2359 VILLERS-BRE-TONNEUX MILI-TARY CEMETERY AND AUSTRALIAN NATIONAL MEMORIAL, FOUILLOY (SOMME). 10½ miles E. of Amiens, 1¼ miles N. of Villers Bretonneux sta., on road to Fouilloy. Records 1,085 U.K., 770 Aust., 263 Can., 4 S.A., 2 N.Z. burials, and 15 special memorials. The Mem. records 18,000 Australian 'Missing'.

1802 PUCHEVILLERS BRITISH CEMETERY (SOMME). 3½ miles S. of Raincheval-Arquêves Sta. and 1,000 yards W. of village. Begun in June 1916 just before Battles of Somme by 3rd and 4th Casualty Clearing Stats. Records 1,132 U.K., 416 Aust., 214 Can., 1 N.Z., 1 French, and 75 German burials.

1961 SAILLY - AU - BOIS MILITARY CEMETERY (P. de C.). 3 miles N. of Mailly-Maillet Sta., W. of village on road to Couin. Used by Field Ambs. and fighting units until March 1917. Records 212 U.K., 24 N.Z., 2 S.A., 1 Aust., and 1 German burials.

562 COUIN BRITISH CEMETERY (P. de C.). 5½ miles SE. of Mondicourt-Pas Sta. The Brit. and New Brit. Cems. are facing each other across road to Souastre at its junction with road to Henu. Used during the Battles of the Somme, Records 397 U.K., 2 S.A. 1 Can., and 1 Ind. burials.

564   COUIN NEW BRITISH CEMETERY (P. de C.).   Facing the British Cem. on Souastre road, used by Field Ambs. from Jan. 1917 to end of War. Records 344 U.K., 14 N.Z., 2 Can., and 2 German burials.

576   COURCELLES-AU-BOIS COMMUNAL CEMETERY EXTENSION (SOMME). 8 miles N. of Albert, 2¾ miles N. of Mailly-Maillet Sta., N. of village. Used until March 1917, also in 1918 during German attack on Amiens. Records 102 U.K., 5 N.Z. 3 S.A., and 2 Can. burials.

256 BERTRANCOURT MILITARY CEMETERY (SOMME). 2¾ miles NE. of Acheux Sta., 400 yards W. of Bertrancourt. Used by Field Ambs. in 1916 and 1917, by Corps and Div. burial parties in June, July and Aug. 1918, when German front line was again within five miles of it. Records 389 U.K., 27 N.Z., and 3 German burials.

1390 MAILLY-MAILLET COMMUNAL CEMETERY EXTENSION (SOMME). 1¼ miles W. of sta., 5½ miles N. of Albert, ⅓ mile N. of village. Was severely shelled and the catacombs under village were prepared for use by troops after March 1918. Cem. used Aug. 1915 to Dec. 1916 and in March–July 1918. Records 122 U.K., 3 N.Z., and 1 Newfld. burials.

1391 MAILLY WOOD CEMETERY (SOMME) 5½ miles N. of Albert, 1 mile SW. of Mailly-Maillet Sta., 400 yards S. of village. Begun by 2nd Seaforths June 1916 and used by 51st (Highland) Div. Nov. 1916, 12th and 21st Divs. in May and Aug. 1918. Records 624 U.K., 27 N.Z., 3 S.A., 41 Unknown burials, and 8 special memorials.

1373 LOUVENCOURT MILITARY CEMETERY (SOMME). SE. of village, ½ mile from sta., on road to Acheux. From July 1915 to Aug. 1916, Field Ambs. were stationed at Louvencourt which was 6 miles behind front line on July 1st 1916. Records 133 U.K., 17 N.Z., 1 Newfld., and 76 German burials.

215 BEAUVAL COMMUNAL CEMETERY (SOMME). 1 mile E. of sta., N. of village. Begun by 4th and 47th Casualty Clearing Stats. Records 234 U.K., 8 Aust., 5 Newfld., and 1 N.Z. burials.

5 ACHEUX BRITISH CEMETERY (SOMME) 1 mile from Acheux Sta., 100 yards N. of Léal-villers road. The VIII Corps Collecting Station was posted here for Battles of the Somme, also centre for Field Ambs. when German offensives brought front line within 5 miles of Acheux in 1918. Records 179 U.K. and 1 Can. burials.

856 FORCEVILLE COMMUNAL CEMETERY EXTENSION (SOMME). W. of village on main road between Doullens and Albert. Nearest sta. Acheux. Third Army took over Forceville from French 1915, Fourth Army occupied until July 20th 1916 when it was included in area of Fifth Army. Records 300 U.K., 2 N.Z., 1 Can., and 7 German burials.

2291 VARENNES MILITARY CEMETERY (SOMME). $1\frac{1}{2}$ miles from Acheux Sta., on N. side of road to Léalvillers, $\frac{1}{2}$ mile from Varennes Church. Begun by the 39th Casualty Clearing Sta. during Battle of Somme 1916. Records 1,190 U.K., 16 N.Z., 5 Can., 4 S.A., 2 Aust., 1 French, 1 Russ., and 42 German burials.

1018 HARPONVILLE COMMUNAL CEMETERY EXTENSION (SOMME). $3\frac{1}{2}$ miles from Acheux Sta., N. side of village on road to Léalvillers, N. of Com. Cem. Made by fighting units during the German advance on the Somme in 1918. Records 138 U.K. burials.

1044   HEDAUVILLE COMMUNAL CEMETERY EXTENSION (SOMME). 5 miles NW. of Albert Sta., N. of village, on road to Forceville. Begun March 1918, when British front line had been consolidated E. of village. Records 168 U.K., 9 N.Z., and 1 Aust. burials.

730   ENGLEBELMER COMMUNAL CEMETERY (SOMME). 4½ miles N. of Albert, 2 miles W. of Mesnil Sta., S. of village, W. of road to Bouzincourt. Englebelmer was 2½ miles behind the front line on July 1st 1916 at beginning of Somme offensive. Records 51 U.K., 1 N.Z., and 6 French burials.

731   ENGLEBELMER COMMUNAL CEMETERY EXTENSION (SOMME). S. of Com. Cem. Used from Oct. 1916 during the Battle of the Ancre Nov. 1916, the German advance of March 1918, and the second Battle of the Somme Aug. 1918. Records 120 U.K., 28 N.Z. burials, and 2 special memorials.

353 BOUZINCOURT COMMUNAL CEMETERY EXTENSION (SOMME). 2½ miles NW. of Albert Sta., on NW. corner of village. Used as a Field Amb. Sta. from early in 1916 to Feb. 1917 when British line went forward from the Ancre. Records 561 U.K., 8 Aust., 7 Can., 2 S.A., 1 N.Z., 8 Unknown, 2 German burials, and 2 special memorials.

2115 SENLIS COMMUNAL CEMETERY EXTENSION (SOMME). 3½ miles NW. of Albert, on NW. edge of village on by-road to Hédauville. Casualties from April to Aug. 1918 the period of German advance and retreat on the Somme. Records 80 U.K., 23 Aust., and 1 S.A. burials.

1485 MILLENCOURT COMMUNAL CEMETERY EXTENSION (SOMME). 3½ miles W. of Albert Sta., on N. Side of road to Hénencourt. Used by Field Ambs. and III Corps Main Dressing Sta. 1916 and 4th Aust. Div., etc., March and April 1918. Records 273 U.K., 50 Aust., 7 Can., 7 N.Z., 1 S.A., and 2 Unknown burials.

2416 WARLOY-BAIL-LON COMMUNAL CEMETERY (SOMME) 3 miles from Contay Sta., 750 yards E. of village on the Albert road. First burial took place in Oct. 1915 and the last on July 1st 1916. Records 46 U.K. burials.

2417 WARLOY-BAIL-LON COMMUNAL CEMETERY EXTENSION (SOMME). In apple orchard on E. side of Com. Cem. Used from July to Nov. 1916, Somme offensive and during German attack in spring of 1918. Records 857 U.K., 318 Aust., 152 Can., 3 Unknown, and 17 German burials.

553 CONTAY BRIT-ISH CEMETERY (SOMME). 7 miles W. of Albert, NE. side of road to Franvillers, beside a quarry. Begun by 49th and 9th Casualty Clearing Stats. in Aug. 1916. Records 686 U.K., 414 Can., 29 Aust., 1 S.A., 3 Unknown, and 40 German burials.

181 BAVELINCOURT COMMUNAL CEMETERY (SOMME). 11 miles from Amiens, 8 miles from Corbie, E. of R. Hallue. Used April to Aug. 1918, and except for 5 Aust. and 13 Art., the casualties are from London Rgts. British plot records 50 U.K. and 4 Aust. burials.

1530 MONTIGNY COMMUNAL CEMETERY (SOMME). 7 miles NE. of Amiens Sta., E. of Béhencourt Sta., on SW. outskirts of village of Montigny. Burials were made during second Battle of Somme 1918, the first step in the advance to Victory. Records 53 U.K. burials.

888 FRECHENCOURT COMMUNAL CEMETERY (SOMME). 8 miles NE. of Amiens, 1½ miles N. of Amiens-Albert road, E. of village, near road to Querrieu. All casualties but 8 are of Aust. Corps who fell April to Aug. 1918. Records 49 Aust. and 8 U.K. burials.

886 FRANVILLERS COMMUNAL CEME-TERY EXTENSION (SOMME). 2¼ miles N. of Heilly Halte, 7 miles W. of Albert, N. of Amiens - Albert road. Used from April to Aug. 1918 by units and Field Ambs. engaged in defence of Amiens. Records 134 Aust., 113 U.K., and 1 N.Z. burials.

37 ALLONVILLE COMMUNAL CEME-TERY (SOMME). 5 miles from Amiens Sta., on E. outskirts of Allon-ville village near road to Querrieu. Burials were made in Cem. from Aug. 1916 to Jan. 1917 and from Jan. 1918 to Jan. 1919. Records 40 Aust. and 38 U.K. burials.

1822 QUERRIEU BRITISH CEMETERY (SOMME). 4 miles N. of Daours Halte, 300 yards S. of village on road to Bussy - lès - Daours. Used by the Divs. taking part in defence of Amiens against German attack 1918. Records 102 U.K., 84 Aust., 1 Chin., and 12 German burials.

1360 LONGUEAU BRITISH CEMETERY (SOMME). 2¾ miles SE. of Amiens Sta., SW. of road to Domart. Begun in April 1918 when Brit. line was re-established before Amiens. Records 68 U.K., 66 Can., 65 Aust., 2 B.W.I., and 1 Unknown burials.

357 BOVES WEST COMMUNAL CEMETERY (SOMME). 4½ miles SE. of Amiens, W. of village and sta., S. of road to Sains-en-Amienois. Used by British March, April and Aug. 1918. Records 44 U.K., 6 Aust., 1 Can., 18 Fr., and 1 U.S.A. burials.

358 BOVES WEST COMMUNAL CEMETERY EXTENSION (SOMME). W. of Com. Cem. Principally Can. casualties Aug. 12th–24th 1918 except for R.F.A. and R.G.A. casualties of April 1918. Records 48 Can., 38 U.K., 4 Aust., and 1 B.W.I. burials.

557 CORBIE COMMUNAL CEMETERY (SOMME). 9 miles E. of Amiens, 1 mile from Corbie Sta., N. of town, between roads to Vaux and Bray. The Third Army taking over from Berles-au-Bois southwards to Somme in 1915 made it a medical centre. Records 246 U.K., 4 Ind., and 15 German burials.

558 CORBIE COMMUNAL CEMETERY EXTENSION (SOMME). E. of Com. Cem. Begun in May 1916 and used during Somme advance 1916 and again during the German offensive of 1918. Records 829 U.K., 57 Aust., 26 S.A., 1 Bermuda, 1 German burials, and 1 special memorial.

288 BLANGY-TRONVILLE COMMUNAL CEMETERY (SOMME) 9 miles E. of Amiens, ¾ mile E. of halte, S. of village, on by-road to Boves. Used March–May 1918. Majority are Aust. casualties who fell during German advance and in fighting around Amiens. Records 27 U.K., 15 Aust., and 1 Fr. burials.

632 DAOURS COM-
MUNAL CEMETERY
E X T E N S I O N
(SOMME). 1 mile N. of
Daours Halte about 300
yards N. of village. From
April to Aug. 1918 the
Ext. was almost a front-
line Cem. Records 754
U.K., 458 Aust., 8 Ind.,
2 Can., 1 N.Z., 1 S.A., 2
Chin., and 25 German
burials.

1236 LA NEUVILLE
BRITISH CEMETERY,
CORBIE (SOMME). 1
mile from Corbie Sta. on
W. side of road to Bon-
nay. No. 21 Casualty
Clearing Sta. was here
throughout the Battles of
the Somme 1916 until
March 1917. The Cem.
was opened for it July
1916. Records 816 U.K.,
24 S.A., 21 Aust., 5 Un-
known, and 30 German
burials.

1237 LA NEUVILLE
COMMUNAL CEME-
TERY, (SOMME).
1 mile from Corbie Sta.,
600 yards N. of La Neu-
ville. Burials from No.
21 Casualty Clearing Sta.
Records 173 U.K. and
13 Aust. burials.

1049 HEILLY STA-TION CEMETERY, MÉRICOURT-L'ABBE (SOMME). 5 miles SW. of Albert, 1½ miles SW. of village, and 500 yards S. of Heilly Halte. 36th Casualty Clearing Sta. was here from April 1st 1916 to April 1917. Records 2,354 U.K., 402 Aust., 118 N.Z., 8 Newfld., 6 Can., 1 Bermuda, 1 B.W.I., 83 German, and 15 special memorials.

1466 MÉRICOURT-L'ABBE COMMUNAL CEMETERY EXTENSION (SOMME). 600 yards S. of sta., E. of village. Summer 1915 Somme front was taken over by British and Méricourt-Ribemont Sta. became a railhead. From March 1918 to Aug. was used by units engaged in defence of Amiens. Records 230 U.K., 122 Aust., 4 Can., 51 Unknown burials, and 2 special memorials.

317 ` BONNAY COMMUNAL CEMETERY EXTENSION (SOMME). 2½ miles N. of Corbie Sta., N. of village, on road to Franvillers. Burials from actions of Villers-Bretonneux by 4th and 5th Aust. and 18th Divs. and later from Battle of Amiens. Records 75 Aust. and 31 U.K. burials.

1888 RIBEMONT COMMUNAL CEMETERY EXTENSION (SOMME). 1 mile NW. of Méricourt-Ribemont Sta., 5 miles SW. of Albert. Used from May to Aug. 1918 by units engaged in defence of Amiens. Records 269 U.K., 178 Aust., 4 Can., 2 S.A., 15 Unknown burials, and 15 special memorials.

2374 VILLE - SUR - ANCRE COMMUNAL CEMETERY EXTEN-SION (SOMME). 4 miles S. of Albert, ½ mile E. of Buire-sur-Ancre Halte, SW. of village on road to Treux. Ville-sur-Ancre was taken by 2nd Aust. Div. May 19th 1918. Records 106 U.K. burials.

191 BEACON CEME-TERY, SAILLY-LAURETTE (SOMME) 3½ miles from Méricourt-Ribemont Sta., S. of road between Bray and Corbie. Fighting took place here March 26th–27th 1918 when 3rd Army withdrew to Albert and Sailly-le-Sec. Records 572 U.K., 195 Aust., 1 S.A. burials, and 4 special memorials.

664   DIVE COPSE BRITISH CEMETERY, SAILLY - LE - SEC (SOMME). 3¼ miles SE. of Méricourt Sta. and 1 mile NE. of Sailly Ch. Burials from XIV Main Corps Dressing Sta. during Somme offensive 1916 and from fighting units in Aug. 1918. Records 498 U.K., 53 Aust., 18 S.A., 10 Unknown burials, and 10 special memorials.

1548 MORLANCOURT BRITISH CEMETERY, No. 1 (SOMME).   4 miles S. of Albert, 1¾ miles SE. of Buire-sur-Ancre Halte, in fields 300 yards W. of church. 2nd Aust. Div. made substantial advance here, taking 300 prisoners in night attack June 10th 1918. Records 74 U.K. and 1 Ind. burials.

1549 MORLANCOURT BRITISH CEMETERY, No. 2 VILLE-SUR-ANCRE (SOMME).   4 miles S. of Albert, 1¾ miles SE. of Buire-sur-Ancre Halte, 500 yards NW. of Morlancourt Church. The III Corps, with aid of a rgt. of 33rd U.S. Div., captured Morlancourt and high ground beyond Aug. 9th 1918. Records 55 U.K. and 1 Aust. burials.

371 BRAY HILL BRITISH CEMETERY, BRAY - SUR - SOMME (SOMME). 1½ miles N. of sta., W. of road to Fricourt. Made by 58th (London) Div. Aug. 31st 1918 in advance from Corbie. Records 102 U.K. and 2 Aust. burials.

372 BRAY MILITARY CEMETERY, BRAY-SUR-SOMME (SOMME). 1 mile N. of Bray Sta. In March 1918 fell into enemy hands but was retaken by 40th Aust. Battn. on Aug. 24th. Records 739 U.K., 31 Aust., 13 Ind., 3 Can., 2 S.A., 79 Unknown, and 8 Egypt. burials.

375 BRAY VALE BRITISH CEMETERY, BRAY - SUR - SOMME (SOMME). 1½ miles N. of sta., E. of road to Albert. Fell into enemy hands March 1918, retaken by 40th Aust. Batt. Aug. 24th. Cem. was begun Aug. 1918, and enlarged after Armistice by concentration of isolated graves. Records 256 U.K., 17 Aust., 3 Newfld., 1 Can., and 2 Unknown burials.

1041 HEATH CEME-
TERY, HARBON-
NIERES (SOMME). 3½
miles NW. of sta. on
Amiens-Péronne road.
Captured by French in
summer 1916 and recap-
tured by Aust. Corps
Aug. 8th 1918. Records
958 Aust., 839 U.K., 9
Can., 6 N.Z., 2 S.A.
burials, and 47 special
memorials.

102 AUBIGNY BRIT-
ISH CEMETERY
(SOMME). 8 miles E. of
Amiens, 1½ miles W. of
Corbie Sta., SE. of vil-
lage on road to Fouilloy.
The Germans were held
April 6th 1918, 4 miles E.
of Aubigny at end of
great offensive on Amiens.
Cem. used from April to
Aug. 1918. Records 88
Aust. and 8 U.K. burials.

2189 SUZANNE
COMMUNAL CEME-
TERY EXTENSION
(SOMME). 8 miles SE.
of Albert, 3 miles E. of
Bray Sta., NW. of village
on track to Brillon Farm.
Begun by 5th Div. 1915–
1916. Burials were of the
Manchester Rgt. and
1918 burials of the Aust.
Corps. Records 141 U.K.
and 14 Aust. burials.

11 ADELAIDE CEMETERY, VILLERS-BRETONNEUX (SOMME). 1½ miles from Villers-Bretonneux Sta., N. side of main Amiens - St. Quentin road. April 24th 1918 the 4th and 5th Aust. Divs., with units of 8th and 18th (British) Divs., carried out 'an enterprise of great daring', recapturing Villers-Bretonneux. Records 519 Aust., 365 U.K., 22 Can., 48 Unknown burials, and 4 special memorials.

616 CRUCIFIX CORNER CEMETERY VILLERS - BRETONNEUX (SOMME). 1 mile S. of sta. on road to Démuin. 4th and 5th Aust. Divs. with units of 8th and 18th Divs. carried whole of the village April 24th 1918. Records 293 Aust., 287 U.K. 76 Can., 241 French, and 10 German burials, also 2 special memorials.

517 CHIPILLY COMMUNAL CEMETERY (SOMME). 7 miles S. of Albert Sta., on N. slopes of R. Somme, N. of village on Etinehem road. Chipilly was captured after stubborn resistance by 58th (Lond.) Div. Aug. 9th 1918. (See Mem. in village.) Records 55 U.K. and 4 French burials.

484 CERISY-GAILLY MILITARY CEME-TERY (SOMME). 120 yards S. of Cerisy-Gailly French Nat. Cem. Used by 13th and 39th Casualty Clearing Stas. which were stationed at Gailly throughout 1917 to Mar. 1918, and used again in Aug. 1918. Records 592 U.K., 81 Aust., 65 Can., 2 S.A. burials, and 5 special memorials.

483 CERISY-GAILLY FRENCH NATIONAL CEMETERY (SOMME) 7 miles S. of Albert, 4 miles NE. of Marcelcave Sta., W. of village and S. of Com. Cem. Made after Armistice from Somme battle-fields (including High Wood and the La Boisselle mine crater). Records 344 U.K., 44 Aust., 4 Can., and 1 N.Z. burials.

2245 TORONTO CEMETERY, DE-MUIN (SOMME). $4\frac{1}{8}$ miles SE. of Villers-Bretonneux Sta.,1 mile N. of village, in fields. Begun by 3rd Can. Batt. (Toronto Rgt.) Aug. 1918. Records 74 Can., 22 U.K., 1 Aust., and 4 German burials.

997 HANGARD COM-
MUNAL CEMETERY
E X T E N S I O N
(SOMME). 3¾ miles S.
of Villers - Bretonneux
Sta., E. of village, on road
to Démuin. 18th Div.
heavily engaged here and
on Aug. 8th 1918 village
was cleared by 1st and
2nd Can. Mtd. Rifles.
Records 427 U.K., 72
Can., 47 Aust., 1 Ger-
man burials, and 17
special memorials.

998 HANGARD WOOD
BRITISH CEMETERY
(SOMME). 2½ miles S.
of Villers - Bretonneux
Sta., N. of village. In
July 1918 was in German
hands, but cleared by
Can. Corps on Aug. 8th
1918. Records 61 Can.,
58 U.K., 17 Aust., 5
S.A., and 20 Fr. burials.

644 DÉMUIN BRIT-
I S H C E M E T E R Y
(SOMME). 2¾ miles S.
of Villers-Bretonneux
Sta., N. of village. Made
by 3rd Can. Batt. Dé-
muin was captured by
58th Can. Batt. Aug. 8th
1918. Records 40 Can.
and 2 U.K. burials.

1116 HOURGES OR-CHARD CEMETERY, DOMART - SUR - LA - LUCE (SOMME). 10 miles SE. of Amiens Sta., SE. of village. April 1st 1918 2nd Cav. Div. (including Can. Cav. Bgde.) took 'Rifle Wood', and retaken by 43rd Can. Batt. Aug. 8th 1918. Records 120 Can., 6 U.K., and 1 special memorial.

1547 MOREUIL COMMUNAL CEME-TERY ALLIED EX-TENSION (SOMME). 11 miles SE. of Amiens, NW. of town opp. sta., 100 yards W. of Com. Cem. Moreuil Wood was counter-attacked by Can. Cav. Bgde., and 3rd Cav. Bgde., during des-perate fighting in Ger-man thrust for Amiens March 1918. Records 171 U.K., 9 Can., and 3 Aust. burials.

1482 MÈZIÈRES COMMUNAL CEME-TERY EXTENSION (SOMME). 13 miles SE. of Amiens, 4 miles E. of Moreuil Sta., 550 yards NE. of Mézières Church, S. of Com. Cem. Begun by Fourth Army and Can. Corps Aug. 1918, and enlarged after Armis-tice. Records 95 U.K., 38 Can., and 1 Aust. burials.

433 CAIX BRITISH CEMETERY (SOMME) 16 miles E. of Amiens, 3 miles W. of Rosierès-en-Santerre Sta., SE. of village on road to Warvillers. Begun in March 1918 and enlarged after Armistice. Caix was taken the night of Aug. 8th 1918 by Can. Corps. Records 219 Can., 129 U.K., and 12 Aust. burials.

478 CAYEUX MILITARY CEMETERY, CAYEUX - EN - SANTERRE (SOMME). 15 miles E. of Amiens, 3 miles SW. of Guillaucourt Sta., $\frac{1}{2}$ mile S. of village off road to Beaucourt - en - Santerre. Cayeux was taken in the stride of the Can. Corps Aug. 8th 1918 in advance to Victory. Records 206 U.K., 5 Can., 2 S.A., 1 Aust., and 1 Ind. burials.

2459 WOOD CEMETERY, MARCELCAVE (SOMME). 16 miles E. of Amiens, S. of Wiencourt l'Equipée Sta., in fields W. of road to Cayeux. Casualties from Can. Corps and Fourth Army who fell Oct. 10th–19th 1918 in the relief of Montdidier. Records 41 Can. and 9 U.K. burials.

1092 HILLSIDE CEMETERY, LE QUESNEL (SOMME). 16½ miles SE. of Amiens, 6 miles SW. of Rosières Sta., N. of village, W. of road to Caix. Majority of casualties from Can. Corps who fell Aug. 8th to 25th 1918. Records 101 Can. and 7 U.K. burials.

193 BEAUCOURT BRITISH CEMETERY, BEAUCOURT - EN - SANTERRE (SOMME). 15 miles SE. of Amiens, 5 miles E. of Moreuil Sta., 300 yards E. of Beaucourt Church on by-road to Le Quesnel. The 3rd Cav. Div. covered by 4th Can. Div. captured village on Aug. 8th 1918. Records 77 Can. and 7 U.K. burials.

1408 MANITOBA CEMETERY, CAIX (SOMME). 15 miles E. of Amiens, 2 miles from Le Quesnel - Beaufort Sta., 2 miles S. of Caix Church. Majority of burials are 8th Can. from Winnipeg (Manitoba). Caix fell to 1st Cav. Div. operating with Can. Corps Aug. 8th 1918. Records 118 Can. and 2 U.K. burials.

2396 VRÉLY COM-
MUNAL CEMETERY
E X T E N S I O N
(SOMME). 21 miles E.
of Amiens, 2 miles S. of
Rosières Sta., NW. of vil-
lage near road to Caix.
Vrély was taken by 2nd
Can. Div. Aug. 9th 1918,
and all casualties are
from that Div. except 3
Tank Corps and 1 Lancer.
Records 39 Can. and 4
U.K. burials.

1918 R O S I È R E S
BRITISH CEMETERY,
V A U V I L L E R S
(SOMME). 21 miles E.
of Amiens, ¾ mile N. of
Rosières - en - Santerre
Sta., on by-road to Fra-
merville. All casualties
buried in Cem. fell be-
tween March 23rd–26th
1918 during German of-
fensive. Records 59 U.K.
burials.

1920 R O S I È R E S
COMMUNAL CEME-
TERY EXTENSION
(SOMME). 21 miles E.
of Amiens, 1 mile from
Rosières Sta., near road to
Caix. Casualties from
Durham L.I. and North.
Fus., who fell in Battle of
Rosières March 27th–
28th 1918; the Cans.
and Austs. were casualties
of the subsequent Brit.
advance. Records 211
U.K., 155 Can., 68 Aust.,
and 1 Chin. burials.

1293 LE QUESNEL COMMUNAL CEMETERY EXTENSION (SOMME). $16\frac{1}{2}$ miles SE. of Amiens, 7 miles SE. of Rosières Sta., NE. of village, E. of Com. Cem. Village was taken before dawn by Can. Corps with the assistance of Tanks, Aug. 9th 1918. Records 54 Can. and 7 U.K. burials.

2422 WARVILLERS CHURCHYARD EXTENSION (SOMME). 3 miles S. of Rosières Sta. and $2\frac{1}{4}$ miles E. of Le Quesnel - Beaufort Sta., S. of Church. Made by fighting units Aug. 1918. Records 35 Can. and 12 U.K. (all but 1 Tank Corps or Cav.) burials.

874 FOUQUESCOURT BRITISH CEMETERY (SOMME). 22 miles E. of Amiens, $1\frac{1}{2}$ miles W. of Hattencourt Sta., N. of village on a track to Chilly. Created after Armistice from battlefields of Aug.–Sept. 1918, the first stages of the advance to Victory. Records 180 U.K., 139 Can., 48 Aust., 2 S.A. burials, and 5 special memorials.

328 BOUCHOIR NEW BRITISH CEMETERY (SOMME). 2½ miles E. of Arvillers-Hangest Sta. on main road from Amiens to Roye, 1 mile SE. of village. Defended by 30th Div. on March 27th 1918; finally recaptured by 8th Can. Inf. Bgde. Records 537 U.K., 214 Can., 6 Aust. burials, and 6 special memorials.

560 CÔTE 80 FRENCH NATIONAL CEMETERY, ETINEHEM (SOMME). 6 miles S. of Albert, 1½ miles W. of Bray-sur-Somme Sta., 1,500 yards N. of Etinehem, E. of Méaulte road. Casualties mostly from Aust. Corps Aug. 1918; village was taken early in that month. Records 29 Aust., 19 U.K., and 1 Can. burials.

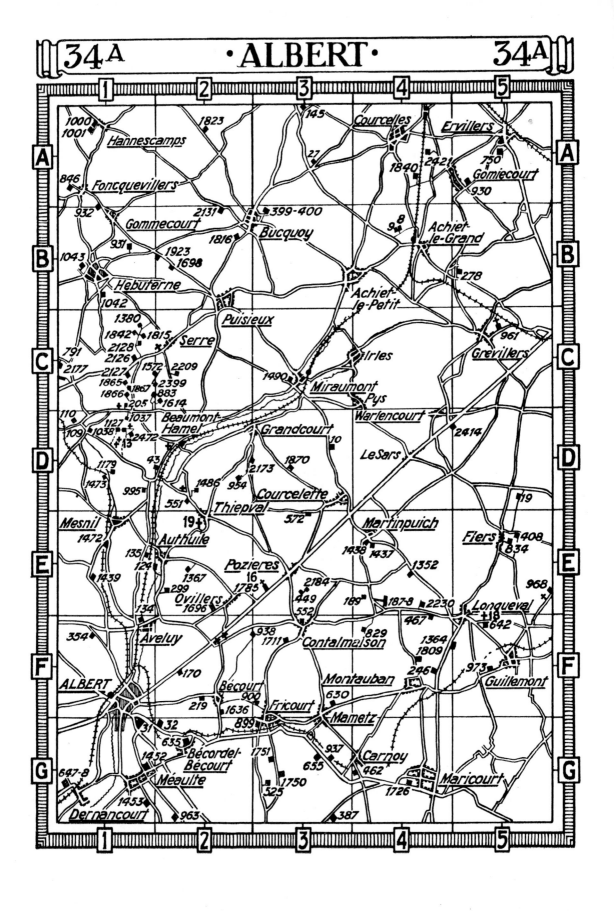

ALBERT

MAP SHEET No. 34A

ALBERT is a town of 7,000 inhabitants on the River Ancre, in the Department of the Somme, with a railway station on the main line from Paris and Amiens to Arras and Lille. It was held by French forces against the German Advance on the Somme in September 1914. It passed into British hands in the summer of 1915; and the first fighting in July 1916 is known as the 'Battle of Albert, 1916'. It was captured by the Germans on the 26th April 1918, and before its recapture by the 8th East Surreys on the following 22nd August (in the Battle of Albert, 1918) it had been completely destroyed by artillery fire.

   The town has been 'adopted' by the City of Birmingham.

THIEPVAL MEMORIAL (SOMME). 5 miles NE. of Albert Sta., $2\frac{1}{2}$ miles S. of Beaucourt-Hamel Sta., S. of Thiepval village near road to Authuile. Records 73,412 'Missing' who fell in the Battles of Albert, Bazentin Ridge, Delville Wood, Pozières Ridge, Guillemont, Ginchy, Flers-Courcelette, Morval, Thiepval Ridge, Transloy Ridges, Ancre Heights and the Ancre 1916, also Miraumont, the Thilloys, Irles and Bapaume 1917.

1785 POZIÈRES BRITISH CEMETERY AND MEMORIAL, OVILLERS - LA - BOISSELLE (SOMME). $3\frac{1}{2}$ miles NE. of Albert, $\frac{1}{2}$ mile SW. of Pozières on Bapaume road. Cem. records 1,809 U.K., 690 Aust., 218 Can., 16 Unknown, 1 German, and 22 special memorials. Memorial records 14,690 'Missing' of the Fifth Army who fell in the Battles of the Somme up to April 5th 1918 and all casualties of this area until Aug. 7th 1918.

SOUTH AFRICAN NATIONAL MEMOR-IAL, DELVILLE WOOD, LONGUEVAL (SOMME). On July 15th 1916 the S.A. Bgde. (9th Div.) captured Delville Wood except for the NW. corner. The Wood was finally taken by 38th (Welsh) Div. Aug. 28th 1918.

MEMORIAL TO NEWFOUNDLAND 'MISSING', BEAUMONT-HAMEL (SOMME). 6 miles N. of Albert, on hill SW. of village, in Newfoundland Mem. Park and on site of front-line trenches of July 1916. The 1st Batt. Newfld. Rgt. reached Beaumont-Hamel July 1st 1916. The Mem. records on cast bronze panels below the Caribou 820 Newfld. 'Missing'.

170 BAPAUME POST MILITARY CEME-TERY, ALBERT (SOMME). 1½ miles E. of Albert Sta. on E. side of Bapaume road. June 1916 British front line crossed the road between the cemetery and village of La Boisselle. Records 243 U.K., 64 Can., 18 Aust., 1 S.A., 83 Unknown burials, and 3 special memorials.

31 ALBERT COM-MUNAL CEMETERY EXTENSION (SOMME). ¾ mile from sta. on SE. side of town at junction of roads to Fricourt and Méaulte. First fighting in July 1916 is known as Battle of Albert 1916. Recaptured April 26th by 8th E. Surreys in Battle of Albert 1918. Records 619 U.K., 202 Can., 39 Aust., 2 B.W.I., 1 Unknown burials, and 5 special memorials.

648 DERNANCOURT COMMUNAL CEME-TERY EXTENSION (SOMME). NW. of Com. Cem.; 3rd Casualty Clearing Sta. was here in March 1918, was evacuated on March 26th, and remained in enemy hands until recapture by 12th Div. and 33rd U.S.A. Div. Aug. 9th. Records 1,503 U.K., 418 Aust., 51 N.Z., 33 S.A., 8 Can., 5 Ind., 1 B.W.I., 112 Unknown, 3 Chin., 3 German burials, and 30 special memorials.

647 DERNANCOURT COMMUNAL CEME-TERY (SOMME). 3 miles S. of Albert Sta., W. of village. Used from Sept. 1915 to Aug. 1916, and again in retreat of March 1918. Records 124 U.K. and 3 Aust. burials.

A

1001 HANNESCAMPS NEW MILITARY CEMETERY (P. de C.). 7¾ miles W. of Miraumont Sta. Is extension of Churchyard on W. of village. Until June 1916, and again in 1918, the village was just behind the British front line. Records 99 U.K., 2 Ind. burials, and 1 special memorial.

B

1923 ROSSIGNOL WOOD CEMETERY, HEBUTERNE (P. de C.). 4 miles NW. of Miraumont Sta., 1½ miles N. of Puisieux on road to Gommecourt. Begun March 14th 1917 by N. and S. Staffs. Rgts. Used again Aug. 1918 by N.Z. Rgts. Records 34 U.K., 7 N.Z., and 70 German burials.

C

2421 WARRY COPSE CEMETERY, COUR-CELLES-LE-COMTE (P. de C.). 10 miles S. of Arras, SE. of village on path 1 mile S. of Cour-celles-le-Comte Halte. Casualties from assault on Aug. 21st–23rd 1918 in Battle of Bapaume, the village of Courcelles being taken on the 21st. Records 40 U.K. burials.

D

930 GOMIECOURT SOUTH CEMETERY (P. de C.). 2 miles NE. of Achiet-le-Grand Sta., SE. of village, near cross-roads to Achiet and Sapignies. Gomiecourt fell to 3rd Div. on Aug. 23rd 1918 in first stages of Third Army's advance. Records 206 U.K. and 27 German burials.

46 FONCQUEVIL-
LERS MILITARY
CEMETERY (P. de C.).
½ miles W. of Miraumont
Sta. on W. outskirts of
village. Begun by French
troops, but taken over by
British in summer of 1915.
In 1915–16 was on Allied
front line.   Records 625
U.K., 12 N.Z., 6 Aust., 2
Chin., 1 French, 4 Ger-
man burials, and 2 special
memorials.

932   GOMMECOURT
WOOD NEW CEME-
TERY, FONCQUE-
VILLERS (P. de C.).   7
miles W. of Achiet Sta.
on road between Fonc-
quevillers and Gomme-
court.   The wood was
attacked by 46th (N.
Mid.) Div. and S. part of
village by 56th (London)
Div. July 1st 1916 in
First Battle of Somme.
Records 682 U.K., 56
N.Z., 1 Aust. burials, and
10 special memorials.

31   GOMMECOURT
BRITISH CEMETERY,
No. 2, HEBUTERNE
(P. de C.).   12 miles SW.
f Arras, 5 miles NW. of
Miraumont Sta., S. of
village near road to Buc-
uoy.   The village and
surrounding woods were
German stronghold and
were attacked by Terri-
torial Divs. in First Battle
f Somme 1916.   Re-
ords 1,291 U.K., 47
N.Z., 26 Aust., and 1
French burials.

1698 OWL TRENCH CEMETERY, HEBUTERNE (P. de C.). 5½ miles W. of Achiet Sta., E. of village. Owl Trench was raided by 4th N.Z.R.B. July 15th 1918 and cleared by 1st Auckland Rgt. five days later, but graves from 31st Div. Feb. 27th 1917 in attack on German rearguard. Records 53 U.K. burials.

1043 HEBUTERNE MILITARY CEMETERY (P. de C.). 9 miles N. of Albert, 5 miles N. of Beaucourt-Hamel Sta., W. of village in orchard. Begun by 48th Div. July 30th 1915 used through Somme offensive July 1916 until Aug. 1918. Records 705 U.K., 48 N.Z., and 5 German burials.

1042 HEBUTERNE COMMUNAL CEMETERY (P. de C.). 9 miles N. of Albert, 5 miles N. of Beaucourt-Hamel Sta., ½ mile S. of village near road to Auchonvillers. In Brit. hands from 1915 to Mar. 1918, Germans held E. of village until Feb. 1917 and again in summer of 1918. Records 54 U.K. and 2 Can. burials.

1823 QUESNOY FARM MILITARY CEMETERY, BUCQUOY (P. de C.). 11 miles S. of Arras, 3½ miles W. of Achiet-le-Grand Sta., 2 miles NW. of village, E. of road to Monchy-au-Bois. Casualties from 15th and 16th Lancs. Fus., and 1/6th and 2nd Manch. Rgt., who fell April 5th–25th 1918. Records 60 U.K. burials.

2131 SHRINE CEMETERY, BUCQUOY (P. de C.). 4¾ miles W. of Achiet Sta. on road to Hannescamps. Begun by 46th (N. Mid.) Div. March 1917, enlarged Aug. 1918. Records 73 U.K., 8 Aust., 7 N.Z., 1 Unknown, and 1 German burials.

400 BUCQUOY COMMUNAL CEMETERY EXTENSION (P. de C.). 4 miles W. of Achiet Sta., E. of village. Made by R.N. Div. Sept. 1918. Occupied by 7th Div. on March 17th 1917, and was scene of very heavy fighting in March and April 1918. Records 68 U.K. burials.

1816 QUEEN'S CEME-TERY, BUCQUOY (P. de C.). 4 miles W. of Achiet Sta., S. of village. Taken by 7th Div. 1917, partly lost after gallant defence by 62nd (W. Riding), 37th and 42nd (E. Lancs.) Divs. April 1918, retaken Aug. 21st. Records 698 U.K., 28 N.Z., 5 French burials, and 10 special memorials.

1840 RAILWAY CUT-TING CEMETERY, COURCELLES - LE - COMTE (P. de C.). 10 miles S. of Arras, 1½ miles N. of Achiet-le-Grand Sta., 1 mile S. of village, E. of road to Achiet. Courcelles was taken Aug. 21st 1918 by Byng's Third Army.   Records 108 U.K. burials.

750   ERVILLERS MILITARY   CEME-TERY (P. de C.). 9 miles S. of Arras, 200 yards SW. of Ervillers Church near road to Achiet-le-Grand. Begun by Germans July 1916, taken by British and used until Dec. 1917. Records 66 U.K. and 1 Aust. burials.

2126 SERRE ROAD CEMETERY, No. 1, HEBUTERNE. 1,000 yards W. of village, on road to Mailly-Maillet, nearest sta. Beaucourt-Hamel. Made by V Corps in May 1917, but enlarged after Armistice. Records 2,106 U.K., 149 Aust., 123 Can., 27 N.Z., 6 S.A., 1 Newfld. burials, and 22 special memorials.

2127 SERRE ROAD CEMETERY No. 2, BEAUMONT - HAMEL (SOMME). 7 miles N. of Albert, 3 miles NW. of Beaucourt-Hamel Sta., 1 mile SW. of Serre on road to Mailly-Maillet. Original burials were made July and Nov. 1916 during Battle of Somme. Enlarged after Armistice by concentration of isolated graves and small Cems. Records 2,931 U.K., 313 Aust., 90 Can., 19 N.Z., 9 S.A., and 3 German burials.

2128 SERRE ROAD CEMETERY No. 3, PUISIEUX (P. de C.). In fields, 300 yards NE. of Serre Road Cem. No. 1. A new road, the Chemin des Cimetières, will lead to it. Records 81 U.K. and 4 special memorials.

9 ACHIET - LE - GRAND COMMUNAL CEMETERY EXTENSION (P. de C.). 600 yards NW. of sta. and village. Occupied by 7th Bedfords March 17th 1917. Lost after defence by 1/6th Manchesters, March 25th 1918, and recaptured Aug. 23rd 1918. Records 1,244 U.K., 94 N.Z., 61 Aust., 4 S.A., 3 Can., 1 Newfld., 40 German burials, and 18 special memorials.

1815 QUEEN'S CEMETERY, PUISIEUX (P. de C.). 8½ miles N. of Albert, 5½ miles from Beaucourt - Hamel Sta., W. of Serre, ½ mile N. of Hebuterne road. Used during first Battle of the Somme July–Nov. 1916, and for a few casualties in 1917. Records 311 U.K. burials.

1380 LUKE COPSE BRITISH CEMETERY, PUISIEUX (P. de C.). 8½ miles N. of Albert, 6 miles from Beaucourt-Hamel Sta., E. of Serre, 600 yards from Hébuterne road. Casualties from attacks on Serre July 1st 1916, Beaucourt and Thiepval Nov. 13th 1916. (Mem. was erected to men of 2nd Suffolk Rgt. who fell Nov. 13th 1916.) Records 72 U.K. burials.

2209   TEN TREE
ALLEY CEMETERY,
PUISIEUX (P. de C.).
8½ miles N. of Albert, 6¼
miles from Beaucourt-
Hamel Sta., S. of Serre,
500 yards from road to
Beaucourt - sur - Ancre.
Burials from Fourth
Army (V Corps) who
fell in fighting prior and
subsequent to German
retirement March 1917.
Records 67 U.K. burials.

791 EUSTON ROAD
CEMETERY, COLIN-
CAMPS (SOMME).   7
miles N. of Albert, 1¾
miles from Mailly-Maillet
Sta. near road junction 1
mile E. of village.   Used
as front-line burial ground
during and after unsuc-
cessful attack on Serre on
July 1st 1916.   Records
866 U.K., 287 N.Z., 26
Aust., 3 Can., 1 Ind., 76
Unknown burials, and 34
special memorials.

2177   SUCRERIE
MILITARY CEME-
TERY, COLINCAMPS
(SOMME).   7 miles N.
of Albert, 1 mile E. of
village. Begun by French
1915, extended by Brit.
1 mile from front line
until spring of 1917.   In
March 1918 the N.Z.
Div. were engaged at
Sucrerie.   Records 827
U.K., 65 N.Z., 2 Can.
burials, and 7 special
memorials.

205 BEAUMONT-HAMEL BRITISH CEMETERY (SOMME) 1½ miles NW. of Beaucourt-Hamel Sta., 500 yards NW. of village. Reached on July 1st 1916 by 29th Div. Attacked and taken on Nov. 13th 1916 by 51st (Highland) Div. Records 111 U.K., 1 Can., 1 Newfld., 63 Unknown burials, and 2 special memorials.

A

A

1842 RAILWAY HOLLOW CEMETERY, HEBUTERNE (P. de C.). 8½ miles N. of Albert, 6¼ miles from Beaucourt-Hamel Sta., W. of Serre, 900 yards N. of Hébuterne road. Burials from Fourth Army (V Corps) who fell in attack on Serre July 1st 1916. Large number of York and Lanc. Rgt. Records 107 U.K. and 2 French burials.

B

B

1572 MUNICH TRENCH BRITISH CEMETERY, BEAUMONT-HAMEL (SOMME). 2¼ miles N. of Beaucourt-Hamel Sta., 150 yards W. of Waggon road. Beaumont-Hamel was captured Nov. 1916, in Battle of Ancre. Records 126 U.K. burials.

1866 REDAN RIDGE CEMETERY, No. 2, BEAUMONT-HAMEL (SOMME). 8 miles N. of Albert, 2 miles NW. of Beaucourt-Hamel Sta., ¾ mile NW. of village, near 'Watling Street.' Cem. on lower ground 100 yards W. of old German front line. Records 279 U.K. burials of the 2nd, 4th and 29th Divs.

1867 REDAN RIDGE CEMETERY, No. 3, BEAUMONT-HAMEL (SOMME). 400 yards N. of Redan Ridge Cem. No. 2. Cem. among old German front-line trenches, and records 67 U.K. burials, mostly of the 2nd Div.

2399 WAGGON ROAD CEMETERY, BEAU-MONT-HAMEL (SOMME). 2 miles N. of Beaucourt-Hamel Sta., E. of Waggon Road, which runs N. to Serre. Beaumont-Hamel was taken Nov. 1916 in Battle of Ancre. Records 195 U.K. burials.

883 FRANKFURT TRENCH BRITISH CEMETERY, BEAU-MONT-HAMEL (SOMME). 1¾ miles NW. of Beaucourt-Hamel Sta., 1 mile NE. of village. Taken on Nov. 13th 1916 by 51st (Highland), and 63rd (R.N.) Divs. Records 161 U.K. burials.

1614 NEW MUNICH TRENCH BRITISH CEMETERY, BEAU-MONT-HAMEL (SOMME). 1¾ miles NW. of Beaucourt-Hamel Sta., N.E. of village. Munich Trench was occupied by 51st (Highland) Div. Nov. 15th 1916; New Munich Trench was dug previous night by 2/2nd Highland Field Co. Records 146 U.K. burials.

1037 HAWTHORN RIDGE CEMETERY No. 1 AUCHONVIL-LERS (SOMME). 6 miles N. of Albert, 1¼ miles NW. of Beaucourt-Hamel Sta., near Newfld. Mem. Park, NW. of 51st (Highland) Div. Mem. Made by V Corps after Somme offensives 1916. Records 152 U.K. and 1 Newfld. burials.

1038 HAWTHORN RIDGE CEMETERY No. 2, AUCHONVILLERS (SOMME). 6 miles N. of Albert, 1¼ miles NW. of Beaucourt-Hamel Sta. in Newfld. Mem. Park, 170 yards W. of 51st (Highland) Div. Mem. Made by V Corps after Somme offensives 1916. Records 191 U.K. and 23 Newfld. burials.

1127 HUNTER'S CEMETERY, BEAUMONT-HAMEL (SOMME). 6 miles N. of Albert, 1 mile NW. of Beaucourt-Hamel Sta. in Newfld. Mem. Park, 75 yards W. of 51st (Highland) Div. Mem. overlooking 'Y' Ravine. Scene of fiercest fighting. Made after capture of Beaumont-Hamel Nov. 13th 1916 by 51st Div. Records 46 U.K. burials.

43 ANCRE BRITISH CEMETERY, BEAUMONT-HAMEL (SOMME). 4½ miles N. of Albert and 1,000 yards SW. of Beaucourt-Hamel Sta., on Albert-Miraumont road. Successfully attacked on Nov. 13th and 14th 1916 by 51st (Highland), 63rd (R.N.) 39th and 19th (Western) Divs. Records 2,446 U.K., 32 Newfld., 2 N.Z., 1 S.A., 1 German burials, and 59 special memorials.

2472 'Y' RAVINE CEMETERY, BEAU-MONT-HAMEL (SOMME). 1¾ miles W. of Beaucourt-Hamel Sta., ½ mile S. of village within the Newfld. Mem. Park. Village was attacked and reached on July 1st 1916 by units of 29th Div. (which included R. New-fld. Rgt.). Records 328 U.K. and 38 Newfld. burials, also 61 special memorials.

110 AUCHONVIL-LERS MILITARY CEMETERY (SOMME) ½ mile from Mailly-Maillet Sta., 300 yards from Auchonvillers Church at end of path leading N. from road to Mailly-Maillet. Begun by French, June 1915. Used by Field Ambs. and fighting units. Records 496 U.K., 24 N.Z., 8 Newfld., and 6 French burials.

1179 KNIGHTS-BRIDGE CEMETERY, MESNIL - MARTIN-SART (SOMME). 1¼ miles N. of Mesnil-Martinsart Sta. Begun during Battles of Somme 1916 and used by fighting units until German re-treat in February 1917; again used from March to July 1918. Records 425 U.K., 39 Newfld., 18 N.Z., 1 Aust., and 65 Unknown burials.

1473 MESNIL RIDGE
CEMETERY, MES-
NIL - MARTINSART
(SOMME). 5 miles N.
of Albert, 1¼ miles N. of
Mesnil village and sta., on
rough field road. Used
from Aug. 1915 to July
1916; contains large
number of 2nd S. Wales
Borderers who fell April
6th 1916. Records 90
U.K. and 1 Newfld.
burials.

995 HAMEL MILI-
TARY CEMETERY,
BEAUMONT-HAMEL
(SOMME). 4 miles N.
of Albert, 1 mile S. of
Beaucourt-Hamel Sta., S.
of village, W. of Albert
road. Beaumont-Hamel
was taken by 51st (High-
land) Div. Nov. 13th
1916. Records 488 U.K.,
1 N.Z., and 4 German
burials.

1486 MILL ROAD
CEMETERY, THIEP-
VAL (SOMME). 2 miles
S. of Beaucourt-Hamel
Sta. between Thiepval
and St. Pierre-Divion.
18th Div. took Thiepval
Sept. 26th 1916 (Mem.
in Chateau grounds),
finally retaken by 38th
(Welsh) and 17th Divs.
March 25th 1918. Re-
cords 1,298 U.K. and 6
special memorials.

551 CONNAUGHT CEMETERY, THIEP-VAL (SOMME). 1¾ miles S. of Beaucourt-Hamel Sta., 3½ miles from Albert. NW. of village. Thiepval was attacked by 36th (Ulster) Div., July 1st 1916 (see Mem.), taken by 18th Div. Sept. 26th, and finally retaken on Aug. 24th 1918 by 17th and 18th (Welsh) Divs. Records 1,278 U.K. burials and 7 special memorials.

2173 STUMP ROAD CEMETERY, GRAND-COURT (SOMME). 1¾ miles E. of Beaucourt-Hamel Sta., ½ mile from village. Occupied by 63rd (R.N.) Div. on Feb. 7th 1917, made by 7th Buffs. following month. Records 237 U.K., 24 Can., and 2 Unknown burials.

1870 REGINA TRENCH CEME-TERY, GRAND-COURT (SOMME). 3 miles E. of Beaucourt-Hamel Sta. NW. of Cour-celette. Was a German work, captured by 5th Can. Bgde. on Oct. 1st 1916; finally cleared by 4th Can. Div. on Nov. 11th 1916. Records 1,667 U.K., 563 Can., 35 Aust. burials, and 14 special memorials.

10 ADANAC MILITARY CEMETERY, MIRAUMONT - PYS (SOMME). 2 miles S. of Miraumont Sta. on road to Courcelette. Miraumont and Pys were occupied on Feb. 24th–25th 1917 in German retreat, and finally fell to the 42nd (E. Lancs.) Div. on Aug. 24th 1918. Records 1,973 U.K., 1,071 Can., 70 N.Z., 53 Aust., 5 Unknown, 1 German burials, and 13 special memorials.

961 GREVILLERS BRITISH CEMETERY (P. de C.). 1½ miles W. of Bapaume Sta., E. of village. From April 1917 to March 1918, the 3rd, 29th, and 3rd Aust. C.C.Ss. were posted here. Grévillers was recaptured by N.Z. Div. Aug. 24th 1918. (Mem. to N.Z. 'Missing' at N. end of Cem.). Records 1,498 U.K., 413 Aust., 153 N.Z., 14 Can., 2 Ind., 1 S.A., 1 B.W.I., 4 Unknown, 18 French burials, and 20 special memorials.

1472 MESNIL COMMUNAL CEMETERY EXTENSION (SOMME). 4¼ miles N. of Albert Sta., ½ mile S. of Mesnil Sta. on road to Martinsart. Begun in July 1916 and used again as a front-line Cem. in 1918. Records 252 U.K., 7 N.Z., 5 Can., 59 Unknown burials, and 10 special memorials.

1439   MARTINSART BRITISH CEMETERY, MESNIL - MARTIN-SART (SOMME). 3¼ miles N. of Albert Sta., 1¼ miles S. of Mesnil Sta., S. of Martinsart. Begun in June 1916 and used as a front-line Cem. until Oct. 1916 and in Sept. 1918. Records 377 U.K., 8 N.Z., 1 Aust., 96 Unknown burials, and 6 special memorials.

135   AVELUY WOOD CEMETERY (LANCA-SHIRE DUMP) MES-NIL - MARTINSART (SOMME).   3 miles N. of Albert Sta., E. of Albert-Hamel road. By side of this road, within N. boundary of wood, 'Lancashire Dump' was made. Begun June 1916. Records 334 U.K., 26 Aust. burials, and 20 special memorials.

134   AVELUY COM-MUNAL CEMETERY EXTENSION (SOMME). 2 miles N. of Albert, ½ mile E. of Aveluy Halte in village. Held by British in succession to French from July 1915 to March 26th 1918. Records 549 U.K., 54 Aust., 7 Can., 2 Ind., 1 S.A. burials, and 3 special memorials.

124 AUTHUILE MILITARY CEMETERY (SOMME). 3 miles N. of Albert, on E. bank of R. Ancre, S. edge of village. Authuile was 1 mile W. of German front-line trenches on July 1st 1916 before Battle of Somme. Casualties from Sept. 1915 to Dec. 1916. Records 451 U.K., 18 Ind., 3 S.A., and 1 German burials.

1367 LONSDALE CEMETERY, AVELUY (SOMME). 4 miles N. of Albert Sta., 1,000 yards E. of Authuile village. July 1st 1916 the 32nd Div., including 1st Dorsets and 11th (Lonsdale) Batt. of the Border Rgt., stormed the Leipzig Salient. Records 1,515 U.K., 4 Aust., 2 French burials, and 22 special memorials.

299 BLIGHTY VALLEY CEMETERY, AUTHUILE WOOD, AVELUY (SOMME). 2½ miles N. of Albert Sta., midway between Authuile and Aveluy. Blighty Valley was for some time an important though dangerous route to trenches. Records 993 U.K., 2 Aust., 1 Can. burials, and 29 special memorials.

354 BOUZINCOURT RIDGE CEMETERY, ALBERT (SOMME). 1¾ miles N. of Albert Sta. near track to Bouzincourt. East end of Albert was attacked June 1918 by 12th and 18th Divs. and cleared in Aug. Cem. begun by V Corps. Records 667 U.K., 35 Aust., 6 Can. burials, and 1 special memorial.

219 BECOURT MILITARY CEMETERY, BECORDEL-BECOURT (SOMME). 2¼ miles E. of Albert Sta. Begun in Aug. 1915 by 51st (Highland) Div., carried on by 18th and other Divs. Records 606 U.K., 72 Aust., 31 Can., 3 S.A. burials, and 1 special memorial.

572 COURCELETTE BRITISH CEMETERY (SOMME). 3½ miles S. of Miraumont Sta., 7 miles NE. of Albert, SW. of village. Stormed in Battle of Flers-Courcelette Sept. 15th 1916 by 2nd Can. Div. and Tanks. Records 780 Can., 657 U.K., 514 Aust., 1 N.Z., 4 Unknown burials, and 9 special memorials.

1696 OVILLERS MILITARY CEMETERY (SOMME). 2½ miles NE. of Albert Sta., SW. of village. Attacked July 1st 1916 by 8th Div., again by 12th (Eastern) and 25th Divs. on July 7th, cleared by 48th (S. Mid.) Div. July 17th, finally retaken Aug. 24th 1918 by 38th (Welsh) Div. Records 3,004 U.K., 88 Can., 42 Aust., 7 S.A., 5 N.Z., 121 French burials, and 60 special memorials.

954 GRANDCOURT ROAD CEMETERY, GRANDCOURT (SOMME). 2⅝ miles SE. of Beaucourt - Hamel Sta., 1 mile S. of village, on 'Stump Road'. Reached July 1st 1916 by 36th (Ulster) Div., but not taken until night of Feb. 5th–6th 1917. Records 389 U.K., 1 Can. burials, and 1 special memorial.

900 FRICOURT NEW MILITARY CEMETERY (SOMME). 1 mile N. of Fricourt Sta. Made by 10th W. Yorks. on old German front line. Attacked on July 1st 1916 by 17th Div. and occupied on following day. Records 208 U.K., and 2 N.Z. burials.

938 GORDON DUMP CEMETERY, OVILLERS-LA-BOISSELLE (SOMME). 4 miles NE. of Albert Sta., ½ mile due E. of La Boisselle. The village was attacked by 34th Div. July 1st 1916, taken by 19th (Western) Div. July 3rd–4th, lost in March 1918, retaken in Aug. Records 1,546 U.K., 92 Aust., 2 Can., 1 Ind. burials, and 34 special memorials.

1711 PEAKE WOOD CEMETERY, FRICOURT (SOMME). 2 miles from Fricourt Sta., on NW. side of Contalmaison road. Peake Wood fell into British hands on July 5th 1916 and was used as a frontline Cem. until Feb. 1917. Records 87 U.K., 7 Aust., 1 Can. burials, and 6 special memorials.

552 CONTALMAISON CHÂTEAU CEMETERY (SOMME). 4 miles NE. of Albert, in village, N. of main street in Château grounds. The Château and village were captured on morning of July 14th 1916 by 1st Black Watch and 1st Camerons with 1st Gloucester Rgt. in support. Records 264 U.K., 21 Aust., and 4 Can. burials.

1437 MARTINPUICH BRITISH CEMETERY (SOMME). 7½ miles NE. of Albert Sta., S. of village. Captured by 15th (Scot.) Div. on Sept. 15th 1916. School playground at Martinpuich presented by 47th (London) Div. as Mem. to those who fell in High Wood. Records 70 U.K., 34 Aust., 1 Can. burials, and 4 special memorials.

2414 WARLENCOURT BRITISH CEMETERY (P. de C.). 3 miles SW. of Bapaume Sta, on Albert-Bapaume road, N. of Butte de Warlencourt. Scene of fierce fighting by 47th (London), 51st (Highland) and 42nd (E. Lancs.) Divs. in 1916 and 1918. Records 2,765 U.K., 461 Aust., 126 S.A., 79 N.Z., 4 Can., and 2 French burials, and 71 special memorials.

1352 LONDON CEMETERY, HIGH WOOD, LONGUEVAL (SOMME). 3¼ miles N. of Montauban Sta., NW. of Longueval opp. High Wood ; group of battlefield graves from 47th (London) Div. (Mem. on SW.), who finally cleared the wood on Sept. 15th 1916. Records 101 U.K. burials.

2230 THISTLE DUMP CEMETERY, HIGH WOOD, LONGUE-VAL (SOMME). 2½ miles N. of Montauban Sta., on NW. of village, ½ mile S. of High Wood. Taken for a day by 7th Div. and Cav. July 14th 1916, partly retaken by 33rd Div. on 20th, struggle continued by 51st (Highland) Div. until Aug. 7th 1916. Records 107 U.K., 37 N.Z., 36 Aust., 12 Unknown, 7 German burials, and 4 special memorials.

19 A.I.F. BURIAL GROUND, GRASS LANE, FLERS (SOMME). 4 miles S. of Bapaume, 1 mile NE. of Flers. Captured on Sept. 15th 1916 by N.Z. and 41st Divs., following the newly revealed Tanks. Records 2,811 U.K., 402 Aust., 84 N.Z., 68 Can., 27 S.A., 55 Unknown, 163 French, 3 German burials, and 26 special memorials.

968 GUARDS' CEME-TERY, LESBŒUFS (SOMME). 2½ miles N. of Combles Sta., 7 miles E. of Albert, ½ mile SW. of village on road to Ginchy. Attacked by Guards Div. on Sept. 15th 1916 and captured by them on 25th. (See Grenadier Guards and Guards Div. Mems. on Ginchy road). Records 2,827 U.K., 202 Aust., 11 N.Z., 4 Newfld., 1 Can. burial, and 88 special memorials.

408 BULLS ROAD CEMETERY, FLERS (SOMME). 3½ miles from Guillemont Sta., E. of village on road to Lesbœufs. Captured by 41st and N.Z. Divs. on Sept. 15th 1916 in Battle of Flers-Courcelette. Records 485 U.K., 148 Aust., 120 N.Z., 2 Unknown burials, and 15 special memorials.

188 BAZENTIN-LE-PETIT COMMUNAL CEMETERY EXTENSION (SOMME). 3 miles N. of Montauban, E. of village. Captured July 14th 1916 by 3rd and 7th Divs., recaptured Aug. 25th 1918 by 38th (Welsh) Div. Records 180 U.K., 5 Can., 1 Aust. burials, and 59 special memorials.

189 BAZENTIN-LE-PETIT MILITARY CEMETERY (SOMME) 3¼ miles N. of Montauban Sta., W. of village. Bazentin Wood was captured July 14th 1916 by 21st Div. Begun July 1916 and used until May 1917 as front-line Cem. Records 116 U.K. 55 Aust., and 10 S.A. burials.

829 FLATIRON COPSE CEMETERY, MAMETZ (SOMME). 2½ miles from Mametz Halte, 4 miles E. of Albert, S. end of Copse. Cleared by 3rd and 7th Divs. on July 14th 1916. Records 1,475 U.K., 30 N.Z., 17 Aust., 1 S.A. burials, and 45 special memorials.

467 CATERPILLAR VALLEY CEMETERY, LONGUEVAL (SOMME). 2 miles NW. of Guillemont Sta., 500 yards W. of village on road to Bazentin. Captured after fierce fighting in July 1916, lost March 1918, recovered Aug. 28th by 38th (Welsh) Div. Mem. to N.Z. 'Missing' on E. of Cem. Records 5,197 U.K., 214 N.Z., 98 Aust., 19 S.A., 6 Can., 2 Newfld. burials, and 38 special memorials.

642 DELVILLE WOOD CEMETERY, LONGUEVAL (SOMME). 2½ miles N. of Montauban Sta., on road to Ginchy, opp. S.A. Mem. and Delville Wood. The 2nd, 14th (Light), 17th and especially the 9th (Scottish) Divs. were heavily engaged within the wood. Records 5,206 U.K., 151 S.A., 81 Aust., 29 Can., 19 N.Z., 3 Unknown burials, and 30 special memorials.

1364 LONGUEVAL ROAD CEMETERY (SOMME). 1½ miles N. of Montauban Sta., S. of village, on road to Bernafay Wood. Cleared by 5th Div. July 1916, finally retaken by 38th (Welsh) Div. and Carabineers on Aug. 28th 1918. Records 182 U.K., 22 Aust., 7 Can., 7 N.Z., 1 Newfld., 1 German burials, and 3 special memorials.

1809 QUARRY CEMETERY, MONTAUBAN (SOMME). 1 mile NW. of sta., on road to Bazentin. Taken by 30th and 18th Divs. July 1st 1916, retaken by 7th Buffs and 11th R. Fus. (18th Div.) Aug. 25th 1918. Records 648 U.K., 36 N.Z., 25 Aust., 6 S.A., 1 Fr., 15 German burials, and 28 special memorials.

246 BERNAFAY WOOD BRITISH CEMETERY, MONTAUBAN (SOMME). 1,100 yards N. of sta., on Longueval - Maricourt road. Taken by 9th (Scot.) Div. July 3rd–4th 1916; same Div. was driven from wood Mar. 25th 1918, recaptured it for a time, finally regained by 18th Div. Aug. 27th. Records 793 U.K., 122 Aust., 4 S.A., 2 N.Z., 1 Ind. burials, and 32 special memorials.

973   GUILLEMONT ROAD CEMETERY, GUILLEMONT (SOMME). 1¼ miles E. of Montauban Sta., between village and Trônes Wood. Important point in German defences July 1916. Retaken on Aug. 29th 1918 by 18th and 38th (Welsh) Divs. Records 2,251 U.K., 1 Can., 1 Aust., 1 S.A., 1 Newfld., 1 French, and 3 German burials, also 8 special memorials.

630 DANTZIG ALLEY BRITISH CEMETERY, MAMETZ (SOMME). ¾ mile NE. of sta., E. of village on N. of road to Montauban. Carried by 7th Div. on July 1st 1916, after hard fighting at Dantzig Alley. Records 1,923 U.K., 17 N.Z., 13 Aust., 10 Can., 3 S.A. burials, and 87 special memorials.

1453   MÉAULTE MILITARY CEMETERY (SOMME). 2½ miles S. of Albert Sta. on W. side of road to Etinehem. Evacuated March 26th 1918 after rearguard fight by 9th (Scot.) Div. Recaptured by 12th (Eastern) Div. and Tanks on Aug. 22nd 1918. Records 283 U.K., 6 Ind., 3 Can., 1 Aust., 7 Unknown burials, and 11 special memorials.

635 DARTMOOR CEMETERY, BECOR-DEL-BÉCOURT (SOMME). 1 mile W. of Fricourt Sta., N. of village on Bécourt road. Named Dartmoor at request of Devon Rgt. Taken by Germans in March 1918, retaken by 12th Div. in Aug. Records 632 U.K., 71 Aust., 59 N.Z., 4 Can., 1 Ind., and 1 Unknown burials.

963 GROVE TOWN CEMETERY, MÉ-AULTE (SOMME). $4\frac{1}{2}$ miles S. of Albert Sta., $1\frac{1}{2}$ miles S. of Méaulte on secondary road to Bray-sur-Somme. 34th and 2/2nd London C.C.S. were posted here Sept. 1916 to deal with casualties from Somme battlefields. Records 1,366 U.K., 14 Aust., 11 New-fld., 1 N.Z., 1 French, and 34 German burials.

525 CITADEL NEW MILITARY CEME-TERY, FRICOURT (SOMME). $1\frac{3}{4}$ miles S. of Fricourt Sta. on road to Bray. Sta. for Field Ambs. before Battle of Somme. Village was captured July 2nd 1916 by 17th Div. Records 379 U.K. burials.

655 DEVONSHIRE CEMETERY, MAMETZ (SOMME). $\frac{1}{2}$ mile SE. of halte and 4 miles E. of Albert. 8th and 9th Devons (7th Div.) attacked here July 1st 1916. Mametz Wood NE. of village was taken on July 7th and following days. Records 163 U.K. burials.

1750 POINT 110 NEW MILITARY CEMETERY, FRICOURT (SOMME). $3\frac{1}{2}$ miles E. of Albert, S. of Fricourt village and sta., E. of rough track to Bray. The strongly fortified Fricourt Salient was cut off and destroyed July 2nd 1916 in the first assaults in Battle of Somme. Records 64 U.K. burials.

1751 POINT 110 OLD MILITARY CEMETERY, FRICOURT (SOMME). $3\frac{1}{2}$ miles E. of Albert, S. of Fricourt village and sta., W. of rough track to Bray, 250 yards N. of New Mil. Cem. Fricourt fell Sunday July 2nd 1916. Records 92 U.K. burials.

937 GORDON CEME-
TERY, MAMETZ
(SOMME). 1,000 yards
E. of Halte, 4 miles E. of
Albert on Péronne road.
Made by 2nd Gordons
(7th Div.) in a British
support trench July 1st
1916, the first day of the
first Battle of the Somme.
Records 102 U.K. burials.

1636 NORFOLK
CEMETERY, BECOR-
DEL-BÉCOURT
(SOMME). 3¼ miles E.
of Albert Sta., N. of vil-
lage on Bécourt road.
Begun by 1st Norfolks
Aug. 1915, and used by
other units until Aug.
1916. Records 407 U.K.,
9 Aust., 3 S.A., 2 Can., 1
N.Z., 1 Ind., and 126
Unknown burials.

899 FRICOURT
BRITISH CEMETERY
(BRAY ROAD)
(SOMME). 250 yards
NE. of Fricourt Sta., 3
miles E. of Albert. S. of
village on road to Bray-
sur-Somme. Made by
7th E. Yorks July 5th–
11th 1916, who erected a
granite Mem. to their
dead in Cem. Records
131 U.K. and 1 N.Z.
burials, and 1 special
memorial.

462 CARNOY MILITARY CEMETERY (SOMME). S. of village alongside halte. Begun in Aug. 1915 by 2nd K.O.S.B. and 2nd K.O. Y.L.I., when village was immediately S. of British front line. Records 828 U.K., 5 N.Z., 2 Can., 1 Aust., 1 S.A. burials, and 18 special memorials.

387 BRONFAY FARM MILITARY CEMETERY, BRAY-SUR-SOMME (SOMME). 3 miles NE. of sta., 5 miles SE. of Albert, on road to Maricourt. Used by British from Aug. 1915 to Feb. 1917, particularly in Battles of the Somme. Records 516 U.K., 15 Aust., 2 Ind., 1 S.A., 1 Unknown burials, and 2 special memorials.

1726 PÉRONNE ROAD CEMETERY, MARICOURT (SOMME). 6½ miles from Albert on Péronne-Albert road. Nearest sta. Montauban. Is a concentration Cem. In first Battle of Somme, the junction of French and British lines was at Maricourt. Records 1,298 U.K., 34 S.A., 14 Aust., 1 Can. burials and 3 special memorials.

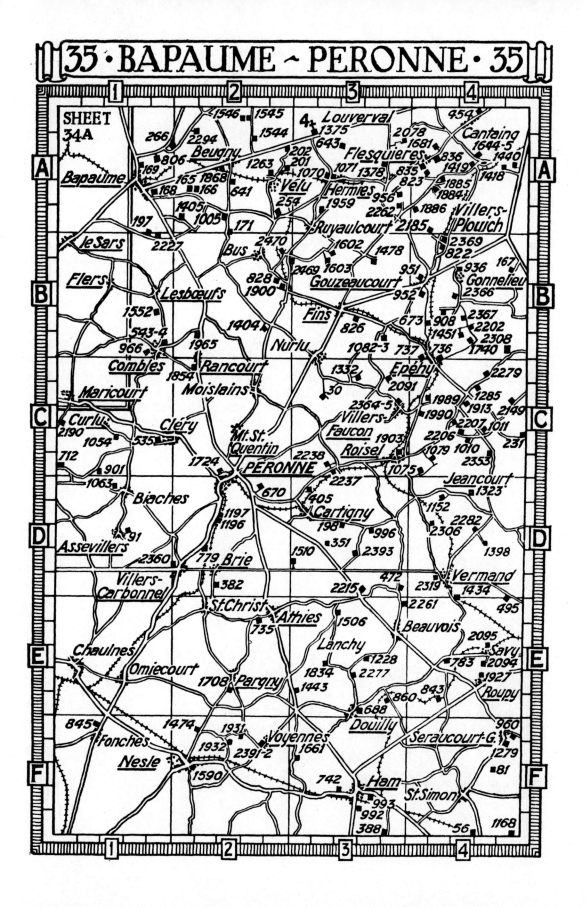

SHEET
34A

BAPAUME—PÉRONNE

MAP SHEET No. 35

BAPAUME is a commune and small town in the Department of the Pas-de-Calais, connected by a light railway with Achiet-le-Grand on the main line from Paris and Amiens to Arras and Douai. It was the scene of a battle on the 3rd January 1871. It was occupied by German forces on the 26th September 1914, and by the British on the 17th March 1917; it was retaken by Germans on the 24th March 1918, and by the New Zealand Division on the following 29th August. It has given its name to the battles of the 24th–25th March 1918 and the 31st August to 3rd September 1918. It was severely damaged by both sides during the War, and it has been 'adopted' by the City of Sheffield.

PÉRONNE is a commune and small town in the Department of the Somme, in the valley of the River Somme. It has a railway station on the main line from Paris to Cambrai and Douai, with light railway connexions.

Péronne has stood many sieges in French and Burgundian history. It was fortified by Vauban. It was captured by the Germans on the 9th January 1871, after a twelve days' siege and a severe bombardment. It fell into German hands again on the 24th September 1914. On the 18th March 1917 the 40th and 48th Divisions entered the town, which had been set on fire by the enemy; and on the 23rd March 1918 the Germans recaptured it. On the 30th August to 1st September 1918 the 2nd Australian Division took Mont-St. Quentin (a feat commemorated by the Battle Memorial erected beside the village street), and on the latter day they entered Péronne.

The town has been 'adopted' by the County Borough of Blackburn.

168 BAPAUME AUSTRALIAN CEMETERY (P. de C.). $\frac{5}{8}$ mile SE. of Bapaume Sta., E. of road to Péronne. Occupied by Brit. March 17th 1917, retaken by N.Z. Div. Aug. 29th 1918. Records 74 Aust., 12 U.K., 1 Ind., 1 Unknown, and 25 German burials.

806 FAVREUIL BRITISH CEMETERY (P. de C.). 1½ miles N. of Bapaume, 500 yards SE. of village, between roads from Favreuil and Bapaume to Beugnâtre. Occupied by British in March 1917, lost in Mar. 1918, and retaken on Aug. 25th by 37th and N.Z. Divs. Records 342 U.K., 26 Aust., 19 N.Z., 3 S.A., 1 Can., 16 German burials, and 5 special memorials.

165 BANCOURT BRITISH CEMETERY (P. de C.). 3 miles E. of Bapaume Sta., E. of village. Recaptured by N.Z. Div. (in particular the 2nd Auck. Batt.) on Aug. 30th 1918. Records 1,999 U.K., 248 Aust., 176 N.Z., 13 Newfld. burials, and 44 special memorials.

1544 MORCHIES AUSTRALIAN CEMETERY (P. de C.). 5 miles NE. of Bapaume Sta., SW. of village on road to Beugny. Captured March 20th 1917, lost March 21st 1918 and retaken Sept. 1918. Begun by Aust. units March 1917. Records 41 U.K., 20 Aust., and 2 German burials.

1546 MORCHIES MILITARY CEMETERY (P. de C.). N. of village and Aust. Cem., W. of road to Noreuil and Lagnicourt. Begun April 1917. Records 128 U.K., 17 Aust., 15 German burials, and 18 special memorials.

1405 MANCHESTER CEMETERY, RIEN-COURT - LES - BA-PAUME (P. de C.). $2\frac{1}{2}$ miles SE. of Bapaume Sta., E. of village. Re-captured by 42nd (E. Lancs.) Div. on evening of Aug. 30th 1918. Re-cords 67 U.K., 1 N.Z., 3 Unknown burials, and 1 special memorial.

197 BEAULENCOURT BRITISH CEMETERY, LIGNY-THILLOY (P. de C.). $2\frac{3}{4}$ miles S. of Bapaume Sta., between villages of Beaulencourt and Ligny-Thilloy. Made by 3rd, 4th, 43rd and 58th Casualty Clearing Stats. Records 564 U.K., 81 N.Z., 51 Aust., 3 Can., 1 Ind., 1 S.A., 14 Chin. burials, and 21 special memorials.

2227 THILLOY ROAD CEMETERY, BEAULENCOURT (P. de C.). 3 miles S. of Bapaume Sta., 1 mile W. of village. Captured in March 1917, lost March 24th–25th 1918 and recovered after severe fighting at end of Aug. Records 230 U.K., 9 N.Z., and 1 B.W.I. burials.

641 DELSAUX FARM CEMETERY, BEUGNY (P. de C.). 700 yards S. of sta., on road to Haplincourt. Lost March 23rd 1918 after gallant defence by 9th Welch Rgt., retaken by 5th Div. Sept. 2nd 1918. Records 482 U.K., 6 N.Z., 3 Can., 2 Aust., and 2 B.W.I. burials.

1263 LEBUCQUIERE COMMUNAL CEMETERY EXTENSION (P. de C.). ½ mile W. of Vélu Sta., on SE. of village. Occupied by Brit. on March 19th 1917, finally re-occupied by 5th Div. on Sept. 3rd 1918. Records 571 U.K., 66 Aust., 21 N.Z., 1 Can., 94 Unknown, 5 German burials, and 21 special memorials.

201 **BEAUMETZ CROSS ROADS CEME-TERY, BEAUMETZ-LES-CAMBRAI** (P. de C.). 7 miles E. of Bapaume, 1 mile N. of Vélu Sta., 500 yards S. of village near Hermies road. Village was evacuated by Germans early in Sept. 1918 consequent to severe attacks by Third Army. Records 211 U.K., 59 Aust., and 12 N.Z. burials.

202 **BEAUMETZ LES-CAMBRAI MILI-TARY CEMETERY, No. 1** (P. de C.). 7 miles E. of Bapaume, 1 mile N. of Vélu Sta., N. of village, near Cambrai road. Scene of heavy fighting in German advance when 25th and 51st Divs. held out all day on March 22nd 1918. Records 257 U.K. burials.

1375 **LOUVERVAL MILITARY CEME-TERY, DOIGNIES, AND MEMORIAL** (Nord). 8 miles E. of Bapaume, 2 miles N. of Hermies Sta.on Bapaume-Cambrai road. Cem. records 118 U.K., 4 Aust., and 2 N.Z. burials. The Mem. records 7,048 'Missing' who fell in the Battle of Cambrai Nov. and Dec. 1917, the Tank Attack, the capture of Bourlon Wood and the German counter-attack.

A

B

A

1868 RED CROSS CORNER CEMETERY, BEUGNY (P. de C.). ½ mile E. of Frémicourt Halte, W. of Beugny village. Made in April 1917 to March 1918 by Field Ambs. and fighting units. Used by Germans March–Aug. 1918. Records 205 U.K., 10 Aust., 4 S.A., 1 German burials, and 1 special memorial.

B

254 BERTINCOURT CHÂTEAU BRITISH CEMETERY (P. de C.). 600 yards W. of Bertincourt Sta., NE. of village on road to Ruyaulcourt. Begun by 7th Batt., K.O.Y.L.I., on March 29th 1917, and used until Sept. 28th 1918. Records 47 U.K. burials.

C

D

C

1070 HERMIES BRITISH CEMETERY (P. de C.). ¼ mile E. of sta. on road to Bertincourt. Seized April 9th 1917 by 2nd and 3rd Aust. Inf. Batts. Held by 17th Div. March 22nd 1918, evacuated and retaken Sept. 1918. Records 81 U.K., 27 Aust. burials, and 1 special memorial.

D

1959 RUYAULCOURT MILITARY CEMETERY (P. de C.). 1 mile E. of Bertincourt Sta., 600 yards NE. of Ruyaulcourt on road to Hermies. Used from April 1917 to March 1918 and again during final advance to Victory Sept. 1918. Records 323 U.K., 20 N.Z., 2 Can., 1 Aust. burials, and 2 special memorials.

1071 HERMIES HILL BRITISH CEMETERY (P. de C.). 84 yards E. of road to Bertincourt, opp. Brit. Cem. Begun Nov. 1917 and used by fighting units until March 1918. Records 949 U.K., 40 Aust., 7 N.Z., 3 Can. burials, and 37 special memorials.

2078 SANDERS KEEP MILITARY CEMETERY, GRAINCOURT LES - HAVRINCOURT (P. de C.). 7 miles W. of Cambrai, 1½ miles N. of Havrincourt Sta., SW. of village, E. of Marquion road. The majority of casualties are from Gds. Div., who fell in storming of Hindenburg Line Sept. 29th 1918. Records 142 U.K. and 49 German burials.

836 FLESQUIÈRES HILL BRITISH CEMETERY (Nord). 6 miles SW. of Cambrai, ¾ mile NW. of Flesquières Sta., E. of village at junction of roads from Anneux and Cantaing. Used as burial ground from Sept. 27th to Oct. 9th during advance to Victory and enlarged after Armistice. Records 820 U.K., 66 N.Z., 20 S.A., 10 Can., 2 Aust. burials, and 3 special memorials.

1378 LOWRIE CEME-
TERY, HAVRIN-
COURT (P. de C.).   ½
mile N. of sta. on E. side
of Canal du Nord, ½ mile
N. of village.   Made by
3rd Div. Burial Officer
Oct. 1918 and named
after him.   Records 251
U.K. burials.

956   GRAND RAVINE
BRITISH CEMETERY,
HAVRINCOURT (P. de
C.).   1 mile SE. of sta., ½
mile SE. of village, in
deep valley.   Made by
62nd (W. Riding) Div.,
who stormed village Nov.
20th 1917 and retook it
Sept. 12th 1918.   Re-
cords 139 U.K. burials.

1885   RIBÉCOURT
RAILWAY CEME-
TERY (Nord).   ½ mile E.
of Flesquières Sta., NE.
of village.   Captured by
9th Norfolks (6th Div.)
Nov. 20th 1917, lost in
March 1918, but recap-
tured by 3rd Div. on
Sept. 27th 1918.   Re-
cords 52 U.K. and 1 N.Z.
burials.

A

A

835 FLESQUIÈRES CHÂTEAU CEMETERY (Nord). 1½ miles N. of Ribécourt Sta., S. of Flesquières village, W. of Château grounds near Ribécourt road. Cem. used from Nov. 1917 to Feb. 1918 (Mem. to 49th Div. at Havrincourt). Records 134 U.K. and 1 Chin. burials.

B

B

1681 ORIVAL WOOD BRITISH CEMETERY, FLESQUIÈRES (Nord). 6 miles SW. of Cambrai, 1½ miles N. of Flesquières Sta., on road to Anneux. Begun during Battle of Cambrai Nov. 1917 and used during Brit. advance Sept.–Oct. 1918. Records 71 U.K. and 20 German burials.

C

1884 RIBÉCOURT BRITISH CEMETERY (Nord). 7 miles SW. of Cambrai, Flesquières Sta., is on N. of village, and Cem. is 200 yards S. on road to Villers-Plouich. Begun Nov. 1917 in first Battle of Cambrai, re-used when 3rd Div. retook village Sept. 27th 1918 in second Battle of Cambrai. Records 267 U.K., 22 N.Z., and 6 German burials.

C

D

D

1886 RIBÉCOURT ROAD CEMETERY, TRESCAULT (P. de C.). 2 miles SW. of Ribécourt Sta., E. of village on road to Ribécourt. The 42nd (E. Lancs.) Div. carried the Hindenburg Line at Trescault Sept. 28th 1918 (Mem. W. of Cem.). Records 255 U.K. and 6 N.Z. burials.

1854 RANCOURT MILITARY CEMETERY (SOMME). 2½ miles E. of Combles Sta. on main Péronne-Bapaume road. In Allied hands until March 24th 1918, was captured by 47th (London) Div. on Sept. 1st 1918. Records 89 U.K. burials and 1 special memorial.

454 CANTAING BRITISH CEMETERY (Nord). 4 miles SW. of Cambrai Sta. on N. outskirts of village. Captured on Nov. 21st 1917 by 51st (Highland) and 6th Divs., with Cavalry and Tanks. Made by 52nd Div. after recapture Sept. 1918. Records 68 U.K. burials.

1418 MARCOING BRITISH CEMETERY (Nord). 4 miles SW. of Cambrai, 1,000 yards E. of Marcoing Sta., on road to Masnières. Created after Armistice from Battles of Cambrai Nov. 1917 and Oct.–Nov. 1918. Contains casualties of 63rd (R.N.) Div. from Villers-Plouich. Records 280 U.K., 58 N.Z., 24 Newfld. and 10 Can. burials.

1440 MASNIÈRES BRITISH CEMETERY, MARCOING (Nord). 4 miles SW. of Cambrai, 1 mile NW. of Masnières Sta., on road from Marcoing to Rumilly. Casualties from Sept. 7th to Oct. 19th 1918, and include Sgt. Neely, V.C., M.M., Roy. Lancs. Rgt. Records 147 U.K., 18 N.Z., and 59 German burials.

2185 SUNKEN ROAD CEMETERY, VILLERS - PLOUICH (Nord). 10 miles SW. of Cambrai, W. of village and sta., N. of road to Beaucamp. Used during first and second Battles of Cambrai Nov. 1917 and Sept. 1918. Records 51 U.K. burials.

826 FINS NEW BRITISH CEMETERY, SOREL - LE - GRAND (SOMME). ½ mile E. of Fins-Sorel Sta., SE. outskirts of village of Fins, on road to Heudecourt. Lost on March 23rd 1918 after stubborn defence by 6th K.O.S.B. and staff of S.A. Bgde. regained following Sept. Records 1,179 U.K., 87 S.A., 5 Can., 3 N.Z., 2 Aust., 1 Guernsey, 234 German burials, and 10 special memorials.

822 FIFTEEN RAVINE BRITISH CEMETERY, VILLERS-PLOUICH (Nord). 1 mile W. of halte in 'Farm Ravine', E. side of rly. Begun by 17th Welch Rgt. in April 1917, after capture of Ravine by 12th S.W. Bordrs., used during Battle of Cambrai. Records 1,139 U.K., 60 N.Z., 10 S.A., 1 Can., 2 German burials, and 54 special memorials.

2369 VILLERS-PLOUICH COMMUNAL CEMETERY (Nord). 10½ miles SW. of Cambrai, N. of Villers-Plouich Sta., in open country 500 yards NE. of village. Majority of Brit. burials date from Nov. and Dec. 1917, many of 63rd (R.N.) Div. Records 52 U.K. and 1 Newfld. burials.

1478 METZ-EN-COUTURE COMMUNAL CEMETERY, BRITISH EXTENSION (P. de C.). 11 miles SW. of Cambrai, 3 miles N. of Fins Sta., ¾ mile W. of village on road to Gouzeaucourt. Begun April 1917 following retreat of Germans to Hindenburg Line. Occupied by Germans March 1918, and enlarged after Armistice. Records 417 U.K., 43 N.Z., 7 S.A., 1 Aust., 1 Can., 1 Chin., 12 German burials, and 4 special memorials.

A

A

1602 NEUVILLE-BOURJONVAL BRIT-ISH CEMETERY (P. de C.).   2½ miles SE. of Bertincourt Sta., E. of village near by-road to Hermies. Begun by 11th Rifle Bgde. April 1917, used by 42nd (E. Lancs.) and other Divs. until March 1918.   Records 198 U.K., 4 N.Z. burials, and 3 special memorials.

B

2366 VILLERS-GUIS-LAIN COMMUNAL CEMETERY (Nord). 12 miles SW. of Cambrai, 2½ miles SE. of Gouzeau-court Sta. on W. out-skirts of village.   The civilian population was completely evacuated early in 1917 and village was heavily shelled. Records 50 U.K. burials.

B

C

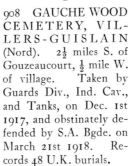

908 GAUCHE WOOD CEMETERY, VIL-LERS-GUISLAIN (Nord).   2½ miles S. of Gouzeaucourt, ½ mile W. of village.   Taken by Guards Div., Ind. Cav., and Tanks, on Dec. 1st 1917, and obstinately de-fended by S.A. Bgde. on March 21st 1918.   Re-cords 48 U.K. burials.

C

D

673 DOMINO BRIT-ISH CEMETERY, EPÉHY (SOMME).   13 miles NE. of Péronne, 1 mile N. of Epéhy Sta., W. of Gouzeaucourt road. The right flank of the 33rd Div. embraced site of cem. at opening of final assault on Hinden-burg Line Sept. 27th 1918.   (Mem. to 12th (Eastern) Div. SE. of vil-lage).   Records 51 U.K. burials.

D

952 GOUZEAUCOURT NEW BRITISH CEMETERY (Nord). 2,000 yards SW. of sta., on road to Heudicourt. Captured by 8th Div. April 12th–13th, recaptured Nov. 30th by Irish Guards, taken by 21st Div. Oct. 8th 1918. Records 1,133 U.K., 72 N.Z., 23 S.A., 2 Can., 1 Newfld., 28 Unknown, 2 Russ. burials, and 35 special memorials.

2367 VILLERS HILL BRITISH CEMETERY, VILLERS - GUISLAIN (Nord). 2½ miles SE. of Gouzeaucourt Sta. on 'Gloucester Road', ½ mile SE. of village. Begun by 33rd Div. Scene of fierce attacks by Gds. Div. and Tanks, Dec. 1st 1917 (Battle of Cambrai). Records 684 U.K., 23 N.Z., 5 Can., 1 Aust., 1 S.A., 13 German, 1 Unknown burials, and 17 special memorials.

2202 TARGELLE RAVINE BRITISH CEMETERY, VILLERS-GUISLAIN (Nord). 11 miles S. of Cambrai, 3 miles NE. of Epéhy Sta., 1 mile S. of village, S of Honnecourt by-road. Used from Sept. 18th to Oct. 8th 1918 during the breaking of Hindenburg Line in final advance to Victory. Records 114 U.K. burials.

A

A

1451 MEATH CEMETERY, VILLERS-GUISLAIN (Nord). 3 miles NE. of Epéhy Sta., S. of village, in field between 'Targelle Ravine' and 'Pigeon Ravine'. Begun by 33rd Div. Records 122 U.K. burials and 3 special memorials.

B

1552 MORVAL BRITISH CEMETERY (P. de C.). 1¾ miles N. of Combles Sta. on W. outskirts of village. Captured by 5th Div. on Sept. 25th 1916. Regained by 38th (Welsh) Div. after fierce fighting on Sept. 1st 1918. Records 54 U.K. and 1 German burials.

C

1063 HERBECOURT BRITISH CEMETERY (SOMME). 5 miles W. of Péronne, 3 miles S. of Hem-Feuillères Sta., W. of village, N. of Amiens road. First casualties from Art. and Sussex Rgt. who fell Feb. and March 1917 prior to German withdrawal to Hindenburg Line. Records 51 Aust. and 8 U.K. burials.

D

860 FORESTE COMMUNAL CEMETERY (AISNE). 8 miles W. of St. Quentin, ¼ mile S. of village church near sta., on road to Villers-St. Cristophe. Burials were casualties during the German retirement of March 1917, and those of Fifth Army who fell on first day of German offensive 1918. Records 94 U.K., 1 Fr. burials, and 23 special memorials.

B

C

D

1740 PIGEON RAVINE CEMETERY, EPÉHY (SOMME). 13 miles NE. of Péronne, 2 miles NE. of Epéhy village and sta., N. of road to Honnecourt. Created Sept. 1918 during final assault on Hindenburg Line. 85 casualties from 2nd Worcesters who fell Sept. 29th. Records 137 U.K. burials.

737 EPÉHY WOOD FARM CEMETERY, EPÉHY (SOMME). ¾ mile W. of sta., on road to Saulcourt. Lost March 22nd 1918 after gallant defence by Leices. Bgde. of 21st Div. and 2nd R. Munster Fus. Retaken in Battle of Epéhy on Sept. 18th 1918 by 12th (Eastern) Div. Records 964 U.K., 1 Malta burials and 31 special memorials.

1083 HEUDICOURT COMMUNAL CEMETERY EXTENSION (SOMME). ¾ miles S. of sta., S. of village. Captured by British in March 1917; it remained in our hands until March 1918, and was retaken in Sept. 1918. Records 82 U.K., 2 Can., and 1 Bermuda burials.

2091 SAULCOURT CHURCHYARD EXTENSION, GUYENCOURT - SAULCOURT (SOMME). 8 miles NE. of Péronne, 3 miles NW. of Villers-Faucon Sta., NW. of village near Gouzeaucourt road. First burials were 3 officers of 6th Warwick Rgt. and one of 143rd M.G.C. April 1917. Used again in Jan. 1918 by Germans in March, April, and finally Sept. 1918. Records 103 U.K. and 7 German burials.

828 FIVE POINTS CEMETERY, LECHELLE (P. de C.). ¾ mile SE. of village near road to Ytres-Etricourt Sta. Village was finally captured Sept. 1918. Cem. made by 53rd Field Amb. and 18th Casualty Clearing Sta. Records 99 U.K. and 1 Ind. burials.

1900 ROCQUIGNY-EQUANCOURT ROAD BRITISH CEMETERY, MANANCOURT (SOMME). ⅝ mile S. of Ytres-Etricourt Sta. near Canal du Nord. Etricourt was occupied by British April 1917 on German retreat to Hindenburg Line. Lost Mar. 1918, regained Sept. Records 1,764 U.K., 22 Newfld., 21 N.Z., 12 Can., 12 S.A., 5 Aust., 2 Guernsey, 10 French, 66 German burials, and 9 special memorials.

1965 SAILLY-SAIL-LISEL BRITISH CEMETERY, (SOMME). 2 miles E. of Combles Sta., on Bapaume-Péronne road. In possession of Allies until March 24th 1918, and on Sept. 1st 1918 was recaptured by 18th and 38th (Welsh) Divs. Records 559 U.K., 12 Aust., 7 Newfld., 185 Unknown burials, and 8 special memorials.

544 COMBLES COMMUNAL CEMETERY EXTENSION (SOMME). 10 miles E. of Albert and 8 miles S. of Bapaume, with sta. on light rly. from Albert to Péronne. Is at back of Com. Cem. Was begun by French troops in Oct. 1916 and enlarged after Armistice. Records 1,041 U.K., 5 Can., 1 S.A. burials, and 13 special memorials.

966 GUARDS' CEMETERY, COMBLES (SOMME). (See Combles Com. Cem. Ext.). On SW. of village, 74 yards from a by-road to Maurepas. Begun in Sept. 1916 by Guards Div. and enlarged after Armistice. Records 152 U.K., 4 Newfld. burials, and 30 special memorials.

1645 NOYELLES-SUR-L'ESCAUT COMMUNAL CEMETERY EXTENSION (Nord). 4 miles SW. of Cambrai, 1½ miles N. of Marcoing Sta., NW. of village on road to Cantaing. Casualties from Sept. 27th to Oct. 9th 1918 when Third Army pierced Hindenburg Line and carried the Marcoing Line. Records 115 U.K. burials.

2190 SUZANNE MILITARY CEMETERY, No. 3 (SOMME). 8 miles SE. of Albert, 3 miles E. of Bray Sta., 1 mile NE. of Suzanne near Maricourt road. Created after the Armistice from isolated graves on the Somme battle-fields. Records 103 U.K., 28 Aust., 8 Can., and 1 German burials.

1054 HEM FARM MILITARY CEMETERY, HEM-MONACU (SOMME). 5 miles W. of Péronne, SW. of Hem-Feuillères Sta. on private by-road to Curlu. The 5th Aust. Div. crossed R. Somme near Hem by hastily constructed bridges to attack Péronne Aug. 30th 1918. Records 367 U.K., 138 Aust., 88 S.A., 4 Can. burials, and 1 special memorial.

1724 PÉRONNE COM-
MUNAL CEMETERY
EXTENSION, STE.
RADEGONDE
(SOMME). 1 mile NW.
of Péronne Sta., near road
to Mont. St. Quentin
(Aust. Mem.). On March
18th 1917 the 40th and
48th Divs. entered town
and on Aug. 30th to
Sept. 1st the 2nd Aust.
Div. took Mont St. Quen-
tin. Records 1,055 U.K.,
512 Aust., 6 S.A., 1 Can.,
97 German burials, and
17 special memorials.

670 DOINGT COM-
MUNAL CEMETERY
EXTENSION
(SOMME). 2 miles E. of
Péronne Sta., ¾ mile N.
of Doingt Halte. Was
captured by 5th Aust.
Div. on Sept. 5th 1918,
village being completely
destroyed in fighting.
Records 342 U.K., 67
Aust., 5 S.A., 2 Can., and
1 Unknown burials.

2238 TINCOURT
NEW BRITISH
CEMETERY
(SOMME). ½ mile W. of
Tincourt-Boucly Halte,
NW. of chyd. Occupied
by British March 1917,
during German retreat to
Hindenburg Line. Re-
cords 1,563 U.K., 226
Aust., 45 Can., 39 S.A.,
15 Ind., 6 Guernsey, 2
Newfld., 58 Chin., 152
German burials, and 33
special memorials.

2364 VILLERS-FAUCON COMMUNAL CEMETERY (SOMME). ¾ mile W. of sta., NW. side of village. Captured by 5th Cav. Div. on March 27th 1917, lost on March 22nd 1918 and retaken by III Corps on Sept. 7th 1918. Records 227 U.K. and 90 German burials.

2365 VILLERS-FAUCON COMMUNAL CEMETERY EXTENSION (SOMME). NW. side of Com. Cem. Used from April 1917 to March 1918, then occupied by Germans, resumed by British in Sept. and Oct. 1918. Records 432 U.K., 10 Aust., 8 Ind., 2 N.Z., 1 S.A., and 66 German burials.

1010 HARGICOURT BRITISH CEMETERY (AISNE). 10 miles NW. of St. Quentin, 4½ miles E. of Roisel Sta., W. of village, near road to Jeancourt. The village of Hargicourt fell at the first assault March 21st 1918 during German offensive. Records 273 U.K., 15 Aust., 22 Ind., and 2 German burials.

1903 ROISEL COMMUNAL CEMETERY EXTENSION (SOMME). 600 yards E. of sta. on road, to Villers-Faucon. Occupied by British April 1917, evacuated March 22nd 1918 after strong defence by 66th (E. Lancs.) Div. Records 721 U.K., 106 Aust., 29 S.A., 6 Can., about 500 German burials, and 15 special memorials.

1152 JEANCOURT COMMUNAL CEMETERY EXTENSION (AISNE). 1¾ miles E. of Hervilly Sta., W. of village on E. side of Protestant Cem. Was a German hosp. centre, and Ext. was used alternately by British and German troops. Records 371 U.K., 113 Aust., 6 Can., 167 German burials, and 2 special memorials.

231 BELLICOURT BRITISH CEMETERY (AISNE). 1,000 yards W. of sta., on Hindenburg Line. 46th (N. Mid.) Div. stormed the line at Bellenglise, 30th U.S. Div. captured Bellicourt and Nauroy, which were cleared by 5th Aust. Div. Records 869 U.K., 305 Aust., 5 S.A., 1 Can., 3 Chin. burials, and 21 special memorials.

A

A

1011 HARGICOURT COMMUNAL CEMETERY EXTENSION (AISNE). 10 miles NW. of St. Quentin, 4½ miles E. of Roisel Sta., N. of village on track to Malakoff Farm. Hargicourt was retaken by Aust. units Sept. 18th 1918. Records 61 U.K. and 12 Aust. burials.

B

992 HAM BRITISH CEMETERY, MUILLE - VILLETTE (SOMME). 14 miles S. of Péronne, 600 yards S. of Ham Sta., on by-road to Golancourt. Village was retaken by French in first stages of Allied advance to Victory, Sept. 6th 1918. Cem. greatly enlarged after Armistice. Records 446 U.K. burials and 30 special memorials.

B

C

1590 NESLE COMMUNAL CEMETERY (SOMME). ⅝ mile SE. of sta., E. of town. Occupied by French and Brit. cav. on March 18th 1917. Taken by Germans on March 25th 1918 but was recaptured by French on following Aug. 28th. Records 135 U.K. burials.

D

56 ANNOIS COMMUNAL CEMETERY (AISNE). 12 miles SW. of St. Quentin, 500 yards W. of Flavy-le-Martel Sta., on E. outskirts of village. Was used by Germans as Prisoners of War Cem. in May and June 1918. Records 61 U.K. burials.

C

D

2206[1] TEMPLEUX-LE-GUERARD BRITISH CEMETERY (SOMME) SE. of village on road to Hargicourt. Begun by 59th (N. Mid.) Div. April 1917, enlarged after Armistice. Village was finally taken by 15th Suffolks of 74th (Yeo.) Div. Records 396 U.K., 22 Aust., 3 Ind., 1 Can. burials, and 16 special memorials.

2207 TEMPLEUX-LE-GUERARD COMMUNAL CEMETERY EXTENSION (SOMME). 2½ miles E. of Roisel Sta., N. of village. Begun by 59th (N. Mid.) Div. after first capture of village April 1917 and carried on by 34th and other Divs. Records 98 U.K., 20 Aust. burials, and 13 special memorials.

1990 STE. EMILIE VALLEY CEMETERY, VILLERS - FAUCON (SOMME). ⅝ mile E. of Villers-Faucon Sta., on E. side of low road from Ste. Emilie to Roisel. British Cem. begun by Germans, and enlarged after Armistice. Records 463 U.K., 25 Aust., 2 S.A., 1 Can., 1 N.Z., 10 German burials, and 21 special memorials.

2279 UNICORN CEMETERY, VEND' HUILE (AISNE). 3½ miles E. of Epéhy Sta., on NW. side of road to Lempire. Taken by the 27th and 30th Amer. Divs. at end of Sept. 1918 and cleared by 12th and 18th Divs. on 30th. Cem. name is taken from 50th Div. mark. Records 689 U.K., 78 Aust., 1 Can., 4 Ind., 218 Unknown burials, and 18 special memorials.

1913 RONSSOY COMMUNAL CEMETERY (SOMME). 12½ miles N. of St. Quentin, 2½ miles E. of Ste. Emilie Sta., N. of village near road to Basse-Boulogne. British burials of Dec. 1917 (mostly 6th Connaught R.) and Sept. 1918. Records 38 U.K., 7 Can., and 1 German burials.

382 BRIE BRITISH CEMETERY (SOMME) 1¾ miles SE. of Pont-lès-Brie Sta., ½ mile S. of village on road to St. Christ. Finally regained Sept. 5th 1918, when 32nd Div. cleared the village. Records 365 U.K., 27 Aust., 1 Can., 1 Unknown, 36 German burials, and 15 special memorials.

996 HANCOURT BRITISH CEMETERY (SOMME). 7 miles E. of Péronne, 3 miles S. of Roisel Sta., E. of village, N. of 'Rue d'Aix'. Begun during German advance March 1918, occupied and used by Germans, retaken and used by British Oct. 1918. Records 86 U.K., 31 Aust., and 1 Can. burials.

2282 VADENCOURT BRITISH CEMETERY, MAISSEMY (AISNE). 8 miles NW. of St. Quentin, 2½ miles N. of Vermand Sta., NW. of village on Bellenglise road. Begun Aug. 1917 and used until March 1918. Reopened in Sept. until Nov. 1918, and enlarged after Armistice. Records 727 U.K., 10 Aust., 7 Can., 2 Ind., 4 Chin. burials, and 5 special memorials.

1434 MARTEVILLE COMMUNAL CEMETERY (AISNE). 12 miles W. of St. Quentin, SE. of village and sta., E. of Attilly road. Cem. was used during German offensive March 1918 and Sept. 1918. Records 76 U.K., 1 French, and 1 German burials.

495 CHAPELLE BRITISH CEMETERY HOLNON (AISNE). 3 miles SW. of St. Quentin, 1 mile N. of Holnon-Savy Sta., S. of St. Quentin-Vermand road. Created after Armistice from isolated battle-field graves around Holnon and woods to the west. Records 617 U.K. burials and 6 special memorials.

2094 SAVY BRITISH CEMETERY (AISNE). 4½ miles W. of St. Quentin, S. of Savy village and sta., on road to Roupy. Created after Armistice from isolated graves and small Cems. (Inniskilling and Lancashire Cems.) in the surrounding battle-fields. Records 799 U.K. and 1 German burials.

2261 TREFCON BRITISH CEMETERY, CAULAINCOURT (AISNE). 3 miles W. of Vermand, in Park of Château de Caulaincourt (Duc de Vicence). Cem. was created during final Allied advance to Victory, Sept. 11th to 30th 1918. Records 281 U.K. and 1 Ind. burials.

2319 VERMAND COMMUNAL CEMETERY (AISNE). $7\frac{1}{2}$ miles NW. of St. Quentin, $\frac{3}{4}$ mile S. of Vermand Sta., SE. of town on road to Attilly. Used for British burials March to May 1917, also March and Sept. 1918. Records 42 U.K. and 1 German burials.

735 ENNEMAIN COMMUNAL CEMETERY EXTENSION (SOMME). 4 miles SE. of Pont-lès-Brie Sta., E. of village on road to Fourques. Made after Armistice from battlefields of March 1917 to Sept. 1918 E. and W. of Ennemain. Records 45 U.K., 4 Aust., 1 Can., 25 Unknown burials, and 2 special memorials.

1708 PARGNY BRITISH CEMETERY (SOMME). $3\frac{1}{2}$ miles NE. of Nesle Sta., $\frac{1}{2}$ mile SW. of village. Made after Armistice from surrounding battle-fields. Reflects stubborn defence of Somme crossings in Mar. 1918 by 61st (S. Mid.) and 8th Divs. Records 611 U.K., 6 Can. burials, and 18 special memorials.

960 GRAND-SERAU-COURT BRITISH CEMETERY (AISNE). 7 miles SW. of St. Quentin, 2 miles W. of Essigny-le-Grand Halte, NE. of village on road to the halte. On line of retreat of II Corps from Mons (the Scots Greys and 12th Lancers charged at Cerizy, 6 miles E., Aug. 27th 1914). Records 1,326 U.K., 1 Can. burials, and 32 special memorials.

ST. QUENTIN
MAP SHEET No. 36

857 FORENVILLE MILITARY CEMETERY (Nord). 3 miles SE. of Cambrai and opp. Com. Cem. Captured on Oct. 8th 1918, and was made by Guards and 2nd Divs. Records 99 U.K. and 2 N.Z. burials.

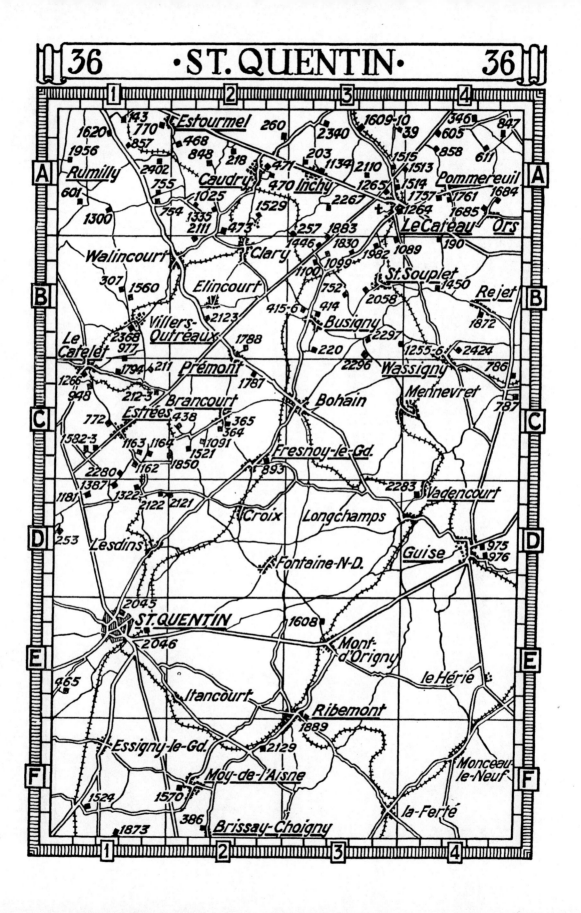

A

A

1956 RUMILLY COMMUNAL CEMETERY EXTENSION (Nord). 4 miles S. of Cambrai, ¾ mile from Rumilly Sta., E. of village, NE. of Com. Cem. Rumilly was captured by 3rd Div. Sept. 30th 1918 in advance to Victory. Records 80 U.K. and 1 N.Z. burials.

B

755 ESNES COMMUNAL CEMETERY (Nord). 5 miles SE. of Cambrai, 2 miles S. of Cattenières Sta., NE. of village on road to Cattenières. Majority of burials were casualties Aug. 26th-27th 1914 in the Retreat from Mons. Esnes was taken by N.Z. Div. Oct. 8th 1918. Records 118 U.K. burials.

B

C

C

260 BETHENCOURT COMMUNAL CEMETERY (Nord). 5 miles W. of Le Cateau, 2 miles N. of Caudry Sta., N. of village near road to Viesly. Burials are casualties of Aug.–Sept. 1914 after Battle of Le Cateau and Oct. 1918 in advance to Victory. Records 80 U.K. and 1 N.Z. burials.

D

1025 HAUCOURT COMMUNAL CEMETERY (Nord). 7 miles SE. of Cambrai, 2 miles S. of Cattenières Sta., E. of village on road to Ligny - en - Cambrésis. Burials were casualties Aug. 26th 1914 in the Retreat from Mons and were buried by the Germans. Records 42 U.K. burials.

D

848 FONTAINE-AU-PIRE COMMUNAL CEMETERY (Nord). 7 miles from Cambrai and Le Câteau, 2 miles W. of Caudry Sta. on NW. outskirts of village. The majority of burials were casualties in the Retreat from Mons Aug. 1914, others were Prisoners of War and all were buried by Germans. Records 168 U.K. and 3 N.Z. burials.

1610 NEUVILLY COMMUNAL CEMETERY EXTENSION (Nord). ¾ mile W. of sta., on NE. side of road to Solesmes. Captured temporarily by 17th Div. on 10th, and finally on Oct. 17th 1918. Records 101 U.K. burials.

470 CAUDRY BRITISH CEMETERY (Nord). 6 miles W. of Le Câteau, E. of town and sta., S. of road to Audencourt. Begun by 2nd Otage Batt. N.Z. E.F. on Oct. 10th 1918, when town was captured by 37th Div. in final advance to Victory. Records 628 U.K., 53 N.Z., 3 S.A., 3 Ind., 2 Can., 1 Aust., 3 French, 19 Chin. burials, and 1 special memorial.

471   CAUDRY OLD COMMUNAL CEMETERY (Nord). 6 miles W. of Le Câteau, 1 mile N. of Caudry Sta., N. of road to Audencourt. Used by Germans from 1914 to 1917 as Prisoners of War Cem., and was constructed by them with forced French labour. Records 128 U.K., 9 Aust., and 2 Can. burials.

1134   INCHY COMMUNAL CEMETERY EXTENSION (Nord). 11½ miles E. of Cambrai, 3¾ miles NW. of Le Câteau, N. of Com. Cem. Inchy fell to 63rd (R.N.) Div. Sept. 3rd 1918. The 'Canal du Nord', under construction at outbreak of War, forms a deep channel with shattered masonry nearby. Records 53 U.K. and 29 German burials.

2110   SELRIDGE BRITISH CEMETERY, MONTAY (Nord). Immediately N. of Le Câteau, near V. of R. Selle. Cem. made by 33rd Div. on Oct. 28th–29th 1918, and is 1 mile W. of village on track leading from Le Câteau to Viesly. Village was reached in Pursuit to Selle on Oct. 10th 1918. Records 147 U.K. burials.

39 AMERVAL COM-
MUNAL CEMETERY
E X T E N S I O N,
SOLESMES (Nord). 3
miles N. of Le Câteau, 1½
miles E. of Neuvilly Sta.,
E. of village on road to
Forest. First casualties
7th Border Rgt. and 10th
Notts and Derbys of
17th Div., who cap-
tured Amerval Oct. 20th
1918. Records 151 U.K.
burials.

A

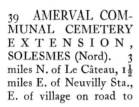

B

A

1513 MONTAY BRIT-
ISH CEMETERY
(Nord). 400 yards N. of
Montay Halte, 2½ miles
N. of Le Câteau. Begun
by 38th (Welsh) Div. and
2nd Argyll and Suther-
land Highs. Records 41
U.K. burials.

B

257 BERTRY COM-
MUNAL CEMETERY
(Nord). 12 miles SE. of
Cambrai, on E. outskirts
of village and 500 yards S.
of Bertry Sta. Burials
were from First Battle of
Le Câteau, Aug. 1914, in
Retreat from Mons, and
Second Battle of Le Câ-
teau Oct. 1918 in advance
to Victory. Records 46
U.K., 10 S.A., and 5 Can.
burials.

1515 MONTAY-NEU-VILLY ROAD CEME-TERY (Nord). ¾ mile NW. of Montay Halte on E. side of Neuvilly road. Begun Oct. 26th and 27th by 23rd Bgde., R.G.A. Records 467 U.K., 2 Can., 27 German burials, and 1 special memorial.

611 CROSS-ROADS CEMETERY, FON-TAINE-AU-BOIS (Nord). 2 miles from Landrecies Sta., 1 mile W. of village, on road to La Câteau. Begun Nov. 1918 by 1/1st Northumbrian Field Amb. Records 629 U.K., 87 N.Z., 1 Aust., 2 S.A., 2 Chin. burials, and 23 special memorials.

1265 LE CÂTEAU MILITARY CEME-TERY (Nord). W. of town, near crossing of Caudry and Montay roads. Scene of battle fought by II Corps on Aug. 26th 1914 against greatly superior German force. Cem. begun by Germans and records 639 U.K., 28 S.A., 6 Aust., 2 Can., 2 N.Z., 1 Newfld., 1 R. Guernsey L.I. burials, and 20 special memorials.

1264 LE CÂTEAU COMMUNAL CEMETERY (Nord). S.E. side of town, immediately N. of light rly. Used during Aug. and Sept. 1914, and last three months of 1918. Records 136 U.K., 13 Aust., and 2 Can. burials.

1757 POMMEREUIL BRITISH CEMETERY (Nord). 3 miles NE. of Le Câteau Sta., on S. side of road from Le Câteau. Was the scene of severe fighting on Oct. 23rd–24th 1918, and after capture of village the Cem. was made by 25th Div. Records 171 U.K. and 2 Aust. burials.

1089 HIGHLAND CEMETERY, LE CÂTEAU (Nord). $\frac{3}{4}$ mile SE. of sta. on W. side of road to Wassigny. After Battle of Le Câteau (Aug. 26th 1914) town remained in German hands until middle of Oct. 1918. Records 549 U.K., 16 S.A., 13 Can., 1 Aust., and 44 Unknown burials.

A

A

847 FONTAINE-AU-BOIS COMMUNAL CEMETERY (Nord). 2 miles NE. of Landrecies Sta., N. of village, E. of road to Robersart. Village was in sector captured by 18th and 50th Divs., Nov. 4th 1918, and Cem. was used for British burials after the attack. Records 89 U.K. and 1 S.A. burials.

B

858 FOREST COMMUNAL CEMETERY (Nord). 3 miles N. of Le Câteau, 2 miles NE. of Montay Halte, 500 yards E. of Forest on road to Landrecies. Contains British casualties who fell in clearing of Forest between Oct. 17th and Nov. 5th 1918. Records 126 U.K. burials.

B

C

C

1685 ORS COMMUNAL CEMETERY (Nord). 3½ miles SW. of Landrecies. NW. of Ors near sta. By hard fighting the 32nd Div. (IX Corps) forced crossing at Ors in final advance Nov. 4th 1918. Records 63 U.K., 6 Russ., and 9 German burials.

D

1684 ORS BRITISH CEMETERY (Nord). ¾ mile NE. of Ors Sta., W. of Sambre Canal. Contains men of Highland L.I., and 218th Co. R.E., who were killed Nov. 4th in bridging the canal, also men of the 1st, 2nd, and 4th S.A. Inf., who fell in relief of Le Câteau Oct. 17th–18th 1918. Records 65 U.K., 41 S.A., and 1 Aust. burials.

D

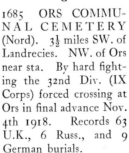

1256 LA VALLEE-MULATRE COMMUNAL CEMETERY EXTENSION (AISNE). 18 miles NE. of St. Quentin, 6 miles S. of Le Câteau, W. of village church and sta. Casualties from final advance to Victory, Oct. 6th to Nov. 4th 1918. Records 47 U.K. and 4 German burials.

1830 QUIETISTE MILITARY CEMETERY, LE CÂTEAU (Nord). 3 miles SW. of Le Câteau, 1¼ miles SW. of Honnechy Sta., on Busigny road. All casualties of Oct. 1918. Named after the Quietistes (18th cent.). The house of Fénelon, Bishop of Cambrai, leader of this Sect, was used as Div. Hdqtrs. Records 52 U.K. and 15 German burials.

2058 ST. SOUPLET BRITISH CEMETERY (Nord). 4 miles S. of Le Câteau, SW. of village and sta. on road to hamlet of La Haie Menneresee. Begun during final advance to Victory Oct. 20th to Nov. 9th 1918 and enlarged after Armistice. Records 680 U.K., 5 Can., 3 Aust., 1 N.Z., 2 Ind., 1 U.S.A. burials, and 55 special memorials.

1099 HONNECHY BRITISH CEMETERY (Nord). 5 miles SW. of Le Câteau, ¾ mile NE. of Honnechy Sta., N. of road to Reumont. Drag. Guards and Can. Div. captured village Oct. 9th 1918 in advance to Victory. Records 415 U.K., 27 N.Z., 3 S.A., 2 Can. burials, and 8 special memorials.

416 BUSIGNY COMMUNAL CEMETERY EXTENSION (Nord). 1½ miles E. of sta., 6 miles SW. of Le Câteau, N. of town. Captured by 30th Amer. Div. and British cavalry on Oct. 9th 1918 in Battle of Cambrai. Records 674 U.K., 24 Aust., 9 Can., and 6 S.A. burials.

2296 VAUX-ANDIGNY BRITISH CEMETERY (AISNE). 6 miles S. of Le Câteau, SW. of village and sta., on road to Mennevret. Casualties from final advance to Victory Oct. 17th to Nov. 3rd 1918. Records 65 U.K. burials.

A

A

1872 LE REJET-DE-BEAULIEU COMMUNAL CEMETERY (Nord). 6 miles SE. of Le Câteau, 2 miles S. of Catillon Sta., S. of village. Casualties from final advance to Victory Oct. 19th to Nov. 9th 1918. Records 49 U.K. and 3 Aust. burials.

B

1446 MAUROIS COMMUNAL CEMETERY (Nord). 4 miles SW. of Le Câteau, 1 mile NE. of Maurois Halte on old Roman road to St. Quentin. 3 Casualties from Aug. 27th 1914, others from final advance to Victory, Oct. 11th to Nov. 2nd 1918. Records 79 U.K., 2 S.A., and 1 Aust. burials.

C

786 ETREUX BRITISH CEMETERY (AISNE). 10 miles SE. of Le Câteau, 400 yards N. of Etreux Sta., E. of road to Landrecies. All burials from the 2nd R. Munster Fus., who fell in the Retreat from Mons Aug. 27th 1914 and were buried by prisoners of the Batt. under German supervision. Records 122 U.K. burials.

D

977 GUIZANCOURT FARM CEMETERY, GOUY (AISNE). 12 miles N. of St. Quentin, 2 miles E. of Le Catelet-Gouy Sta., near road to Guizancourt Farm. Casualties from Fourth Army mostly North Country and Welsh Rgts., who fell on Oct. 4th and 8th 1918 in clearing Guizancourt Farm. Records 140 U.K. burials.

B

C

D

307 BOIS-DES-ANGLES BRITISH CEMETERY, CREVE-CŒUR-SUR-L'ES-CAUT (Nord). 9½ miles S. of Cambrai, 1¾ miles N. of Villers-Outréaux Sta., 4½ miles S. of Crevecœur on road to Lesdain. Created during victorious advance in Oct. 1918. Records 176 U.K. burials and 1 special memorial.

1560 MOULIN-DE-PIERRE BRITISH CEMETERY, VILLERS-OUTREAU (Nord). 11 miles S. of Cambrai, 1 mile N. of village and sta., on road to Lesdain. Casualties from Welsh Rgt. and Roy. Welsh Fus., who fell when village was taken by 38th Div. Oct. 8th 1918. Records 49 U.K. burials.

1794 PROSPECT HILL CEMETERY, GOUY (AISNE). 1¼ miles E. of Le Catelet-Gouy Sta., E. of village. On Oct. 3rd 1918 the 1st K.O.Y.L.I. captured Prospect Hill, after Le Catelet and Gouy had been taken by the 59th (Northumbrian) Div., 6th R. Innis. Fus., and 4th K.R.R.C. Records 450 U.K., 77 Aust., 10 S.A. burials, and 1 special memorial.

1787 PREMONT BRITISH CEMETERY (AISNE). 2 miles NW. of Bohain Sta., 1 mile SE. of village on road to Bohain. Captured by 30th Amer. Div. on Oct. 8th 1918. Records 521 U.K., 7 Aust., 6 Can., 1 S.A., 1 Ind., and 36 German burials.

211 BEAUREVOIR BRITISH CEMETERY (AISNE). 2½ miles E. of Le Catelet, ¾ mile N. of Beaurevoir Sta., on road to Malincourt. Created during British advance in Oct. 1918. Records 222 U.K., 64 S.A., and 3 Aust. burials.

1181 LA BARAQUE BRITISH CEMETERY, BELLENGLISE (AISNE). 6 miles N. of St. Quentin, ½ mile NE. of village at cross-roads to Le Câteau and Joncourt. Siegfried Line by Bellenglise was broken by 46th (N. Mid.) Div. by wading the Scheldt Canal and scaling the walls, Sept. 29th 1918. Records 61 U.K. burials and 1 special memorial.

A

213 BEAUREVOIR COMMUNAL CEMETERY EXTENSION (AISNE). 2½ miles E. of Le Catelet, SE. of village and sta., on road to hamlet of Geneve. Created by Fourth Army following the final breach of the Hindenburg Line by 50th Div. at Le Catelet on Oct. 3rd 1918. Records 73 U.K., 18 S.A., and 5 Aust. burials.

B

2123 SERAIN COMMUNAL CEMETERY EXTENSION (Nord). 12 miles SE. of Cambrai, 4 miles W. of Busigny Sta., NE. of village on road to Walincourt. Cem. was used Oct. 1918 in final advance to Victory, and enlarged after Armistice. Records 100 U.K., 5 Aust., 1 Can., 1 S.A., and 2 German burials.

B

C

1162 JONCOURT BRITISH CEMETERY (AISNE). ¾ mile S. of Joncourt Sta., 350 yards S. of village, on road to Levergies. All burials, with the exception of six, are casualties of the 10th Argyll and Sutherland Highlanders. Records 61 U.K. burials.

D

1164 JONCOURT EAST BRITISH CEMETERY (AISNE). 1½ miles E. of Joncourt Sta., E. of village, 500 yards from Ramicourt road. All casualties, mostly Lancs. Fus. and Manchester Rgt., fell between Sept. 30th and Oct. 3rd 1918 in advance to Victory. Records 71 U.K. burials.

C

D

A

A

2280 UPLANDS CEMETERY, MAGNY-LA-FOSSE (AISNE). $1\frac{1}{4}$ miles S. of Joncourt Sta., on high ground N. of village. Captured by 46th (N. Mid.) Div. Sept. 29th 1918, but Cem. belongs rather to 32nd Div. who followed after them. Records 43 U.K. burials.

B

365 BRANCOURT-LE-GRAND MILITARY CEMETERY (AISNE). 3 miles SW. of Bohain, 250 yards NW. of Brancourt Sta., near road to Fresnoy - le - Grand. Created during victorious advance in Oct. 1918. Records 41 U.K. burials, and 1 special memorial.

B

C

C

1091 HIGH TREE CEMETERY, MONT-BREHAIN (AISNE). $1\frac{1}{4}$ miles E. of sta., NE. of Brit. Cem. in field SE. of village, near farm ' de l'Arbre Haut'. Records 44 U.K. and 4 Aust. burials who fell Oct. 1918.

D

893 FRESNOY-LE-GRAND COMMUNAL CEMETERY EXTENSION (AISNE). 9 miles NE. of St. Quentin, NE. of village and sta., on road to Etâves. Fresnoy-le-Grand was taken by 46th Div. Oct. 8th 1918. (Mem. to Div. at Bellenglise 7 miles W.). Records 64 U.K. and 5 German burials.

D

438   CALVAIRE CEMETERY, MONT-BREHAIN (AISNE). ¾ mile NW. of sta., NW. of Brit. Cem. near village, opp. Com. Cem. Records 48 Aust., and 20 U.K. burials, who fell Sept.–Oct. 1918.

1521 MONTBREHAIN BRITISH CEMETERY (AISNE). ½ mile S. of sta., on road to Fontaine-Uterte. First taken by 3 Batts. of Sherwood Fors. (46th Div.) Oct. 3rd 1918, finally captured by 21st and 24th Aust. Inf. Batts. 2 days later. Records 86 U.K. and 3 Aust. burials.

1850 RAMICOURT BRITISH CEMETERY (AISNE). 1 mile S. of Ramicourt Sta., S. of village on road to Levergies. Captured by 1/5th, 1/6th and 1/8th Sher. Foresters on Oct. 3rd 1918. Records 97 U.K., 18 Aust., and 3 Unknown burials.

253 BERTHAUCOURT COMMUNAL CEME-TERY, PONTRU (AISNE). 6 miles NW. of St. Quentin, 550 yards W. of village of Berthaucourt, E. of road to Maissemy. (Mem. to 4th Aust. Div. N. of Pontru). Cem. was used Sept. 18th to Oct. 7th 1918 during advance to Victory. Records 71 U.K. burials.

976 GUISE (LA DESOLATION) FRENCH NATIONAL CEMETERY, FLA-VIGNY - LE - PETIT (AISNE). 2 miles S. of Guise, near hamlet of La Desolation on road to Marle. Begun by Germans Aug. 1914 and used as Prisoners of War Cem. Enlarged after Armistice. British Plot records 46 U.K., 1 Can. burials, and 1 special memorial.

1335 LIGNY - EN - CAMBRESIS COM-MUNAL CEMETERY (Nord). 9 miles SE. of Cambrai, 1 mile S. of Fontaine-au-Piré Halte, W. of village. There are 33 casualties of Aug. 26th to Sept. 7th 1914 in the Retreat from Mons, and 7 Prisoners of War who died 1917–1918. Records 40 U.K. burials.

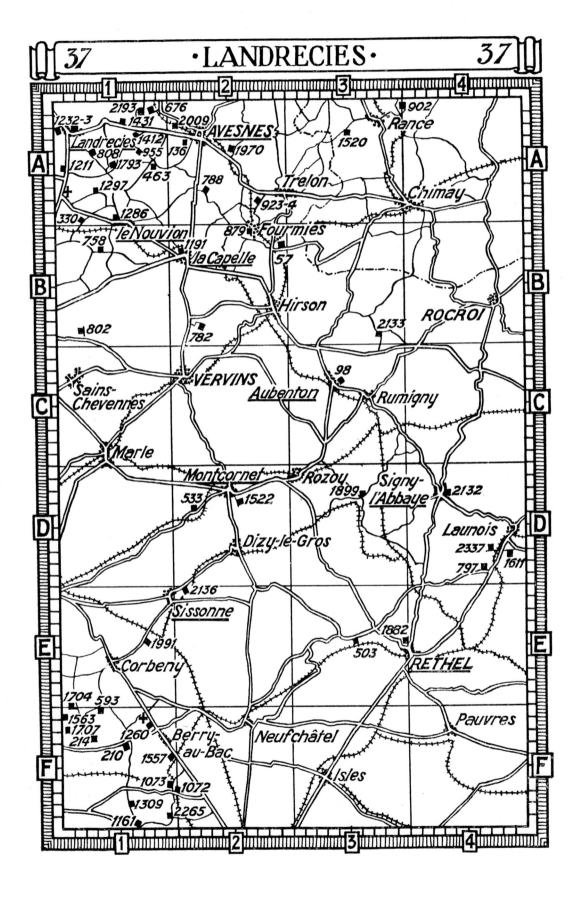

1232 LANDRECIES BRITISH CEMETERY (Nord). 6 miles E. of Le Câteau, NW. of Landrecies Sta., on road to Le Câteau. Captured in final advance by 25th Div., who crossed R. Sambre N. and S. of town by rafts Nov. 4th 1918. Records 163 U.K. burials.

A

A

1233 LANDRECIES COMMUNAL CEME-TERY (Nord). SE. of town and sta., on road to Maroilles and Avesnes. Occupied by Germans greater part of War, and Cem. used by them to bury British who fell in fighting of Aug. 1914 and Oct. 1918. Records 55 U.K., 1 Aust., 1 French, and 1 Russ. burials.

B

136 AVESNES-SUR-HELPE COMMUNAL CEMETERY (Nord). SW. of town and sta., on road to Cartignies. Avesnes was Hdqtrs. of German 18th Army and advanced Hdqtrs. of Hindenburg and Ludendorff 1918. Taken by British Nov. 8th 1918. Records 77 U.K. burials and 5 special memorials.

B

923 GLAGEON COM-
MUNAL CEMETERY
(Nord). 8 miles SE. of
Avesnes - sur - Helpe, 3
miles N. of Fourmies Sta.,
SW. of Glageon on road
to Fourmies. Used by
Germans for burial of
British Prisoners of War
June – Aug. 1918. Re-
cords 59 U.K. and other
Allied burials.

924 GLAGEON COM-
MUNAL CEMETERY
EXTENSION (Nord). 8
miles SE. of Avesnes-sur-
Helpe, 3 miles N. of
Fourmies Sta., SW. of
Glageon, on road to
Fourmies, S. of Com.
Cem. Used by Germans
for burial of British Pris-
oners of War from Aug.
to Oct. 1918. Records
300 U.K., 1 Aust., 1
S.A., and 2 French burials.

1522 MONTCORNET
MILITARY CEME-
TERY (AISNE). 21
miles E. of Laon, S. of
Montcornet Sta., on road
to Lislet. Used by Ger-
mans as Prisoners of War
Cem. from Montcornet
Hosp. between May and
Oct. 1918. Records 56
U.K. burials and 3 special
memorials.

2136 S I S S O N N E
BRITISH CEMETERY
(AISNE). 10 miles E. of
Laon, 1½ miles NE. of
Sissonne on road to Lap-
pion. All Prisoner of
War graves regrouped
from large German Cem.
(10,700 graves) adjoining,
and from other German
Cems. Casualties from
Nov. 1914 to March
1916. Records 286 U.K.
burials and 4 special
memorials.

1991 ST. ERME COM-
MUNAL CEMETERY
EXTENSION (AISNE).
12 miles E. of Laon, ¾
miles W. of St. Erme
Sta., near road to sta. and
Ramecourt. Casualties
from May to Nov. 1918.
Cem. enlarged after
Armistice. Records 64
U.K. burials.

1260 LA VILLE-AUX-
B O I S B R I T I S H
CEMETERY (AISNE).
14 miles NW. of Reims, 2½
miles NW. of Pontavert
Sta., on Reims-Laon
road. Created after
Armistice from battle-
fields of May 1918. Mem.
to 2nd Devon Rgt. at La
Musette who fell May
27th 1918 in gallant de-
fence. Records 548 U.K.
burials and 18 special
memorials.

210 BEAUREPAIRE FRENCH NATIONAL CEMETERY, PONTAVERT (AISNE). 16 miles NW. of Reims, $\frac{3}{4}$ mile E. of Pontavert village and sta., S. of road to Bourg-et-Comin near the 'Chemin des Dames'. All identified casualties fell May – June 1918. British plot records 65 U.K. burials and 2 special memorials.

1073 HERMONVILLE MILITARY CEMETERY (MARNE). $9\frac{1}{2}$ miles NW. of Reims, 750 yards SW. of Hermonville Sta., in field N. of village. Created after the Armistice from isolated graves and Cems. in the battle-fields of May 1918 in the vicinity. Records 238 U.K. burials and 5 special memorials.

1161 JONCHERY-SUR-VESLE BRITISH CEMETERY (MARNE) $10\frac{1}{2}$ miles W. of Reims, $\frac{3}{4}$ mile W. of Jonchery Sta., on by-road N. of Reims road. Created after the Armistice from isolated graves and cems. in the battle-fields of May to Aug. 1918 in the vicinity. Records 360 U.K., 1 Can. burials, and 5 special memorials.

1882 RETHEL FRENCH NATIONAL CEMETERY (ARDENNES). NW. of town and sta. on road to Montcornet. Town was 20 miles behind German front line until released by Gen. Gouraud's Army Nov. 6th 1918. Cem. was begun after Armistice from isolated Prisoner of War graves. Records 108 U.K. burials, French, and other Allies.

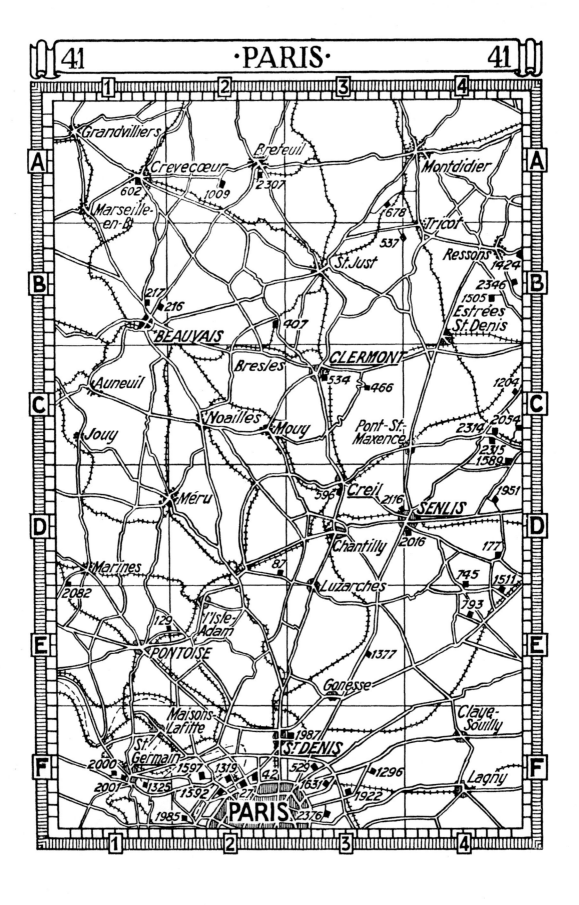

PARIS

MAP SHEET No. 41

PARIS. The British War Graves in the neighbourhood of Paris fall into three main groups. The earliest are those of soldiers who died of wounds in French and British hospitals in or near Paris in 1914, when the ambulance trains ran south-westward from the Aisne and the Marne. The second group is due to the presence of British troops in the Aisne and the Marne in the summer of 1918. The third is a number of graves of men who died after the Armistice.

529 CITY OF PARIS CEMETERY, PANTIN. NE. of city, 1½ miles from Porte de la Villette on road to Le Bourget. British graves in small plot (Div. 6) at W. end of Cem. among French Mil. graves. Records 71 U.K., 11 Can., and 11 Aust. burials.

1302 LES GONARDS CEMETERY, VERSAILLES. 1 mile SE. of Rive Gauche Sta., in Bois des Gonards, on R. of main avenue, 150 yards from entrance. From No. 4 Gen. Hosp. 1914–1915. Records 167 U.K. and 3 Can. burials.

2315 VERBERIE FRENCH NATIONAL CEMETERY (OISE). 9½ miles SW. of Compiègne, S. of Verberie Sta., E. of village. Contains burials from 'L' Battery, R.H.A., 2nd and 5th Dragoon Guards who fell in the affair of Néry Sept. 1st 1914. British plot records 52 U.K., 1 Can. burials, and 26 special memorials.

2116 SENLIS FRENCH NATIONAL CEMETERY (OISE). 1 mile W. of Senlis Sta., on N. outskirts of town, N. of road to Creil. British burials were mostly casualties from July 24th to Aug. 11th 1918. British plot records 135 U.K. burials.

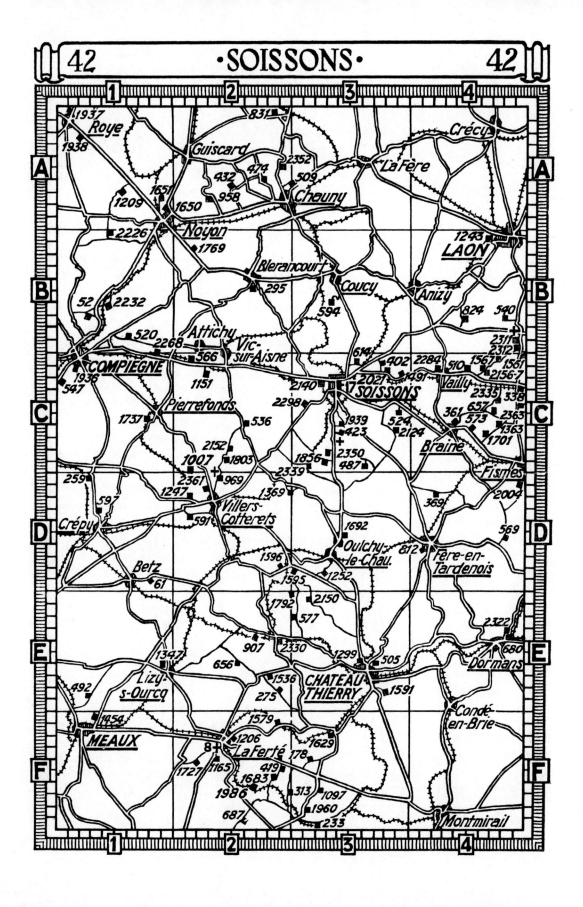

SOISSONS
MAP SHEET No. 42

SOISSONS stands on the left bank of the Aisne, between wooded hills rising north and south from the wide valley.

The original British Expeditionary Force crossed the Aisne in August 1914 a few miles west of Soissons, and re-crossed it in September a few miles east.

At the end of April 1918 five Divisions, forming the IX Corps, were transferred to the French Sixth Army to rest and refit. They were the 8th, 19th (Western), 21st, 25th, and 50th (Northumbrian) Divisions. The 19th, 21st, 25th, and 50th had within the last two months helped to withstand the two great German offensives on the Somme on the Lys, while the 8th had been heavily engaged in the fighting on the Somme. All of them had very recently received young and partly trained drafts from England.

During the first fortnight in May the 21st, 8th, and 50th Divisions were put into the line on a front of fifteen miles running east and west between Reims and Soissons, with their left flank close to the eastern end of the Chemin des Dames. On these Divisions, as well as on the French troops for twenty miles on their left, there fell, in the early morning of the 27th May, the German attack called the 'Offensive in Champagne'.

The German infantry attack was preceded by a bombardment of intense severity lasting three and a half hours, and it was immediately and overwhelmingly successful. But the British Divisions were not driven back without adding to the great reputation which each of them had already acquired, and the self-sacrifice of the 2nd Devons and the 5th Battery Royal Field Artillery was the subject of special Orders of the Day issued later by the French Fifth Army Commander.

On the 6th June a fierce German attack on the Montagne de Bligny, immediately north-east of the river, was repulsed by the 1st/4th King's Shropshire Light Infantry, to whom as a unit the French Croix de Guerre was afterwards awarded.

The IX Corps was withdrawn from the French Front in the first days of July 1918. It had lost by death about 15,000 officers and men, but it had gained the warm appreciation of its French comrades and added another to the list of heroic defensive battles fought by British troops.

On the 13th July, for reasons connected with the disposition of the German forces near Reims, General Headquarters agreed to send four Divisions—the 15th (Scottish), 34th, 51st (Highland), and 62nd (West Riding)—constituting the XXII Corps, to the French Front. The fighting from the 20th July to the 2nd August, so far as the British forces are concerned, is known as the 'Counter-Attack in Champagne', and it is divided into the two Battles of the Marne 1918.

The Battle of Tardenois lasted from 20th to the 31st July. The 51st and 62nd Divisions attacked in the neighbourhood where the 19th Division had fought on June 6th; they took Marfaux on the 23rd July and the Montagne de Bligny on the 28th, capturing 1,200 prisoners and advancing four miles; and it should be added that the New Zealand Cyclist Battalion (twelve of whose dead are named on a memorial in Marfaux British Cemetery) played a distinguished part in the capture of Marfaux.

On the 23rd July the 15th and 34th Divisions, as part of the French Tenth Army, attacked the west side of the German Salient about Berzy-le-Sac and Parcy-Tigny. This engagement, known as the 'Battle of the Soissonnais and of the Ourcq', lasted until the 2nd August, and the 15th Division in particular was prominent in the capture of Buzancy on the 28th July.

SOISSONS MEMOR-IAL (AISNE). 1 mile N. of station between the Cathedral and Pont des Anglais, E. of R. Aisne. Records 3,987 'Missing' who fell in the Battles of the Aisne and Marne 1918, which include the Battle of the Soissonnais and the Ourcq July 20th–Aug. 2nd. (Attack on Buzancy July 28th and Capture of Beugneux Ridge). The Battle of Tardenois (fighting for the Ardre Valley July 20th to 31st 1918).

LA FERTE-SOUS-JOUARRE MEMO-RIAL (SEINE-ET-M.). $\frac{5}{8}$ mile S. of Sta. on S. bank of R. Marne by bridge on Paris road. Records 3,888 'Missing' who fell in the Battles of Mons, Le Câteau, the Marne and the Aisne 1914. Also Mem. on R. banks to R.E.'s of 4th Div.

1938 ROYE NEW BRITISH CEMETERY (SOMME). 25 miles SE. of Amiens, SE. of Roye town and sta., S. of Noyon road. On March 26th 1918 the depleted 20th and 36th Divs. retired through Roye after the 61st Bgde. (20th Div.) had fought a gallant rearguard action at Liancourt. Recaptured by First French Army Aug. 1918. Records 358 U.K., 64 Can., 7 S.A., 1 Aust., 2 German burials, and 117 special memorials.

1651 NOYON NEW BRITISH CEMETERY (OISE). 15 miles NE. of Compiegne, 1 mile N. of Noyon Sta., near road to Guiscard. Noyon was Brit. Hdqtrs. Aug. 26th–28th 1914, but was occupied by Germans Sept. 1st, finally recaptured by Third French Army Aug. 1918. Records 241 U.K., 8 Can., and 1 U.S.A. burials.

509 CHAUNY COMMUNAL CEMETERY BRITISH EXTENSION (AISNE). 1½ miles N. of Chauny Sta., NE. of town, N. of road to La Fère. Created after the Armistice from isolated graves and small Cems. on the battle-fields of Feb. to July 1918 in the vicinity. Records 909 U.K., 21 Can. burials, and 22 special memorials.

361 BRAINE COMMUNAL CEMETERY (AISNE). 10 miles E. of Soissons, ¾ mile N. of Braine Sta., near road to Vieil-Arcy. All casualties from original B.E.F. who fell Sept. and Oct. 1914. Records 143 U.K. burials.

2284 VAILLY BRIT-ISH CEMETERY, VAILLY - SUR - AISNE (AISNE). 10 miles E. of Soissons, W. of Vailly village and sta. on road to Celles. Created after the Armistice from isolated graves and small Cems. on the battle-fields in vicinity and adjoins a large French National Cem. Capt. Theodore Wright, V.C., R.E., is buried here. Records 678 U.K., 1 Can., 1 French, 1 German burials, and 2 special memorials.

2311 VENDRESSE BRITISH CEMETERY (AISNE). 12 miles S. of Laon, 3 miles N. of Bourg-et-Comin Sta., ½ mile N. of village on road to Cerny - en - Laonnois. The 8th, 21st and 50th Divs. were heavily attacked here by Germans May 27th 1918. Cem. was made after Armistice from isolated graves. Records 657 U.K. burials and 49 special memorials.

2312 VENDRESSE CHURCHYARD (AISNE). 12 miles S. of Laon, 2½ miles N. of Bourg-et-Comin Sta., on N. edge of village. Burials from 1st Div., who took Vendresse in attack on Courtecon Ridge Sept. 13th–15th 1918. Records 84 U.K. burials.

614　CROUY-VAUX-ROT FRENCH NATIONAL CEMETERY (AISNE). 3¾ miles N. of Soissons Sta., ½ mile W. of Crouy Sta., on road to Vauxrot. Graves re-grouped from surrounding battle-fields. Contains large number of Seaforth Highldrs., who fell Sept. 1914. British plot records 50 U.K. burials.

2298　VAUXBUIN FRENCH NATIONAL CEMETERY (AISNE). 3¼ miles SW. of Soissons, SW. of village, W. of main road to Villers Cotterêts. Cem. reflects successful attack of 15th (Scot.) and 34th Divs. in this Sector July 23rd 1918. British plot records 284 U.K. burials.

423　BUZANCY MILITARY CEMETERY (AISNE). 4½ miles S. of Soissons, 2 miles S. of Berzy-le-Sec Sta., on by-road 200 yards W. of village. Begun by 15th (Scot.) Div. July 1918, who earned great distinction in fierce struggle for Buzancy July 23rd 1918. (Mem. erected to this Div. by French Command 300 yards N. of Cem.). Records 330 U.K. burials.

1936 ROYALLIEU FRENCH NATIONAL CEMETERY, COMPIÈGNE (OISE). 2 miles S. of Compiègne Sta., ¾ mile NE. of Royallieu, E. of road to Senlis. British burials from Sept. 1914 and July–Aug. 1918. British plot records 80 U.K. burials.

1856 RAPERIE BRITISH CEMETERY, VILLEMONTOIRE (AISNE). 2½ miles E. of Vierzy Sta., S. of village and sugar factory. Is connected entirely with victorious advance of 15th (Scot.) and 34th Divs. July 23rd to Aug. 2nd 1918. Records 600 U.K. burials and 12 special memorials.

969 GUARDS' GRAVE, VILLERS - COTTERETS FOREST (AISNE). 2½ miles N. of Villers-Cotterets on road to Viviers in heart of forest. Casualties from Grenadier, Irish, Coldstream and Life Guards, who fell Sept. 1st–19th 1914. Records 98 U.K. burials.

1692 OULCHY - LE - CHÂTEAU CHURCH-YARD EXTENSION (AISNE). 13 miles S. of Soissons, 12 miles N. of Château - Thierry, $1\frac{1}{2}$ miles NE. of Oulchy-Breny Sta. British burials made July–Aug. 1918 (large number of 1/5th Argyl. and Suth. Hdrs.), also three 1914 burials. Records 124 U.K. burials.

1536 MONTREUIL-AUX-LIONS BRITISH CEMETERY (AISNE). $6\frac{1}{2}$ miles NE. of La-Ferté-sous-Jouarre Sta., E. of village on road to Château-Thierry. Created after Armistice from isolated graves mostly from battle-fields of 1914. Records 139 U.K. burials.

1727 PERREUSE CHÂTEAU FRENCH NATIONAL CEME-TERY, SIGNY - SIG-NETS (SEINE - ET - MARNE). $4\frac{1}{2}$ miles SW. of La Ferté-sous-Jouarre Sta., E. of village in Château grounds. British casualties occurred in fighting at Signy-Signets Sept. 1914, and burials were made by 11th Field Amb. British plot records 54 U.K. burials.

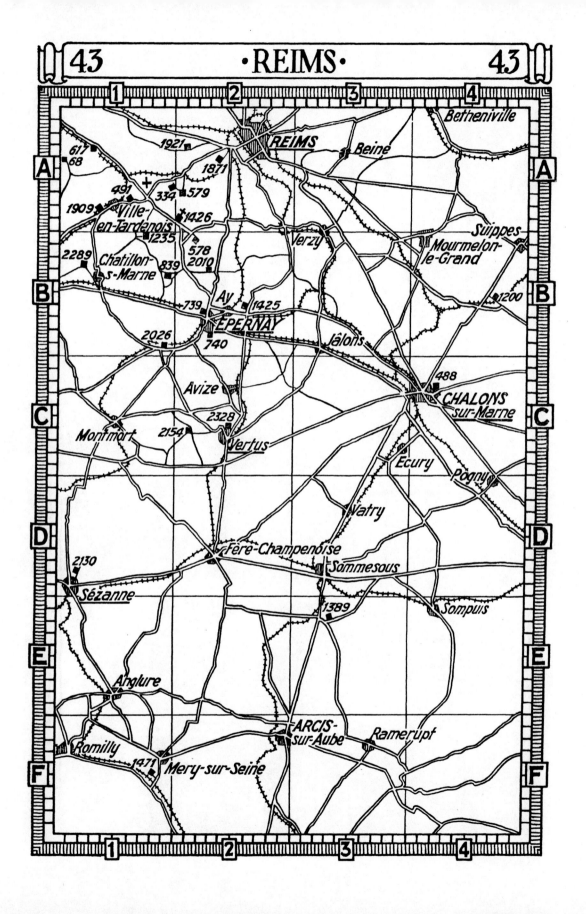

491 CHAMBRECY BRITISH CEMETERY (MARNE). 11 miles SW. of Reims, 1¾ miles E. of Ville-en-Tardenois Sta., E. of village on road to Reims. Made after Armistice mostly from casualties of the 9th Div., who fell June 1918, and the 51st and 62nd Divs. in July 1918 in fighting around Montagne de Bligny. Records 433 U.K., 1 N.Z., 1 Ind. burials, and 1 special memorial.

334 BOUILLY CROSS-ROADS MILITARY CEMETERY (MARNE) 7 miles SW. of Reims, 1 mile S. of Clairizet-Ste. Euphraise Sta., 400 yards E. of village. Begun by the Braucardiers of the French 45th Div. Aug. 1918. Records 136 U.K. burials and 5 special memorials.

579 COURMAS BRITISH CEMETERY (MARNE). 7 miles SW. of Reims, 1¾ miles S. of Clairizet-Ste. Euphraise Sta., ½ mile SW. of Courmas. On line taken by XXII Corps (15th, 34th, 51st and 62nd Divs.) July 1918. Records 207 U.K. burials.

1426 MARFAUX BRITISH CEMETERY (MARNE). 11½ miles from Reims, 10 from Epernay, 4½ from Chambrecy Sta., on Fismes-Epernay road. Marfaux was taken July 23rd 1918 by 51st (Highland) and 62nd Divs. against rigorous and determined resistance. Records 1,102 U.K., 15 N.Z. burials, and 12 special memorials. (Mem. to N.Z. 'Missing' in Record Building.)

1235 LA NEUVILLE-AU-LARRIS MILITARY CEMETERY (MARNE). 13 miles SW. of Reims, 3½ miles SE. of Ville-en-Tardenois Sta., E. of village, on road to Paradis. Begun by French Senégalais, and used by British after Armistice. Records 98 U.K. burials.

2010 ST. IMOGE CHURCHYARD (MARNE). 6 miles N. of Epernay, in Forest of Reims, ¾ mile W. of Epernay-Reims road. Burials from 51st (Highland) Div. who fell Aug. 19th–28th 1918 in fighting before village of St. Imoge. Records 78 U.K. and 2 French burials.

740 EPERNAY FRENCH NATIONAL CEMETERY (MARNE) S. of town, in Avenue Louise, which runs E. off Rue de l'Hôpital Auban-Moet. First burials made in Sept. 1914, but majority are 1918 casualties. Cem. was enlarged after Armistice. Records 265 U.K. and 2 N.Z. burials.

2130 SÉZANNE COMMUNAL CEMETERY (MARNE). 38 miles E. of Paris, 1 mile N. of Sézanne Sta., on NE. outskirts of town, E. of road to Epernay. British casualties died June–July and Aug. 1918. Records 126 U.K. and 1 N.Z. burials.

CEMETERIES OUTSIDE THE BATTLE AREA

1330 LIÉGE COMMUNAL CEMETERY (LIEGE). E. of town and sta., in suburb of Robermont. Tram service from Liége to Bois de Breux stops at Cem. gates. Used by Germans as Prisoners of War Cem. The forts of Liége proved a serious obstacle to German advance through France and Belgium in 1914. Records 44 U.K., 3 Can., 1 Aust., 1 N.Z., and 1 Russ. burials.

2108 SEDAN (ST. CHARLES) COMMUNAL CEMETERY, FRENCH MILITARY EXTENSION (ARDENNES). ¾ mile N. of sta., on NE. outskirts of town, N. of road to Charleville. All burials are those who died as Prisoners of War from April 9th to Oct. 30th 1918. British graves record 50 U.K. burials.

490 CHAMBIERE FRENCH NATIONAL CEMETERY, METZ (MOSELLE). 2 miles NE. of Metz Sta., N. of road to Thionville. Majority of casualties died as Prisoners of War between May and Oct. 1918. Records 71 U.K., 2 Can. burials, and 7 special memorials.

2085 SARRALBE MILITARY CEMETERY (MOSELLE). 9½ miles from Sarreguemines, 3 miles from Sarralbe Sta., SW. of village, near Com. Cem. on road to Rech. Used by Germans from Feb. 1917 as Prisoners of War Cem., and enlarged after Armistice. Records 94 U.K. burials and 11 special memorials.

500 CHARMES MILITARY CEMETERY, ESSEGNY (VOSGES). 2½ miles from town and sta. Records 201 burials who died between Nov. 1917 and Feb. 1919; of these there are 106 officers and men of the R.A.F. and R.N.A.S. The original war Cem. was enlarged by concentrations from smaller cems. in the vicinity. Records 143 U.K., 11 Can., 40 Ind., 4 Chin., 1 Russ., 2 German burials, and 1 special memorial.

1282 LE MANS GRAND CEMETERY (SARTHE). 1 mile from centre of town, with halte on tramway from sta. British plot in centre of Cem. near to French military graves. Burials from hospitals in vicinity. Records 60 U.K. and 1 Can. burials.

2251 TOURLAVILLE COMMUNAL CEMETERY, CHERBOURG (MANCHE). 3 miles E. of Cherbourg, S. of Tourlaville. British plot in centre of Cem., W. of main path. Used for British burials from May 1918 to Feb. 1919 from hospital in vicinity. Records 55 U.K., 2 S.A., and 2 German burials.

2258 TOUTES-AIDES CEMETERY, ST. NAZAIRE (LOIRE-INF.). ¾ mile W. of St. Nazaire Sta., W. of Boulevard Victor Hugo, N. of road to Vannes. Burials from original B.E.F., Sept. - Oct. 1914. Records 82 U.K., 23 French, and 10 German burials.

1999 ST. GERMAIN-AU-MONT D'OR COMMUNAL CEMETERY EXTENSION (RHÔNE). 9 miles N. of Lyon, SE. of St. Germain Sta., E. of village on hill overlooking R. Saone. Burials were made from a British camp and hospital near village from Nov. 1917 until end of War. Records 80 U.K., 2 Aust., 7 Ind., and 6 B.W.I. burials.

CEMETERY

MEMORIAL

1447 MAZARGUES CEMETERY AND MEMORIAL TO 'MISSING', MARSEILLE (BOUCHES-DU-RHÔNE). 6½ miles S. of St. Charles Sta. Marseille. (Tram service from town to village of Mazargues.) Burials represent nearly every British Possession and include victims of the *Majestic* and *Arcadian* torpedoed off Marseilles. Cem. records 230 U.K., 14 Aust., 3 S.A., 3 N.Z., 984 Ind., 188 B.W.I., 13 Nat. Sea., 11 Egypt., 4 Fiji, 6 Chin., 1 French, 1 Jap. burials, and 2 special memorials. Mem. records 125 'Missing'.

THE SILENT CITIES

[For various reasons the following Cemeteries have not yet been constructed.]

91   Assevillers New British Cemetery.

120   Aulnoye Communal Cemetery.

428   Caestre Military Cemetery.

449   2/Canadian Cemetery (Sunken Road), Contalmaison.

823   51/Divisional Cemetery, Flesquières.

948   Gouy British Cemetery.

1196   La Chapellette British and Indian Cemetery, Péronne.

1865   Redan Ridge Cemetery No. 1, Beaumont-Hamel.

1989   Ste. Emilie British Cemetery, Villers-Faucon.

2121–2   Sequehart British Cemeteries, No. 1 and No. 2.

2184   Sunken Road Cemetery, Contalmaison.

2293   Vaulx A.D.S. Cemetery, Vaulx-Vraucourt.

2294   Vaulx Australian Field Ambulance Cemetery, Vaulx-Vraucourt.

2394   Vraucourt Copse British Cemetery, Vaulx-Vraucourt.

INDEX TO MAPS (DIAGRAM)

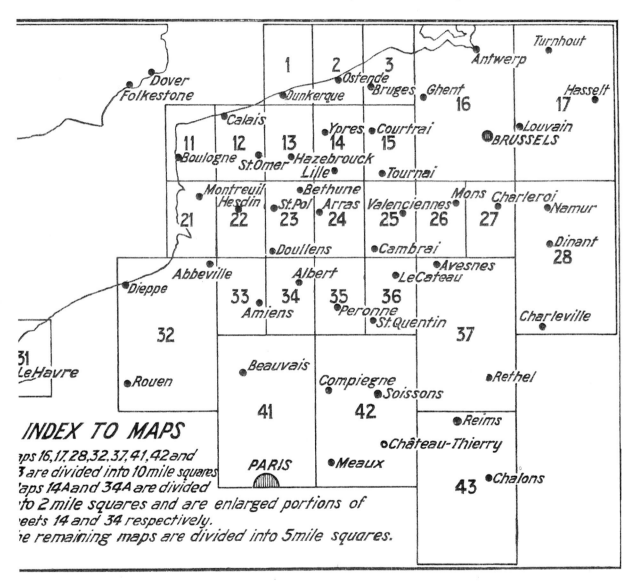

Dover
Folkestone

Turnhout
Antwerp
Hasselt

1   2   3
Ostende
Dunkerque   Bruges   Ghent   16   17

Calais   Ypres   Courtrai   Louvain
11   12   13   14   15   BRUSSELS
Boulogne   St.Omer   Hazebrouck
Lille   Tournai

Montreuil   Bethune   Mons   Charleroi
Hesdin   St.Pol   Arras   Valenciennes   Namur
21   22   23   24   25   26   27

Doullens   Cambrai   Dinant
28

Abbeville   Albert   Avesnes
Dieppe   LeCateau   Charleville
33   34   35   36
Amiens   Peronne
St.Quentin   37
32

Beauvais
Rouen   Compiegne   Rethel
Soissons
41   42   Reims
Château-Thierry
PARIS   Meaux   Chalons
43

INDEX TO MAPS

aps 16,17,28,32,37,41,42 and
3 are divided into 10 mile squares
aps 14A and 34A are divided
to 2 mile squares and are enlarged portions of
eets 14 and 34 respectively.
he remaining maps are divided into 5 mile squares.

31
LeHavre

INDEX TO CEMETERIES

The Cemeteries are shown thus ■ *2216* on the maps.

The reference number in the first column of this index corresponds with the number of the cemetery on the map.

The map location in the second column gives the number of the map and the square in which the cemetery will be found.

* Denotes cemeteries in Belgium.

REFERENCE NUMBER	MAP LOCATION	MAP PAGE	ILLUSTRA-TION PAGE	NAME OF CEMETERY
37	34.C.1	222	232	Allonville Communal Cemetery
38	23.A.2	109	—	Allouagne Communal Cemetery
39	36.A.3	315	319	Amerval Communal Cemetery Extension, Soleames
40	23.A.2	109	—	Ames Communal Cemetery
41	34.A.1	222	—	Amplier Communal Cemetery (St. Nazaire)
43	34A.D.2	250	265	Ancre British Cemetery, Beaumont Hamel
44	34.F.4	222	—	Andechy Communal Cemetery
45	16.E.3	100	—	*Anderlecht Communal Cemetery
46	27.C.2	202	—	*Anderlues Communal Cemetery
47	—	—	—	Angers West Cemetery, 50 miles NE. of Nantes
48	—	—	—	*Angleur Communal Cemetery, 2½ miles SE. of Liege
49	26.D.1	196	—	*Angre Communal Cemetery
50	26.D.1	196	—	*Angreau Communal Cemetery
51	14.F.4	34	—	Annappes Churchyard
52	42.B.1	341	—	Annel Communal Cemetery, Longueil-Annel (Oise)
53	23.B.4	109	—	Annequin Communal Cemetery
54	24.F.4	137	175	Anneux British Cemetery
55	23.A.3	109	—	Annezin Communal Cemetery
56	35.F.4	285	308	Annois Communal Cemetery
57	37.B.2	332	—	Anor Communal Cemetery
58	15.C.3	97	—	*Anseghem Communal Cemetery
59	15.E.3	97	—	*Anserœul Communal Cemetery
60	28.A.3	205	—	*Antheit Communal Cemetery
61	42.D.1	341	—	Antilly Churchyard
62	25.A.3	180	—	*Antoing Communal Cemetery
1177	16.B.4	100	—	*Antwerp (Kiel) Town Cemetery
63	15.E.4	97	—	*Anvaing Churchyard
64	22.B.4	106	—	Anvin Churchyard
65	14.F.1	34	87	Anzac Cemetery, Sailly-sur-la-Lys
66	23.D.4	109	134	Anzin-St. Aubin British Cemetery
67	—	—	—	Arcachon Communal Cemetery (Gironde), 32 miles SW. of Bordeaux
68	43.A.1	349	—	Arcis le Ponsart Communal Cemetery
69	—	—	—	Argentan Communal Cemetery, 34 miles SE. of Caen
70	33.C.4	216	—	Argœuvres Communal Cemetery
71	24.E.4	137	—	Arleux Communal Cemetery
72	—	—	—	*Arlon Communal Cemetery, 15 miles NW. of Luxembourg
73	—	—	—	Arnaville Communal Cemetery, 10 miles SW. of Metz
74	13.C.2	18	22	Arneke British Cemetery
75	13.C.2	18	—	Arneke Churchyard
76	32.B.1	210	213	Arques-la-Bataille British Cemetery
77	24.D.1	137	147	Arras Road British Cemetery, Roclincourt
78	—	—	—	Arry Churchyard, 10 miles SW. of Metz
79	21.D.3	104	—	Arry Communal Cemetery
80	—	—	—	Ars-sur-Moselle Churchyard, 5 miles SE. of Metz
81	35.F.4	285	—	Artemps Communal Cemetery
82	14.B.2	34	75	*Artillery Wood Cemetery, Bœsinghe
83	—	—	—	Artolsheim Communal Cemetery, 30 miles SW. of Strasbourg
84	25.E.3	180	—	Artres Communal Cemetery
85	34.F.3	222	—	Arvillers Communal Cemetery
86	14.F.4	34	96	Ascq Communal Cemetery
87	41.D.2	338	—	Asnières-sur-Oise Communal Cemetery
88	26.C.3	196	—	*Asquillies Churchyard
89	26.C.3	196	—	*Asquillies Communal Cemetery
90	26.E.4	196	—	Assevent French National Cemetery

REFERENCE NUMBER	MAP LOCATION	MAP PAGE	ILLUSTRA- TION PAGE	NAME OF CEMETERY
				B
148	23.E.3	109	128	Bac-du-Sud British Cemetery, Bailleulval.
149	26.F.2	196	—	Bachant Communal Cemetery
150	3.F.4	8	—	*Baerle Churchyard
151	33.A.4	216	220	Bagneux British Cemetery, Gézaincourt
152	13.D.4	18	25	Bailleul Communal Cemetery
153	13.D.4	18	25	Bailleul Communal Cemetery Extension
154	23.F.3	109	—	Bailleulmont Communal Cemetery
155	24.D.1	137	151	Bailleul Road East Cemetery, St. Laurent-Blangy
156	24.D.1	137	147	Bailleul Road West Cemetery, St. Laurent-Blangy
157	23.E.3	109	—	Bailleulval Communal Cemetery
158	15.F.1	97	—	Baisieux Churchyard
159	26.C.1	196	—	*Baisieux Communal Cemetery
161	34.C.2	222	—	Baizieux New Communal Cemetery
162	23.C.2	109	—	Bajus Churchyard
163	28.A.1	205	—	*Balâtre Communal Cemetery
164	3.D.3	8	—	*Balgerhœk Communal Cemetery
165	35.A.2	285	287	Bancourt British Cemetery
166	35.A.2	285	—	Bancourt Communal Cemetery
168	35.A.1	285	286	Bapaume Australian Cemetery
170	34A.F.2	250	252	Bapaume Post Military Cemetery, Albert
171	35.A.2	285	—	Barastre Communal Cemetery
173	14A.A.3	36	44	*Bard Cottage Cemetery, Bœsinghe
174	23.B.3	109	120	Barlin Communal Cemetery Extension
175	23.E.3	109	—	Barly French Military Cemetery
176	—	—	—	Bar-le-Duc French National Cemetery, 47 miles W. of Nancy
177	41.D.4	338	—	Baron Communal Cemetery
178	42.F.3	341	—	Bassevelle Communal Cemetery
179	—	—	—	Baulme-la-Roche Communal Cemetery (Cote d'Or), 13 miles W. of Dijon
180	26.E.2	196	—	Bavay Communal Cemetery
181	34.C.2	222	231	Bavelincourt Communal Cemetery
182	23.E.3	109	—	Bavincourt Communal Cemetery
183	12.C.3	14	—	Bayenghem-les-Eperlecques Churchyard
184	12.E.3	14	—	Bayenghem-les-Seninghem Churchyard
185	—	—	—	Bayonne (St. Léon) Cemetery (Basses Pyrénées), 5 miles E. of Biarritz
187	34A.E.4	250	—	Bazentin-le-Petit Communal Cemetery
188	34A.E.4	250	277	Bazentin-le-Petit Communal Cemetery Extension
189	34A.E.4	250	277	Bazentin-le-Petit Military Cemetery
190	36.B.4	315	—	Bazuel Communal Cemetery
191	34.C.3	222	237	Beacon Cemetery, Sailly-Laurette
192	32.D.3	210	—	Beaubec-la-Rosière Communal Cemetery
193	34.E.3	222	246	Beaucourt British Cemetery, Beaucourt-en-Santerre
194	34.E.3	222	—	Beaucourt-en-Santerre Churchyard
195	25.E.4	180	—	Beaudignies Communal Cemetery
196	34.F.3	222	—	Beaufort Churchyard
197	35.A.1	285	288	Beaulencourt British Cemetery, Ligny-Thilloy
198	35.D.3	285	—	Beaumetz Communal Cemetery, Cartigny
200	22.F.3	106	—	Beaumetz Communal Cemetery
199	23.E.4	109	—	Beaumetz-les-Loges Communal Cemetery
201	35.A.2	285	290	Beaumetz Cross Roads Cemetery, Beaumetz-les-Cambrai
202	35.A.2	285	290	Beaumetz-les-Cambrai Military Cemetery No. 1
203	36.A.3	315	—	Beaumont Communal Cemetery

REFERENCE NUMBER	MAP LOCATION	MAP PAGE	ILLUSTRATION PAGE	NAME OF CEMETERY
204	24.C.2	137	—	Beaumont (Pas de Calais) Communal Cemetery
205	34A.C.1	250	262	Beaumont-Hamel British Cemetery
206	34.A.1	222	—	Beauquesne Communal Cemetery
207	25.F.3	180	194	Beaurain British Cemetery
208	28.D.2	205	—	*Beauraing Communal Cemetery
209	24.E.1	137	155	Beaurains Road Cemetery, Beaurains
210	37.F.1	332	336	Beaurepaire French National Cemetery, Pontavert
211	36.C.1	315	327	Beaurevoir British Cemetery
212	36.C.1	315	—	Beaurevoir Communal Cemetery
213	36.C.1	315	328	Beaurevoir Communal Cemetery, British Extension
214	37.F.1	332	—	Beaurieux Churchyard
215	34.A.1	222	226	Beauval Communal Cemetery
216	41.B.1	338	—	Beauvais-Marissel French National Cemetery
217	41.B.1	338	—	Beauvais Communal Cemetery (Oise)
218	36.A.2	315	—	Beauvois-en-Cambresis Communal Cemetery
219	34A.F.2	250	272	Bécourt Military Cemetery, Bécordel-Bécourt
220	36.B.3	315	—	Becquigny Communal Cemetery
221	14A.C.3	36	54	*Bedford House Cemetery, Zillebeke
222	24.D.1	137	148	Beehive Cemetery, Willerval
223	34.C.2	222	—	Behencourt Churchyard
224	14A.B.2	36	47	*Belgian Battery Corner Cemetery, Ypres
225	28.A.2	205	206	*Belgrade Communal Cemetery, Namur
226	—	—	·	Beliet Communal Cemetery (Gironde), 26 miles SW. of Bordeaux
227	23.E.4	109	128	Bellacourt Military Cemetery, Rivière
228	25.D.2	180	—	Bellaing Churchyard
229	15.D.1	97	—	*Belleghem Churchyard
230	25.F.3	180	193	Belle Vue British Cemetery, Briastre
231	35.C.4	285	307	Bellicourt British Cemetery
232	26.D.1	196	—	Bellignies Churchyard
233	42.F.3	341	—	Bellot Communal Cemetery
234	16.B.4	100	—	*Berchem Communal Cemetery (Antwerp)
235	15.D.3	97	—	*Berchem-les-Audenarde Communal Cemetery
237	14A.F.3	36	72	*Berks Cemetery Extension, Plœgsteert
238	13.F.2	18	—	Berguette Churchyard
239	26.F.2	196	—	Berlaimont Communal Cemetery
240	26.F.2	196	201	Berlaimont Communal Cemetery Extension
241	23.F.3	109	131	Berles-au-Bois Churchyard Extension
242	23.F.3	109	131	Berles New Military Cemetery, Berles-au-Bois
243	23.F.3	109	131	Berles Position Military Cemetery, Berles-au-Bois
244	25.E.3	180	187	Bermerain Communal Cemetery
245	26.E.1	196	—	Bermeries Communal Cemetery
246	34A.F.4	250	279	Bernafay Wood British Cemetery, Montauban
247	33.A.3	216	—	Bernaville Communal Cemetery
248	23.E.4	109	—	Berneville Communal Cemetery
249	33.A.3	216	—	Berneuil Communal Cemetery
150	33.C.4	216	—	Bertangles Communal Cemetery
251	33.B.3	216	—	Berteaucourt-les-Dames Churchyard
252	13.D.4	18	28	Bertenacre Military Cemetery, Flêtre
253	36.D.1	315	331	Berthaucourt Communal Cemetery, Pontru
254	35.A.2	285	291	Bertincourt Château British Cemetery
255	34.A.3	222	—	Bertrancourt Communal Cemetery
256	34.A.3	222	225	Bertrancourt Military Cemetery
257	36.A.3	315	319	Bertry Communal Cemetery
258	—	—	—	Besançon (St. Claude) Communal Cemetery (Doubs), 46 miles E. of Dijon
259	42.D.1	341	—	Bethancourt Communal Cemetery
260	36.A.2	315	316	Bethencourt Communal Cemetery

REFERENCE NUMBER	MAP LOCATION	MAP PAGE	ILLUSTRA-TION PAGE	NAME OF CEMETERY
261	14A.E.3	36	70	*Bethleem Farm East Cemetery, Messines
262	14A.E.3	36	70	*Bethleem Farm West Cemetery, Messines
263	23.A.4	109	110	Bethune Town Cemetery
264	33.B.1	216	—	Bettencourt Rivière Churchyard
265	26.D.1	196	—	Bettrechies Communal Cemetery
266	35.A.1	285	—	Beugnâtre Communal Cemetery
267	21.A.4	104	—	Beussent Churchyard
268	23.A.4	109	111	Beuvry Communal Cemetery
269	23.A.4	109	111	Beuvry Communal Cemetery Extension
270	25.B.1	180	—	Beuvry-les-Orchies Communal Cemetery
271	13.A.4	18	—	*Beveren-sur-Yser Churchyard
272	15.B.2	97	—	*Beveren-les-Courtrai Churchyard
273	25.F.2	180	—	Bevillers Communal Cemetery
274	14.B.4	34	—	*Beythem Communal Cemetery, Rumbeke
275	42.E.2	341	—	Bezu-le-Guèry Communal Cemetery
276	23.F.3	109	132	Bienvillers Military Cemetery
277	—	—	—	Biganos Communal Cemetery (Gironde), 25 miles SW. of Bordeaux
278	34A.B.5	250	—	Bihucourt Communal Cemetery
279	24.C.2	137	—	Billy-Montigny Communal Cemetery
280	27.B.1	202	—	*Binche Communal Cemetery
281	14A.B.4	36	50	*Birr Cross-Roads Cemetery, Zillebeke
282	—	—	—	Biscarosse-Bourg Communal Cemetery (Landes), 42 miles SW. of Bordeaux
283	15.C.1	97	—	*Bisseghem Communal Cemetery
284	23.E.4	109	—	Blairville Churchyard
285	—	—	—	Blaisy Bas Churchyard (Côte d'Or), 13 miles W. of Dijon
286	15.F.1	97	—	*Blandain Churchyard
287	32.B.3	210	—	Blangy-sur-Bresle Communal Cemetery
288	34.D.1	222	234	Blangy-Tronville Communal Cemetery
289	2.C.4	6	—	*Blankenberghe Communal Cemetery
290	32.D.4	210	214	Blargies Communal Cemetery Extension
291	13.E.2	18	—	Blaringhem Churchyard
292	26.D.2	196	—	*Blaugies Communal Cemetery
293	14A.C.3	36	56	*Blauwepoort Farm Cemetery, Zillebeke
294	25.A.2	180	—	*Bleharies Communal Cemetery
295	42.B.2	341	—	Blerancourt Communal Cemetery
296	12.C.4	14	16	Bleue Maison Military Cemetery, Eperlecques
297	14A.A.2	36	38	*Bleuet Farm Cemetery, Elverdinghe
298	31.D.1	207	—	Bléville Communal Cemetery, Le Havre
299	34A.E.2	250	271	Blighty Valley Cemetery, Authuile Wood, Aveluy
300	13.E.2	18	—	Boëseghen Churchyard
301	14.B.2	34	—	*Bœsinghe Churchyard
302	28.F.1	205	—	Bogny-Braux Communal Cemetery
303	24.D.1	137	148	Bois Carré British Cemetery, Thélus
304	24.B.1	137	141	Bois Carré Military Cemetery, Haisnes
305	27.B.2	202	—	*Bois d'Haine Communal Cemetery
306	23.C.4	109	119	Bois de Noulette British Cemetery, Aix Noulette
307	36.B.1	315	326	Bois des Angles British Cemetery, Crèvecœur-sur-L'Escaut
308	14.F.2	34	89	Bois Grenier Communal Cemetery
309	32.E.1	210	213	Boisguillaume Communal Cemetery, Rouen
310	32.E.1	210	213	Boisguillaume Communal Cemetery Extension, Rouen
311	24.F.1	137	—	Boisleux-au-Mont Communal Cemetery
313	42.F.2	341	—	Boitron Churchyard
314	13.B.1	18	—	Bollezeele Communal Cemetery
315	12.F.4	14	—	Bomy Churchyard
317	34.C.2	222	236	Bonnay Communal Cemetery Extension

REFERENCE NUMBER	MAP LOCATION	MAP PAGE	ILLUSTRA- TION PAGE	NAME OF CEMETERY
374	34.C.4	222	—	Bray-sur-Somme French National Cemetery
375	34.C.4	222	239	Bray Vale British Cemetery, Bray-sur-Somme
376	24.D.3	137	169	Brebières British Cemetery
377	2.D.3	6	—	*Breedene Churchyard
378	34.C.2	222	—	Bresle Communal Cemetery
1175	—	—	—	Brest (Kerfautras) Cemetery, Lambèzeele (Finisterè). 320 miles W. of Paris
2268	42.B.1	341	—	Breuil Churchyard, Trosly-Breuil
379	14.F.2	34	89	Brewery Orchard Cemetery, Bois Grenier
380	25.F.3	180	—	Briastre Communal Cemetery
381	14A.A.4	36	51	*Bridge House Cemetery, Langemarck
382	35.D.2	285	310	Brie British Cemetery
385	25.C.1	180	—	Brillon Communal Cemetery
386	36.F.2	315	—	Brissay-Choigny Churchyard
387	34A.G.3	250	284	Bronfay Farm Military Cemetery, Bray-sur-Somme
388	35.F.3	285	—	Brouchy Churchyard
389	23.E.1	109	—	Brouilly Churchyard
390	24.D.2	137	153	Brown's Copse Cemetery, Rœux
391	23.A.4	109	114	Brown's Road Military Cemetery, Festubert
392	13.C.1	18	—	Broxeele Churchyard
393	23.B.3	109	116	Bruay Communal Cemetery Extension
394	25.C.3	180	—	Bruay-sur-l'Escaut Communal Cemetery
395	3.D.1	8	—	*Bruges General Cemetery, Assebrouck
396	25.B.3	180	—	Bruille St. Amand Churchyard
397	16.E.4	100	101	*Brussels Communal Cemetery, Evère
398	25.A.2	180	—	*Bruyelle Communal Cemetery
399	34A.B.3	250	—	Bucquoy Communal Cemetery
400	34A.B.3	250	257	Bucquoy Communal Cemetery Extension
401	23.E.4	109	135	Bucquoy Road Cemetery, Ficheux
402	42.C.3	341	—	Bucy-le-Long Communal Cemetery
403	14A.A.4	36	51	*Buffs Road Cemetery, St. Jean-lès-Ypres
405	35.D.3	285	—	Buire Communal Cemetery
406	34.C.3	222	—	Buire-sur-Ancre Communal Cemetery
407	41.B.2	338	—	Bulles Communal Cemetery
408	34A.E.5	250	277	Bulls Road Cemetery, Flers
409	23.B.4	109	121	Bully-Grenay Communal Cemetery, French Extension
410	23.B.4	109	121	Bully-Grenay Communal Cemetery, British Extension
411	24.E.1	137	156	Bunyans Cemetery, Tilloy-les-Mofflaines
412	23.A.2	109	—	Burbure Communal Cemetery
413	14A.C.3	36	56	*Bus House Cemetery, Voormezeele
415	36.B.3	315	—	Busigny Communal Cemetery
416	36.B.3	315	324	Busigny Communal Cemetery Extension
417	34.A.3	222	—	Bus-lès-Artois Communal Cemetery
418	13.F.2	18	—	Busnes Communal Cemetery
419	42F.2	341	—	Bussières Communal Cemetery
420	34.D.1	222	—	Bussy-lès-Daours Communal Cemetery
421	14.C.3	34	78	*Buttes New British Cemetery, Polygon Wood, Zonnebeke
422	13.C.1	18	—	Buysscheure Churchyard
423	42.C.3	341	346	Buzancy Military Cemetery

C

424	23.C.4	109	123	Cabaret Rouge British Cemetery, Souchez
425	14A.E.3	36	70	*Cabin Hill Cemetery, Wytschæte
426	34.E.2	222	—	Cachy Communal Cemetery
427	13.D.3	18	—	Cæstre Communal Cemetery

REFERENCE NUMBER	MAP LOCATION	MAP PAGE	ILLUSTRA- TION PAGE	NAME OF CEMETERY
428	13.D.3	18	—	Cæstre Military Cemetery. See page 357
429	24.F.3	137	171	Cagnicourt British Cemetery
430	25.F.1	180	—	Cagnoncles Communal Cemetery
431	34.D.1	222	—	Cagny Communal Cemetery
432	42.A.2	341	—	Caillouel Churchyard
433	34.E.3	222	245	Caix British Cemetery
434	34.E.3	222	—	Caix Communal Cemetery
436	12.A.1	14	15	Calais Southern Cemetery
437	13.F.3	18	—	Calonne-sur-la-Lys Communal Cemetery
438	36.C.2	315	330	Calvaire Cemetery, Montbréhain
439	14.E.2	34	79	*Calvaire (Essex) Military Cemetery, Plœgsteert
440	25.F.1	180	190	Cambrai East Military Cemetery
441	23.B.4	109	115	Cambrin Churchyard Extension
442	23.A.4	109	115	Cambrin Military Cemetery
443	34.D.1	222	—	Camon Communal Cemetery
444	12.F.2	14	—	Campagne-les-Boulonnais Churchyard
445	13.D.1	18	—	Campagne-les-Wardrecques Churchyard
446	15.F.1	97	—	Camphin-en-Pévèle Communal Cemetery
447	25.F.1	180	189	Canada Cemetery, Tilloy-les-Cambrai
448	14A.A.1	36	37	*Canada Farm Cemetery, Elverdinghe
449	34A.E.3	250	—	2/Canadian Cemetery (Sunken Road), Contalmaison. See page 357
451	24.C.1	137	145	Canadian Cemetery No. 2, Neuville St. Vaast
452	33.A.4	216	—	Candas Communal Cemetery
453	25.E.3	180	186	Canonne Farm British Cemetery, Sommaing
454	35.A.4	285	295	Cantaing British Cemetery
455	24.F.4	137	173	Cantimpré Canadian Cemetery, Sailly (Nord)
456	25.E.4	180	188	Capelle-Beaudignies Road Cemetery, Capelle
457	—	—	—	Cap-d'Ail Communal Cemetery (Alpes Maritimes), 5 miles E. of Nice
458	15.C.1	97	—	*Capelle Ste. Catherine Communal Cemetery
459	—	—	—	Carling Communal Cemetery, 25 miles E. of Metz
460	11.E.3	10	—	Carly Communal Cemetery
461	25.F.2	180	194	Carnières Communal Cemetery Extension
462	34A.G.4	250	284	Carnoy Military Cemetery
463	37.A.1	332	—	Cartignies Communal Cemetery
464	24.B.2	137	179	Carvin Communal Cemetery
465	36.E.1	315	—	Castres Communal Cemetery
466	41.C.3	338	—	Catenoy French National Cemetery
467	34A.F.4	250	278	Caterpillar Valley Cemetery, Longueval
468	36.A.2	315	—	Cattenières Churchyard
469	—	—	—	Caucade British Civil Cemetery, Nice, 100 miles NE. of Marseille
470	36.A.2	315	317	Caudry British Cemetery
471	36.A.2	315	318	Caudry Old Communal Cemetery
472	35.D.3	285	—	Caulaincourt Communal Cemetery
473	36.A.2	315	—	Caullery Communal Cemetery
474	42.A.2	341	—	Caumont Churchyard
475	25.F.1	180	—	Cauroir Communal Cemetery
476	33.D.2	216	—	Cavillon Communal Cemetery
477	34.E 3	222	—	Cayeux-en-Santerre Communal Cemetery
478	34.E.3	222	245	Cayeux Military Cemetery, Cayeux-en-Santerre
479	21.F.1	104	—	Cayeux-sur-Mer Churchyard
480	14.B.2	34	75	*Cement House Cemetery, Langemarck
481	—	—	—	Censeau Communal Cemetery (Jura), 60 miles SE. of Dijon
483	34.D.3	222	242	Cerisy-Gailly French National Cemetery
484	34.D.3	222	242	Cerisy-Gailly Military Cemetery

REFERENCE NUMBER	MAP LOCATION	MAP PAGE	ILLUSTRATION PAGE	NAME OF CEMETERY
485	—	—	—	Cernay French National Cemetery, 85 miles E. of Dijon
486	—	—	—	Cette (Le Py) Communal Cemetery (Herault), 17 miles SW. of Montpellier
487	42.C.3	341	—	Chacrise Communal Cemetery
488	43.C.4	349	—	Châlons-sur-Marne Communal Cemetery
489	—	—	—	Châlon-sur-Sâone Communal Cemetery (Sâone-et-Loire), 38 miles S. of Dijon
490	—	—	353	Chambière French National Cemetery, Metz, 2¼ miles N. of Metz
491	43.A.1	349	350	Chambrecy British Cemetery
—	—	—	—	Champagnole Communal Cemetery (Jura), 57 miles SE. of Dijon
494	24.F.4	137	173	Chapel Corner Cemetery, Sauchy-Lestrée
495	35.E.4	285	312	Chapelle British Cemetery, Holnon
496	14.E.2	34	84	Chapelle d'Armentières New Military Cemetery
497	14.E.2	34	84	Chapelle d'Armentières Old Military Cemetery
498	27.C.4	202	203	*Charleroi Communal Cemetery
499	28.F.1	205	206	Charleville Communal Cemetery
500	—	—	354	Charmes Military Cemetery, Essegny, 30 miles S. of Nancy
501	—	—	—	Chartres (Saint Chèron) Communal Cemetery, 50 miles SW. of Paris
502	—	—	—	Château-du-Loir Communal Cemetery, 24 miles SE. of Le Mans
503	37.E.3	332	—	Château-Porcien Communal Cemetery
504	28.F.1	205	—	Château-Regnault Communal Cemetery
505	42.E.3	341	—	Château-Thierry Communal Cemetery
506	27.C.4	202	—	*Chatelet Communal Cemetery
507	—	—	—	Châtenois Communal Cemetery, 30 miles SW. of Nancy
508	—	—	—	Chaumont (St. Aignan) Churchyard, 55 miles N. of Dijon
509	42.A.3	341	344	Chauny Communal Cemetery British Extension
510	42.C.4	341	—	Chavonne Communal Cemetery
511	32.A.4	210	—	Chepy Churchyard
512	—	—	—	Cherbourg Town Cemetery (Manche), ¾ mile W. of station
513	15.F.2	97	—	*Chercq Churchyard
514	24.E.2	137	160	Chèrisy Road East Cemetery, Héninel
515	14A.C.3	36	55	*Chester Farm Cemetery, Zillebeke
516	24.D.2	137	150	Chili Trench Cemetery, Gavrelle
517	34.D.3	222	241	Chipilly Communal Cemetery
518	34.D.3	222	—	Chipilly Communal Cemetery Extension
519	23.A.3	109	112	Chocques Military Cemetery
520	42.B.1	341	—	Choisy-au-Bac Communal Cemetery
521	—	—	—	Choloy French National Cemetery, 16 miles W. of Nancy
522	13.D.2	18	19	Cinq Rues British Cemetery, Hazebrouck
523	26.C.3	196	—	*Ciply Communal Cemetery
524	42.C.3	341	—	Ciry Salsogne Communal Cemetery
525	34A.G.3	250	281	Citadel New Military Cemetery, Fricourt
526	14.E.2	34	83	Cité Bonjean Military Cemetery, Armentières
530	32.B.4	210	—	Citerne Communal Cemetery
527	—	—	—	City of Paris Cemetery, Bagneux, 1¼ miles S. of Porte de Montrouge, Paris
27	41.F.2	338	—	City of Paris Cemetery, Batignolles Clichy
528	—	—	—	City of Paris Cemetery, Ivry, ½ mile S. of Porte de Choisy, Paris
529	41.F.3	338	339	City of Paris Cemetery, Pantin

REFERENCE NUMBER	MAP LOCATION	MAP PAGE	ILLUSTRATION PAGE	NAME OF CEMETERY
42	41.F.2	338	—	City of Paris Cemetery, St. Ouen-sur-Seine
531	33.D.3	216	—	Clairy-Saulchoy Communal Cemetery
532	2.C.3	6	—	*Clemskerke Churchyard
533	37.D.2	332	—	Clermont Churchyard (Aisne)
534	41.C.3	338	—	Clermont Communal Cemetery (Oise)
535	35.C.1	285	—	Cléry-sur-Somme Communal Cemetery
536	42.C.2	341	—	Cœuvres-et-Valsery Communal Cemetery
537	41.B.3	338	—	Coivrel Communal Cemetery
538	24.F.1	137	179	Cojeul British Cemetery, St. Martin-sur-Cojeul
539	34.A.3	222	—	Colincamps Communal Cemetery
540	42.B.4	341	—	Colligis Communal Cemetery
541	—	—	—	Colmar Communal Cemetery (Bas Rhin), 40 miles SW. of Strasbourg
542	14A.A.3	36	46	*Colne Valley Cemetery, Bœsinghe
543	35.B.1	285	—	Combles Communal Cemetery
544	35.B.1	285	303	Combles Communal Cemetery Extension
545	14.D.3	34	—	Comines (France) Communal Cemetery
546	—	—	—	Commercy French National Cemetery, 28 miles W. of Nancy
547	42.C.1	341	—	Compiègne (South) Communal Cemetery
548	—	—	—	Conches Communal Cemetery (Eure), 11 miles SW. of Evreux
549	25.B.4	180	182	Condé-sur-l'Escaut Communal Cemetery
550	33.B.2	216	—	Condé-Folie Communal Cemetery
551	34A.D.2	250	268	Connaught Cemetery, Thiepval
552	34A.F.3	250	274	Contalmaison Château Cemetery
553	34.B.2	222	230	Contay British Cemetery
554	22.F.2	106	—	Conteville Churchyard
—	—	—	—	Contrexeville Communal Cemetery, 38 miles S. of Nancy
555	33.F.3	216	—	Conty Communal Cemetery
556	24.D.3	137	—	Corbehem Communal Cemetery
557	34.D.2	222	234	Corbie Communal Cemetery
558	34.D.2	222	234	Corbie Communal Cemetery Extension
559	—	—	—	Corbeil Communal Cemetery, 15 miles SE. of Porte de Choisy, Paris
560	34.C.4	222	249	Côte 80 French National Cemetery, Etinehem
561	34.E.1	222	—	Cottenchy Churchyard
562	34.A.2	222	224	Couin British Cemetery
563	34.A.2	222	—	Couin Communal Cemetery
564	34.A.2	222	224	Couin New British Cemetery
565	23.F.2	109	—	Coullemont Churchyard
566	42.C.2	341	—	Couloisy Churchyard
567	12.E.2	14	—	Coulomby Churchyard
568	—	—	—	Coulommiers Communal Cemetery, 35 miles E. of Paris
569	42.D.4	341	—	Coulonges-en-Tardenois Communal Cemetery
570	22.F.2	106	—	Coulonvillers Churchyard
571	—	—	—	Courban R.A.F. Cemetery (Côte d'Or), 44 miles NW. of Dijon
572	34A.E.3	250	272	Courcelette British Cemetery
573	42.C.4	341	—	Courcelles Communal Cemetery (Aisne)
574	27.B.3	202	—	*Courcelles Communal Cemetery (Hainault)
575	34.A.3	222	—	Courcelles-au-Bois Communal Cemetery
576	34.A.3	222	224	Courcelles-au-Bois Communal Cemetery Extension
577	42.E.3	341	—	Courchamps Churchyard
578	43.B.2	349	—	Courtagnon Churchyard
579	43.A.2	349	350	Courmas British Cemetery
580	24.B.2	137	—	Courrières Communal Cemetery

REFERENCE NUMBER	MAP LOCATION	MAP PAGE	ILLUSTRA- TION PAGE	NAME OF CEMETERY
581	15.C.1	97	—	*Courtrai Communal Cemetery (La Madeleine)
582	15.C.1	97	98	*Courtrai Communal Cemetery (St. Jean)
584	27.E.1	202	—	Cousolre Communal Cemetery
585	16.F.4	100	—	*Couture St. Germain Churchyard, Nivelles
586	24.B.4	137	—	Coutiches Churchyard
587	23.F.2	109	—	Couturelle Communal Cemetery
588	1.E.4	2	4	*Coxyde Military Cemetery
590	15.D.2	97	—	*Coyghem Churchyard
591	42.D.2	341	—	Coyolles Communal Cemetery
592	22.F.2	106	—	Cramont Communal Cemetery
593	37.F.1	332	—	Craonnelle French National Cemetery
594	42.B.3	341	—	Crecy-au-Mont Military Cemetery
595	22.E.1	106	—	Crecy-en-Ponthieu Communal Cemetery
596	41.D.3	338	—	Creil Communal Cemetery
597	42.D.1	341	—	Crepy-en-Valois Communal Cemetery
598	26.C.1	196	—	Crespin Communal Cemetery
599	24.F.4	137	176	Crest Cemetery, Fontaine-Notre-Dame
600	14.E.4	34	—	Cretinier Cemetery, Wattrelos
601	36.A.1	315	—	Crêvecœur Communal Cemetery
602	41.A.1	338	—	Crêvecœur-le-Grand Communal Cemetery
603	24.F.1	137	167	Croisilles British Cemetery
604	24.F.2	137	167	Croisilles Railway Cemetery
605	36.A.4	315	—	Croix Churchyard
606	14.E.4	34	—	Croix Communal Cemetery
607	14.E.1	34	83	Croix-du-Bac British Cemetery, Steenwerck
608	13.A.2	18	22	Croix Rouge Military Cemetery, Quædypre
609	—	—	—	Cronenbourg French National Cemetery, Strasbourg, 250 miles E. of Paris
610	14A.D.3	36	66	*Croonært Chapel Cemetery, Wytschæte
611	36.A.4	315	320	Cross-Roads Cemetery, Fontaine-au-Bois
612	33.C.2	216	218	Crouy British Cemetery
613	33.C.2	216	—	Crouy Communal Cemetery
614	42.C.3	341	346	Crouy-Vauxrot French National Cemetery, Crouy
615	25.E.3	180	186	Crucifix Cemetery, Vendegies-sur-Ecaillon
616	34.D.2	222	241	Crucifix Corner Cemetery, Villers-Bretonneux
617	43.A.1	349	—	Crugny Churchyard
618	24.D.2	137	154	Crump Trench British Cemetery, Fampoux
619	24.E.2	137	161	Cuckoo Passage Cemetery, Héninel
620	15.C.1	97	—	*Cuerne Churchyard
621	26.C.3	196	198	*Cuesmes Communal Cemetery
622	24.A.1	137	140	Cuinchy Communal Cemetery
623	25.D.4	180	—	Curgies Communal Cemetery

D

625	14.C.4	34	—	*Dadizeele Communal Cemetery
626	14.C.4	34	78	*Dadizeele New British Cemetery
627	23.E.4	109	127	Dainville British Cemetery
628	23.E.4	109	—	Dainville Communal Cemetery
629	34.F.4	222	—	Damery Communal Cemetery
630	34A.F.3	250	280	Dantzig Alley British Cemetery, Mametz
631	34.D.2	222	—	Daours Communal Cemetery
632	34.D.2	222	235	Daours Communal Cemetery Extension
635	34A.G.2	250	281	Dartmoor Cemetery, Bécordel-Bécourt
636	—	—	—	Dax Communal Cemetery (Landes), 30 miles NE. of Biarritz
637	31.F.1	207	—	Deauville Communal Cemetery (Calvados)

REFERENCE NUMBER	MAP LOCATION	MAP PAGE	ILLUSTRATION PAGE	NAME OF CEMETERY
638	23.F.4	109	132	De Cusine Ravine British Cemetery, Basseux
639	15.C.2	97	—	Deerlyck Churchyard
640	12.F 4	14	—	Delettes Communal Cemetery
641	35.A.2	285	289	Delsaux Farm Cemetery, Beugny
642	34A.F.5	250	278	Delville Wood Cemetery, Longueval
643	35.A.3	285	—	Demicourt Communal Cemetery, Boursies
644	34.E.2	222	243	Démuin British Cemetery
645	25.D.2	180	182	Denain Communal Cemetery
646	12.F.3	14	—	Dennebrœucq Churchyard
647	34A.G.1	250	253	Dernancourt Communal Cemetery
648	34A.G.1	250	253	Dernancourt Communal Cemetery Extension
649	14A.D.3	36	67	*Derry House Cemetery No. 2, Wytschæte
650	—	—	—	*Desnié Churchyard, La Reid, 16 miles SE. of Liege
651	14.E.2	34	92	Desplanque Farm Cemetery, La Chapelle d'Armentières
652	15.B.2	97	—	*Desselghem Churchyard
653	12.E.1	14	—	Desvres Communal Cemetery
654	28.E.1	205	—	Deville Communal Cemetery
655	34A.G.3	250	282	Devonshire Cemetery, Mametz
656	42.E.2	341	—	Dhuisy Communal Cemetery
657	42.C.4	341	—	Dhuizel Churchyard
658	14A.C.2	36	—	*Dickebusch Churchyard
659	14A.C.2	36	58	*Dickebusch New Military Cemetery
660	14A.C.2	36	58	*Dickebusch New Military Cemetery Extension
661	14A.C.2	36	62	*Dickebusch Old Military Cemetery
662	—	—	—	Dijon (les Pejoces) Communal Cemetery, 165 miles SE. of Paris
663	28.C.2	205	—	*Dinant Communal Cemetery
664	34.D.3	222	238	Dive Copse British Cemetery, Sailly-le-Sec
665	23.B.2	109	—	Divion Communal Cemetery
666	14A.B.2	36	47	*Divisional Cemetery, Dickebusch Road, Vlamertinghe
667	14A.A.3	36	43	*Divisional Collecting Post Cemetery, Bœsinghe
667	14A.A.3	36	43	*Divisional Collecting Post Cemetery Extension, Bœsinghe
669	14.B.2	34	78	*Dochy Farm New British Cemetery, Langemarck
670	35.D.2	285	305	Doingt Communal Cemetery Extension
671	33.A.3	216	—	Domart-en-Ponthieu Communal Cemetery
672	34.E.2	222	—	Domart-sur-La Luce Communal Cemetery
673	35.B.4	285	298	Domino British Cemetery, Epéhy
674	24.F.2	137	170	Dominion Cemetery, Hendecourt-les-Cagnicourt
675	34.E.1	222	—	Dommartin Communal Cemetery
676	37.A.1	332	—	Dompierre Communal Cemetery
678	41.A.3	338	—	Dompierre French National Cemetery (Oise)
679	24.A.2	137	143	Don Communal Cemetery, Annœullin
680	42.E.4	341	—	Dormans French National Cemetery
681	15.E.1	97	—	*Dottignies Communal Cemetery
682	24.C.3	137	144	Douai British Cemetery, Cuincy
683	24.D.3	137	143	Douai Communal Cemetery
684	23.F.4	109	133	Douchy-lès-Ayette British Cemetery
685	23.F.4	109	—	Douchy-lès-Ayette Communal Cemetery
686	32.A.4	210	—	Doudelainville Communal Cemetery
687	42.F.2	341	—	Doué Communal Cemetery
688	35.E.3	285	—	Douilly Communal Cemetery
689	23.F.1	109	130	Doullens Communal Cemetery Extension No. 1
690	23.F.1	109	130	Doullens Communal Cemetery Extension No. 2
691	26.C.2	196	—	*Dour Communal Cemetery
693	26.F.3	196	201	Dourlers Communal Cemetery Extension
694	13.B.4	18	21	*Dozinghem Military Cemetery, Westvleteren

REFERENCE NUMBER	MAP LOCATION	MAP PAGE	ILLUSTRATION PAGE	NAME OF CEMETERY
695	14A.A.3	36	42	*Dragoon Camp Cemetery, Bœsinghe
696	14A.E.1	36	62	*Dranoutre Churchyard
697	14A.E.1	36	63	*Dranoutre Military Cemetery
698	33.C.1	216	—	Dreuil Hamel Churchyard
699	—	—	—	Dreux Communal Cemetery (Eure-et-Loir), 46 miles E. of Paris
700	32.B.4	210	—	Dromesnil Communal Cemetery
701	24.F.4	137	175	Drummond Cemetery, Raillencourt
702	24.B.1	137	139	Dud Corner Cemetery, Loos
703	14A.B.3	36	42	*Duhallow A.D.S. Cemetery, Ypres
704	23.D.4	109	126	Duisans British Cemetery, Etrun
705	1.F.2	2	3	Dunkerque Town Cemetery
706	24.E.3	137	171	Dury Crucifix Cemetery (Pas de Calais)
708	24.E.3	137	172	Dury Mill British Cemetery (Pas de Calais)
				E
709	13.D.2	18	19	Ebblinghem Military Cemetery
711	—	—	—	Eclaron Communal Cemetery, 19 miles SW. of Bar-le-Duc
712	35.C.1	285	—	Eclusier Communal Cemetery, Eclusier-Vaux
713	23.D.4	109	125	Ecoivres Military Cemetery, Mont St. Eloi
715	24.F.2	137	166	Ecoust Military Cemetery, Ecoust St. Mein
716	24.F.2	137	166	Ecoust St. Mein British Cemetery
717	23.A.2	109	—	Ecquedecques Communal Cemetery
718	26.F.3	196	—	Ecuelin Churchyard
719	13.D.3	18	—	Eecke Churchyard
720	28.A.4	205	—	*Ellemelle Churchyard
721	26.A.1	196	—	*Ellignies Ste. Anne Communal Cemetery
722	26.C.1	196	199	*Elouges Communal Cemetery
723	15.C.3	97	—	*Elsegem Churchyard
724	14A.A.1	36	—	*Elverdinghe Churchyard
725	14A.C.2	36	57	*Elzenwalle Brasserie Cemetery, Voormezeele
726	22.B.2	106	—	Embry Churchyard
727	25.D.1	180	—	Emerchicourt Churchyard
728	16.F.2	100	—	*Enghien Communal Cemetery
729	28.A.4	205	—	*Engis Communal Cemetery
730	34.B.3	222	228	Englebelmer Communal Cemetery
731	34.B.3	222	228	Englebelmer Communal Cemetery Extension
732	25.F.4	180	192	Englefontaine British Cemetery
733	25.F.4	180	—	Englefontaine Churchyard
734	14.F.2	34	—	Englos Churchyard
735	35.E.2	285	313	Ennemain Communal Cemetery Extension
736	35.B.4	285	—	Epéhy Communal Cemetery
737	35.B.4	285	301	Epéhy Wood Farm Cemetery, Epéhy
738	12.C.3	14	—	Eperlecques Churchyard
739	43.B.2	349	—	Epernay Communal Cemetery
740	43.B.2	349	352	Epernay French National Cemetery
742	35.F.3	285	—	Eppeville Churchyard
743	25.A.2	180	—	*Ere Churchyard
745	41.D.4	338	—	Ermenonville Communal Cemetery
746	26.D.2	196	—	*Erquennes Communal Cemetery
747	27.D.1	202	204	*Erquelinnes Communal Cemetery
748	14.E.1	34	86	Erquinghem-Lys Churchyard Extension
744	—	—	—	Erquy Communal Cemetery, 16 miles NW. of St. Brieuc
749	—	—	—	Erstein Communal Cemetery (Bas Rhin), 12 miles S. of Strasbourg

REFERENCE NUMBER	MAP LOCATION	MAP PAGE	ILLUSTRATION PAGE	NAME OF CEMETERY
750	34A.A.5	250	258	Ervillers Military Cemetery
751	15.D.3	97	—	*Escanaffles Communal Cemetery
752	36.B.3	315	—	Escaufourt Communal Cemetery
753	12.D.1	14	—	Escœuilles Churchyard
754	36.A.1	315	—	Esnes Churchyard
755	36.A.1	315	316	Esnes Communal Cemetery
756	15.E.2	97	—	*Espierres Churchyard
757	25.A.1	180	—	*Esplechin Churchyard
758	37.B.1	332	—	Esqueheries Communal Cemetery
759	13.B.2	18	—	Esquelbecq Communal Cemetery
760	13.B.2	18	17	Esquelbecq Military Cemetery
761	15.E.2	97	—	*Esquelmes Churchyard
762	24.C.3	137	—	Esquerchin Communal Cemetery
763	12.E.4	14	—	Esquerdes Churchyard
764	14A.A.3	36	46	*Essex Farm Cemetery, Bœsinghe
765	15.E.2	97	—	*Estaimbourg Churchyard
766	13.F.4	18	28	Estaires Communal Cemetery
767	13.F.4	18	28	Estaires Communal Cemetery Extension
768	24.B.2	137	—	Estevelles Communal Cemetery
769	26.C.4	196	—	*Estinnes-au-Mont Communal Cemetery
770	36.A.1	315	—	Estourmel Churchyard
771	13.F.1	18	—	Estrée Blanche Communal Cemetery
772	36.C.1	315	—	Estrées Communal Cemetery
773	24.D.3	137	—	Estrées German Cemetery
775	25.D.4	180	—	Estreux Churchyard
776	24.E.3	137	—	Etaing Communal Cemetery, German Extension
777	21.A.3	104	105	Etaples Military Cemetery
778	24.E.2	137	171	Eterpigny British Cemetery
779	35.D.2	285	—	Eterpigny Communal Cemetery Extension
780	26.D.1	196	—	Eth Communal Cemetery
781	34.D.4	222	—	Etinehem Communal Cemetery
782	37.B.2	332	—	Etreaupont Communal Cemetery
774	23.E.1	109	—	Etrée-Wamin Churchyard
783	35.E.4	285	—	Etreillers Communal Cemetery
784	31.A.2	207	209	Etretat Churchyard
785	31.A.2	207	209	Etretat Churchyard Extension
786	36.C.4	315	325	Etreux British Cemetery
787	36.C.4	315	—	Etreux Communal Cemetery
788	37.A.2	332	—	Etroeungt Communal Cemetery
789	32.A.3	210	—	Eu Communal Cemetery
790	14.F.1	34	93	Euston Post Cemetery, Laventie
791	34A.C.1	250	261	Euston Road Cemetery, Colincamps
792	24.C.3	137	—	Evin-Malmaison Communal Cemetery
793	41.E.4	338	—	Eve Communal Cemetery
794	—	—	—	Evreux Communal Cemetery (Eure), 56 miles W. of Paris
795	16.C.2	100	—	*Exærde Communal Cemetery
796	15.C.4	97	—	*Eyne Churchyard
				F
797	37.D.4	332	—	Faissault Churchyard
798	—	—	—	Falaise Communal Cemetery (Calvados), 22 miles SE. of Caen
799	25.D.3	180	183	Famars Communal Cemetery Extension
800	27.B.1	202	—	*Familleureux Communal Cemetery (Hainaut)
801	24.D.1	137	150	Fampoux British Cemetery

REFERENCE NUMBER	MAP LOCATION	MAP PAGE	ILLUSTRA- TION PAGE	NAME OF CEMETERY
802	37.B.1	332	—	Faty Churchyard
803	24.E.1	137	138	Faubourg d'Amiens Cemetery, Arras
804	12.F.3	14	—	Fauquembergues Communal Cemetery
805	14.F.1	34	94	Fauquissart Military Cemetery, Laventie
806	35.A.1	285	287	Favreuil British Cemetery
808	37.A.1	332	—	Favril Churchyard
809	26.D.2	196	—	*Fayt-le-Franc Churchyard
810	31.A.4	207	—	Fécamp Communal Cemetery
811	26.E.3	196	—	Feignies Communal Cemetery
812	42.D.4	341	—	Fère-en-Tardenois Communal Cemetery
813	23.A.2	109	—	Ferfay Communal Cemetery
814	14.E.2	34	92	Ferme Buterne Military Cemetery, Houplines
815	14A.A.1	36	37	*Ferme Olivier Cemetery, Elverdinghe
816	26.E.4	196	—	Ferrière-la-Petite Communal Cemetery
817	24.E.1	137	152	Feuchy British Cemetery
818	24.E.1	137	153	Feuchy Chapel British Cemetery, Wancourt
820	32.A.3	210	—	Feuquières-en-Vimeu Communal Cemetery
821	33.A.4	216	220	Fienvillers British Cemetery
822	35.B.4	285	297	Fifteen Ravine British Cemetery, Villers Plouich
823	35.A.4	285	—	51/Divisional Cemetery, Flesquières.　See page 357
824	42.B.4	341	—	Filain Churchyard
825	22.D.3	106	107	Fillièvres British Cemetery
826	35.B.3	285	296	Fins New British Cemetery, Sorel-le-Grand
827	14A.C.4	36	56	*1st D.C.L.I. Cemetery, The Bluff, Zillebeke
828	35.B.2	285	302	Five Points Cemetery, Lechelle
829	34A.F.4	250	278	Flatiron Copse Cemetery, Mametz
831	42.A.2	341	—	Flavy-le-Martel Communal Cemetery
832	26.C.3	196	—	*Flenu Communal Cemetery
834	34A.E.5	250	—	Flers Communal Cemetery
835	35.A.4	285	294	Flesquières Château Cemetery
836	35.A.4	285	292	Flesquières Hill British Cemetery
837	13.D.4	18	—	Flêtre Churchyard
838	27.B.4	202	—	*Fleurus Communal Cemetery
839	43.B.1	349	—	Fleury-la-Rivière Communal Cemetery
840	25.B.3	180	—	Flines-les-Mortagne Churchyard
841	24.C.4	137	—	Flines-les-Râches Churchyard
842	26.F.3	196	—	Floursies Churchyard
843	35.E.4	285	—	Fluquières Communal Cemetery
844	34.F.3	222	—	Folies Communal Cemetery
845	35.F.1	285	—	Fonchette Churchyard
846	34A.A.1	250	255	Foncquevillers Military Cemetery
847	36.A.4	315	322	Fontaine-au-Bois Communal Cemetery
848	36.A.2	315	317	Fontaine-au-Pire Communal Cemetery
849	—	—	—	Fontainebleau Communal Cemetery, 32 miles S. of Paris
850	32.B.4	210	—	Fontaine-le-Sec Communal Cemetery
851	22.D.2	106	—	Fontaine l'Etalon Churchyard
852	24.F.4	137	—	Fontaine-Notre Dame Communal Cemetery
853	27.D.1	202	—	*Fontaine-Valmont Communal Cemetery
854	—	—	—	Forbach Military Cemetery, 32 miles E. of Metz
855	34.B.3	222	—	Forceville Communal Cemetery
856	34.B.3	222	227	Forceville Communal Cemetery Extension
857	36.A.1	315	314	Forenville Military Cemetery
858	36.A.4	315	322	Forest Communal Cemetery (Nord)
859	16.E.3	100	—	*Forest Communal Cemetery
860	35.E.3	285	300	Foreste Communal Cemetery
861	21.E.4	104	—	Forest-l'Abbaye Churchyard
862	21.E.3	104	—	Forest Montiers Churchyard
863	32.D.3	210	—	Forges-les-Eaux Communal Cemetery

REFERENCE NUMBER	MAP LOCATION	MAP PAGE	ILLUSTRA-TION PAGE	NAME OF CEMETERY
864	32.D.3	210	—	Forges-les-Eaux Communal Cemetery Extension
865	28.A.2	205	—	*Forville Churchyard
866	24.B.1	137	142	Fosse No. 7 Military Cemetery (Quality Street), Mazingarbe
867	23.B.4	109	—	Fosse No. 10 Communal Cemetery, Sains-en-Gohelle
868	23.B.4	109	122	Fosse No. 10 Communal Cemetery Extension, Sains-en-Gohelle
869	34.D.4	222	—	Foucaucourt Communal Cemetery
870	23.D.1	109	—	Foufflin-Ricametz Churchyard
871	34.D.2	222	—	Fouilloy Communal Cemetery
872	32.C.4	210	—	Fouilloy-sous-Poix Communal Cemetery
873	23.A.3	109	—	Fouquereuil Communal Cemetery
874	34.F.4	222	248	Fouquescourt British Cemetery
875	34.F.4	222	—	Fouquescourt Churchyard
876	23.A.3	109	—	Fouquières Churchyard
877	23.A.3	109	112	Fouquières Churchyard Extension
878	24.C.2	137	—	Fouquières-lès-Lens Communal Cemetery
879	27.B.2	332	—	Fourmies Communal Cemetery
880	—	—	—	Fraize Churchyard, 52 miles SE. of Nancy
881	26.C.3	196	198	*Frameries Communal Cemetery
882	34.D.4	222	—	Framerville Communal Cemetery
883	34A.C.2	250	264	Frankfurt Trench British Cemetery, Beaumont-Hamel
884	33.A.2	216	—	Fransu Churchyard
885	34.C.2	222	—	Franvillers Communal Cemetery
886	34.C.2	222	232	Franvillers Communal Cemetery Extension
887	26.E.1	196	—	Frasnoy Communal Cemetery
888	34.C.2	222	231	Frechencourt Communal Cemetery
890	32.B.4	210	—	Fresnes-Tilloloy Communal Cemetery
891	32.B.4	210	—	Fresnoy-Andainville Communal Cemetery
892	34.F.3	222	—	Fresnoye-en-Chausée Churchyard
893	36.C.2	315	329	Fresnoy-le-Grand Communal Cemetery Extension
894	34.F.4	222	—	Fresnoy-les-Roye Communal Cemetery
895	24.A.4	137	—	Frétin Communal Cemetery
896	—	—	—	Fretoy Communal Cemetery, 40 miles E. of Paris
897	32.B.4	210	—	Frette-Cuisse Churchyard
898	—	—	—	Freyming Communal Cemetery, 25 miles E. of Metz
899	34A.G.3	250	283	Fricourt British Cemetery (Bray Road)
900	34A.F.3	250	273	Fricourt New Military Cemetery
901	35.C.1	285	—	Frise Communal Cemetery
902	37.A.4	332	—	*Froidchappelle Communal Cemetery
903	25.A.2	180	—	*Froidmont Communal Cemetery
904	27.D.4	202	—	*Fromiée Communal Cemetery
905	22.A.3	106	—	Fruges Communal Cemetery
906	1.F.4	2	—	*Furnes Communal Cemetery
				G
907	42.E.2	341	—	Gandelu Communal Cemetery
908	35.B.4	285	298	Gauche Wood Cemetery, Villers-Guislain
909	—	—	—	Geffosses Churchyard (Manche), 37 miles S. of Cherbourg
910	16.F.4	100	—	*Genappe Communal Cemetery
911	24.A.4	137	—	Genech Communal Cemetery
912	34.E.2	222	—	Gentelles Communal Cemetery
913	23.F.1	109	—	Gezaincourt Communal Cemetery
914	23.F.1	109	130	Gezaincourt Communal Cemetery Extension
915	16.C.1	100	102	*Ghent City Cemetery (Bruges Gate)

REFERENCE NUMBER	MAP LOCATION	MAP PAGE	ILLUSTRATION PAGE	NAME OF CEMETERY
916	25.E.4	180	187	Ghissignies British Cemetery
917	25.F.4	180	—	Ghissignies Churchyard
918	26.B.3	196	—	*Ghlin Communal Cemetery
—	—	—	—	Giens Communal Cemetery, Hyères (Var.), 42 miles SE. of Marseille
—	—	—	—	Gièvres Communal Cemetery, 45 miles S. of Orléans
920	24.C.1	137	144	Givenchy-en-Gohelle Canadian Cemetery, Souchez
921	24.C.1	137	144	Givenchy Road Canadian Cemetery, Neuville-St.-Vaast
919	26.C.4	196	—	*Givry Communal Cemetery
923	37.A.2	332	334	Glageon Communal Cemetery
924	37.A.2	332	334	Glageon Communal Cemetery Extension
925	34.D.1	222	—	Glisy Communal Cemetery
926	13.D.4	18	24	Godewaersvelde British Cemetery
927	13.C.4	18	—	Godewaersvelde Churchyard
928	14A.D.2	36	63	*Godezonne Farm Cemetery, Kemmel
929	—	—	—	Golbey Communal Cemetery (Vosges), 37 miles S. of Nancy
930	34A.A.5	250	254	Gomiécourt South Cemetery
931	34A.B.1	250	255	Gommecourt British Cemetery No. 2, Hebuterne
932	34A.B.1	250	255	Gommecourt Wood New Cemetery, Foncquevillers
933	26.E.1	196	—	Gommegnies Communal Cemetery
934	23.A.3	109	117	Gonnehem British Cemetery
935	23.A.3	109	—	Gonnehem Churchyard
936	35.B.4	285	—	Gonnelieu Communal Cemetery
937	34A.G.3	250	283	Gordon Cemetery, Mametz
938	34A.F.3	250	274	Gordon Dump Cemetery, Ovillers-La-Boisselle
939	33.A.2	216	—	Gorenflos Communal Cemetery
940	23.A.4	109	112	Gorre British Cemetery, Beuvry
941	23.A.4	109	112	Gorre Indian Cemetery, Beuvry
942	23.B.3	109	—	Gosnay Communal Cemetery
943	27.B.3	202	—	*Gosselies Communal Cemetery
944	28.B.1	205	—	*Gougnies Communal Cemetery
945	32.E.4	210	—	Gournay-en-Bray Communal Cemetery
946	24.D.1	137	151	Gourock Trench Cemetery, Tilloy-les-Mofflaines
947	—	—	—	*Gouvy Churchyard, Limerle, 36 miles SE. of Liege
948	36.C.1	315	—	Gouy British Cemetery.　See page 357
949	23.E.3	109	127	Gouy-en-Artois Communal Cemetery Extension
950	23.C.4	109	—	Gouy-Servins Communal Cemetery
952	35.B.4	285	299	Gouzeaucourt New British Cemetery
954	34A.D.2	250	273	Grandcourt Road Cemetery, Grandcourt
955	37.A.1	332	—	Grand Fayt Communal Cemetery
956	35.A.3	285	293	Grand Ravine British Cemetery, Havrincourt
957	26.D.4	196	—	*Grand Reng Communal Cemetery
958	42.A.2	341	—	Grandru Communal Cemetery
959	23.E.2	109	—	Grand Rullecourt Communal Cemetery
960	35.F.4	285	314	Grand Seraucourt British Cemetery
961	34A.C.5	250	269	Grévillers British Cemetery
962	14A.C.1	36	59	*Grootebeek British Cemetery, Reninghelst
963	34A.G.2	250	281	Grove Town Cemetery, Méaulte
964	—	—	—	Gruissan Communal Cemetery (Aude), 45 miles SW. of Montpellier
965	13.F.2	18	—	Guarbecque Churchyard
966	35.B.1	285	303	Guards' Cemetery, Combles
967	23.A.4	109	114	Guards' Cemetery, Windy Corner, Cuinchy
968	34A.E.5	250	276	Guards' Cemetery, Les Bœufs
969	42.D.2	341	347	Guards' Grave, Villers Cotterêts Forest
970	24.E.2	137	157	Guémappe British Cemetery, Wancourt
971	33.D.3	216	—	Guignemicourt Communal Cemetery

REFERENCE NUMBER	MAP LOCATION	MAP PAGE	ILLUSTRA- TION PAGE	NAME OF CEMETERY
972	25.A.2	180	—	*Guignies Communal Cemetery
973	34A.F.5	250	280	Guillemont Road Cemetery, Guillemont
974	—	—	—	Guilvinec Communal Cemetery (Finistère), 16 miles S. of Quimper
975	36.D.4	315	—	Guise Communal Cemetery
976	36.D.4	315	331	Guise (La Désolation) French National Cemetery, Flavigny-le-Petit
977	36.B.1	315	325	Guizancourt Farm Cemetery, Gouy
978	14.E.2	34	79	*Gunners' Farm Cemetery, Plœgsteert
979	26.D.1	196	—	Gussignies Churchyard
980	14.B.1	34	37	*Gwalia Cemetery, Poperinghe
981	16.D.1	100	—	*Gysenzeele Churchyard

H

982	23.D.3	109	136	Habarcq Communal Cemetery Extension
983	24.F.2	137	165	H.A.C. Cemetery, Ecoust St. Mein
984	14A.B.1	36	41	*Hagle Dump Cemetery, Elverdinghe
—	—	—	—	Haguenau Communal Cemetery, 15 miles N. of Strasbourg
1573	27.D.3	202	—	*Haies Communal Cemetery, Nalines
985	34.E.1	222	—	Hailles Communal Cemetery
986	23.B.3	109	—	Haillicourt Communal Cemetery
987	27.B.1	202	—	*Haine St. Paul (Bouly) Communal Cemetery
988	16.E.3	100	102	*Hal Communal Cemetery
989	32.A.4	210	—	Hallencourt Communal Cemetery
990	12.E.4	14	—	Hallines Churchyard
991	14.D.4	34	—	Halluin Communal Cemetery
992	35.F.3	285	308	Ham British Cemetery, Muille Villette
993	35.F.3	285	—	Ham Communal Cemetery
995	34A.D.1	250	267	Hamel Military Cemetery, Beaumont-Hamel
996	35.D.3	285	311	Hancourt British Cemetery
997	34.E.2	222	243	Hangard Communal Cemetery Extension
998	34.E.2	222	243	Hangard Wood British Cemetery, Hangard
999	33.C.2	216	—	Hangest-sur-Somme Communal Cemetery
1000	34A.A.1	250	—	Hannescamps Churchyard
1001	34A A.1	250	254	Hannescamps New Military Cemetery
1002	17.F.3	103	—	*Hannut Communal Cemetery
1003	28.A.2	205	—	*Hanret Communal Cemetery
1004	27.E.1	202	—	*Hantes-Wiheries Communal Cemetery
1005	35.A.2	285	—	Haplincourt Communal Cemetery
1006	24.E.2	137	154	Happy Valley British Cemetery, Fampoux
1007	42.C.2	341	—	Haramont Communal Cemetery
1008	26.B.1	196	—	*Harchies Communal Cemetery
1009	41.A.2	338	—	Hardivillers Communal Cemetery
1010	35.C.4	285	306	Hargicourt British Cemetery
1011	35.C.4	285	308	Hargicourt Communal Cemetery Extension
1012	26.E.2	196	—	Hargnies Communal Cemetery
1013	13.B.3	18	21	*Haringhe (Bandaghem) Military Cemetery, Rousbrugge-Haringhe
1014	15.C.2	97	—	*Harlebeke Churchyard
1015	15.C.2	97	99	*Harlebeke New British Cemetery
1016	26.C.4	196	—	*Harmignies Churchyard
1017	34.B.2	222	—	Harponville Communal Cemetery
1018	34.B.2	222	227	Harponville Communal Cemetery Extension
1019	26.C.3	196	—	*Harvengt Churchyard
1020	25.C.2	180	—	Hasnon Communal Cemetery

REFERENCE NUMBER	MAP LOCATION	MAP PAGE	ILLUSTRA- TION PAGE	NAME OF CEMETERY
1021	25.E.2	180	—	Haspres Communal Cemetery
1022	25.E.2	180	184	Haspres Coppice Cemetery, Haspres
1024	14.F.3	34	—	Haubourdin Communal Cemetery
1025	36.A.2	315	316	Haucourt Communal Cemetery
1026	25.F.3	180	—	Haussy Communal Cemetery
1027	23.D.3	109	125	Haute-Avesnes British Cemetery
1029	26.E.3	196	200	Hautmont Communal Cemetery
1031	26.B.2	196	—	*Hautrage Communal Cemetery
1032	26.B.2	196	201	*Hautrage Military Cemetery
1033	26.D.3	196	—	*Havay Communal Cemetery
1034	13.F.3	18	31	Haverskerque British Cemetery
1035	13.F.3	18	—	Haverskerque Churchyard
1036	26.B.4	196	—	*Havré Communal Cemetery
1037	34A.D.1	250	264	Hawthorn Ridge Cemetery No. 1, Auchonvillers
1038	34A.D.1	250	265	Hawthorn Ridge Cemetery No. 2, Auchonvillers
1039	24.F.4	137	172	Haynecourt British Cemetery
1040	13.E.3	18	17	Hazebrouck Communal Cemetery
1041	34.D.4	222	240	Heath Cemetery, Harbonnières
1042	34A.B.1	250	256	Hébuterne Communal Cemetery
1043	34A.B.1	250	256	Hébuterne Military Cemetery
1044	34.B.3	222	228	Hédauville Communal Cemetery Extension
1045	14A.C.4	36	54	*Hedge Row Trench Cemetery, Zillebeke
1046	15.D.2	97	—	*Heestert Churchyard
1047	15.D.2	97	98	*Heestert Military Cemetery
1048	34.C.2	222	—	Heilly Churchyard
1049	34.C.2	222	236	Heilly Station Cemetery, Méricourt l'Abbé
1050	15.E.2	97	—	*Helchin Churchyard
1051	14.F.4	34	—	Hellemmes Communal Cemetery
1052	22.F.4	106	—	Hem Communal Cemetery
1053	14.F.4	34	—	Hem Communal Cemetery
1054	35.C.1	285	304	Hem Farm Military Cemetery, Hem-Monacu
1055	25.E.1	180	—	Hem-Lenglet Communal Cemetery
1056	24.F.1	137	159	Hénin Communal Cemetery Extension, Hénin-sur-Cojeul
1057	24.E.1	137	160	Hénin Crucifix Cemetery
1058	24.E.1	137	158	Héninel Communal Cemetery Extension
1059	24.E.2	137	158	Héninel-Croisilles Road Cemetery, Héninel
1060	16.F.3	100	—	*Hennuyères Communal Cemetery
1061	26.C.1	196	—	*Hensies Churchyard
1062	23.F.2	109	—	Hénu Churchyard
1063	35.D.1	285	300	Herbécourt British Cemetery
1064	26.A.2	196	—	*Herchies Communal Cemetery
1065	26.D.2	196	—	Hergies Communal Cemetery, Hon-Hergies
1066	16.F.2	100	—	*Herinnes Churchyard (Brabant)
1067	15.E.2	97	—	*Herinnes Communal Cemetery (Hainault)
1068	34.B.1	222	—	Hérissart Communal Cemetery
1069	34.D.4	222	—	Herleville Churchyard
1070	35.A.3	285	291	Hermies British Cemetery
1071	35.A.3	285	292	Hermies Hill British Cemetery
1072	37.F.2	332	—	Hermonville Communal Cemetery
1073	37.F.1	332	336	Hermonville Military Cemetery
1074	23.B.4	109	121	Hersin Communal Cemetery Extension
1075	35.C.4	285	—	Hervilly Churchyard
1076	24.D.1	137	150	Hervin Farm British Cemetery, St. Laurent-Blangy
1077	13.B.3	18	—	Herzeele Churchyard
1078	16.D.2	100	—	*Herzele Churchyard
1079	35.C.4	285	—	Hesbécourt Communal Cemetery
1080	22.C.2	106	—	Hesdin Communal Cemetery, Marconne

REFERENCE NUMBER	MAP LOCATION	MAP PAGE	ILLUSTRATION PAGE	NAME OF CEMETERY
1081	27.F.1	202	—	Hestrud Churchyard
1082	35.B.3	285	—	Heudicourt Communal Cemetery
1083	35.B.3	285	301	Heudicourt Communal Cemetery Extension
1084	15.C.1	97	—	*Heule Churchyard
1085	12.E.4	14	—	Heuringhem Churchyard
1086	22.F.3	106	—	Heuzecourt Churchyard
1087	3.B.1	8	—	*Heyst Communal Cemetery
1088	24.E.1	137	157	Hibers Trench Cemetery, Wancourt
1089	36.B.3	315	321	Highland Cemetery, Le Câteau
1090	24.D.1	137	150	Highland Cemetery, Roclincourt
1091	36.C.2	315	329	High Tree Cemetery, Montbréhain
1092	34.E.3	222	246	Hill Side Cemetery, Le Quesnel
1093	23.A.3	109	117	Hinges Military Cemetery
1094	16.E.4	100	—	*Hoeylært Communal Cemetery
1095	—	—	—	Homecourt Communal Cemetery, 11 miles NW. of Metz
1096	13.D.3	18	—	Hondeghen Churchyard
1097	42.F.3	341	—	Hondevilliers Communal Cemetery
1098	26.D.2	196	—	Hon-Hergies Communal Cemetery
1099	36.B.3	315	324	Honnechy British Cemetery
1100	36.B.3	315	—	Honnechy Churchyard
1101	14A.B.4	36	52	*Hooge Crater Cemetery, Zillebeke
1102	14.A.4	34	—	*Hooghlede Churchyard
1103	13.A.4	18	—	*Hoogstæde Belgian Military Cemetery
1104	14A.B.1	36	38	*Hop Store Cemetery, Vlamertinghe
1105	25.E.1	180	—	Hordain Communal Cemetery
1107	25.D.2	180	—	Hornaing Communal Cemetery
1108	14A.A.1	36	38	*Hospital Farm Cemetery, Elverdinghe
1109	23.B.3	109	116	Houchin British Cemetery
1110	23.B.3	109	—	Houchin Communal Cemetery
1111	26.D.2	196	—	Houdain Communal Cemetery
1113	24.E.1	137	156	Houdain Lane Cemetery, Tilloy-les-Mofflaines
1114	12.C.4	14	—	Houlle Churchyard
1115	14.E.2	34	82	Houplines Communal Cemetery Extension
1116	34.E.2	222	244	Hourges Orchard Cemetery, Domart-sur-la-Luce
1117	13.B.3	18	—	Houtkerque Churchyard
1118	2.D.4	6	—	*Houttave Churchyard
1119	23.D.1	109	—	Houvin Communal Cemetery, Houvin-Houvigneul
1121	22.C.2	106	107	Huby-St. Leu British Cemetery
1122	22.C.2	106	—	Huby-St. Leu Churchyard
1123	12.F.1	14	—	Hucqueliers Churchyard
1124	15.B.1	97	—	*Hulste Churchyard
1125	23.F.3	109	—	Humbercamps Communal Cemetery
1126	23.F.3	109	132	Humbercamps Communal Cemetery Extension
1127	34A.D.1	250	265	Hunter's Cemetery, Beaumont-Hamel
1128	14A.C.2	36	58	*Huts Cemetery, Dickebusch
1129	28.A 4	205	206	*Huy (la Sarte) Communal Cemetery
1130	14A.F.3	36	72	*Hyde Park Corner (Royal Berks) Cemetery, Plœgsteert
1131	—	—	—	Hyères Communal Cemetery (Var.), 42 miles SE. of Marseille

I

1132	34.E.3	222	—	Ignaucourt Churchyard
1134	36.A.3	315	318	Inchy Communal Cemetery Extension
1136	15.B.1	97	—	*Inglemunster German Military Cemetery
1137	15.C.3	97	99	*Ingoyghem Military Cemetery

REFERENCE NUMBER	MAP LOCATION	MAP PAGE	ILLUSTRA- TION PAGE	NAME OF CEMETERY
1138	—	—	—	Ingwiller Communal Cemetery, 25 miles NW. of Strasbourg
1139	16.F.1	100	—	*Irchonwelz Communal Cemetery
1140	14A.D.2	36	66	*Irish House Cemetery, Kemmel
1141	13.F.2	18	—	Isbergues Communal Cemetery
1142	—	—	—	Ivry-sur-Seine Communal Cemetery, 1 mile SE. of Porte de Choisy, Paris
1144	25.E.1	180	184	Iwuy Communal Cemetery
1145	16.E.4	100	—	*Ixelles Communal Cemetery
1146	24.D.2	137	—	Izel-lès-Equerchin Communal Cemetery
1147	23.D.2	109	—	Izel-lès-Hameau Communal Cemetery
				J
1148	28.B.2	205	—	*Jambes Communal Cemetery
1149	32.B.1	210	212	Janval Cemetery, Dieppe
1150	—	—	—	Jarville Communal Cemetery, 2 miles SE. of Nancy
1151	42.C.2	341	—	Jaulzy Churchyard
1152	35.D.4	285	307	Jeancourt Communal Cemetery Extension
1153	26.C.3	196	—	*Jemappes Communal Cemetery
1156	25.D.4	180	—	Jenlain Communal Cemetery
1157	26.E.4	196	—	Jeumont Communal Cemetery
1158	—	—	—	Jœuf Communal Cemetery, 11 miles NW. of Metz
1159	—	—	—	Joinville-le-Pont Communal Cemetery, 3½ miles SE. of Porte de Picpus, Paris
1160	26.E.1	196	—	Jolimetz Communal Cemetery
1161	37.F.1	332	336	Jonchery-sur-Vesle British Cemetery
1162	36.C.1	315	328	Joncourt British Cemetery
1163	36.C.1	315	—	Joncourt Communal Cemetery
1164	36.C.1	315	328	Joncourt East British Cemetery
1165	42.F.2	341	—	Jouarre Communal Cemetery
1166	34.F.1	222	—	Jumel Communal Cemetery
1167	26.A.3	196	—	*Jurbise Churchyard
1168	35.F.4	285	—	Jussy Communal Cemetery
1169	—	—	—	Juvisy-sur-Orge Communal Cemetery, 9 miles S. of Porte de Choisy, Paris
				K
1170	—	—	—	Kalhouse Communal Cemetery, 50 miles E. of Metz
1171	14A.E.2	36	69	*Kandahar Farm Cemetery, Neuve Eglise
1172	14A.D.2	36	64	*Kemmel Château Military Cemetery
1173	14A.D.2	36	—	*Kemmel Churchyard
1174	14A.D.2	36	64	*Kemmel No. 1 French Cemetery
1176	14.C.4	34	79	*Kezelberg Military Cemetery, Moorseele
1178	14A.D.2	36	64	*Klein Vierstraat British Cemetery, Kemmel
1179	34A.D.1	250	266	Knightsbridge Cemetery, Mesnil-Martinsart
1180	3.B.1	8	—	*Knocke Churchyard
				L
1181	36.D.1	315	327	La Baraque British Cemetery, Bellenglise
1182	14A.A.3	36	41	*La Belle Alliance Cemetery, Bœsinghe
1183	16.F.2	100	—	*Labliau Communal Cemetery
1185	23.B.4	109	—	Labourse Communal Cemetery

REFERENCE NUMBER	MAP LOCATION	MAP PAGE	ILLUSTRA- TION PAGE	NAME OF CEMETERY
1186	26.C.2	196	—	*La Bouverie New Communal Cemetery
1187	14A.A.3	36	44	*La Brique Military Cemetery No. 1, St. Jean-lès-Ypres
1188	14A.A.3	36	44	*La Brique Military Cemetery No. 2, St. Jean-lès-Ypres
1189	22.D.2	106	—	Labroye Churchyard
1191	37.B.2	332	—	La Capelle-en-Thiérache Communal Cemetery
1192	23.F.3	109	—	La Cauchie Communal Cemetery
1193	14.E.2	34	85	La Chapelle d'Armentières Communal Cemetery
1194	—	—	—	La Chapelle-St. Mesmin Communal Cemetery, Orléans, 3 miles E. of Orléans
1195	—	—	—	La Chapelle-St. Mesmin Communal Cemetery Extension, Orléans, 3 miles E. of Orléans
1196	35.D.2	285	—	La Chapellette British and Indian Cemetery, Peronne. See page 357
1198	24.C.1	137	145	La Chaudière Military Cemetery, Vimy
1199	33.C.3	216	—	La Chaussée Tirancourt Communal Cemetery
1201	14A.D.1	36	59	*La Clytte Military Cemetery, Reninghelst
1202	14A.F.1	36	—	La Crèche Communal Cemetery, Bailleul
1203	11.F.4	10	—	Lacres Churchyard
1204	41.C.4	338	—	La Croix St. Ouen Communal Cemetery
1205	—	—	—	La Ferté-Alais Communal Cemetery, 26 miles S. of Paris
1206	42.F.2	341	—	La Ferté-sous-Jouarre Communal Cemetery
1207	25.A.1	180	—	*La Glanerie Churchyard
1208	24.F.2	137	168	Lagnicourt Hedge Cemetery
1209	42.A.1	341	—	Lagny Churchyard
1210	13.F.4	18	27	La Gorgue Communal Cemetery
1211	37.A.1	332	—	La Groise Communal Cemetery
1212	—	—	—	La Guillotière Old Communal Cemetery, Lyon (Rhône), 250 miles SE. of Paris
1213	23.F.3	109	—	Laherlière Communal Cemetery
1214	16.E.4	100	—	*La Hulpe Communal Cemetery
1215	—	—	—	Laigle Communal Cemetery, 30 miles SW. of Evreux
1216	22.A.4	106	—	Laires Churchyard
1217	13.D.3	18	19	La Kreule Military Cemetery, Hazebrouck
1218	14A.D.2	36	63	*La Laiterie Military Cemetery, Kemmel
1219	33.C.1	216	—	Laleu Communal Cemetery
1220	24.C.4	137	—	Lallaing Communal Cemetery
1221	16.E.3	100	—	La Longueville Communal Cemetery
1222	27.B.1	202	203	*La Louvière Communal Cemetery
1386	33.D.4	216	—	La Madeleine Cemetery, Amiens
1223	15.F.1	97	—	*Lamain Communal Cemetery
1224	13.F.1	18	—	Lambres Churchyard
1225	34.D.1	222	—	Lamotte-Brebière Communal Cemetery
1226	—	—	—	Lampaul Churchyard (Ile de Ouessant), 27 miles W. of Brest
1227	14A.F.3	36	74	*Lancashire Cottage Cemetery, Plœgsteert
1228	35.E.3	285	—	Lanchy Churchyard
1229	3.F.4	8	—	*Landeghem Churchyard
1230	27.D.3	202	—	*Landelies Communal Cemetery
1231	28.A.3	205	—	*Landen-les-Couthuin Churchyard
1232	37.A.1	332	333	Landrecies British Cemetery
1233	37.A.1	332	333	Landrecies Communal Cemetery
1234	—	—	—	La Neuve Lyre Communal Cemetery (Eure), 20 miles SW. of Evreux
1235	43.B.1	349	351	La Neuville-aux-Larris Military Cemetery
1236	34.D.2	222	235	La Neuville British Cemetery, Corbie
1237	34.D.2	222	235	La Neuville Communal Cemetery
1238	34.D.4	222	—	La Neuville-les-Bray Communal Cemetery

REFERENCE NUMBER	MAP LOCATION	MAP PAGE	ILLUSTRA- TION PAGE	NAME OF CEMETERY
1239	—	—	—	Lanildut Churchyard (Finistère), 13 miles NW. of Brest
1240	15.E.1	97	—	Lannoy-du-Nord Communal Cemetery
1241	1.E.3	2	—	*La Panne Communal Cemetery
1242	—	—	—	Lanton Churchyard (Gironde), 25 miles SW. of Bordeaux
1243	42.B.4	341	—	Laon (St. Just) Communal Cemetery
1244	14A.E.2	36	71	*La Plus Douve Farm Cemetery, Plœgsteert
1245	23.A.3	109	113	Lapugnoy Military Cemetery
1246	14A.C.4	36	53	*Larch Wood (Railway Cutting) Cemetery, Zillebeke
1247	42.D.2	341	—	Largny Churchyard
1248	—	—	—	*Laroche Communal Cemetery, 8 miles E. of Evreux
1249	25.D.3	180	—	La Sentinelle Communal Cemetery
1250	16.F.4	100	—	*Lasne Communal Cemetery
1251	23.D.4	109	134	La Targette British Cemetery (Aux Rietz)
1252	42.D.3	341	—	Latilly Communal Cemetery
1253	—	—	—	Latour-en-Wœvre Communal Cemetery, 17 miles W. of Metz
1254	14.D.4	34	—	*Lauwe Churchyard
1255	36.B.3	315	—	La Vallée Mulâtre Communal Cemetery
1256	36.B.3	315	323	La Vallée Mulâtre Communal Cemetery Extension
1257	14.F.1	34	—	Laventie Communal Cemetery
1258	14.F.1	34	86	Laventie Military Cemetery, La Gorgue
1259	34.C.3	222	—	La Viéville Communal Cemetery
1260	37.F.1	332	335	La Ville-aux-Bois British Cemetery
1261	14.E.2	34	—	Le Bizet Communal Cemetery
1262	22.E.2	106	—	Le Boisle Communal Cemetery
1263	35.A.2	285	289	Lebucquière Communal Cemetery Extension
1264	36.A.3	315	321	Le Câteau Communal Cemetery
1265	36.A.3	315	320	Le Câteau Military Cemetery
1266	36.C.1	315	—	Le Catelet Churchyard
1267	23.E.2	109	—	Le Cauroy Communal Cemetery, Berlencourt
1268	25.B.2	180	—	Lecelles Churchyard
1200	43.B.4	349	—	Le Cheppe (Mont Frenet) French National Cemetery
1269	24.E.3	137	—	Lecluse Communal Cemetery
1270	21.E.2	104	—	Le Crotoy Communal Cemetery
1271	14.C.4	34	—	*Ledeghem Churchyard
1272	14.C.4	34	79	*Ledeghem Military Cemetery
1273	13.C.1	18	—	Lederzeele Churchyard
1274	15.E.1	97	—	Leers Communal Cemetery
1275	15.E.1	97	—	*Leers-Nord Communal Cemetery
1276	23.E.4	109	128	Le Fermont Military Cemetery, Rivière
1277	14.E.1	34	82	Le Grand Beaumart British Cemetery, Steenwerck
1278	13.E.3	18	29	Le Grand Hasard Military Cemetery, Morbecque
1280	34.D.3	222	—	Le Hamel Communal Cemetery (Somme)
1281	—	—	—	Le Lavandou Communal Cemetery (Var), 52 miles E. of Marseille
1282	—	—	354	Le Mans Grand Cemetery (Sarthe), 115 miles SW. of Paris
1283	16.D.1	100	—	*Lemberge Churchyard
1284	22.F.4	106	—	Le Meillard Communal Cemetery
1285	35.C.4	285	—	Lempire Communal Cemetery
1286	37.A.1	332	—	Le Nouvion Communal Cemetery
1287	24.C.1	137	—	Lens Communal Cemetery, Sallaumines
1288	—	—	—	Léon Communal Cemetery (Landes), 18 miles NW. of Dax
1290	—	—	—	Le Palais Communal Cemetery, Belle-Isle-en-Mer (Morbihan), 76 miles W. of Nantes

REFERENCE NUMBER	MAP LOCATION	MAP PAGE	ILLUSTRA-TION PAGE	NAME OF CEMETERY
1289	13.D.3	18	27	Le Peuplier Military Cemetery, Cæstre
1291	11.D.2	10	—	Le Portel Communal Cemetery
1292	34.F.3	222	—	Le Quesnel Communal Cemetery
1293	34.F.3	222	248	Le Quesnel Communal Cemetery Extension
1294	25.E.4	180	188	Le Quesnoy Communal Cemetery
1295	25.E.4	180	188	Le Quesnoy Communal Cemetery Extension
1296	41.F.3	338	—	Le Raincy Communal Cemetery
1872	36.B.4	315	325	Le Rejet-de-Beaulieu Communal Cemetery
1297	37.A.1	332	—	Le Sart Churchyard
1298	12.A.1	14	16	Les Baraques Military Cemetery, Sangatte
1299	42.E.3	341	—	Les Chesneaux French National Cemetery, Château-Thierry
1300	36.A.1	315	—	Lesdain Churchyard
1301	25.A.2	180	—	*Lesdain Communal Cemetery
1302	—	—	339	Les Gonards Cemetery, Versailles, 6 miles SW. of Porte de St. Cloud, Paris
1303	—	—	—	Les Moutiers Hubert Churchyard (Calvados), 40 miles E. of Evreux
1304	23.E.1	109	—	Le Souich Communal Cemetery
1305	—	—	—	Lespéron Communal Cemetery (Landes), 20 miles N. of Dax
1306	22.B.1	106	—	Lespinoy-sur-Canche Communal Cemetery
1307	16.F.1	100	—	*Lessines Communal Cemetery
1308	13.F.4	18	—	Lestrem Communal Cemetery
1310	33.B.2	216	—	L'Etoile Churchyard
1311	21.A.2	104	105	Le Touquet-Paris-Plage Communal Cemetery
1312	14.E.2	34	88	*Le Touquet Railway Crossing Cemetery, Warneton
1313	23.A.4	109	110	Le Touret Military Cemetery, Richebourg l'Avoué
1314	32.A.2	210	212	Le Tréport Military Cemetery
1315	14.F.1	34	93	Le Trou Aid Post Cemetery, Fleurbaix
1316	—	—	—	Leucate Communal Cemetery (Aude), 16 miles NE. of Perpignan
1317	15.F.4	97	98	*Leuze Communal Cemetery
1318	26.F.2	196	—	Leval Communal Cemetery
1319	41.F.2	338	—	Levallois-Perret Communal Cemetery
1320	24.D.2	137	154	Level Crossing Cemetery, Fampoux
1321	—	—	—	Le Verdon-sur-Mer Communal Cemetery (Gironde), 55 miles NW. of Bordeaux
1322	36.D.1	315	—	Levergies Communal Cemetery
1323	35.D.4	285	—	Le Verguier Churchyard
1324	23.A.3	109	117	Le Vertannoy British Cemetery, Hinges
1325	41.F.1	338	—	Le Vesinet Temporary Hospital Cemetery
1326	24.F.1	137	166	L'Homme Mort British Cemetery, Ecoust St. Mein
1328	28.E.4	205	—	*Libramont Communal Cemetery
1329	24.D.1	137	146	Lichfield Crater (C.B. 2a), Thélus
1330	—	—	353	*Liège Communal Cemetery, 1¾ miles E. of Liège
1331	23.E.2	109	—	Liencourt Communal Cemetery
1332	35.C.3	285	—	Lieramont Communal Cemetery
1333	33.B.1	216	—	Liercourt Churchyard
1334	24.C.1	137	143	Liévin Communal Cemetery Extension
1335	36.A.2	315	331	Ligny-en-Cambrésis Communal Cemetery
1336	23.D.2	109	124	Ligny-St. Flochel British Cemetery, Averdoingt
1337	22.D.4	106	107	Ligny-sur-Canche British Cemetery
1338	34.E.4	222	—	Lihons French National Cemetery
1339	13.C.4	18	24	*Lijssenthœk Military Cemetery, Poperinghe
1340	14.F.3	34	95	Lille Southern Cemetery
1341	23.A.2	109	113	Lillers Communal Cemetery
1342	23.A.2	109	113	Lillers Communal Cemetery Extension

REFERENCE NUMBER	MAP LOCATION	MAP PAGE	ILLUSTRA- TION PAGE	NAME OF CEMETERY
1343	14A.E.2	36	67	*Lindenhœk Châlet Military Cemetery, Kemmel
1344	14.D.3	34	—	Linselles Communal Cemetery
1345	—	—	—	L'Isle de Sein Communal Cemetery (Finistère), 35 miles W. of Quimper
1346	28.A.2	205	—	*Lives Churchyard
1347	42.E.1	341	—	Lizy-sur-Ourcq Communal Cemetery
1348	26.F.1	196	—	Locquignol Communal Cemetery
1349	14A.D.1	36	61	*Locre Churchyard
1350	14A.E.1	36	61	*Locre No. 10 Cemetery
1351	14A.E.1	36	61	*Locre Hospice Cemetery
1352	34A.E.4	250	275	London Cemetery, High Wood, Longueval
1353	24.E.1	137	159	London Cemetery, Neuville-Vitasse
1354	14A.F.3	36	75	*London Rifle Brigade Cemetery, Plœgsteert
1355	14A.E.2	36	68	*Lone Tree Cemetery, Wytschæte
1356	33.B.1	216	—	Long Churchyard
1357	33.C.4	216	—	Longpré Communal Cemetery
1358	33.B.2	216	219	Longpré-les-Corps-Saints British Cemetery
1359	33.B.1	216	—	Longpré-les-Corps-Saints Communal Cemetery
1360	34.D.1	222	233	Longueau British Cemetery
1361	34.D.1	222	—	Longueau Communal Cemetery
1362	12.D.4	14	16	Longuenesse (St. Omer) Souvenir Cemetery
1363	42.C.4	341	—	Longueval Communal Cemetery
1364	34A.F.4	250	279	Longueval Road Cemetery
1365	17.F.1	103	—	*Longueville Churchyard
1366	—	—	—	Longwy (Haut) Communal Cemetery, 17 miles SW. of Luxembourg
1367	34A.E.2	250	271	Lonsdale Cemetery, Aveluy
1368	24.B.1	137	140	Loos British Cemetery
1369	42.D.2	341	—	Louâtre Churchyard
1370	23.D.4	109	126	Louez Military Cemetery, Duisans
1371	25.D.2	180	—	Lourches Communal Cemetery
1372	17.E.1	103	—	*Louvain Communal Cemetery
1373	34.A.2	222	226	Louvencourt Military Cemetery
1375	35.A.3	285	290	Louverval Military Cemetery, Doignies
1376	25.F.4	180	—	Louvignies Churchyard
1377	41.E.3	338	—	Louvres Communal Cemetery
1378	35.A.3	285	293	Lowrie Cemetery, Havrincourt
1379	23.A.2	109	—	Lozinghem Communal Cemetery
1380	34A.C.1	250	260	Luke Copse British Cemetery, Puisieux
1381	12.E.3	14	—	Lumbres Communal Cemetery
1382	27.B.3	202	—	*Luttre Communal Cemetery
1383	—	—	—	Luxeuil-les-Bains Communal Cemetery, 25 miles S. of Epinal
1384	13.E.2	18	—	Lynde Churchyard

M

1385	21.D.4	104	—	Machy Churchyard
1387	36.D.1	315	—	Magny-la-Fosse Churchyard
1388	28.B.2	205	—	*Maillen Communal Cemetery
1389	43.E.3	349	—	Mailly-le-Camp French Military Cemetery
1390	34.A.3	222	225	Mailly-Maillet Communal Cemetery Extension
1391	34.B.3	222	225	Mailly Wood Cemetery
1392	25.E.3	180	185	Maing Communal Cemetery Extension
1393	—	—	—	Maintenon Communal Cemetery, 40 miles SW of Paris
1394	26.D.3	196	—	Mairieux Churchyard
1395	26.B.3	196	—	*Maisières Communal Cemetery

REFERENCE NUMBER	MAP LOCATION	MAP PAGE	ILLUSTRATION PAGE	NAME OF CEMETERY
1396	23.D.1	109	—	Maisnil St. Pol Churchyard
1397	33.A.2	216	—	Maison Roland Churchyard
1398	35.D.4	285	—	Maissemy Communal Cemetery
1399	23.D.2	109	—	Maizières Churchyard
1400	1.F.2	2	—	Malo-les-Bains Communal Cemetery
1401	28.B.1	205	—	*Malonne Communal Cemetery
1402	26.D.2	196	—	Malplaquet Communal Cemetery
1403	13.F.1	18	—	Mametz Churchyard
1404	35.B.2	285	—	Manancourt Communal Cemetery
1405	35.A.2	285	288	Manchester Cemetery, Riencourt-lès-Bapaume
1406	—	—	—	Mandelieu Communal Cemetery (Alpes Maritimes), 17 miles SW. of Nice
1407	—	—	—	Mandres-sur-Vair Communal Cemetery, 35 miles SW. of Nancy
1408	34.E.3	222	246	Manitoba Cemetery, Caix
1409	—	—	—	Mantes Communal Cemetery, 30 miles NW. of Paris
1410	14A.F.2	36	77	*Maple Leaf Cemetery, Romarin
1411	14A.C.4	36	52	*Maple Copse Cemetery, Zillebeke
1412	37.A.1	332	—	Marbaix Communal Cemetery
1413	28.C.4	205	—	Marche Communal Cemetery, German Extension
1414	22.E.1	106	—	Marcheville Communal Cemetery
1415	25.C.1	180	—	Marchiennes New Communal Cemetery
1416	27.D.3	202	203	*Marcinelle New Communal Cemetery
1417	15.C.1	97	—	*Marcke Churchyard
1418	35.A.4	285	295	Marcoing British Cemetery
1419	35.A.4	285	—	Marcoing Communal Cemetery
1420	25.E.1	180	—	Marcq Churchyard
1421	1.F.1	2	—	Mardyck Churchyard
1422	25.E.4	180	—	Maresches Communal Cemetery
1423	22.C.1	106	—	Maresquel Churchyard
1424	41.B.4	338	—	Mareuil-la-Motte Churchyard
1425	43.B.2	349	—	Mareuil-sur-Ay Communal Cemetery
1426	43.A.2	349	351	Marfaux British Cemetery
1427	23.B.2	109	—	Marles-les-Mines Communal Cemetery
1428	28.C.4	205	—	*Marloie Churchyard, Waha
1429	23.B.4	109	121	Maroc British Cemetery, Grenay
1430	23.D.4	109	119	Marœuil British Cemetery
1431	37.A.1	332	—	Maroilles Communal Cemetery
1432	26.E.4	196	—	Marpent Communal Cemetery
1433	14.E.3	34	—	Marquette Communal Cemetery
—	—	—	—	Marson Churchyard, 9 miles SE. of Chalons-sur-Marne
1434	35.D.4	285	311	Marteville Communal Cemetery
1435	13.F.1	18	—	Marthes Churchyard, Mametz
1436	—	—	—	Martigny-les-Bains Communal Cemetery (Vosges), 45 miles SW. of Nancy
1437	34A.E.4	250	275	Martinpuich British Cemetery
1438	34A.E.4	250	—	Martinpuich Communal Cemetery
1439	34A.E.1	250	270	Martinsart British Cemetery, Mesnil-Martinsart
1440	35.A.4	285	296	Masnières British Cemetery, Marcoing
1441	26.A.3	196	—	*Masnuy St. Pierre New Communal Cemetery
1442	24.D.4	137	—	Masny Churchyard
1443	35.E.3	285	—	Matigny Communal Cemetery
1444	22.A.3	106	—	Matringhem Churchyard
1445	26.E.3	196	200	Maubeuge Centre Cemetery
2158	26.E.3	196	200	Maubeuge (Sous-le-Bois) Cemetery
1446	36.B.3	315	325	Maurois Communal Cemetery
1447	—	—	356	Mazargues Cemetery Extension, Marseille 6½ miles S. of St. Charles Station, Marseille

REFERENCE NUMBER	MAP LOCATION	MAP PAGE	ILLUSTRA- TION PAGE	NAME OF CEMETERY
1448	23.B.4	109	119	Mazingarbe Communal Cemetery
1449	23.B.4	109	120	Mazingarbe Communal Cemetery Extension
1450	36.B.4	315	—	Mazinghien Communal Cemetery
1451	35.B.4	285	300	Meath Cemetery, Villers Guislain
1452	34A.G.1	250	—	Méaulte Churchyard
1453	34A.G.1	250	280	Méaulte Military Cemetery
1454	42.F.1	341	—	Meaux Communal Cemetery
1455	26.E.2	196	—	Mecquignies Churchyard
1456	3.F.4	8	—	*Meerendre Churchyard
1457	11.D.3	10	12	Meerut Military Cemetery, St. Martin-lès-Boulogne
1458	—	—	—	Melun North Communal Cemetery, 26 miles SE. of Paris
1459	13.B.4	18	21	*Mendinghem British Cemetery, Proven
1460	14 D.4	34	—	*Menin Communal Cemetery
1461	14A.B.3	36	49	*Menin Road South Military Cemetery, Ypres
1462	—	—	—	Menton (Trabuquet) New Communal Cemetery (Alpes Maritimes), 14 miles NE. of Nice
1464	12.F.3	14	—	Merck-St. Lievin Churchyard
1465	33.D.1	216	—	Méricourt-en-Vimeux Communal Cemetery
1466	34.C.3	222	236	Méricourt-l'Abbé Communal Cemetery Extension
1467	34.F.1	222	—	Merville-au-Bois Churchyard
1468	—	—	—	Merville Churchyard (Calvados), 8 miles NE. of Caen
1469	13.F.4	18	27	Merville Communal Cemetery
1470	13.F.4	18	28	Merville Communal Cemetery Extension
1471	43.F.1	349	—	Mesgrigny French Military Cemetery
1472	34A.E.1	250	269	Mesnil Communal Cemetery Extension, Mesnil-Martinsart
1473	34A.D.1	250	267	Mesnil Ridge Cemetery, Mesnil Martinsart
1474	35.F.2	285	—	Mesnil-St. Nicaise Churchyard
1475	14A.E.3	36	69	*Messines Ridge British Cemetery, Messines
1476	13.D.4	18	26	Méteren Military Cemetery
1477	33.C.1	216	—	Métigny Communal Cemetery
1478	35.B.3	285	297	Metz-en-Couture Communal Cemetery, British Extension
1480	22F.4	106	—	Mézerolles Communal Cemetery
1481	28.F.1	205	—	Mézières Communal Cemetery (Ardennes)
1482	34.E.2	222	244	Mézières Communal Cemetery Extension (Somme)
1483	27.A.1	202	—	*Mignault Communal Cemetery
1484	12.C.4	14	—	Millain Churchyard
1485	34.B.3	222	229	Millencourt Communal Cemetery Extension
1486	34A.D.2	250	267	Mill Road Cemetery, Thiepval
1487	24.F.4	137	173	Mill Switch British Cemetery, Tilloy-les-Cambrai
1488	24.D.1	137	151	Mindel Trench British Cemetery, St. Laurent-Blangy
1489	14A.A.3	36	46	*Minty Farm Cemetery, St. Jean-lès-Ypres
1490	34A.C.3	250	—	Miraumont Communal Cemetery
1491	42.C.3	341	—	Missy-sur-Aisne Communal Cemetery
1492	—	—	—	Modane Communal Cemetery (Savoie), 45 miles E. of Grenoble
1493	24.F.3	137	178	Mœuvres British Cemetery
1494	24.F.3	137	177	Mœuvres Communal Cemetery Extension
1495	28.A.3	205	—	*Moha Communal Cemetery
1496	13.F.2	18	—	Molinghem Communal Cemetery
1497	34.C.1	222	—	Molliens-au-Bois Communal Cemetery
1498	—	—	—	Molsheim Communal Cemetery, 12 miles W. of Strasbourg
1499	—	—	—	Monaco Principality Cemetery, La Condamine, 8 miles NE. of Nice
1500	26.F.2	196	—	Monceau St. Waast Communal Cemetery

REFERENCE NUMBER	MAP LOCATION	MAP PAGE	ILLUSTRATION PAGE	NAME OF CEMETERY
1501	25.E.3	180	—	Monchaux-sur-Ecaillon Communal Cemetery
1502	25.D.1	180	—	Monchecourt Communal Cemetery
1503	23.C.2	109	—	Monchy-Breton Churchyard
1504	24.E.2	137	164	Monchy British Cemetery, Monchy-le-Preux
1505	41.B.4	338	—	Monchy-Humières Communal Cemetery
1506	35.E.3	285	—	Monchy-Lagache New Communal Cemetery
1507	23.F.2	109	—	Mondicourt Communal Cemetery
1508	26.B.3	196	198	*Mons Communal Cemetery
1509	14.F.4	34	—	Mons-en-Baroeul Communal Cemetery
1510	35.D.3	285	—	Mons-en-Chaussée Communal Cemetery
1511	41.E.4	338	—	Montagny Ste. Félicité Churchyard
1512	—	—	—	Montargis Communal Cemetery, 62 miles SE. of Paris
1513	36.A.3	315	319	Montay British Cemetery
1514	36.A.3	315	—	Montay Communal Cemetery
1515	36.A.3	315	320	Montay-Neuvilly Road Cemetery, Montay
1516	—	—	—	Montbard Communal Cemetery (Côte d'Or), 38 miles NW. of Dijon
1517	—	—	—	Montbéliard Communal Cemetery (Doubs), 42 miles NE. of Besançon
1518	13.F.3	18	31	Mont Bernenchon British Cemetery, Gonnehem
1519	13.F.3	18	—	Mont Bernenchon Churchyard
1520	37.A.3	332	—	*Monbliart Communal Cemetery
1521	36.C.2	315	330	Montbrehain British Cemetery
1522	37.D.2	332	334	Montcornet Military Cemetery
1523	—	—	—	Montereau Communal Cemetery, 40 miles SE. of Paris
1524	36.F.1	315	—	Montescourt-Lizerolles Communal Cemetery
1525	32.E.1	210	—	Mont Gargan Communal Cemetery, Rouen
1526	28.E.1	205	—	Monthermé (Laval-Dieu) Communal Cemetery
1527	32.A.2	210	212	Mont Huon Military Cemetery, Le Tréport
1528	26.D.1	196	—	*Montignies-sur-Roc Churchyard
1529	36.A.2	315	—	Montigny Communal Cemetery (Nord)
1530	34.C.2	222	231	Montigny Communal Cemetery (Somme)
1531	34.C.2	222	—	Montigny Communal Cemetery Extension
1532	22.F.3	106	—	Montigny-les-Jongleurs Churchyard
1533	—	—	—	Montmédy German Cemetery No. 3, 33 miles SE. cf Mezières
1534	13.D.4	18	22	Mont Noir Military Cemetery, St. Jans-Cappel
1536	42.E.2	341	348	Montreuil-aux-Lions British Cemetery
1537	17.F.2	103	—	*Mont St. André Churchyard
1538	15.C.4	97	—	*Mooreghem Churchyard
1540	14.C.4	34	80	*Moorseele Military Cemetery
1541	14.B.3	34	—	*Moorslede Communal Cemetery
1542	13.E.3	18	29	Morbecque British Cemetery
1543	13.E.3	18	—	Morbecque Churchyard
1544	35.A.2	285	287	Morchies Australian Cemetery
1545	35.A.2	285	—	Morchies Communal Cemetery
1546	35.A.2	285	288	Morchies Military Cemetery
1547	34.E.2	222	244	Moreuil Communal Cemetery Allied Extension
1548	34.C.3	222	238	Morlancourt British Cemetery No. 1
1549	34.C.3	222	238	Morlancourt British Cemetery No. 2, Ville-sur-Ancre
1551	25.B.3	180	—	Mortagne-du-Nord Communal Cemetery
1552	35.B.1	285	300	Morval British Cemetery
1553	—	—	—	Morvillars French National Cemetery, 7 miles SE. of Belfort
1554	28.C.1	205	—	*Morville Communal Cemetery
1555	24.F.1	137	165	Mory Abbey Military Cemetery, Mory
1556	24.F.1	137	165	Mory Street Military Cemetery, St. Léger
1557	37.F.1	332	—	Moscou French National Cemetery, Berry-au-Bac

REFERENCE NUMBER	MAP LOCATION	MAP PAGE	ILLUSTRATION PAGE	NAME OF CEMETERY
1558	14.E.2	34	88	*Motor Car Corner Cemetery, Plœgsteert
1559	25.A.1	180	—	Mouchin Churchyard
1560	36.B.1	315	326	Moulin de Pierre British Cemetery, Villers Outreau
1561	42.C.4	341	—	Moulins Churchyard
1562	—	—	—	Moulins-lès-Metz Communal Cemetery (Moselle), 3½ miles W. of Metz
1563	37.F.1	332	—	Moulins New Communal Cemetery
1564	—	—	—	Moulins-sur-Allier Communal Cemetery (Allier), 57 miles SE. of Bourges
1565	—	—	—	Mouroux Communal Cemetery, 32 miles E. of Paris
1566	15.D.1	97	—	*Mouscron Communal Cemetery
1567	42.C.4	341	—	Moussy-sur-Aisne Churchyard
1568	—	—	—	Moutiers Communal Cemetery, 93 miles SE. of Paris
1569	14.E.4	34	—	Mouvaux New Communal Cemetery
1570	36.F.2	315	—	Moy Communal Cemetery
1571	14A.F.3	36	77	*Mud Corner Cemetery, Warneton
1572	34A.C.2	250	262	Munich Trench British Cemetery, Beaumont Hamel

N

1574	21.C.3	104	—	Nampont-St. Firmin Churchyard
1575	33.E.2	216	218	Namps-au-Val British Cemetery
1576	—	—	—	Nancy Southern Cemetery, 2¾ miles SE. of Nancy Station
1577	—	—	—	Nangis Communal Cemetery, 35 miles SE. of Paris
1578	—	—	—	Nantes (La Bouteillerie) Communal Cemetery, 214 miles SW. of Paris
1579	42.F.2	341	—	Nanteuil-sur-Marne Communal Cemetery
1580	33.B.4	216	—	Naours Churchyard
1581	—	—	—	Narbonne East Cemetery (Aude), 53 miles SW. of Montpellier
1582	36.C.1	315	—	Nauroy Churchyard
1583	36.C.1	315	—	Nauroy Communal Cemetery
1584	24.D.2	137	152	Naval Trench Cemetery, Gavrelle
1585	25.F.1	180	190	Naves Communal Cemetery Extension
1586	15.A.4	97	—	*Nazareth Churchyard
1587	15.E.1	97	—	*Néchin Communal Cemetery
1588	23.A.1	109	—	Nédonchel Churchyard
1589	41.C.4	338	—	Néry Communal Cemetery
1590	35.F.2	285	308	Nesle Communal Cemetery
1591	42.E.3	341	—	Nesles Communal Cemetery
—	—	—	—	Neuf-Brisach Communal Cemetery Extension, 40 miles S. of Strasbourg
1593	11.F.3	10	—	Neufchâtel Churchyard
1594	26.E.3	196	—	Neufmesnil Communal Cemetery
1595	42.D.3	341	—	Neuilly St. Front Communal Cemetery
1596	42.D.2	341	—	Neuilly St. Front French National Cemetery
1597	41.F.2	338	—	Neuilly-sur-Seine New Communal Cemetery
1592	41.F.2	338	—	Neuilly-sur-Seine Old Communal Cemetery
1598	14.F.1	34	94	Neuve Chapelle British Cemetery
1599	24.A.1	137	—	Neuve Chapelle Churchyard
1600	14.F.1	34	94	Neuve Chapelle Farm British Cemetery
1601	14A.F.2	36	85	*Neuve-Eglise Churchyard
1602	35.B.3	285	298	Neuville-Bourjonval British Cemetery
1603	35.B.3	285	—	Neuville-Bourjonval Communal Cemetery
1604	14.D.4	34	—	Neuville-en-Ferrain Communal Cemetery
1605	25.F.1	180	—	Neuville-St. Remy Churchyard

REFERENCE NUMBER	MAP LOCATION	MAP PAGE	ILLUSTRA-TION PAGE	NAME OF CEMETERY
1606	21.B.4	104	—	Neuville-sous-Montreuil Indian Cemetery
1607	24.E.1	137	162	Neuville-Vitasse Road Cemetery, Neuville Vitasse
1608	36.E.3	315	—	Neuvillette Churchyard
1609	36.A.3	315	—	Neuvilly Communal Cemetery
1610	36.A.3	315	317	Neuvilly Communal Cemetery Extension
1611	37.D.4	332	—	Neuvizy Communal Cemetery
1612	—	—	—	Nevers Communal Cemetery (Nièvres), 134 miles SE. of Paris
1613	14A.A.3	36	44	*New Irish Farm Cemetery, St. Jean-lès-Ypres
1614	34A.C.2	250	264	New Munich Trench British Cemetery, Beaumont Hamel
1615	25.F.2	180	191	Niagara Cemetery, Iwuy
1616	—	—	—	Nice Communal Cemetery (Caucade), (Alpes Maritimes), 100 miles NE. of Marseille
1617	12.E.2	14	—	Nielles-lez-Bléquin Churchyard
1618	13.E.3	18	26	Nieppe-Bois (Rue-du-Bois) British Cemetery, Vieux-Berquin
1619	14.E.1	34	81	Nieppe Communal Cemetery
1620	36.A.1	315	—	Niergnies Communal Cemetery
1621	2.E.1	6	7	*Nieuport Communal Cemetery
1622	17.F.1	103	—	*Nil-St. Vincent Communal Cemetery
1623	13.C.4	18	23	*Nine Elms British Cemetery, Poperinghe
1624	24.D.1	137	146	Nine Elms Military Cemetery, Thélus
1625	24.B.1	137	141	Ninth Avenue Cemetery, Haisnes
1626	27.A.2	202	—	*Nivelles Communal Cemetery
1627	23.B.4	109	118	Nœux-les-Mines Communal Cemetery
1628	23.B.4	109	117	Nœux-les-Mines Communal Cemetery Extension
1629	42.F.3	341	—	Nogent-l'Artaud Communal Cemetery
1630	26.C.3	196	—	*Noirchain Churchyard
1631	41.F.3	338	—	Noisy-le-Sec Communal Cemetery
1632	25.B.1	180	—	Nomain Churchyard
1633	14A.A.3	36	43	*No Man's Cot Cemetery, Bœsinghe
1634	13.C.2	18	—	Noordpeene Churchyard
1635	24.F.2	137	167	Noreuil Australian Cemetery
1636	34A.F.2	250	283	Norfolk Cemetery, Bécordel-Bécourt
1637	13.F.2	18	—	Norrent-Fontes Churchyard
1463	12.D.3	14	—	Nortbécourt Churchyard, Mentque-Nortbécourt
1638	12.C.3	14	—	Nortleulinghem Churchyard
1639	23.B.4	109	—	North Maroc Intercommunal Cemetery, Grenay
1641	26.C.3	196	—	*Nouvelles Communal Cemetery
1642	21.E.4	104	—	Nouvion-en-Ponthieu Churchyard
1643	24.C.3	137	—	Noyelles-Godault Communal Cemetery
1644	35.A.4	285	—	Noyelles-sur-l'Escaut Communal Cemetery
1645	35.A.4	285	304	Noyelles-sur-l'Escaut Communal Cemetery Extension
1646	21.F.3	104	105	Noyelles-sur-Mer Chinese Cemetery
1647	26.F.2	196	—	Noyelles-sur-Sambre Communal Cemetery
1648	25.E.2	180	—	Noyelles-sur-Selle Communal Cemetery
1649	—	—	—	Noyers Communal Cemetery, 50 miles SW. of Orléans
1650	42.A.1	341	—	Noyon Communal Cemetery
1651	42.A.1	341	344	Noyon New British Cemetery
1652	—	—	—	Nuits-St. George's New Communal Cemetery (Côte d'Or), 14 miles SW. of Dijon

O

1653	14A.C.3	36	55	*Oak Dump Cemetery, Voormezeele
1654	26.E.2	196	—	Obies Communal Cemetery

REFERENCE NUMBER	MAP LOCATION	MAP PAGE	ILLUSTRATION PAGE	NAME OF CEMETERY
1655	15.E.2	97	—	*Obigies Communal Cemetery
1656	—	—	—	Ochey Churchyard, 13 miles SW. of Nancy
1657	25.B.3	180	—	Odomez Communal Cemetery
1658	—	—	—	*Odrimont Churchyard, Lierneux, 25 miles SE. of Liège
1659	16.E.2	100	—	*Oetinghen Churchyard
1661	35.F.3	285	—	Offoy Communal Cemetery
1662	24.B.3	137	—	Oignies Communal Cemetery
1664	32.B.4	210	—	Oisemont Communal Cemetery
1665	33.D.2	216	—	Oissy Churchyard
1666	16.F.1	100	—	*Ollignies Communal Cemetery
1667	—	—	—	Omont Communal Cemetery, 11 miles S. of Mezières
1668	25.C.4	180	—	Onnaing Communal Cemetery
1669	26.D.1	196	—	*Onnezies Churchyard
1670	24.F.3	137	174	Ontario Cemetery, Sains-les-Marquion
1671	3.E.1	8	—	*Oostcamp Churchyard
1672	14.B.3	34	—	*Oostnieuwkerke Churchyard
1673	15.B.2	97	—	*Oostroosebeke Communal Cemetery
1674	14A.D.3	36	65	*Oosttaverne Wood Cemetery, Wytschæte
1675	—	—	—	Orange Communal Cemetery (Vaucluse), 15 miles N. of Avignon
1676	24.E.1	137	156	Orange Hill Cemetery, Feuchy
1677	24.E.2	137	157	Orange Trench Cemetery, Monchy-le-Preux
1678	24.D.1	137	148	Orchard Dump Cemetery, Arleux-en-Gohelle
1679	15.F.2	97	—	*Orcq Communal Cemetery
1680	33.F.4	216	—	Oresmaux Communal Cemetery
1681	35.A.4	285	294	Orival Wood British Cemetery, Flesquières
1682	—	—	—	Orléans Main Cemetery (Loiret), 70 miles S. of Paris
1683	42.F.2	341	—	Orly-sur-Morin Communal Cemetery
1684	36.A.4	315	322	Ors British Cemetery
1685	36.A.4	315	322	Ors Communal Cemetery
1686	25.E.4	180	—	Orsinval Communal Cemetery
1687	2.D.2	6	7	*Ostende New Communal Cemetery
1689	23.C.1	109	—	Ostreville Churchyard
1690	14.B.4	34	—	*Ouckene Churchyard
1692	42.D.3	341	348	Oulchy-le-Château Churchyard Extension
1693	22.F.4	106	—	Outrebois Churchyard
1694	13.E.4	18	25	Outtersteene Communal Cemetery Extension, Bailleul
1695	16.E.4	100	—	*Overyssche Communal Cemetery
1696	34A.E.2	250	273	Ovillers Military Cemetery, Ovillers-la-Boisselle
1697	25.F.3	180	195	Ovillers New Communal Cemetery, Solesmes
1698	34A.B.2	250	256	Owl Trench Cemetery, Hébuterne
1699	14A.A.4	36	45	*Oxford Road Cemetery, Ypres
1700	12.A.3	14		Oye Plage Churchyard

P

1701	42.C.4	341	—	Paars Churchyard
1702	14A.E.2	36	70	*Packhorse Farm Shrine Cemetery, Wulverghem
1703	25.E.1	180	—	Paillencourt Churchyard
1704	37.E.1	332	—	Paissy Churchyard
1705	—	—	—	Paray-le-Monial Communal Cemetery (Saône-et-Loire), 75 miles SW. of Dijon
1706	—	—	—	Parentis-en-Born Communal Cemetery (Landes), 42 miles SW. of Bordeaux
1707	37.F.1	332	—	Pargnan Churchyard
1708	35.E.2	285	313	Pargny British Cemetery
1709	23.F.2	109	—	Pas-en-Artois Communal Cemetery

REFERENCE NUMBER	MAP LOCATION	MAP PAGE	ILLUSTRATION PAGE	NAME OF CEMETERY
1710	14.B.3	34	76	*Passchendaele New British Cemetery
1711	34A.F.3	250	274	Peake Wood Cemetery, Fricourt
1712	15.E.2	97	—	*Pecq Communal Cemetery
1713	24.C.4	137	—	Pecquencourt Communal Cemetery
1714	—	—	—	Pécy Communal Cemetery, 37 miles SE. of Paris
1716	24.E.2	137	—	Pelves Communal Cemetery
1717	23.D.2	109	—	Penin Churchyard
1718	—	—	—	*Pepinster Communal Cemetery, 11 miles SE. of Liège
1719	23.B.1	109	116	Pernes British Cemetery, Pernes-en-Artois
1720	23.B.1	109	—	Pernes Churchyard
1721	33.B.3	216	220	Pernois British Cemetery, Halloy-les-Pernois
1722	33.B.3	216	—	Pernois Communal Cemetery
1724	35.C.2	285	—	Péronne Communal Cemetery
1724	35.C.2	285	305	Péronne Communal Cemetery Extension, Ste. Radegonde
1725	24.A.4	137	—	Péronne-en-Melantois Churchyard
1726	34A.G.4	250	284	Péronne Road Cemetery, Maricourt
1727	42.F.2	341	348	Perreuse Château French National Cemetery, Signy-Signets
1728	14A.B.4	36	53	*Perth Cemetery, China Wall, Zillebeke
1729	15.C.4	97	—	*Peteghem-lès-Audenarde Churchyard
1730	24.C.1	137	145	Petit Vimy British Cemetery, Vimy
1731	—	—	—	Pézarches Communal Cemetery, 31 miles E. of Paris
1732	24.B.3	137	156	Phalempin Communal Cemetery
1733	23.B.4	109	120	Philosophe British Cemetery, Mazingarbe
1734	33.C.3	216	218	Picquigny British Cemetery
1735	33.C.3	216	—	Picquigny Communal Cemetery
1736	32.B.4	210	—	Pierrecourt Communal Cemetery
1737	42.C.1	341	—	Pierrefonds-les-Bains Communal Cemetery
1738	—	—	—	Pierrelatte Communal Cemetery (Drome), 30 miles N. of Avignon
1743	—	—	—	Pierrepont French National Cemetery, 24 miles NE. of Verdun
1739	17.F.1	103	—	*Piétrebais Churchyard
1740	35.B.4	285	301	Pigeon Ravine Cemetery, Epéhy
1741	33.E.3	216	—	Plachy-Buyon Communal Cemetery
1742	—	—	—	Plaine French National Cemetery, 30 miles SW. of Strasbourg
1744	14A.F.3	36	—	*Plœgsteert Churchyard
1745	14A.F.3	36	73	*Plœgsteert Wood Military Cemetery, Warneton
1746	—	—	—	Ploudalmézeau Communal Cemetery (Finistère), 15 miles NW. of Brest
1747	—	—	—	Plouescat Communal Cemetery (Finistère), 24 miles NE. of Brest
1748	—	—	—	Plouguerneau Communal Cemetery (Finistère), 17 miles N. of Brest
1749	14.B.3	34	76	*Poelcapelle British Cemetery
1750	34A.G.3	250	282	Point 110 New Military Cemetery, Fricourt
1751	34A.G.3	250	282	Point 110 Old Military Cemetery, Fricourt
1752	24.D.1	137	155	Point-du-Jour Military Cemetery, Athies-lès-Arras
1753	25.F.4	180	—	Poix-du-Nord Communal Cemetery
1754	25.F.4	180	195	Poix-du-Nord Communal Cemetery Extension
1755	—	—	—	Poix-Terron Communal Cemetery (Ardennes), 8 miles SW. of Mezières
1756	14.C.3	34	77	*Polygon Wood Cemetery, Zonnebeke
1757	36.A.4	315	321	Pommereuil British Cemetery
1761	36.A.4	315	—	Pommereuil Communal Cemetery
1758	—	—	—	Pommeuse Communal Cemetery, 31 miles E. of Paris

REFERENCE NUMBER	MAP LOCATION	MAP PAGE	ILLUSTRA- TION PAGE	NAME OF CEMETERY
1759	23.F.3	109	—	Pommier Communal Cemetery
1760	14A.E.2	36	67	*Pond Farm Cemetery, Wulverehem
—	—	—	—	Pontarlier Communal Cemetery (Doubs), 28 miles SE. of Besançon
1762	24.B.2	137	—	Pont-à-Vendin Communal Cemetery
1763	—	—	—	Pontcarré Communal Cemetery, 17 miles E. of Paris
1764	14.E.1	34	81	Pont-d'Achelles Military Cemetery, Nieppe
1765	33.D.4	216	—	Pont-de-Metz Churchyard
1766	14.E.1	34	81	Pont-de-Nieppe Communal Cemetery, Nieppe
1767	13.F.4	18	32	Pont-du-Hem Military Cemetery, La Gorgue
1768	34.C.2	222	—	Pont-Noyelle Communal Cemetery
1769	42.B.2	341	—	Pontoise Communal Cemetery
1770	33.A.1	216	219	Pont-Remy British Cemetery
1771	33.B.1	216	—	Pont-Remy Communal Cemetery
1772	26.E.2	196	200	Pont-sur-Sambre Communal Cemetery
1773	13.C.4	18	—	*Poperinghe Communal Cemetery
1774	13.C.4	18	23	*Poperinghe New Military Cemetery
1775	13.C.4	18	23	*Poperinghe Old Military Cemetery
1776	—	—	—	Porquerolles Communal Cemetery, Hyères (Var), 47 miles SE. of Marseille
1777	25.F.1	180	189	Porte-de-Paris Cemetery, Cambrai
1778	23.A.4	109	114	Post Office Rifles Cemetery, Festubert
1779	14A.B.3	36	50	*Potijze Burial Ground, Ypres
1780	14A.B.4	36	50	*Potijze Château Grounds Cemetery, Ypres
1781	14A.B.4	36	50	*Potijze Château Lawn Cemetery, Ypres
1782	14A.B.4	36	51	*Potijze Château Wood Cemetery, Ypres
1783	15.E.2	97	—	*Pottes Communal Cemetery
1784	—	—	—	Pouru-aux-Bois Communal Cemetery, 7 miles E. of Sedan
1785	34A.E.3	250	251	Pozières British Cemetery, Ovillers-la-Boisselle
1786	13.D.3	18	—	Pradelles Churchyard
1787	36.C.2	315	327	Prémont British Cemetery
1788	36.B.2	315	—	Prémont Communal Cemetery
1789	25.D.4	180	183	Préseau Communal Cemetery Extension
1790	25.F.4	180	194	Preux-au-Bois Communal Cemetery
1791	26.E.1	196	—	Preux-au-Sart Churchyard
1792	42.E.2	341	—	Priez Communal Cemetery
1793	37.A.1	332	—	Prisches Communal Cemetery
1794	36.C.1	315	326	Prospect Hill Cemetery, Gouy
1795	22.F.3	106	—	Prouville Churchyard
1796	25.D.3	180	—	Prouvy Communal Cemetery
1797	13.B.4	18	—	*Proven Churchyard
1798	24.F.4	137	174	Proville British Cemetery
1799	—	—	—	Provins (Haute-Ville) Communal Cemetery, 48 miles SE. of Paris
1800	14A.F.3	36	73	*Prowse Point Military Cemetery, Warneton
1801	34.D.4	222	—	Proyart Communal Cemetery
1802	34.B.1	222	223	Puchevillers British Cemetery
1803	42.C.2	341	—	Puiseux Communal Cemetery

Q

1805	26.C.2	196	—	*Quaregnon Communal Cemetery
1806	25.C.4	180	—	Quarouble Communal Cemetery
1807	24.F.3	137	178	Quarry Cemetery, Marquion
1808	24.B.1	137	142	Quarry Cemetery, Vermelles
1809	34A.F.4	250	279	Quarry Cemetery, Montauban

REFERENCE NUMBER	MAP LOCATION	MAP PAGE	ILLUSTRATION PAGE	NAME OF CEMETERY
1858	14.E.2	34	84	Ration Farm Military Cemetery, La Chapelle-d'Armentières
1859	—	—	—	Rebais New Communal Cemetery, 40 miles E. of Paris
1860	16.F.1	100	—	*Rebaix Communal Cemetery
1861	16.F.3	100	—	*Rebecq-Rognon Communal Cemetery
1862	—	—	—	Réchicourt-le-Château Communal Cemetery, 30 miles E. of Nancy
1863	12.F.4	14	—	Reclinghem Churchyard
1864	12.C.3	14	—	Recques Churchyard
1865	34A.C.1	250	—	Redan Ridge Cemetery No. 1, Beaumont Hamel. See page 357
1866	34A.C.1	250	263	Redan Ridge Cemetery No. 2, Beaumont Hamel
1867	34A.C.1	250	263	Redan Ridge Cemetery No. 3, Beaumont Hamel
1868	35.A.2	285	291	Red Cross Corner Cemetery, Beugny
1869	14A.B.1	36	41	*Red Farm Military Cemetery, Vlamertinghe
1870	34A.D.3	250	268	Regina Trench Cemetery, Grandcourt
1871	43.A.2	349	—	Reims West Communal Cemetery
1873	36.F.1	315	—	Remigny Churchyard
1874	12.E.3	14	—	Remilly-Wirquin Churchyard
1875	—	—	—	Remiremont Communal Cemetery Extension (Vosges), 50 miles SE. of Nancy
1876	15.D.4	97	—	*Renaix Communal Cemetery
1877	—	—	—	*Rendeux-Bas Churchyard, 28 miles S. of Liège
1878	14.C.1	34	—	*Reninghelst Churchyard
1879	14.C.1	34	62	*Reninghelst Churchyard Extension
1880	14.C.1	34	59	*Reninghelst New Military Cemetery
1881	12.F.3	14	—	Renty Churchyard
1882	37.E.3	332	337	Rethel French National Cemetery
1883	36.A.3	315	—	Reumont Churchyard
1884	35.A.4	285	294	Ribécourt British Cemetery
1885	35.A.4	285	293	Ribécourt Railway Cemetery
1886	35.A.4	285	294	Ribécourt Road Cemetery, Trescault
1887	34.C.3	222	—	Ribemont Communal Cemetery
1888	34.C.3	222	237	Ribemont Communal Cemetery Extension
1889	36.E.3	315	—	Ribemont Communal Cemetery Extension (Aisne)
1890	14A.C.2	36	60	*Ridge Wood Military Cemetery, Voormezeele
1891	33.C.2	216	—	Riencourt Churchyard
1892	14A.F.3	36	74	*Rifle House Cemetery, Warneton
1893	22.A.2	106	—	Rimboval Churchyard
1895	25.F.4	180	—	Robersart Churchyard
1896	24.D.1	137	149	Roclincourt Military Cemetery
1897	24.D.1	137	149	Roclincourt Valley Cemetery
1898	26.E.4	196	—	Rocq Churchyard, Marpent
1899	37.D.3	332	—	Rocquigny Communal Cemetery
1900	35.B.2	285	302	Rocquigny-Equancourt Road British Cemetery, Manancourt
1901	25.D.1	180	—	Rœulx Communal Cemetery
1902	24.E.2	137	153	Rœux British Cemetery
1903	35.C.3	285	307	Roisel Communal Cemetery Extension
1904	26.D.1	196	—	*Roisin Communal Cemetery
1905	15.D.1	97	—	*Rolleghem Churchyard
1906	22.C.3	106	—	Rollencourt Churchyard
1907	25.F.3	180	193	Romeries Communal Cemetery Extension
1908	32.C.4	210	—	Romescamps Churchyard
1909	43.A.1	349	—	Romigny Churchyard
1910	14.F.3	34	—	Ronchin Communal Cemetery
1911	14.D.4	34	—	Roncq Communal Cemetery
1913	35.C.4	285	310	Ronssoy Communal Cemetery

REFERENCE NUMBER	MAP LOCATION	MAP PAGE	ILLUSTRA-TION PAGE	NAME OF CEMETERY
1966	14.E.1	34	88	Sailly-sur-la-Lys Churchyard
1967	14.F.1	34	87	Sailly-sur-la-Lys Canadian Cemetery
1968	14.F.4	34	—	Sainghin-en-Mélantois Churchyard
1969	24.A.2	137	—	Sainghin-en-Weppes Communal Cemetery
1970	37.A.2	332	—	Sains-du-Nord Communal Cemetery
1971	33.E.4	216	—	Sains-en-Amiénois Communal Cemetery
1972	24.F.3	137	174	Sains-les-Marquion British Cemetery
1973	33.D.4	216	—	St. Acheul French National Cemetery, Amiens
1974	23.F.3	109	129	St. Amand British Cemetery
1975	25.B.3	180	—	St. Amand-les-Eaux Communal Cemetery
1976	14.E.3	34	85	St. André Communal Cemetery
1977	25.F.2	180	191	St. Aubert British Cemetery
1978	25.F.2	180	—	St. Aubert Churchyard
1979	26.F.3	196	—	St. Aubin Churchyard
1980	—	—	—	St. Avold Military Cemetery, 25 miles E. of Metz
1981	25.C.4	180	—	St. Aybert Communal Cemetery
1982	36.B.3	315	—	St. Benin Communal Cemetery
1983	—	—	—	St. Brieuc (St. Michel) Cemetery (Côtes-du-Nord), 58 miles NW. of Rennes
1984	23.D.4	109	135	Ste. Catherine British Cemetery
1985	41.F.2	338	—	St. Cloud Communal Cemetery (Seine-et-Oise)
1986	42.F.2	341	—	St. Cyr-sur-Morin Communal Cemetery
1987	41.F.3	338	—	St. Denis-sur-Seine Communal Cemetery
1988	—	—	—	St. Dizier (la Noue) Communal Cemetery, 14 miles SW. of Bar-le-Duc
1989	35.C.4	285	—	Ste. Emilie British Cemetery, Villers-Faucon. See page 357
1990	35.C.4	285	309	Ste. Emilie Valley Cemetery, Villers-Faucon
1991	37.E.1	332	335	St. Erme Communal Cemetery Extension
1992	11.E.2	10	12	St. Etienne-au-Mont Communal Cemetery
1993	—	—	—	St. Florentin Communal Cemetery, 86 miles SE. of Paris
1994	33.E.4	216	—	St. Fuscien Communal Cemetery
1995	15.D.2	97	—	*St. Genois Churchyard
1996	22.C.3	106	—	St. Georges Churchyard
1997	—	—	—	St. Georges-Motel Communal Cemetery, 45 miles W. of Paris
1998	—	—	—	St. Germain-au-Mont d'Or Communal Cemetery (Rhône), 9 miles N. of Lyon
1999	—	—	355	St. Germain-au-Mont d'Or Communal Cemetery Extension (Rhône), 9 miles N. of Lyon
2000	41.F.1	338	—	St. Germain-en-Laye New Communal Cemetery
2001	41.F.1	338	—	St. Germain-en-Laye Old Communal Cemetery
2002	32.E.4	210	—	St. Germer-de-Fly Communal Cemetery
2003	26.C.2	196	—	*St. Ghislain Communal Cemetery
2005	22.E.4	106	108	St. Hilaire Cemetery, Frévent
2006	22.E.4	106	108	St. Hilaire Cemetery Extension, Frévent
2007	13.F.2	18	—	St. Hilaire-Cottes Churchyard
2008	25.F.2	180	—	St. Hilaire-lès-Cambrai British Cemetery
2009	37.A.2	332	—	St. Hilaire-sur-Helpe Churchyard
2010	43.B.2	349	351	St. Imoge Churchyard
2011	13.C.4	18	—	*St. Jan-ter-Biezen Communal Cemetery, Poperinghe
2012	13.D.4	18	—	St. Jans Cappel Churchyard
2013	—	—	—	St. Jean-Cap-Ferrat Communal Cemetery (Alpes Maritimes), 4 miles SE. of Nice
2014	—	—	—	St. Jean-de-Maurienne Communal Cemetery (Savoie), 30 miles E. of Grenoble
2015	14A.A.4	36	46	*St. Julien Dressing Station Cemetery, Langemarck

REFERENCE NUMBER	MAP LOCATION	MAP PAGE	ILLUSTRATION PAGE	NAME OF CEMETERY
2016	41.D.4	338	—	St. Lazare Hospital Cemetery, Senlis
2017	24.F.1	137	164	St. Léger British Cemetery
2018	15.E.1	97	—	*St. Léger Churchyard
2019	33.B.3	216	—	St. Léger-les-Domart Communal Cemetery
2020	—	—	—	St. Mandrier Hospital Cemetery, La Seyne-sur-Mer (Var), 28 miles SE. of Marseille
2021	42.C.3	341	—	Ste. Marguerite Churchyard
2022	31.D.2	207	208	Ste. Marie Cemetery, Le Havre, Graville-Ste-Honorine
2023	13.D.3	18	—	Ste. Marie Cappel Churchyard
2025	24.E.1	137	162	St. Martin Calvaire British Cemetery, St. Martin-sur-Cojeul
2026	43.B.1	349	—	St. Martin-d'Ablois Communal Cemetery
2027	24.B.1	137	141	St. Mary's Advance Dressing Station Cemetery, Haisnes
2028	32.B.4	210	—	St. Maulvis Communal Cemetery
2029	25.A.2	180	—	*St. Maur Churchyard
2030	—	—	—	St. Maurice Communal Cemetery (Seine), 2 miles SE. of Porte de Picpus, Paris
2031	—	—	—	St. Michel de Maurienne Communal Cemetery, French Military Extension (Savoie), 35 miles E. of Grenoble
2032	24.D.1	137	147	St. Nicolas British Cemetery
2033	16.C.3	100	—	*St. Nicholas Communal Cemetery
2034	24.F.4	137	176	St. Olle British Cemetery, Raillencourt
2035	24.F.4	137	—	St. Olle Communal Cemetery, Raillencourt
2036	33.B.3	216	—	St. Ouen Communal Cemetery
2037	24.B.1	137	142	St. Patrick's Cemetery, Loos
2038	33.D.4	216	217	St. Pierre Cemetery, Amiens
2039	—	—	—	St. Pierre Jewish Cemetery, Marseille, 2 miles SE. of St. Charles Station, Marseille
2040	—	—	—	St. Pierre le Moutier Communal Cemetery (Nièvre), 40 miles SE. of Bourges
2041	23.C.1	109	124	St. Pol British Cemetery, St. Pol-sur-Ternoise
2042	23.C.1	109	124	St. Pol Communal Cemetery Extension
2047	14A.E.2	36	69	*St. Quentin Cabaret Military Cemetery, Plœgsteert
2046	36.E.1	315	—	St. Quentin (Faubourg d'Isle) Communal Cemetery
2045	36.E.1	315	—	St. Quentin (North) Communal Cemetery
2048	—	—	—	St Raphaël Communal Cemetery (Var), 70 miles E. of Marseille
2049	26.F.2	196	—	St. Remy-Chaussée Communal Cemetery
2050	26.F.3	196	—	St. Rémi-du-Nord Communal Cemetery
2051	22.F.1	106	108	St. Riquier British Cemetery
2052	—	—	—	Ste. Ruffine Communal Cemetery (Moselle), 4 miles W. of Metz
2053	33.E.4	216	—	St. Sauflieu Communal Cemetery
2054	41.C.4	338	—	St. Sauveur Communal Cemetery
2055	32.E.1	210	214	St. Sever Cemetery, Rouen
2056	32.E.1	210	214	St. Sever Cemetery Extension, Rouen
2057	—	—	—	St. Siméon Communal Cemetery, 40 miles E. of Paris
2058	36.B.3	315	323	St. Souplet British Cemetery
2059	26.C.4	196	199	*St. Symphorien Military Cemetery
2060	25.F.2	180	—	St. Vaast Communal Cemetery
2061	25.F.2	180	192	St. Vaast Communal Cemetery Extension
2062	13.F.4	18	29	St. Vaast Post Military Cemetery, Richebourg l'Avoué
2063	21.F.2	104	—	St. Valery-sur-Somme Communal Cemetery
2064	13.F.3	18	30	St. Venant Communal Cemetery
2065	13.F.3	18	30	St. Venant Communal Cemetery Extension
2066	13.F.3	18	30	St. Venant-Robecq Road British Cemetery, Robecq
2067	—	—	—	*St. Vith Communal Cemetery, 35 miles SE. of Liège
2068	26.E.1	196	—	St. Waast-la-Vallée Communal Cemetery

REFERENCE NUMBER	MAP LOCATION	MAP PAGE	ILLUSTRA- TION PAGE	NAME OF CEMETERY
2069	16.F.3	100	—	*Saintes Communal Cemetery
2070	33.D.4	216	—	Saleux Communal Cemetery
2072	24.C.2	137	—	Sallaumines Communal Cemetery
2073	—	—	—	Salmaise Communal Cemetery (Côte-d'Or), 40 miles NW. of Dijon
2074	25.B.2	180	—	Saméon Churchyard
2075	11.E.4	10	—	Samer Communal Cemetery
2076	24.E.4	137	172	Sancourt British Cemetery
2077	14A.B.4	36	52	*Sanctuary Wood Cemetery, Zillebeke
2078	35.A.3	285	292	Sanders Keep Military Cemetery, Graincourt-lès-Havrincourt
2079	23.A.3	109	115	Sandpits British Cemetery, Labeuvrière
2080	—	—	—	Sanguinet Communal Cemetery (Landes), 40 miles SW. of Bordeaux
2081	14.F.2	34	—	Santes Churchyard
2082	41.E.1	338	—	Santeuil Churchyard
2083	31.D.1	207	—	Sanvic Communal Cemetery
2084	16.E.1	100	—	*Sarlardinghe Churchyard
2085	—	—	354	Sarralbe Military Cemetery, 38 miles E. of Metz
2086	26.F.4	196	—	Sars-Poteries Communal Cemetery
2087	26.F.2	196	—	Sassegnies Communal Cemetery
2088	24.E.3	137	—	Sauchy-Cauchy Communal Cemetery
2089	24.E.3	137	163	Sauchy-Cauchy Communal Cemetery Extension
2090	24.E.4	137	—	Sauchy-Lestrée Communal Cemetery
2091	35.C.3	285	302	Saulcourt Churchyard Extension, Guyencourt-Saulcourt
2092	25.D.4	180	—	Saultain Communal Cemetery
2093	—	—	—	Savigny Churchyard (Vosges), 24 miles S. of Nancy
2094	35.E.4	285	312	Savy British Cemetery
2095	35.E.4	285	—	Savy Communal Cemetery
2096	16.E.4	100	—	*Schaerbeck Communal Cemetery
2097	—	—	—	Schaeferhof Communal Cemetery, Dabo, 50 miles E. of Nancy
2099	16.D.1	100	—	*Scheldewindeke Churchyard
2098	16.E.3	100	—	*Schepdael Churchyard
2100	—	—	—	Scherwiller Communal Cemetery, 25 miles SW. of Strasbourg
2101	16.C.4	100	102	*Schoonselhof Cemetery, Antwerp
2102	28.A.3	205	—	*Sclayn Communal Cemetery
2103	14A.A.4	36	51	*Seaforth Cemetery, Cheddar Villa, Langemarck
2105	25.D.4	180	185	Sebourg British Cemetery
2106	25.D.4	180	—	Sebourg Communal Cemetery
2107	13.E.3	18	—	Sec Bois Communal Cemetery, Vieux Berquin
2108	—	—	353	Sedan (St. Charles) Communal Cemetery, French Military Extension, 11 miles SE. of Charleville
2109	—	—	—	Selestat Communal Cemetery, 25 miles SW. of Strasbourg
2110	36.A.3	315	318	Selridge British Cemetery, Montay
2111	36.A.2	315	—	Selvigny Communal Cemetery
2112	26.F.3	196	—	Semousies Churchyard
2113	—	—	—	Sénas Communal Cemetery (Bouches-du-Rhone), 16 miles SE. of Avignon
2114	12.E.1	14	—	Senlecques Churchyard
2115	34.B.3	222	229	Senlis Communal Cemetery Extension
2116	41.D.3	338	340	Senlis French National Cemetery
2118	—	—	—	Sens-sur-Yonne Communal Cemetery, 62 miles SE. of Paris
2119	28.B.4	205	—	*Seny Communal Cemetery
2117	—	—	—	Senonches Communal Cemetery, 22 miles NW. of Chartres

REFERENCE NUMBER	MAP LOCATION	MAP PAGE	ILLUSTRA-TION PAGE	NAME OF CEMETERY
2120	25.E.4	180	—	Sepmeries Communal Cemetery
2121	36.D.2	315	—	Sequehart British Cemetery No. 1. See page 357
2122	36.D.1	315	—	Sequehart British Cemetery No. 2. See page 357
2123	36.B.2	315	328	Serain Communal Cemetery Extension
1279	35.F.4	285	—	Seraucourt-le-Grand Communal Cemetery
2124	42.C.3	341	—	Serches Communal Cemetery
2125	12.C.4	14	—	Serques Churchyard
2126	34A.C.1	250	259	Serre Road Cemetery No. 1, Hébuterne
2127	34A.C.1	250	259	Serre Road Cemetery No. 2, Beaumont Hamel
2128	34A.C.1	250	259	Serre Road Cemetery No. 3, Puisieux
2129	36.F.2	315	—	Séry-les-Mézières Communal Cemetery
--	---	—	—	Seurre Communal Cemetery (Côte-d'Or), 23 miles S. of Dijon
2130	43.D.1	349	352	Sézanne Communal Cemetery
2131	34A.B.2	250	257	Shrine Cemetery, Bucquoy
2132	37.D.4	332	—	Signy-l'Abbaye Communal Cemetery
2133	37.B.3	332	—	Signy-Le-Petit Communal Cemetery
2134	15.F.1	97	—	Sin Churchyard
2135	24.D.4	137	—	Sin-le-Noble Communal Cemetery
2136	37.E.2	332	335	Sissonne British Cemetery
2137	27.F.1	202	—	*Sivry Communal Cemetery
2138	14.C.4	34	—	*Slypskappelle Churchyard, Moorslede
2139	26.A.4	196	—	*Soignies Communal Cemetery
2140	42.C.3	341	—	Soissons Communal Cemetery
2141	25.F.3	180	193	Solesmes British Cemetery
2142	25.F.3	180	—	Solesmes Communal Cemetery
2143	14A.A.2	36	40	*Solferino Farm Cemetery, Brielen
2144	26.F.4	196	—	Solre-le-Château Communal Cemetery
2145	27.F.2	202	—	*Solre-St. Géry Communal Cemetery
2146	25.D.1	180	—	Somain Communal Cemetery
2147	14A.D.3	36	65	*Somer Farm Cemetery, Wytschæte
2148	25.E.3	180	—	Sommaing Churchyard
2149	35.C.4	285	—	Somme American Cemetery, Bony
2150	42.E.3	341	—	Sommelans Churchyard
2151	23.F.3	109	—	Souastre Churchyard
2152	42.C.2	341	—	Soucy Communal Cemetery
2153	33.C.2	216	—	Soués Churchyard
2154	43.C.2	349	—	Soulières Churchyard
2155	27.F.3	202	—	*Soumoy Communal Cemetery
2156	42.C.4	341	---	Soupir Churchyard (Aisne)
2157	42.C.4	341	—	Soupir Communal Cemetery (Aisne)
2159	---	—	—	*Spa Communal Cemetery, 17 miles S. of Liège
2160	14A.E.3	36	66	*Spanbroekmolen British Cemetery, Wytschæte
2161	26.C.3	196	—	*Spiennes Churchyard
2162	26.C.3	196	—	*Spiennes Communal Cemetery
2163	14A.C.3	36	55	*Spoilbank Cemetery, Zillebeke
2164	28.A.1	205	—	*Spy Communal Cemetery
2165	15.C.1	97	—	*Staceghem Communal Cemetery
2166	2.D.4	6	—	*Stalhille Churchyard
2167	13.D.2	18	—	Staple Churchyard
2168	13.E.2	18	—	Steenbecque Churchyard
2169	1.F.4	2	—	*Steenkerke Belgian Military Cemetery
2170	13.C.3	18	—	Steenvoorde Communal Cemetery
2171	14.E.1	34	—	Steenwerck Communal Cemetery
2172	14A.F.3	36	74	*Strand Military Cemetery, Plœgsteert Wood
2173	34A.D.3	250	267	Stump Road Cemetery, Grandcourt
2174	24.E.4	137	174	Sucrerie Cemetery, Epinoy
2175	24.F.3	137	177	Sucrerie British Cemetery, Graincourt-les-Havrincourt

REFERENCE NUMBER	MAP LOCATION	MAP PAGE	ILLUSTRATION PAGE	NAME OF CEMETERY
2176	23.C.4	109	123	Sucrerie Cemetery, Ablain St. Nazaire
2177	34A.C.1	250	261	Sucrerie Military Cemetery, Colincamps
2179	14A.D.2	36	62	*Suffolk Cemetery, Vierstraat, Kemmel
2178	14.E.1	34	86	Suffolk Cemetery, La Rolanderie Farm, Erquinghem-Lys
2180	—	—	—	Suippes Communal Cemetery Extension, 15 miles NE. of Chalons-sur-Marne
2181	24.F.1	137	162	Summit Trench Cemetery, Croisilles
2182	24.D.1	137	152	Sunken Road Cemetery, Fampoux
2183	24.F.1	137	160	Sunken Road Cemetery, Boisleux St. Marc
2184	34A.E.3	250	—	Sunken Road Cemetery, Contalmaison. See page 357
2185	35.A.4	285	296	Sunken Road Cemetery, Villers Plouich
2186	24.E.2	137	170	Sun Quarry Cemetery, Chérisy
2187	—	—	—	Supt Churchyard, near Andelot (Jura), 30 miles S. of Besançon
2188	23.E.2	109	—	Sus-St. Léger Churchyard
2189	34.C.4	222	240	Suzanne Communal Cemetery Extension
2190	35.C.1	285	304	Suzanne Military Cemetery No. 3
2191	15.C.2	97	—	*Sweveghem Churchyard

T

REFERENCE NUMBER	MAP LOCATION	MAP PAGE	ILLUSTRATION PAGE	NAME OF CEMETERY
2192	25.A.2	180	—	*Taintegnies Communal Cemetery
2193	37.A.1	332	—	Taisnières-en-Thierache Communal Cemetery
2194	14A.A.2	36	40	*Talana Farm Cemetery, Bœsinghe
2195	—	—	—	Talence Communal Cemetery Extension (Gironde), 2 miles S. of Bordeaux
2196	34.B.1	222	—	Talmas Communal Cemetery
2197	28.B.1	205	—	*Tamines Communal Cemetery
2198	14.E.2	34	80	*Tancrez Farm Cemetery, Plœgsteert
2199	24.E.2	137	158	Tank Cemetery, Guémappe
2200	13.F.2	18	20	Tannay British Cemetery, Thiennes
2201	—	—	—	Tannay Communal Cemetery (Ardennes), 17 miles S. of Mezières
2202	35.B.4	285	299	Targelle Ravine British Cemetery, Villers Guislain
2203	24.A.3	137	—	Templemars Communal Cemetery
2204	15.F.1	97	—	*Templeuve Communal Cemetery
2205	24.A.4	137	—	Templeuve Communal Cemetery
2206	35.C.4	285	309	Templeux-le-Guérard British Cemetery
2207	35.C.4	285	309	Templeux-le-Guérard Communal Cemetery Extension
2208	22.B.4	106	—	Teneur Churchyard
2209	34A.C.2	250	261	Ten Tree Alley Cemetery, Puisieux
2211	13.C.3	18	—	Terdeghem French Military Cemetery
2212	11.D.3	10	13	Terlincthun British Cemetery, Wimille
2213	16.D.2	100	—	*Termonde Communal Cemetery Extension
2214	34.A.1	222	—	Terramesnil Communal Cemetery
2215	35.D.3	285	—	Tertry Communal Cemetery
2216	24.D.1	137	146	Thélus Military Cemetery
2217	34.E.2	222	—	Thennes Communal Cemetery
2218	—	—	—	*Theux Communal Cemetery, 13 miles SE. of Liège
2219	34.E.1	222	—	Thésy-Glimont Communal Cemetery
2220	25.E.3	180	184	Thiant Communal Cemetery
2221	—	—	—	Thiaucourt Communal Cemetery, 18 miles SW. of Metz
2223	12.F.2	14	—	Thiembronne Communal Cemetery
2224	13.E.2	18	20	Thiennes British Cemetery
2225	13.E.2	18	—	Thiennes Churchyard
2226	42.B.1	341	—	Thiescourt French National Cemetery

REFERENCE NUMBER	MAP LOCATION	MAP PAGE	ILLUSTRATION PAGE	NAME OF CEMETERY
2278	14A.F.2	36	72	*Underhill Farm Cemetery, Plœgsteert
2279	35.C.4	285	310	Unicorn Cemetery, Vendhuile
2280	36.C.1	315	329	Uplands Cemetery, Magny-la-Fosse
2281	24.E.2	137	170	Upton Wood British Cemetery, Hendecourt-les Cagnicourt
				V
2282	35.D.4	285	311	Vadencourt British Cemetery, Maissemy
2283	36.D.4	315	—	Vadencourt-et-Bohéries Communal Cemetery
2284	42.C.4	341	345	Vailly British Cemetery, Vailly-sur-Aisne
2285	34.D.2	222	—	Vaire-sous-Corbie Communal Cemetery
2286	—	—	—	Valence sur Rhône Communal Cemetery (Drôme), 60 miles S. of Lyon
2287	25.D.3	180	182	Valenciennes Communal Cemetery
2288	24.E.2	137	163	Valley Cemetery, Vis-en-Artois
2289	43.B.1	349	—	Vandières Churchyard
2290	34.B.2	222	—	Varennes Communal Cemetery
2291	34.B.2	222	227	Varennes Military Cemetery
2292	—	—	—	Vaudoy Communal Cemetery, 36 miles SE. of Paris
2293	24.F.2	137	—	Vaulx A.D.S. Cemetery, Vaulx-Vraucourt. See page 357
2294	35.A.2	285	—	Vaulx Australian Field Ambulance Cemetery, Vaulx-Vraucourt. See page 357
2295	24.F.2	137	168	Vaulx Hill Cemetery, Vaulx-Vraucourt
2296	36.B.3	315	324	Vaux-Andigny British Cemetery
2297	36.B.3	315	—	Vaux-Andigny Communal Cemetery
2298	42.C.3	341	346	Vauxbuin French National Cemetery
2299	33.C.4	216	—	Vaux-en-Amiénois Communal Cemetery
2300	14.F.1	34	90	V.C. Corner, Australian Cemetery, Fromelles
2301	—	—	—	*Veldwezelt Communal Cemetery, 16 miles N. of Liège
2302	25.A.2	180	—	*Velvain Churchyard, Wez-Velain
2303	25.F.4	180	192	Vendegies-au-Bois British Cemetery
2304	25.F.4	180	—	Vendegies-au-Bois Churchyard
2305	25.E.3	180	187	Vendegies Cross-Roads British Cemetery, Bermerain
2306	35.D.4	285	—	Vendelles Churchyard
2307	41.A.2	338	—	Vendeuil-Caply Churchyard
2308	35.B.4	285	—	Vendhuile Communal Cemetery
2310	—	—	—	Vendôme Town Cemetery, 50 miles SW. of Chartres
2311	42.B.4	341	345	Vendresse British Cemetery
2312	42.B.4	341	345	Vendresse Churchyard
2313	—	—	—	Vendresse Communal Cemetery (Ardennes), 11 miles S. of Mezières
2314	41.C.4	338	—	Verberie Communal Cemetery
2315	41.C.4	338	340	Verberie French National Cemetery
2316	25.E.3	180	186	Verchain British Cemetery, Verchain-Maugré
2317	22.B.4	106	—	Verchin Churchyard
2318	32.B.4	210	—	Vergies Churchyard
2319	35.D.4	285	313	Vermand Communal Cemetery
2320	23.B.4	109	118	Vermelles British Cemetery
2321	23.B.4	109	—	Vermelles Communal Cemetery
2322	42.E.4	341	—	Verneuil Churchyard
2323	—	—	—	Vernon Communal Cemetery (Eure), 15 miles NE. of Evreux
2324	23.B.4	109	—	Verquigneuil Communal Cemetery
2325	23.B.4	109	—	Verquin Communal Cemetery
2326	25.F.3	180	192	Vertain Communal Cemetery Extension

REFERENCE NUMBER	MAP LOCATION	MAP PAGE	ILLUSTRATION PAGE	NAME OF CEMETERY
2327	25.F.3	180	—	Vertigneul Churchyard, Romeries
2328	43.C.2	349	—	Vertus Communal Cemetery
2329	—	—	—	*Verviers Communal Cemetery, 14 miles SE. of Liège
2330	42.E.2	341	—	Veuilly-La-Poterie Communal Cemetery
2331	15.C.2	97	—	*Vichte Churchyard
2332	15.C.2	97	99	*Vichte Military Cemetery
2333	25.C.3	180	—	Vicoigne Communal Cemetery, Raismes
2334	25.C.4	180	—	Vicq Communal Cemetery
2335	42.C.4	341	—	Vieil-Arcy Communal Cemetery
2336	22.C.3	106	—	Vieil-Hesdin Churchyard
2337	37.D.4	332	—	Vieil-St. Remy Communal Cemetery
2338	13.F.4	18	31	Vieille-Chapelle New Military Cemetery, Lacoutre
2339	42.C.3	341	—	Vierzy Communal Cemetery
2340	36.A.3	315	—	Viesly Communal Cemetery
2341	13.E.4	18	—	Vieux-Berquin Communal Cemetery
2343	25.B.4	180	—	Vieux-Condé Communal Cemetery
2344	26.E.3	196	—	Vieux-Mesnil Churchyard
2345	33.B.3	216	219	Vignacourt British Cemetery
2346	41.B.4	338	—	Vignemont French National Cemetery
2347	—	—	—	Villé Communal Cemetery (Weiler), (Bas Rhin), 25 miles SW. of Strasbourg
2348	—	—	—	Villé French National Cemetery (Weiler), (Bas Rhin), 25 miles SW. of Strasbourg
2349	26.B.4	196	—	*Ville-sur-Haine Churchyard
2350	42.C.3	341	—	Villemontoire Communal Cemetery
2351	—	—	—	Villeneuve-St. Georges Communal Cemetery, 8 miles S. of Porte de Picpus, Paris
2352	42.A.2	341	—	Villequier-Aumont Communal Cemetery
2353	35.C.4	285	—	Villeret Churchyard
2354	26.B.2	196	—	*Villerot Communal Cemetery
2355	24.D.4	137	—	Villers-au-Tertre Communal Cemetery
2356	33.B.4	216	—	Villers-Bocage Communal Cemetery
2357	33.B.4	216	221	Villers-Bocage Communal Cemetery Extension
2358	34.D.2	222	—	Villers-Bretonneux Communal Cemetery
2359	34.D.2	222	223	Villers-Bretonneux Military Cemetery, Fouilloy
2360	35.D.1	285	—	Villers-Carbonnel Communal Cemetery
2361	42.D.2	341	—	Villers-Cotterêts French National Cemetery
2362	25.E.2	180	—	Villers-en-Cauchies Communal Cemetery
2363	42.C.4	341	—	Villers-en-Prayères Communal Cemetery
2364	35.C.3	285	306	Villers-Faucon Communal Cemetery
2365	35.C.3	285	306	Villers-Faucon Communal Cemetery Extension
2366	35.B.4	285	298	Villers-Guislain Communal Cemetery
2367	35.B.4	285	299	Villers Hill British Cemetery, Villers-Guislain
2368	36.B.1	315	—	Villers-Outreaux Communal Cemetery
2369	35.B.4	285	297	Villers-Plouich Communal Cemetery
2370	25.E.4	180	188	Villers-Pol Communal Cemetery Extension
2371	26.D.4	196	—	Villers-sire-Nicole Communal Cemetery
2372	23.C.4	109	123	Villers Station Cemetery, Villers-au-Bois
2373	34.C.3	222	—	Ville-sur-Ancre Communal Cemetery
2374	34.C.3	222	237	Ville-sur-Ancre Communal Cemetery Extension
2375	24.C.1	137	—	Vimy Communal Cemetery, Farbus
2376	41.F.3	338	—	Vincennes New Communal Cemetery
2377	24.E.2	137	140	Vis-en-Artois British Cemetery, Haucourt
2378	24.E.2	137	—	Vis-en-Artois Communal Cemetery
2379	32.A.4	210	—	Vismes Communal Cemetery
2380	—	—	—	Vitry-le-François French National Cemetery, 19 miles SE. of Chalons-sur-Marne
2381	—	—	—	Vittel Communal Cemetery (Vosges), 35 miles S. of Nancy

REFERENCE NUMBER	MAP LOCATION	MAP PAGE	ILLUSTRA- TION PAGE	NAME OF CEMETERY
2382	15.B.2	97	—	*Vive St. Bavon Churchyard
2383	14A.B.2	36	41	*Vlamertinghe Military Cemetery
2384	14A.B.2	36	40	*Vlamertinghe New Military Cemetery
2385	27.F.3	202	—	*Vogenée Communal Cemetery
2386	—	—	—	Voinsles Communal Cemetery, 33 miles SE. of Paris
2387	14A.C.3	36	57	*Voormezeele Enclosures No. 1 and No. 2
2389	14A.C.3	36	57	*Voormezeele Enclosure No. 3
2390	—	—	—	Vouziers Communal Cemetery, 33 miles NE. of Reims
2392	35.F.2	285	—	Voyennes Communal Cemetery
2393	35.D.3	285	—	Vraignes Communal Cemetery
2394	24.F.2	137	—	Vraucourt Copse British Cemetery, Vaulx-Vraucourt. See page 357
2395	25.C.1	180	—	Vred Communal Cemetery
2396	34.E.4	222	247	Vrély Communal Cemetery Extension

W

2397	15.B.2	97	—	*Waereghem Communal Cemetery
2398	15.D.3	97	—	*Waermaerde Churchyard
2399	34A.C.2	250	263	Waggon Road Cemetery, Beaumont-Hamel
2400	23.E.4	109	129	Wailly Orchard Cemetery
2401	13.D.2	18	—	Wallon-Cappel Churchyard
2402	36.A.1	315	—	Wambaix Communal Cemetery
2404	14.E.3	34	—	Wambrechies Communal Cemetery
2405	24.E.2	137	159	Wancourt British Cemetery
2406	23.B.1	216	—	Wanel Communal Cemetery
2407	25.A.1	180	—	Wannehain Churchyard
2408	23.E.3	109	—	Wanquetin Communal Cemetery
2409	23.E.3	109	127	Wanquetin Communal Cemetery Extension
2410	15.E.2	97	—	*Warcoing Churchyard
2411	13.E.1	18	—	Wardrecques Churchyard
2412	25.D.4	180	—	Wargnies-le-Grand Churchyard
2413	26.E.1	196	—	Wargnies-le-Petit Communal Cemetery
2414	34A.D.5	250	275	Warlencourt British Cemetery
2415	23.F.2	109	129	Warlincourt Halte British Cemetery, Saulty
2416	34.B.2	222	230	Warloy Baillon Communal Cemetery
2417	34.B.2	222	230	Warloy Baillon Communal Cemetery Extension
2418	33.C.1	216	—	Warlus Churchyard
2419	23.E.4	109	—	Warlus Communal Cemetery
2420	26.C.2	196	—	*Warquignies Communal Cemetery
2421	34A.A.4	250	254	Warry Copse Cemetery, Courcelles-le-Comte
2422	34.F.4	222	248	Warvillers Churchyard Extension
2423	—	—	—	Wasselonne Communal Cemetery (Protestant) (Bas Rhin), 15 miles W. of Strasbourg
2424	36.B.4	315	—	Wassigny Communal Cemetery
2425	13.C.3	18	—	*Watou Churchyard
2426	12.C.4	14	—	Watten Churchyard
2427	15.E.1	97	—	Wattrelos Old Communal Cemetery
2428	22.E.3	106	108	Wavans British Cemetery
2429	12.E.3	14	—	Wavrans-sur-l'Aa Churchyard
2430	17.F.1	103	—	*Wavre Communal Cemetery
2431	24.A.2	137	—	Wavrin Communal Cemetery
2432	27.B.4	202	—	*Wayaux Communal Cemetery
2433	25.F.2	180	190	Wellington Cemetery, Rieux-en-Cambresis
2434	14A.A.3	36	42	*Welsh Cemetery (Caesar's Nose), Bœsinghe
2435	2.C.4	6	—	*Wenduyne Churchyard

REFERENCE NUMBER	MAP LOCATION	MAP PAGE	ILLUSTRA-TION PAGE	NAME OF CEMETERY
2487	14.D.3	34	—	*Wervicq Communal Cemetery, German Eastern Extension
2488	14.D.3	34	—	*Wervicq Communal Cemetery, German Western Extension
2437	14A.F.1	36	71	*Westhof Farm Cemetery, Neuve-Eglise
2438	14.C.1	34	60	*Westoutre British Cemetery
2439	14.C.1	34	—	*Westoutre Churchyard
2440	14.C.1	34	60	*Westoutre Churchyard Extension
2441	13.B.4	18	—	*Westvleteren Belgian Military Cemetery
2442	16.D.2	100	—	*Wetteren Communal Cemetery
2443	14.C.4	34	—	*Wevelghem Communal Cemetery
2444	25.A.2	180	—	*Wez-Velvain Churchyard
2445	14.F.2	34	89	White City Cemetery, Bois-Grenier
2446	14A.B.3	36	45	*White House Cemetery, St. Jean-lès-Ypres
2447	24.A.2	137	—	Wicres Churchyard
2448	15.B.2	97	—	*Wielsbeke Churchyard
2449	14A.A.4	36	45	*Wieltje Farm Cemetery, St. Jean-lès-Ypres
2450	26.C.1	196	—	*Wiheries Communal Cemetery
2451	15.F.1	97	—	Willems Communal Cemetery (Nord)
2452	11.C.3	10	13	Wimereux Communal Cemetery
2453	24.E.2	137	163	Windmill British Cemetery, Monchy-le-Preux
2454	14.C.4	34	—	*Winkel-St. Eloi Churchyard
2455	13.C.3	18	—	Winnezeele Churchyard
2456	—	—	—	Wissembourg Communal Cemetery, 30 miles N. of Strasbourg
2457	12.E.4	14	—	Wizernes Churchyard
2458	24.A.1	137	143	Woburn Abbey Cemetery, Cuinchy
2459	34.E.3	222	245	Wood Cemetery, Marcelcave
2460	14A.C.4	36	54	*Woods Cemetery, Zillebeke
2461	13.B.2	18	—	Wormhoudt Communal Cemetery
2462	14A.E.2	36	—	*Wulverghem Churchyard
2463	14A.E.2	36	68	*Wulverghem-Lindenhœk Road Military Cemetery, Wulverghem
2464	14A.D.3	36	65	*Wytschæte Military Cemetery

X

2465	14.E.2	34	87	'X' Farm Cemetery, La Chapelle-d'Armentières

Y

2466	14A.B.3	36	48	*Ypres Reservoir Cemetery
2467	14A.B.3	36	48	*Ypres Town Cemetery (Menin Gate)
2468	14A.B.3	36	48	*Ypres Town Cemetery Extension (Menin Gate)
2469	35.B.3	285	—	Ytres Churchyard
2470	35.B.2	285	—	Ytres Communal Cemetery
2471	14.F.1	34	92	'Y' Farm Military Cemetery, Bois-Grenier
2472	34A.D.1	250	266	'Y' Ravine Cemetery, Beaumont-Hamel
2473	25.E.2	180	185	York Cemetery, Haspres
2474	—	—	—	Yutz-Basse New Communal Cemetery (Moselle), 17 miles N. of Metz
2475	—	—	—	Yvetot Communal Cemetery (Seine-Inférieure), 20 miles NW. of Rouen

REFERENCE NUMBER	MAP LOCATION	MAP PAGE	ILLUSTRA- TION PAGE	NAME OF CEMETERY
				Z
2476	14.C.3	34	80	*Zantvoorde British Cemetery
2477	14.C.3	34	—	*Zantvoorde Churchyard
2478	3.B.1	8	—	*Zeebrugge Churchyard
2479	13.F.4	18	32	Zelobes Indian Cemetery, Lacouture
2480	14A.C.4	36	—	*Zillebeke Churchyard
2481	24.D.1	137	147	Zivy Crater, Thélus
2482	12.C.2	14	—	Zouafques Churchyard
2483	23.C.4	109	135	Zouave Valley Cemetery, Souchez
2484	12.D.3	14	—	Zudausques Churchyard
2485	1.F.2	2	3	Zuydcoote Military Cemetery

INDEX TO MEMORIALS TO THE 'MISSING'

The Memorials are shown thus ✚ 12 on the maps. The reference number in the first column of this index corresponds with the number of the memorial on the map.

The map location in the second column gives the number of the map and the square in which the memorial will be found.

* Denotes memorials in Belgium.

REFERENCE NUMBER	MAP LOCATION	MAP PAGE	ILLUSTRA-TION PAGE	NAME OF MEMORIAL
1	24.E.1	137	138	Arras Memorial and Faubourg d'Amiens Cemetery
2	34.D.2	222	223	Australian National Memorial and Villers-Bretonneux Military Cemetery, Fouilloy
3	14.F.1	34	90	Australian Memorial and V.C. Corner Australian Cemetery, Fromelles
4	35.A.3	285	290	Cambrai Memorial and Louverval Military Cemetery, Doignies
5	24.C.1	137	139	Canadian National Memorial, Vimy Ridge
6	11.A.4	10	11	Dover Patrol Memorial, Cap Blanc-Nez, Escalles. (Not to 'Missing')
7	24.A.1	137	139	Indian Memorial, Neuve-Chapelle
8	42.F.2	341	343	La Ferté-sous-Jouarre Memorial
9	23.A.4	109	110	Le Touret Memorial and Cemetery, Richebourg-l'Avoué
10	24.B.1	137	139	Loos Memorial and Dud Corner Cemetery
11	—	—	356	Mazargues Memorial and Cemetery, Marseille
12	14A.B.3	36	33	*Menin Gate Memorial, Ypres
13	34A.D.1	250	252	Newfoundland National Memorial, Beaumont-Hamel
14	2.E.1	6	5	*Nieuport Memorial
15	14A.F.3	36	72	*Plœgsteert Memorial and Berks Cemetery Extension
16	34A.E.3	250	251	Pozières Memorial and Cemetery
17	42.C.3	341	343	Soissons Memorial
18	34A.F.5	250	252	South African National Memorial, Delville Wood. (Not to 'Missing')
19	34A.E.2	250	251	Thiepval Memorial
20	14.B.3	34	76	*Tyne Cot Memorial and Cemetery, Passchendaele
21	24.E.2	137	140	Vis-en-Artois Memorial and Cemetery, Haucourt
22	3.B.1	8	9	*Zeebrugge Memorial. (Not to 'Missing')

The New Zealand Expeditionary Force 'Missing' are commemorated on memorials in the following Cemeteries :

*Buttes New British Cemetery, Polygon Wood, Zonnebeke
Caterpillar Valley Cemetery, Longueval
Cité Bonjean Military Cemetery, Armentières
Grévillers British Cemetery
Marfaux British Cemetery
*Messines Ridge British Cemetery, Messines
*Tyne Cot Cemetery, Passchendaele

Printed in the United Kingdom
by Lightning Source UK Ltd.
118391UK00001B/91-94